MIXED MATCHES

I0086242

SPEKTRUM: Publications of the German Studies Association
Series Editor: David M. Luebke, University of Oregon

Published under the auspices of the German Studies Association, *Spektrum* offers current perspectives on culture, society, and political life in the German-speaking lands of central Europe—Austria, Switzerland, and the Federal Republic—from the late Middle Ages to the present day. Its titles and themes reflect the composition of the GSA and the work of its members within and across the disciplines to which they belong—literary criticism, history, cultural studies, political science, and anthropology.

For a complete series listing, please see page 247.

Mixed Matches

Transgressive Unions in Germany
from the Reformation to the Enlightenment

~:~

Edited by

DAVID M. LUEBKE and MARY LINDEMANN

berghahn

NEW YORK · OXFORD

www.berghahnbooks.com

First edition published in 2014 by

Berghahn Books

www.berghahnbooks.com

© 2014, 2017 David M. Luebke and Mary Lindemann
First paperback edition published in 2017

All rights reserved. Except for the quotation of short passages
for the purposes of criticism and review, no part of this book
may be reproduced in any form or by any means, electronic or
mechanical, including photocopying, recording, or any information
storage and retrieval system now known or to be invented,
without written permission of the publisher.

Library of Congress Cataloging-in-Publication Data

Mixed matches : transgressive unions in Germany from the Reformation to the
Enlightenment / edited by David Luebke and Mary Lindemann.
    pages cm. — (Spektrum: publications of the German Studies Association ; volume 8)
Includes bibliographical references and index.
ISBN 978-1-78238-409-0 (hardback : alk. paper) — ISBN 978-1-78533-524-2
(paperback) — ISBN 978-1-78238-410-6 (ebook)
1. Marriage—Germany—History. 2. Germany—History—1517–1871. 3. Germany—
Civilization. I. Luebke, David Martin, 1960– II. Lindemann, Mary.
HQ625.M59 2014
306.810943—dc23

                                                                          2014000991

British Library Cataloguing in Publication Data

A catalogue record for this book is available from the British Library

ISBN: 978-1-78238-409-0 hardback
ISBN: 978-1-78533-524-2 paperback
ISBN: 978-1-78238-410-6 ebook

❧ CONTENTS ❧

INTRODUCTION

~:~

Transgressive Unions

DAVID M. LUEBKE

In our time, and on both sides of the Atlantic, barriers to marriage crumble
and fall. When the Supreme Court of the United States overturned anti-
miscegenation laws in 1967, seventeen states still forbade marriages that crossed
the color line. Most of these states had been on the losing side of the Civil War,
but such legislation was no Southern monopoly. Only nine states had *never*
enacted such laws.[1] Public attitudes toward mixed-race unions have softened
as well. At the time of the court's decision in *Loving v. Virginia*, large majori-
ties still disapproved of them; today, among Americans born after 1981, such
unions meet with near universal acceptance.[2] Religious impediments to marriage have eroded, too. In the American experience, such barriers were never as
rigid as the legal bans against interracial unions. Nevertheless, throughout the
nineteenth century, official antipathy toward interfaith marriages remained intense, even panicky, especially among Catholic clergy and the rabbinate.[3] Even
so, rates of religious exogamy in the United States have risen steadily among
all denominations. Among White Catholics, for example, the rate swelled from
18 to over 40 percent between 1930 and 1980.[4] In Germany, historically, marriages between the Christian religions were rare, even in confessionally mixed
jurisdictions. From the 1850s on, however, their number increased—and in
Prussia were up to 10 percent of all unions by 1912.[5] Where law reinforced
social taboos against interfaith marriage, increased rates of conversion could result.[6] The same goes for barriers to remarriage: over the past century and a half,
divorce laws have liberalized throughout Europe and North America, and with
that liberalization divorce rates have surged.[7] To be sure, some taboos have
fallen away, only to reemerge. From the mid-eighteenth century through the
nineteenth century, for example, cousin marriage enjoyed a degree of respect-
ability that it subsequently lost.[8] But the broader trend is clear: legal barriers to
marriage fall down, and social acceptance grows for unions that once provoked
horror and ostracism.

The most dramatic change has been the advent of same-sex marriage, a phenomenon without obvious precedent in European history.[9] The pace of legalization has been swift: no country recognized such marriages until the Netherlands broke the mold in 2001. As of this writing, same-sex couples enjoy full and equal marriage rights in fifteen countries, and many more recognize some form of protected, same-sex union.[10] In the United States, same-sex marriage has been introduced in seventeen U.S. states and the District of Columbia, all since 2004.[11] On 26 June 2013, the U.S. Supreme Court declared unconstitutional the 1996 Defense of Marriage Act, which had restricted federal marriage benefits to opposite-sex unions and forbidden interstate recognition of same-sex marriages. In another decision issued the same day, the Supreme Court effectively reinstated a lower court decision making same-sex marriage legal in the state of California. Compared with interracial marriage, public attitudes on same-sex marriage have evolved even more rapidly than the pace of legal change: since the twenty-first century began, the percentage of Americans who favor full marriage rights for gay couples has grown from 35 to 47 percent—a slender plurality over those who oppose same-sex unions.[12]

Although they culminate a long progress toward the liberalization of marriage law, same-sex unions nevertheless represent a profound departure from an ancient heterosexual norm. That fact reverberates through the vehement language of opponents to same-sex marriage, a rhetoric that draws heavily on arguments once raised in support of anti-miscegenation laws. Thus in the debate surrounding California's Proposition 8—an effort to ban same-sex marriage by plebiscite—many claimed that parents in a transgressive union placed their own children at an unfair emotional or psychological disadvantage.[13] Others railed against same-sex marriage as a violation of "divine law as expressed in nature."[14] Both arguments had also been advanced in support of anti-miscegenation laws during the post-Reconstruction era.[15]

Deriving continuity and stability from the norm of heterosexual marriage, however, obscures the wide variety of historical forms that marriage has taken. Explicitly or implicitly, the exponents of Proposition 8 assumed that the norm of *heterosexual monogamy* is a historical and cultural constant, self-evident in biblical Scripture and the law of nature. To be sure, the dominance of heterosexual normativity has been overwhelming. In the Holy Roman Empire, for example, the Criminal Constitution of 1532 made sexual relations between two men or two women a capital offense.[16] But the case for monogamy, by comparison, has been surprisingly precarious. As Bernardino Ochino (1487–1565) pointed out in 1563, the Bible neither endorses monogamy to the exclusion of other forms of marital union, nor does it condemn polygamy.[17] Ochino's scripturalist case for polygamy put the lie to Geneva's magistrates, who punished his challenge with exile.[18] Likewise the argument from natural law offers cold comfort at best: while no natural law theorists advocated same-sex marital unions, they found it difficult to identify any rational justification for upholding monogamy as the sole legitimate form. Hugo Grotius (1583–1645) and Samuel Pufendorf (1632–1694) agreed that both nature and Scripture permitted a man to marry multiple wives; the great jurist Christian Thomasius (1655–1728) argued that natural law allowed women to engage in plural marriage. As Stephan Buchholz and others have observed, their deliberations reflected a systemic differentiation of religion from law and politics that began when evangelical reformers deprived marriage of its sacramental status.[19]

As for theological constants, the opponents of same-sex marriage invoke an ideal that has its modern origins in the Protestant Reformation, with its elevation of the married estate, its spiritualization of affective bonds between husband and wife, and its concomitant downgrading of clerical celibacy.[20] But as David Whitford notes in his contribution to this volume, Luther's thoughts on heterosexual monogamy were anything but simple or consistent. To be sure, the Wittenberg reformer heartily endorsed monogamous marriage. But he also assigned to heterosexuality an ontological position in the order of creation anterior to that of original sin, lending it a disruptive potency that, under the right pastoral circumstances, might warrant polygamy as the best constraint on male sexual urges.[21] For this reason Luther secretly endorsed the bigamous marriage of Landgrave Philipp of Hessen to Margarete von der Saale on 4 March 1540. Thus in William Rockwell's memorable phrase, "the first political protagonist of German Protestantism was, with Luther's blessing, a bigamist."[22]

Marriage, in other words, never possessed the unity and stability in law, theology, or social practice that the modern defenders of tradition assume. Indeed, if there is any constant in the history of marriage, it is *variety*—the sheer number and diversity of sexual pair-bonds that Western societies have recognized, formally or informally. The essays assembled here expose that variety by exploring the margins of marriage during the three centuries that began with the Protestant Reformation—a period, like the present time, of rapid cultural pluralization in which parameters of marriage were redrawn. All of them draw on evidence from the German-speaking lands, where the Reformation began, but their focus is not confined to the effects of religious reform. Nor is the goal to erect a new teleology to replace the current opposition between tradition and liberalization. Rather, the aim of these essays is to explore the variety of early modern marriage by examining unions that violated some sort of taboo—be it religious, social, ethnic, or related to kin. "Only by historicizing," writes Ruth Mazo Karras, "can we see the inherent illogic of claims that there is only one 'real' form."[23]

As the first three chapters show, the Protestant Reformation, far from defining marriage more clearly, superimposed new marital norms on communities that were at best half-ready to accept them in full. The trouble began almost as soon as evangelical reforms were introduced. Reluctantly, Luther allowed divorce on the grounds of adultery, desertion, and sexual impotence. But as Whitford reminds us, Protestants who divorced and remarried became bigamists to those who did not accept the evangelical doctrines: in their eyes, serial monogamy punctuated by divorce was no less bigamous than concurrent marriage to multiple spouses. The Protestants' introduction of clerical marriage, similarly, raised fundamental questions of spiritual authority. Wolfgang Breul analyzes the impact of clerical marriage on the Hessian town of Hersfeld, which in 1523 issued a municipal decree—the first of its kind—against priests who lived in sexual union with concubines, obligating them to marry their partners or abandon them. Such unmarriages (*Unehen*) were nothing new, of course: the papal archives bulge with petitions from the sons of priests seeking retroactive legitimation.[24] Nor had civic authorities been lax in prosecuting clerical sexual misconduct.[25] But no medieval town had forced priests to marry or depart if they refused. Hersfeld's decree, and many more that followed it, constituted an assault both on ecclesiastical jurisdiction and on the canonical principle of clerical celibacy. By legalizing clerical marriage, Hersfeld erased status distinctions between laity and clergy, assimilating the latter into communal polity and the "priesthood of all believers."

This appropriation of ecclesiastical jurisdictions had been deliberate and intentional. But clerical marriage also stirred a hornet's nest of unintended consequences. As Beth Plummer's chapter reveals, few experienced those consequences more keenly than monks and nuns who, like Luther himself and his wife, Katharina von Bora, had abjured vows of celibacy that bound them as in marriage to God. Although the unmarriages of parish clergy frequently aroused indignation, their ubiquity also eased the integration of priests as husbands and citizens into the secular world. Monastics enjoyed no such advantage. Abjuration made them "whores and knaves"; by marrying they became bigamists. Because vows of chastity bound them in spiritual kinship, moreover, ex-nuns who married ex-monks compounded bigamy with incest.[26] The practical difficulties they faced were legion—some of which anyone in a same-sex marriage today would recognize. Imperial law still forbade monastics to marry, for example, even if individual Protestant jurisdictions allowed it. Would the marriage be regarded as valid in a Catholic territory?

Plummer charts the proliferation of their marriages, beginning in 1521 with that of Bartholomäus Bernhardi (1487–1551)—the first monk, as far as we know, to marry on the basis of the new teachings. That Catholics shunned monks who married is not surprising. But even among Protestants, the fate of married ex-nuns and former monks was by no means as easy as Luther's unequivocal endorsement of clerical marriage might have suggested. More fundamentally, married ex-monastics entered a world that depended vitally on the sacrosanctity of vows.[27] As self-perjurers, they found themselves the targets of suspicion from their evangelical coreligionists. All too often their full integration proved elusive.[28]

The essays of Ralf-Peter Fuchs and Michael Sikora probe a different sort of constraint on marriage, one associated with social inequality. In order to legitimate the social inequalities on which their elevated rank and honor depended, Sikora reminds us, nobles and princes relied on the heritability of their status. And because German society traced status inheritance through women as well as men, the integrity of every noble lineage hinged on the choice of equal or superior inherited rank. As the preoccupation of nobles with documenting lineage intensified during the fifteenth and sixteenth centuries, misalliances became the object of literary fascination—one thinks here of the large corpus of poems, plays, and biographies devoted to Agnes Bernauer, the daughter of a bath attendant whom Duke Albrecht of Bavaria kept as lover and, perhaps, as his clandestine wife from 1428 on.[29] So grave was the threat she posed to the Wittelsbach dynasty that on 12 October 1435 Albrecht's father, according to one contemporary account, had her thrown to her death from the Danube River bridge at Straubing.[30]

Less well appreciated are constraints on misalliances from below. To elucidate them, Ralf-Peter Fuchs analyzes a series of defamation cases brought before the Imperial Chamber Court—one of two tribunals with jurisdiction, theoretically, over the entire Holy Roman Empire. Applying Pierre Bourdieu's concept of habitus, Fuchs exposes the risks that socially transgressive misalliances involved. Throughout the sixteenth and seventeenth centuries, the combined pressures of social stratification, sexual disciplining, and the reform of religion heightened the likelihood that matchmaking across the social divide between noble and non-noble would injure the honor of kin-groups on one or both sides, thereby damaging the social capital available to them for subsequent matches. Such were the stakes, Fuchs shows, that when socially transgressive matchmaking fell apart, nobles and commoners alike defended their honor to the top of the empire's judicial hierarchy. Much the same tension between sex and status that doomed Agnes Bernauer kept imperial tribunals busy with trials of honor.

A similar dynamic operated at the top of the social hierarchy, as Sikora shows, in marital ties between princely families and nobles of lesser, non-sovereign rank. Here too, social distinction depended on an exclusivity that sexual attraction sometimes confounded. Concubinage was one solution, but like commoners, the families of noblewomen proved increasingly unwilling to allow sexual unions with princes that, in the absence of any public recognition, impugned their honor. Such pressure helps to explain Landgrave Philipp of Hessen's eagerness to enter a bigamous marriage; it also gave emperors reason to elevate the socially inferior wives of imperial princes. But such interventions were politically difficult and, in Pierre Bourdieu's terms, risked exhausting the

social capital available to emperors who indulged in rank-elevation too lib-
erally. Princely dynasties resolved the conundrum by crafting a new type of
marriage—morganatic marriage (*Friedelehe*)—which rather like today's same-
sex civil unions, conferred some, but not all the rights of full-fledged marriage.
Left out of such unions was the morganatic wife's right to participate in her
husband's rank or to claim a portion of his inheritance. But the marriage did
not injure the wife's honor or that of her family, and the children were considered legitimate. Thus the innovation granted recognition while shielding
princely lineages from the taint of marrying down.

An analogous set of innovations defined marriage across confessional
lines—a new barrier to marriage in the sixteenth century, and the subject of
three contributions to this volume.[31] Paradoxically, legal barriers to marriage
between Catholics, Lutherans, and Reformed Protestants were few and far between during the sixteenth century. Luther, for his part, had discarded any impediment to marriage on the basis of disparate belief as contrary to the words
of the Apostle Paul in 1 Corinthians 7:13.[32] A few Protestant states tried to
prevent interconfessional marriage by pastoral means, but none banned it outright.[33] Less equivocal was the decree *Tametsi*, promulgated at the Council of
Trent in 1563, that stipulated that a valid marriage could only be performed by
an ordained Catholic priest. But even the Roman Catholic church also recognized the validity of marriages not performed by its own clergy and regarded
as binding unions between Catholics and so-called heretics. The situation was
made no clearer by a decision of the Imperial Diet in 1555 to recognize the
Augsburg Confession—the basic transcript of Lutheran beliefs—as a lawful
form of Christian worship in the Holy Roman Empire. Nevertheless, as a small
but growing body of research shows, by 1600 or so confessional divisions had
hardened to the extent that confessional endogamy was the norm—even in cities such as Augsburg or territories such as the prince-bishopric of Osnabrück,
in which more than one form of Christian observance enjoyed official status. In
eighteenth-century Augsburg, for example, the number of confessionally mixed
marriages made up barely 1 percent of the total.[34] When they formed, such
unions posed novel questions of confessional adhesion: Where would the family worship? In what religion would the children be raised?

Dagmar Freist shows that ordinary peasants exhibited as much ingenuity
as princely dynasts in crafting broadly acceptable solutions to the problems
that transgressive unions generated. As with misalliances, the main obstacles
to inter-confessional marriage were not legal but social. With respect to the
education of children, however, imperial law seemed to assert the right of fathers to determine the religion of their children (the *patria potestas*). In her
case studies from the prince-bishopric of Osnabrück, however, Freist finds that
mixed couples typically obeyed a customary maxim that held that confessional
adhesion should follow gender—that sons would be raised in the religion of

their father, and daughters in the religion of their mother. This solution and the families it generated were not without conflict; they also faced constant pressure from magistrates, kin, and clergy whose interest lay not in preserving domestic peace, but in pressing one confession's advantage over the other. Even so, it is noteworthy that religious difference did not dissuade ordinary parishioners from forming marital unions, if some other rationale made them compelling, and that they found pragmatic and broadly equitable solutions to the problems that inter-confessional marriage posed.

How princely families managed to traverse the confessional gap are the subject of essays by Daniel Riches and Alexander Schunka. Riches examines an attenuated marriage negotiation during the 1630s and early 1640s that, had it succeeded, would have united Queen Christina of Sweden, who at that point had not yet converted to Catholicism, with Elector Friedrich Wilhelm of Brandenburg-Prussia. In the end, a combination of obstacles—confessional difference, divergent customs, inequality of rank, and rumors of Christina's lesbianism—proved insuperable. Of these, religion and rank were the most damaging: owing to the Queen's superior rank, Swedish diplomats demanded that Friedrich Wilhelm, a Calvinist, convert to the Lutheran creed. This he was unwilling to do, but Riches insists that this should not distract us from the transformative potential that such negotiations carried. Marriage negotiations were characterized by a liminality, he argues, that joined all parties to the negotiation in kind of suspended reality, in which everyday constraints are exposed as arbitrary and the potential for radical transformation seems unbounded. In this case, the marriage promised to resolve the two states' competing claims over the Duchy of Pomerania; more fundamentally, it raised the prospect of reconciliation between the two main branches of Protestant faith. That these hopes were dashed is less significant than the fact that between sovereign dynasties, inter-confessional matchmaking was capable of raising them at all.

Indeed, the implications of dynastic marriages that crossed confessional lines reverberated throughout the European political system—as Alexander Schunka shows in his analysis of unions between the British and German ruling houses. The number of inter-confessional dynastic marriages increased significantly after 1700, but unlike similar unions in the seventeenth century, did not necessarily involve conversion. Mixed marriages therefore produced confessionally plural courts and enlivened the hopes of irenicists for reunion among the Protestant faiths. In Berlin, the Calvinist court preacher, Daniel Ernst Jablonski, looked to George I, king of England and elector of Hanover, as a model for reconciliation: If George could be an Anglican in England and a Lutheran in Hanover, what was to prevent his subjects from rapprochement? Perhaps the practices of accommodation that characterized the court of St. James might also function in Berlin, where George's Lutheran sister Sophia Charlotte had reigned as Prussia's first queen. Unfortunately for irenicism, the softening of confessional barriers to marriage among the high and mighty held little promise for Protestant reunion, and Jablonski's hopes were dashed.

Given the paramount status that race acquired in the nineteenth century, it is ironic that such differences presented relatively minor obstacles to marriage, at least for sailors and merchants overseas, in comparison with the barriers of religion and social inequality. In her contribution to this volume, Antje Flüchter explores interethnic unions between Europeans and South Asians, as they were described in German-language travel literature of the seventeenth and eighteenth centuries—a genre dominated by men of little education, written as much for entertainment as instruction—and in novelistic accounts of South Asia. Even more than ethnicity and social rank, religion placed strict limits on who could marry whom. This is not to say that ethnic difference counted for nothing. Some evaded the problem by taking native women as concubines. But Flüchter warns that we must not assume this was the norm, for to do so would involve viewing interethnic unions anachronistically, from the perspective of a scientific and biological worldview. For contemporaries, only the barrier separating Christianity from so-called heathen religions could not be transgressed: as long as both parties were Christian, the remaining obstacles to marriage— status inequality, ethnicity—were subject to negotiation.

If post-Reformation Europe said little about race as an obstacle to marriage, it spoke great volumes on the incest taboo. Here the reformers' interventions were ample and explicit: Luther, characteristically, insisted that a man was forbidden to marry only those enumerated in Leviticus 18:6–13, namely, "my mother, my stepmother; my sister, my stepsister; my child's daughter or step-daughter; my father's sister; my mother's sister."[35] Anyone else, in his view, was fair game. On the whole, Protestant authorities were more cautious and tended to reinforce existing, canonical prohibitions against marriages within the third degree of consanguinity—and to threaten offenders with capital punishment.[36] But as Claudia Jarzebowski shows in her contribution to this volume, we must not conclude that their redefinition of incest taboos was any less profound. On the contrary: the early reformers narrowed the definition of incest by sweeping aside whole categories of spiritual kinship (*cognatio spiritualis*) and focusing instead on questions of consanguinity in marriage, subject to the adjudication of secular authority. The result was a drastic reduction in the number of spiritual impediments to marriage. Shaping the entire discourse, Jarzebowski argues, was a shift in understandings of love and its relationship to sexuality, friendship, and power. Reformers redefined love, separating its godly manifestations from the so-called natural and devil-inspired drives. Thus incest became the proper object of natural law. The Enlightenment redefined incest yet again, this time giving a positive valence to the natural.

The volume concludes with Mary Lindemann's essay on the Guyard affair of 1765—a cause célèbre in Hamburg that raised a host of questions about the nature of incest, the effects of reading and, ultimately, the meaning of Enlightenment. The incident, which involved the alleged molestation of a young woman by her father—or was it perhaps a consensual incestuous relationship?—threw into turmoil all the parties involved: Charlotte Guyard, her father Denys Martin (a French immigrant), her husband Jean-François, as well as the citizens of Hamburg and their magistrates. Charlotte first embellished the charge of incest, then recanted and accused her newlywed husband of stirring up the trouble. The resulting cause célèbre expressed anxieties that laxer attitudes toward incest taboos had generated. Even more profoundly, it articulated fears over the potentially disruptive effects of reading on sexual morality. Books, especially "dirty books," were blamed for the corruption of the daughter; worse, it was her father who had put these books into her hands. Thus did the pedagogic initiatives of Enlightenment clash with sexual mores: as never before, fathers were expected to serve as preceptor to their children and cultivate their daughters in reason and chastity through proper reading. The Guyard affair turned such expectations on their head, showing how the wrong books could just as surely be blamed for leading a young woman down a path toward immorality, sin, and sexual depravity.

* * * * *

With Charlotte Guyard, we stand at the threshold of modern marriage, its freedoms and constraints. Some of the older impediments would soon disappear, or had already. In the nineteenth century, as David Sabean, Simon Teuscher, and Jon Matheiu have argued, marriage became far more endogamous, in relation both to class and kin.[37] Cousin marriage, which the incest norms of the sixteenth century had forbidden, became more common in all social strata as a means of consolidating material resources and conveying them from one generation to the next. Gone too were the impediments of spiritual kinship. With the eclipse of serfdom in its many guises, the ancient obligation of bonded men and women to marry within the circle (*familia*) of persons subject to the same serf-lord likewise disappeared.[38] Other constraints were new, or nearly so. Among them was the barrier posed by race—in part because the occasions for interethnic union were more numerous, in part owing to the emergence of race as an organizing category in law, science, anthropology, and social thought. The consolidation of nations and modern citizenship redefined and encumbered the formation of marriages between the citizens of one country and those of another. Still other constraints remained firmly in place: the social barrier to marriage imposed by religious difference, already established by the eighteenth century, persisted well into the nineteenth. Likewise the prohibitions against bigamy and polygamy—however ill-grounded in theology and natural law, and no matter how poorly enforced among the high and mighty— remained in effect. Morganatic marriage continued right along, enabling the

sovereign dynasties of Europe to replenish their supply of child-bearing females without exposing princely lineages to the taint of lesser blood. The most
famous morganatic pair—Archduke Franz Ferdinand of Austria and his lower-
ranking wife, Sophie von Chotkowa—died at the hand of an assassin in Sara-
jevo on 28 June 1914.

Joel Harrington's afterword to this volume summarizes the transformations
that span the preceding period, between the late Middle Ages and the Enlightenment, and suggests how these essays adjust our understanding of them. For
present purposes, then, it is enough to stress again that if there is a constant
in marriage since the Reformation, it is the persistence of change. Definitions
of marriage, its purpose and ideal constitution, have altered radically over
time, leaving behind older forms with each transformation. The Reformation
changed marriage profoundly, giving rise to an ideal that the modern protagonists of traditional take for eternal. The Enlightenment, too, exposed marriage
to thorough-going critique. Since the nineteenth century, we have been in an
era in which the impediments of race, religion, and sex have slowly but surely
withered away. One can only guess what the future will bring.

Notes

1. The seventeen states that in 1967 still forbade interracial marriage were Alabama,
   Arkansas, Delaware, Florida, Georgia, Kentucky, Louisiana, Maryland, Mississippi,
   Missouri, North Carolina, Oklahoma, South Carolina, Tennessee, Texas, Virginia,
   and West Virginia. Maryland repealed its law in 1967, after the Supreme Court had
   begun deliberations on the Loving case. The nine that never enacted miscegenation
   laws were Alaska, Connecticut, Hawaii, Minnesota, New Hampshire, New Jersey,
   New York, Vermont, and Wisconsin. On the Loving decision, see Fay Botham, *Almighty God Created the Races: Christianity, Interracial Marriage, and American Law*
   (Chapel Hill, 2009); and Peter Wallenstein, "Interracial Marriage on Trial: Loving v.
   Virginia (1967)," in *Race on Trial: Law and Justice in American History*, ed. Annette
   Gordon-Reed (Oxford, 2002), 177–96. On the enactment and repeal of racial barriers
   to marriage generally, see Peggy Pascoe, *What Comes Naturally: Miscegenation Law and
   the Making of Race in America* (Oxford, 2009).
2. According to a survey conducted in 2010 by the Pew Research Center for the People and the Press, 85 percent of Americans born in or after 1981 "would be fine with
   a family member"s marriage to someone of a different racial or ethnic group." See
   "Almost All Millenials Accept Interracial Dating and Marriage," Pew Research Center Publications (1 February 2010), http://pewresearch.org/pubs/1480/millennials-
   accept-interracial-dating-marriage-friends-different-race-generations.
3. Anne C. Rose, *Beloved Strangers: Interfaith Families in Nineteenth-Century America*
   (Cambridge, UK, 2001), 50–66.
4. Allan McCutcheon, "Denominations and Religious Intermarriage: Trends among
   White Americans in the Twentieth Century," *Review of Religious Research* 29 (1988):
   213–27.

5. See Christopher Clark, "Religion and Confessional Conflict," in *Imperial Germany, 1871–1918*, ed. James Retallack (Oxford, 2008), 83–105, here 94–95. On the near disappearance of interconfessional marriage during the eighteenth century, see Étienne François, *Die unsichtbare Grenze: Protestanten und Katholiken in Augsburg, 1647–1806* (Sigmaringen, 1991), 190–204.
6. Among the highest rates of conversion from Judaism to Christianity, for example, were in Austria, where law forbade such unions; see Avraham Barkai, "Bevölkerungsrück-gang und wirtschaftliche Stagnation," in *Deutsch-Jüdische Geschichte in der Neuzeit*, ed. Michael A. Meyer, Michael Brenner, Avraham Barkai, Paul Mendes-Flohr, and Steven M. Lowenstein, 4 vols. (Munich, 1996–2000), vol. 4, 37–49, here 39; and Steven M. Lowenstein, "Jewish Intermarriage and Conversion in Germany and Austria," *Modern Judaism* 25 (2005): 23–61.
7. Roderick Philips, *Putting Asunder: A History of Divorce in Western Society* (Cambridge, UK, 1988), 185–251.
8. David Warren Sabean, *Kinship in Neckarhausen, 1700–1870* (Cambridge, UK, 1998).
9. John Boswell argued, famously, that medieval liturgies for "brother-making" attest to formal recognition for affective, personal unions between males that were parallel to heterosexual marriage; see Boswell, *Same-Sex Unions in Premodern Europe* (New York, 1994). Boswell's critics argued that his analytic language obscured alternative interpretations of "brotherhood" in favor of marriage-like sexual union; see Joan Cadden's review in *Speculum* 71 (1996): 693–96. Better documented is the quasi-legal recognition accorded to same-sex male households in southern France through the device of *affrèrement* contracts; see Allan Tulchin, "Same-Sex Couples Creating Households in Old Regime France: The Uses of *Affrèrement*," *Journal of Modern History* 79 (2007): 613–47.
10. These are Argentina, Belgium, Brazil, Canada, Denmark, France, Iceland, the Netherlands, New Zealand, Norway, Portugal, South Africa, Spain, Sweden and Uruguay. In Mexico, same-sex unions are recognized everywhere but performed only in the capital city. The parliament of the United Kingdom passed a bill legalizing same-sex marriage in July 2013 that will take effect in mid-2014. Israel recognizes same-sex unions, but does not allow them to be performed.
11. The thirteen states are Massachusetts (2004), Connecticut (2008), Iowa (2009), Vermont (2009), New Hampshire (2010), New York (2011), Maine (2012), Maryland (2012), Washington (2012), Rhode Island (2013), Delaware (2013), Minnesota (2013), California (2013), New Jersey, (2013), Hawaii (2013), Illinois (2014), and New Mexico (2014). Another three states—Nevada, Oregon, and Wisconsin—have passed "domestic partnership" or "civil union" laws that confer rights similar, but not equal, to marriage.
12. "Religion and Attitudes toward Same-Sex Marriage," The Pew Forum on Religion and Public Life (7 February 2012), http://www.pewforum.org/2012/02/07/religion-and-attitudes-toward-same-sex-marriage/.
13. "Official Prop. 8 Proponent Claims Same-Sex Marriage Can Harm Children," *Los Angeles Times* (22 January 2010), http://articles.latimes.com/2010/jan/22/local/la-me-prop8-trial22-2010jan22.
14. Thus a pamphlet by Paul Thigpen, "Same-Sex Unions: A Catholic Response" (2004); accessible at http://www.paulthigpen.com/?page_id=522.
15. Pascoe, *What Comes Naturally*, 69–74.

16. "Straff der Unkeuschheit / so wider die Natur geschicht," §116, *Peinliche Halßgericht des . . . Keyser Carols deß Fünfften und des Heyligen Romischen Reichs peinlich Gerichts ordnung, auff den Reichstag zu Augspurg und Regenspurg in den Jaren dreyssig und zwey und dreyssig gehalten auffgericht und beschlossen* (Frankfurt, 1609), 54.

17. Bernardino Ochino, *Dialogi XXX in duos libros diuisi* (Basel, 1563), translated as *A Dialogue of Polygamy, Written Originally in Italian* (London, 1657).

18. On Ochino, see Roland H. Bainton, *The Travail of Religious Liberty; Nine Biographical Studies* (Philadelphia, 1951), 139–76.

19. See Stephan Buchholz, *Recht, Religion, und Ehe: Orientierungswandel und gelehrte Kontroversen im Übergang vom 17. zum 18. Jahrhundert* (Frankfurt, 1988), 27 and 374–406; and Paul Mikat, *Die Polygamiefrage in der frühen Neuzeit* (Opladen, 1988), 8 et passim. See also Manuel Braun, "Tiefe oder Oberfläche? Zur Lektüre der Schriften des Christian Thomasius über Polygamie und Konkubinat," *Internationales Archiv für Sozialgeschichte der deutschen Literatur* 30 (2005): 28–54.

20. Steven Ozment, *When Fathers Ruled: Family Life in Reformation Europe* (Cambridge, US, 1983); for a more sober assessment, see Joel F. Harrington, *Reordering Marriage and Society in Reformation Germany* (Cambridge, UK, 1995).

21. Martin Luther, *Vom Eelichen Leben* (Wittenberg, 1522), Aiii^v; translated as "The Estate of Marriage," in Helmut T. Lehmann, ed., *Luther's Works*, vol. 45, *The Christian in Society II* (Philadelphia, 1962), 11–49.

22. William W. Rockwell, *Die Doppelehe des Landgrafen Philipp von Hessen* (Marburg, 1904), 1. See also Buchholz, *Recht, Religion, und Ehe*, 382–86.

23. Ruth Mazo Karras, *Unmarriages: Women, Men and Sexual Unions in the Middle Ages* (Philadelphia, 2012), 1.

24. See Ludwig Schmugge, Patrick Hersperger, and Béatrice Wiggenhauser, *Die Supplikenregister der päpstlichen Pönitentiarie aus der Zeit Pius II (1458–1464)* (Tübingen, 1996). On medieval concubinage see most recently Karras, *Unmarriages*, 115–64.

25. Marjorie Elizabeth Plummer, *From Priest's Whore to Pastor's Wife: Clerical Marriage and the Process of Reform in the Early German Reformation* (Farnham, UK, 2012), 11–50.

26. See Claudia Jarzebowski's contribution to this volume.

27. See the essays collected in *Glaube und Eid: Treuformeln, Glaubensbekenntnisse und Sozialdisziplinierung zwischen Mittelalter und Neuzeit*, ed. Paolo Prodi and Elisabeth Müller-Luckner (Munich, 1993); and in *Serment, promesse et engagement: Rituels et modalités au Moyen Âge*, ed. Françoise Laurent (Montpellier, 2008).

28. See also Amy Leonard, *Nails in the Wall: Catholic Nuns in Reformation Germany* (Chicago, 2005).

29. On noble obsession with documenting lineage, see the essays contained in *Dynastie und Herrschaftssicherung in der Frühen Neuzeit: Geschlechter und Geschlecht*, ed. Heide Wunder (Berlin, 2002). For a case study, see Erica Bastress-Dukehart, *The Zimmern Chronicle: Nobility, Memory and Self-Representation in Sixteenth-Century Germany* (Aldershot, UK, 2002).

30. Andreas von Regensburg (1380–1442), "Chronica de principibus terrae Bavarorum," in *Andreas von Regensburg, Sämtliche Werke*, ed. Georg Leidinger (Munich, 1903), 503–87, here 583–84. Literary treatments commence with Hans Sachs'"Die ertrenkt Jungfrau" (1546); see Alfons Huber, "Ein bislang unbekanntes Meisterlied, die älteste faßbare literarische Bearbeitung des Bernauerstoffes," *Jahresbericht des Historischen Vereins für Straubing und Umgebung* 86 (1984): 453–66.

31. On the novelty of confession as an impediment to marriage, see David M. Luebke, "Making Marriages Mixed: Religious Pluralization, Ritual, and the Formation of Intra-Christian Marriage Barriers in Germany," in *Gemischte Ehen im Europa: Politik und Praxis der religiösen Pluralität (14.–19. Jh.)*, ed. Cecilia Cristellon (forthcoming); and Dagmar Freist, "One Body, Two Confessions: Mixed Marriages in Germany," in Ulinka Rublack, ed., *Gender in Early Modern Germany* (Cambridge, UK, 2002), 275–304.

32. Luther, *Vom Eelichen Leben*, Bii.

33. See, for example, "Des . . . herrn Augusten, herzog zu Sachsen u.s.w. Ordnung" (1580), in *Die evangelischen Kirchenordnungen des XVI. Jahrhunderts*, vol. 1/1, *Sachsen und Thüringen nebst angrenzenden Gebieten*, ed. Emil Sehling et al. (Leipzig, 1902), 359–457, here 436.

34. François, *Die unsichtbare Grenze*, 192. See also Paul Warmbrunn, *Zwei Konfessionen in einer Stadt: Das Zusammenleben von Katholiken und Protestanten in den paritätischen Reichsstädten Augsburg, Biberach, Ravensburg und Dinkelsbühl von 1548 bis 1648* (Wiesbaden, 1993), 332–55; and Peter Zschunke, *Konfession und Alltag in Oppenheim: Beiträge zur Geschichte von Bevölkerung und Gesellschaft einer gemischtkonfessionellen Kleinstadt in der Frühen Neuzeit* (Wiesbaden, 1984), 102–4. See also Elisabeth Homing, "Konfession und demographisches Verhalten: Oberkassel, 1670–1810," *Historical Social Research /Historische Sozialforschung* 23 (1998): 275–98. On confessional intermarriage rates in the prince-bishopric of Osnabrück, see Jürgen Schlumbohm, *Lebensläufe, Familien, Höfe: Die Bauern und Heuerleute des Osnabrückischen Kirchspiels Belm in proto-industrieller Zeit, 1650–1860* (Göttingen, 1994), 419; and Dagmar Freist's contribution to this volume.

35. Luther, *Vom Eelichen Leben*, Aiv^v.

36. On Protestant marriage law in general, see Hartwig Dieterich, *Das protestantische Eherecht in Deutschland bis zur Mitte des 17. Jahrhunderts* (Munich, 1970); and John Witte Jr., *Law and Protestantism: The Legal Teachings of the Lutheran Reformation* (Cambridge, UK, 2002), 214–55. For the ban against incest, see "Straff de Unkeuscheit mit nahenden Gesipten Freunden," §117 in *Peinliche Halßgericht des . . . Keyser Carols*, 54.

37. David Sabean, Simon Teuscher, and Jon Mathieu, "Outline and Summaries," in their *Kinship in Europe: Approaches to Long-Term Development (1300–1900)* (New York, 2007), 187–92.

38. See Peter Blickle, *Von der Leibeigenschaft zu den Menschenrechten: Eine Geschichte der Freiheit in Deutschland* (Munich, 2003). For the particulars of servile marriage prohibitions, see Walter Müller, *Entwicklung und Spätformen der Leibeigenschaft am Beispiel der Heiratsbeschränkungen: Die Ehegenoßsame im alemannisch-schweizerischen Raum* (Sigmaringen, 1974).

CHAPTER 1

~: :~

"It Is Not Forbidden that a Man May Have More Than One Wife"
Luther's Pastoral Advice on Bigamy and Marriage

DAVID M. WHITFORD

In 1522 Martin Luther published a short treatise on the estate of marriage.[1] It was based on a series of sermons on the subject and covered the negative impediments to marriage, possible reasons one might terminate a marriage, and the positive benefits of marriage. This was not a topic he relished. "How I dread preaching on the estate of marriage! I am reluctant to do it because I am afraid if I once get really involved in the subject it will make a lot of work for me and for others. The shameful confusion wrought by the accursed papal law has occasioned so much distress and the lax authority of both the spiritual and temporal swords had given rise to so many dreadful abuses and false situations that I would much prefer neither to look into the matter nor hear of it."[2] Though Luther lay blame for confused consciences at the feet of papal law, it might just as easily be placed upon the human condition, for, as we shall see, Luther's own advice concerning marital affairs was no less confusing or contradictory than was medieval canon law.[3]

Luther always saw himself primarily as a pastor who was appointed by God to care for souls. The care of souls governed his approach to marriage matters not appeals to legal formulations or cultural traditions. He always saw marriage through the lens of pastoral care, and if there was a conflict between the law or tradition and a troubled conscience, then Luther believed that one must "tear through the law confidently like a millstone ripping through a spider web, and act as if the law had never been born."[4] Though he often spoke of marriage as a public act, Luther's pastoral advice focused on the private nature of the marriage bond. Understanding these two patterns of behavior helps explain the seeming inconsistencies of his counsel. First, by treating each marriage as unique, he created a dynamic that encouraged hypersensitivity to the powers of sexual drive and to the soteriological consequences of allowing that drive to go unchecked.[5] Luther believed that lust and fornication led inevitably to damnation; marriage provided a necessary outlet for sexual desire. He therefore sought to open up rather than foreclose opportunities for people to marry. Second, Luther's pastoral impulses toward those who sought his counsel often overwhelmed sound judgment or theological consistency.

Nowhere are these two patterns of behavior more clearly demonstrated than in his advice on bigamy.[6] Luther wrote and offered advice on bigamous marriage from the 1520s through the 1540s. At times the persons involved were ordinary people, sometimes they were fellow clergy; most famously, the subject of bigamy came up in advice offered to Henry VIII of England and Philipp, Landgrave of Hesse. Through all these writings a clear tendency reveals itself: Luther consistently offered overly permissive counsel for those he cared about and severe or harsh counsel for those with whom he disagreed or those he regarded as foes.[7]

Luther's Theological Approach to Marriage and Bigamy in the 1520s

Luther's earliest comprehensive examination of marriage is a sermon from early 1519.[8] The sermon has as its focus Genesis 2:18–24, which recounts the creation of Eve and begins with God's declaration, "It is not good for man to be alone." Using that divine decree, Luther instructs his hearers to pray for a spouse earnestly because a spouse is a good gift from God. He then recapitulates much of medieval theology on marriage that the original benefits of marriage, established by God before the Fall, are companionship (fidelity) and children (procreation). After the Fall, God added a third benefit—restraint of sin.[9] Marriage provides an outlet for sexual desire because the "temptation of the flesh has become so strong and consuming that marriage may be likened to a hospital for incurables which prevents inmates from falling into graver sin."[10] Here, Luther connects the power of lust with the need for marriage. Lust is not just a simple human temptation, as one might assume from reading the text in the American edition translation. The term he used—*Anfechtung*—is more than temptation: it is a powerful, even existential force that can overwhelm a person. It is satanic in origin and destructive to the soul.[11] For Luther, lust is an *Anfechtung* that is "great and raging" (*gross und wütend*).

Marriage overcomes this great and raging force in human beings by creating a "community of fidelity" (*eyn vorbuntnuß . . . der trew*).[12] This devoted community binds one to the other and makes clear that "the way is barred to the body of anyone else, and they content themselves in the marriage bed with their one companion. In this way God sees to it that the flesh is subdued so as to not rage wherever and however it pleases, and within this plighted troth, permits even more occasion than is necessary for the begetting of children."[13] The question of curbing lust and providing an outlet for sexual desire becomes especially pronounced in the question of bigamy.

Luther's writings on marriage and bigamy must be seen in light of his belief that marriage was ordered according to God's Two Kingdoms, the doctrine that guided Luther's approach to nearly all social and political institutions.[14] According to Luther, God worked in the world in two distinct but complementary ways: through civil orders and estates, and through the church. Thus Luther argued that the church and pastors ought to speak to married persons regarding God's plan—that one should be faithful and multiply—and about God's expectations within marriage—thou shall not commit adultery. As a public institution, marriage is an "external, worldly matter like clothing and food, house and property, subject to temporal authority, as the many imperial laws enacted on the subject prove."[15] According to Luther, therefore, bigamy was subject to civil law. Though not always enforced, bigamy was outlawed throughout the Christian West. As early as the sixth century, the Justinian Code had declared that "our citizens are forbidden to contract more than one marriage at a time."[16] In the early thirteenth century, Eike von Repgau made clear that digamy—sequential marriage—was permitted but otherwise described marriage as monogamous.[17] The gloss accompanying Eike's discussion notes that marriage is the "oldest, the most holy, the most beneficial of all orders" and one "established at the beginning of creation when the first rules were given to the first people."[18] When people fail to honor marriage, the glossator continued, they bring asunder all the orders of creation.[19] Likewise in the sixteenth century, civil law condemned bigamy harshly. In Germany, the influential Criminal Code of Bamberg (1507) and the Imperial Criminal Code of 1532 both continued the prohibition of "a married man taking another wife or of a married woman taking another husband." The punishment for bigamy could include death.[20] Canon law on the question of plural marriage was equally censorious. The *Decretals* forbade bigamy and provided for only a single exception—a divine mandate, such as was given to the patriarchs of the Old Testament. Even then, however, it was recognized that this was contrary to natural law.[21]

Luther was conversant with both secular and canon law, but his discussions of bigamy vacillated between consistency with tradition, modification, and complete rejection. His earliest comments that challenge traditional views of marriage and bigamy appeared in the 1520 treatise, *On the Babylonian Captivity of the Church* (De captivitate Babyonicae ecclesiae), where he observes that if marriage is a "hospital for lust," then one party's inability to copulate denied the other much needed medicine.[22] If this medicinal nature of marriage could not be found in one place, people would seek it in another, thereby putting their souls in jeopardy. The traditional solution was to dissolve the marriage through public testimony. If, however, the parties did not wish to publicize the man's impotence and the wife could not remain continent, Luther recommended that the wife enter into a secret, bigamous marriage, for the reason that impotence had disqualified the first husband and rendered him "only a dweller under the same roof with her."[23] Here, clearly, Luther departs from tradition. While impotence justified the dissolution of a marriage, nothing in the *Decretals* or other pastoral advice manuals recommends a secret, plural marriage as the solution to impotence. In fact the twelfth-century scholastic, Peter Lombard, explicitly denied this possibility.[24] Luther rejected the church's tradition on pastoral grounds because the wife's soul was jeopardized by the adultery that would likely result from her husband's incapacity. But he does not explain why a secret marriage was better than a public dissolution of the marriage despite the embarrassment that would be inflicted upon the husband. Over the next twenty years, the question of plural marriage discussed in the *Babylonian Captivity* in the abstract would give way to actual examples of bigamy, the earliest of which appeared just a few years later.

These early discussions of plural marriage are found in Luther's letters to civil and ecclesiastical officials.[25] The first was written to the Saxon chancellor Gregor Brück (1484–1557) in 1524 and concerned events surrounding Andreas Bodenstein von Karlstadt (1486–1541) in Orlamünde. The exact nature of what happened in Orlamünde is unclear, but it appears that Karlstadt—Luther's erstwhile colleague and rival—had given permission to a man whose wife was ill to marry a second woman. Luther begins by noting that while bigamy is not "repugnant to scripture," he does not think it advisable that it be "introduced among Christians" because not everything that is permissible to a Christian "ought to be seized upon even if [Christian] freedom allows it." Furthermore, he did not believe that the man's soul was truly endangered by his wife's illness and her inability to have a sexual relationship with him. "I scarcely believe that God would so desert a Christian, because of some divinely imposed impediment to conjugal rights [the wife's illness], that he would be unable to remain continent."[26]

The second letter (August 1525) concerns Pastor Michael Kramer of Dommitsch.[27] Kramer was an avid supporter of Luther. In 1523 he had married a servant from Eisenberg named Dorothea. Sometime shortly thereafter, the bishop of Naumburg had him arrested for violating his oath of chastity, but Kramer escaped and fled to Wittenberg. In the meantime, Dorothea grew tired of him and sought companionship with another. When Kramer returned from Wittenberg in 1524 to retrieve her and bring her to his pastoral appointment, she balked. Later she would marry another man after the city council in her new town refused to acknowledge the legitimacy of her marriage to Kramer. Kramer, in the meantime, had also remarried. By August 1525, however, this second wife had also left Kramer.

The status of twice-abandoned Kramer became the subject of controversy in Dommitsch. Urged to respond, Luther wrote a short letter to the city council, in which he blames Kramer's abandonment on the women, stating that they have been "very dishonest wives" toward Kramer, and that if one of them will not return to him, Luther has nothing to add beyond what God's word had already declared in 1 Corinthians 7 ("But if the unbelieving partner desires to separate, let it be so; in such a case the brother or sister is not bound. For God has called us to peace"). Two years earlier, Luther had written a commentary on 1 Corinthians 7, in which he discussed whether one who had been abandoned by a wife or husband might remarry. According to Luther, Paul "releases the Christian spouse, once the non-Christian partner has separated himself or will not permit his mate to lead a Christian life," even if this meant that a Christian might have "ten or more wives who are still living" because this is far better than falling into a "heathen or unchristian way of life."[28] Luther's interpretation of this text departs dramatically from tradition. Throughout the medieval era, 1 Corinthians 7 was used as a justification for the superiority of celibacy over marriage. Luther rejected that reading earlier and offers in its place an almost entirely novel understanding of the term "unbeliever." In 1 Corinthians 7, Paul is speaking of Christians married to non-Christians; in Luther's new view, unbelieving spouses cannot really be said to be a pagan. Rather, the act of leaving and refusing to return to their spouse marks them as "truly a heathen and unchristian." Kramer's two wives both fit this category. Thus, if Pastor Kramer "cannot live without a wife, then he is free, in the Name of God, to take another."[29]

In these first two examples of Luther's pastoral advice concerning bigamy and marital fidelity, a pattern emerges: his advice varies depending not on the congruity of the situation to his previously stated position, but rather according to the theological position of the actors involved. The difference between his advice regarding Pastor Kramer and the un-named Orlamünde parishioner is striking. Both scenarios mirror hypothetical situations earlier outlined by Luther. In the first case, however, Luther not only condemns the proposed bigamous marriage as contrary to true Christianity and scripture, but also even denies that a person in such a situation would be unable to remain sexually faithful to his sickly wife—the very justification for secret plural marriage he had advocated in the *Babylonian Captivity*. In the second case, Luther's opinion is exactly in keeping with his position in the 1523 commentary on 1 Corinthians 7. The only discernable difference is that while Kramer was an active supporter of Luther, Karlstadt was by then a theological adversary.[30] This pattern of altering advice to suit not the situation but the actors continued into the 1530s.

Bigamy and the Marriage of Henry VIII

Luther's habit of adapting his pastoral advice to fit his interlocutor is also evident in his relationship with King Henry VIII. Henry apparently first learned some specifics of Luther's theology in 1519. In 1521 Henry published his famous retort to Luther's *Babylonian Captivity*. The two men continued to quarrel throughout the 1520s. Their debates were acrimonious and marked by personal invective. Thus, it is somewhat surprising that as part of his campaign to secure support for the annulment of his marriage or his divorce from Catherine of Aragon, Henry sought the opinion of Protestant theologians on his "great matter." Simon Gryneaus, a Basel professor visiting in England, was dispatched back to the Continent where he secured the opinions of the reformers Huldrych Zwingli, Martin Bucer, Johannes Oecolampadius, and Philip Melanchthon. Robert Barnes was delegated to secure the opinion of Martin Luther.[31]

"Much ill-will" greeted his opinion in England.[32] Luther completely rejected the possibility of divorce and added that if Henry proceeded to divorce Catherine, he would violate the law of God and the queen would still remain both his wife and the legitimate queen.[33] As already noted, Luther was generally opposed to divorce except in cases of adultery, abandonment, or incapacity. None of those conditions applied to Henry. Furthermore, the birth of Mary Tudor ruled out divorce even if Levitical law had been broken. On this point Luther was consistent. A year earlier, in *On Marriage Matters*, he had noted that forcing a divorce would destroy the woman's honor and therefore the marriage ought to be maintained out of "mercy and to prevent greater calamity."[34] The greater calamity Luther saw in the case of Henry VIII was that it would "make the mother as well as the daughter into incestuous women."[35] Just a few weeks before Luther and Melanchthon were approached about Henry VIII's marriage difficulties, they wrote an opinion on marriage matters and consanguinity for some Protestant princes. In that memorandum they noted that people are often confused by the rules of affinity and are even more perplexed by malleable papal dispensations that sometimes annul these rules.

Nevertheless, there could never be a case "when one should leave a marriage for God's sake."[36] Thus, Luther's reticence to endorse the divorce is not terribly surprising. As an alternative he held out the possibility of Henry taking a second queen: "Before I would approve of such a divorce," he wrote, "I would rather permit the King to marry still another woman and to have, according to the examples of the patriarchs and kings, two women or queens at the same time."[37] This suggestion was in keeping with the literary device he had used a decade earlier and had already been raised elsewhere.[38] Where Luther did alter his opinion relative to Henry VIII was in his complete dismissal of the purported foundation of Henry's anxiety: the prohibition of his marriage by Leviticus 18.

Luther consistently opposed marriages of affinity and specifically a marriage between a man and his brother's wife. In 1522 he wrote on the issue of consanguinity twice and forbid such a marriage in each: "God has forbidden these persons [from marrying], namely, my father's brother's wife; my son's wife; my brother's wife."[39] Four years after his opinion on Henry's marriage, Luther produced a theological opinion on a proposed marriage in Zwickau in which a man had already lain with his deceased wife's sister and now sought to marry her. In that memorandum, Luther declared that the couple must separate because "God's command forbids it . . . as is made clear in Leviticus 18, in this case it is a *primo gradu affinitatis* . . . which is also forbidden by imperial law." Furthermore, if the couple continued to live together as married, they will suffer "very troubled consciences."[40]

Luther could have passed over Leviticus 18 in his answer to Henry VIII. He had already declared why, even if Leviticus did forbid the marriage, it was no longer binding because of the birth of Mary. Instead, he spent nearly four pages laying out exactly why Leviticus 18 bore no relevance to Henry's case: "Therefore on the basis of this passage the doctors of the opposition [those supporting Henry's divorce] could accomplish nothing that is sound, even if the law of Moses [still] bound us Gentiles. How much less can they accomplish now since Moses' law does not bind us Gentiles!" While Luther does not betray his earlier theological commitments to the same extent that he did in the mid-1520s cases, the long history of personal attacks between Henry VIII and Luther seems to have colored his response to the questions of divorce or annulment.

Polygamy and the Kingdom on Münster

Perhaps the most notorious example of polygamy in the sixteenth century was the Anabaptist kingdom of Münster. Beyond its simple notoriety, however, Münster is important to Luther's discussion of polygamy because the advocates of polygamy in the kingdom used both scriptural and theological arguments on their behalf. How Luther dealt with those arguments and the consistency of his opinion after Münster follow the same tendency of fitting his advice to the persons involved, and not to the subject.

Polygamy was first introduced in Münster in July of 1534 and came to an end nearly a year later when the city fell to the armies of Münster's bishop and his allies. Luther kept himself informed about events in Münster but, surprisingly, wrote on them only twice.[41] Both writings are short prefaces appended to larger works by others.

The first prefaces Urbanus Rhegius' (1489–1541) *Confutation of the New Valentinian and Donatist Teachings in Münster* (Widderlegung der Münsterischen newen Valentinianer und Donatisten bekentnus).[42] The *Confutation* responds to Bernhard Rothmann's *Restoration of True and Sound Christian Doctrine* (Restitution Rechter und gesunder christlicher Lehre), a defense and apology of Anabaptist theology that appeared in 1534. Rhegius refutes Rothmann's theology point by point and argues that the religious innovations in Münster were not a restoration of true Christian teachings but in reality nothing more than repristinated heresies. Luther heartily approves of Rhegius' refutation but, perhaps because Rhegius was so thorough, waited until the second preface to clearly delineate his own position on some of Rothmann's theological arguments.

This second preface was written immediately after the first and was attached to a sensational account of the events in Münster. Published in 1535, the *New Report on the Anabaptists in Münster* (Newe Zeitung von den Widerteuffern zu Münster) focuses almost exclusively on the "Prophet and King of Münster," Jan of Leiden, who had decreed "all the men have five, six, seven or eight wives, each according to his own pleasure."[43] In his preface, Luther homed in on polygamy and mocked Jan of Leiden's gross excesses. His behavior and Rothmann's justifications of polygamy are so contrary to tradition and morality, Luther argued, as to reveal their allegiance to the devil. But it is a comically incompetent "kindergartner devil . . . just learning his ABC's." A truly smart devil would have told Rothmann and Leiden to dress humbly and flee the company of women, but he prodded them to take "not just one wife but as many as lust and appetite demand."[44] To their theological arguments he is equally dismissive and mocking, noting that if Rothmann was correct in saying that only Anabaptist marriages were holy and that all other marriages made women whores, are not all the leaders in Münster nothing more than "the children of whores" and if so, "what right do they have to the city or the belongings of their ancestors?"[45]

Luther was not alone in his strident condemnation of the kingdom of Münster.[46] In 1535 Philip Melanchthon wrote two treatises on the kingdom.[47] In the both responses, the malleability of early Protestant thought on plural marriage is apparent. In 1531, Philip Melanchthon confidently declared to Henry VIII that "polygamy is not prohibited by divine law."[48] In 1535, however, after branding Anabaptism a "satanic sect," Melanchthon confidently declared, "The Lord Jesus Christ will have the married estate as it was first established by God as he said in Matthew 18, 'and the two shall become one flesh,' so will he now have the estate of marriage: it shall be between two persons and no other way."[49] In the next paragraph, he elaborated, "even though the Jews might have had many wives [*viel weiber*], it still violates natural law [*wider das gesetz der natur*]."[50]

The Landgrave's Great Matter

In 1539 Luther became embroiled in Philipp of Hesse's pursuit of a second wife. The eventual bigamous marriage and Luther's advice regarding it scandalized many in the Holy Roman Empire when it was revealed less than a year later.

Though Luther will later claim that pastoral concern guided all of his actions, a close examination reveals a far more complicated and contradictory story.

In December 1523 Philipp of Hesse (just turned nineteen) married Christina of Saxony (almost eighteen). Over the next sixteen years, they would have seven children. Despite this prodigious procreativity, in 1539 Philipp began to claim that he had never found his wife appealing nor was he ever faithful to her:

> Since the very beginning, when I first took the Landgravine [as my wife], I have had neither desire nor longing for her because of her unattractive appearance, her disposition, her smell, and also because she is often drunk, as many of her ladies, maidens, and other people can attest. . . . But my physical constitution, as my doctors know, is such that I cannot live without a wife and so I have gone to many other women. . . . I was unfaithful to my marriage just three weeks after getting married.[51]

That Philipp was unfaithful to his wife is undoubtedly true. In 1539 he suffered two severe bouts of syphilis, which he contracted neither from his wife nor his mother.[52] The first bout of syphilis made him fear for his life. His illness seems to have awakened his conscience; he believed it was a punishment for his sinful sexual habits. However, and although he later claimed having considered taking a second wife years earlier, the precipitating factor was probably his first meeting with Margarete von der Saale in August 1539.[53] Her mother would not allow her to become a concubine, nor would the mother settle for anything less than a marriage sanctioned by Lutheran clergy, Duke Maurice of Saxony (the Landgravine's cousin), and Elector John Frederick.[54] Philipp had no grounds for divorcing Christine and so he set his mind to a second marriage. To that end, he summoned Martin Bucer and together they began to lobby for a bigamous marriage to Margarete.

Their argument on behalf of his bigamy was contained in a letter that Bucer brought with him to Wittenberg in December 1539. It has eight points. The most important for Luther was the first, which claimed that Philipp never found his wife attractive and that his physical nature required that he have female companionship. The letter ended with an implied threat that if Philipp did not receive the answer he sought he would be left with no other option than to look to the emperor and the pope for succor. In 1539 this was no negligible threat. The emperor, Charles V, was finally poised to resolve the Luther Affair that he had pledged to do nearly twenty years earlier. The defection of one of Protestantism's most senior nobles would have greatly increased Charles' ability to suppress Luther's reforms.

Bucer arrived in Wittenberg on 9 December 1539. Philipp's letter, and no doubt Philipp's implied threat, made a significant impression. The theologians began drawing up a response to Philipp that day and Bucer had a finished copy of their memorandum the next day. That the theologians were trapped in a snare of political reality and their previous positions is certainly clear. An outright denial of Philipp's claim would have painted them as duplicitous and would have placed their lives and their lives' work in great jeopardy. Nevertheless, Philipp's letter also struck chords that resonated on pastoral and theological levels. Thus, though Luther later makes clear that political necessity motivated the decision to support Philipp, he also believed that he and the other theologians acted in the Landgrave's best interests and that he would have taken the same position again.[55]

Luther, as we have seen, viewed marriage as a hospital for sin and lust as a powerful, even existential, urge that without the benefit of marriage leads one to sin and perdition. Under normal circumstances, Luther was willing to make exceptions for people trapped by lust and in danger of damnation. His overarching concern was their soul. Philipp's case was anything but ordinary. Philipp believed, and argued that his doctors concurred, that his physical nature required female companionship as a treatment for a serious medical condition. This is probably a veiled reference to the fact that he was a triorchid. Triorchidism is a rare condition in which some men are born with three testicles. From the time of Polybius, triorchidism was associated with a lecherous nature.[56] In the sixteenth century, triorchidism was sometimes seen as a manifestation of monstrosity and at other times as a symbol of virility. Perhaps the most famous triorchid known in the sixteenth century was the fifteenth-century Italian *condottiero*, Bartolomeo Colleoni, who had his coat of arms fashioned with three testes and was revered for his virility.[57] Though not widely discussed, Philipp's special condition was known in the sixteenth century and formed the subject of a heated argument at the 1514 Hessian territorial diet.[58] A few months after offering his opinion to Philipp, Luther noted that Bucer had discussed the Landgrave's inability to remain chaste under the seal of the confessional.[59] It is impossible to know whether Bucer explained the Landgrave's unique physicality to Luther. But because the condition would certainly have greatly strengthened his case for a second wife in the eyes of Luther, it is likely that Bucer made Luther aware of Philipp's condition.

Luther's response, cosigned by Melanchthon, Bucer, Antonius Corvinus, and two other clergy, excels in the art of plausible deniability. The essay begins with a revealing sentence that then undermines all the carefully crafted caveats that lie between it and the memorandum's final paragraph. Luther asserts that his advice in this case must not be understood as the creation of a new general law (*gemein gesetz*) but ought to be better understood as a "dispensation according to God's permission" (*gottlicher zulassung ein dispensation zu brauchen*). His opinion cannot be a new general law because as such it would scandalize not just the landgrave but marriage itself. Luther recognizes that God did not condemn polygamy in the Old Testament and even seemed to countenance it because of humanity's "weak nature" (*suachen natur*). He then returns to his belief that any advice offered to the landgrave cannot be construed as a new law and quotes Jesus from Matthew 19 that the "two shall become one flesh." At the end of his memorandum, he returns to the reality of the situation: the prince will take another wife. Given this fact, he required that Philipp keep this marriage a secret and encouraged the landgrave to treat the new wife as a concubine before the world because many princes have concubines. To the world having a concubine will seem normal, while Philipp will know in his heart that he is actually married to her.[60]

On 4 March 1540 Philipp of Hesse married Margarete von der Saale. The marriage was not secret and was attended by both Martin Bucer and Philip Melanchthon. In less than three weeks, news of the marriage spread. In early April Luther wrote the landgrave demanding that he be more discreet. By May the marriage had become a public scandal. In June Luther received an angry letter from John Frederick of Saxony demanding an explanation for his involvement in the affair. In a letter of 10 June, Luther acknowledged his involvement and asked the elector to understand why he had to keep it secret.[61] Luther argued that Bucer shared information with him under the seal of the confessional and thus could say nothing. Once Philipp acknowledged the marriage and stated publicly that Luther supported it, Luther felt free to discuss his advice with the elector but refused to reveal further confessional information. Luther is defensive but also invokes righteous indignation. He notes the landgrave's threat to abandon Protestantism; thus he felt it necessary to support Philipp. Nevertheless, considering the information he had at hand, he gave the right advice. The patriarchs, after all, had multiple wives. Moreover, he had already offered the similar advice to bishops in ducal Saxony to marry their cooks—in other words, their concubines—secretly. The main portion of the letter, however, accuses the landgrave of lying to him. Philipp, he suggested, had concealed not only the fact that he already had a concubine, but also that the proposed new wife was of noble birth and therefore scandalously inappropriate for a bigamous wife.

Luther's letter to John Frederick is one of Luther's least effective missives. His angry denunciations of the landgrave ring hollow. It is clear that Luther's anger with the landgrave has little to do with any deception on Philipp's part. Rather, it has everything to do with the landgrave's failure to maintain the deception that the marriage to Margarete was not a marriage but simple concubinage. Luther is angry that the landgrave's great matter has become public. It is not terribly surprising that Luther wished the entire affair to remain secret or that he was infuriated when it became public. It also not terribly surprising that confessionally oriented historians have passed over or explained away Luther's opinion in this matter, because it presents him in a particularly unflattering light. Not only did he endorse behavior he had recently condemned, but he also advised lying and treating a young woman as a concubine.

Luther treated Philipp of Hesse's marital problems in 1539 with typical inconsistency. Unlike the abandoned pastors, the son-less and conflicted Henry VIII, or the secretly married bishops to whom he had offered advice, Philipp of Hesse already had a caring wife. Furthermore, Philipp failed to meet any of the conditions that Luther had previously allowed for a dispensation. His wife was not ill or unable to attend the marriage bed. In fact, Philipp and Christine had three more children after he took Margarete as his second wife. Unlike Jan of Leiden, Philipp never claimed that, like the Old Testament patriarchs, he had a special call from God to "be fruitful and multiply." Philipp's only true justification was lust.

In 1531 Luther was involved in a similar case that also focused almost exclusively on lust, but he then offered strikingly different advice. The major difference in the two episodes was not the predicament of the tormented soul before Luther, but rather Luther's personal regard for the person. The 1531 case involved Hans von Metzsch, a Wittenberg city official and the elector's high bailiff for Wittenberg. Metzsch was a well-known womanizer. In a letter to John of Saxony discussing Metzsch, Luther relates that Metzsch told him in pastoral confidence that he "cannot be without women." Nevertheless, Luther admonished him to abandon his whoring. He also explained to the elector that he had forbidden Metzsch from taking the sacrament and planned to condemn him from the pulpit for his illicit behavior.[62] At the same time, he and Metzsch were involved in an often heated dispute over Metzsch's leadership in the refortification of the city's walls.[63] In both Metzsch's case and Philipp's, the men in question maintained that they could not live without the company of women and that lust was the fundamental urge that had to be satisfied. Luther understood the power of lust. The only significant difference between the two men was that while Luther was involved in a heated argument with one, he held the other in good regard.[64] The same might be said for Luther's condemnation of Jan of Leiden, which focused almost exclusively on Leiden's lustful appetite for women. In the end, it was neither consistency nor political necessity that motivated Luther to support Philipp. He had previously shown willful disregard for political necessity when it suited him. The only consistent motivation present in Luther's advice on many marital issues was his closeness and affection for the persons involved. This was certainly true in Philipp of Hesse's case.

Conclusion

In 1528 Johannes Cochlaeus wrote to Willibald Pirkheimer concerning a recent publication by Luther on the question of successive marriages. According to Cochlaeus, the clear implication of Luther's writings on marriage was that, "contrary to Christ, the church, even contrary to temporal imperial law, he grants to the laity the right that a husband may have two, or three, or as many wives as he wants."[65] Cochlaeus was one of Luther's most virulent critics and a very close reader of Luther's writings; he was prone to hyperbole but did not misquote Luther simply to serve his own purposes. In this case, Cochlaeus captured a kernel of truth. Luther always claimed that the individual soul in jeopardy was more important than the law that jeopardized them. "The law," he wrote, "exists for the sake of the conscience, not the conscience for the sake of the law. If one cannot help both at the same time, then help the conscience and oppose the law."[66] In his attempt to aid his parishioners' consciences, however, a pattern of accepting or accommodating those with whom he agreed or liked emerges. In the end, it was not consciences that he soothed, but colleagues, compatriots, and friends. It was not behavior that he evaluated, but relationships. Luther was not a sex-obsessed former friar who brazenly endorsed bigamy as some of his confessional critics accused. Neither was he a consistent spiritual caregiver (*Seelsorger*), who assuaged guilty consciences and led the lost back to the flock. He was not guided by theological principle. Rather, Luther's advice on bigamy embodies that most common of human frailties, in which one condemns one's enemies and forgives one's friends.

Notes

1. The quotation in this chapter's title is taken from Luther's 1523 Sermon on Genesis 16. Martin Luther, *D. Martin Luthers Werke: Kritische Gesamtausgabe*, 120 vols. (Weimar, 1883–2007), vol. 24, 300–316, here 305. The *Kritische Gesamtausgabe* is composed of generic divisions, each with its own sequence of volume numbers. Following scholarly convention, volumes in the division containing Luther's published "writings and works" (*Schriften/Werke*) are cited hereafter as WA (for "Weimarer Ausgabe"); volumes of his correspondence (*Briefwechsel*) are cited as WA BR (for "Weimarer Ausgabe Briefe").
2. Martin Luther, "Vom ehelichen Leben" (1522), WA, vol. 10/II, 275–304. See also the English translation in *Luther's Works*, ed. Jaroslav Pelikan and Helmut T. Lehmann, 55 vols. (St. Louis and Minneapolis, 1955–1986), vol. 45, 17–56. Volumes in the English translation are cited hereafter as LW.
3. Olavi Lähteenmäki, *Sexus und Ehe bei Luther* (Turku, 1955), 18.
4. Martin Luther, "Von Ehesachen" (1530), WA, vol. 30/III, 205-248, here 247; translated as "On Marriage Matters," LW, vol. 46, 259–320, here 319.
5. Luther's own sexuality has loomed over anti-Luther propaganda from the very beginnings of the Reformation. Here I am not claiming that Luther himself was hypersexualized, rather that he had a tendency to amplify sexual desire in others. For an excellent study of Luther and human sexuality, see Merry E. Wiesner-Hanks, "Lustful Luther: Male Libido in the Writings of the Reformer," in *Masculinity in the Reformation Era*, ed. Scott H. Hendrix and Susan C. Karant-Nunn (Kirksville, 2008).
6. In the early modern era, there were no set, common terms when discussing polygamy and bigamy. Possibilities ranged from the Latin *bigamia* and *digamia*, to various Latin phrases denoting multiple wives: *plures uxores*, for example. In German, *zweifacher ehe*

and *doppelverlobung* were sometimes used, but more often phrases were used that included a multiplier *zwie* or *viel* and either marriage (*ehe*) or wife (*Weib*) were used. For consistency's sake, I use bigamy and polygamy to refer to marital situations that involved a single man or woman being married simultaneously to more than one living spouse. Digamy will be used to denote marriages in which one man or woman was married to multiple spouses in succession following either formal divorce or the death of a spouse.

7. Luther's opinions on bigamy have been a boon to his critics and a source of embarrassment to his theological heirs, so it is not surprising that interpretations of his writings on bigamy have traditionally followed the confessional allegiance of the author. For example Hartmann Grisar, a nineteenth-century Roman Catholic biographer of Luther, devotes seventy-nine pages to Luther's opinions on bigamy, presenting him in the worst possible light. On the other side of the confessional divide, Heinrich Böhmer dismissed Luther's opinion as nothing more than a traditional pastoral dispensation excusing a secret impediment to a marriage. See Hartmann Grisar, *Luther*, 6 vols. (London, 1913–17), vol. 5, 4; and Heinrich Böhmer, *Luther in Light of Recent Research* (New York, 1916), 237. Needless to say, the intent of this chapter is neither to laud Luther nor to condemn him.

8. The traditional view of Luther's theology of marriage is that he desacramentalized it while simultaneously bestowing on both its members a higher station and calling than was represented in medieval theology. But as both Susan Karant-Nunn and Joel Harrington have demonstrated, the positive benefits of Luther's views of marriage have been overstated, especially as they relate to the status and role of women. Harrington, *Reordering Marriage and Society*; Susan C. Karant-Nunn, *The Reformation of Ritual* (New York, 1997).

9. Augustine, "De Bono Coniugali," in *Corpus Scriptorum Ecclesiasticorum Latinorum*, ed. Joseph Zycha (Vienna, 1900), translated as "On the Good Marriage," in *Treatises on Marriage and Other Subjects*, ed. Roy J. Deferrari (New York, 1955).

10. Martin Luther, "A Sermon on the Estate of Marriage" (1519), LW, vol. 44, 3–14, here 9. Luther would remain consistent on rehabilitative nature of marriage throughout his career. In 1535 in his Genesis Lectures (which would occupy his time from 1535 until 1545, just before his death), he writes, "Marriage was ordained by God as a remedy for our weak nature"; LW, vol. 1, 167.

11. Martin Luther, "Eyn Sermon von dem Elichen Standt" (1519), WA, vol. 2, 166–79, here 168.

12. Ibid.

13. Luther, "Sermon on the Estate of Marriage," LW, vol. 44, 11.

14. The literature on the Two Kingdoms is vast; the most recent significant examination of the topic is William J. Wright, *Luther's Two Kingdoms* (Grand Rapids, 2009).

15. Luther, "Von Ehesachen," WA, vol. 30/III, 205; LW, vol. 46, 265.

16. *The Civil Law*, ed. Samuel P. Scott, 17 vols. (Cincinnati, 1932), vol. 15, 12 (Book 9, Title 9.18).

17. Eike von Repgau, *Sachsenspiegel Landrecht*, 2nd ed. (Göttingen, 1955), vol. 2, 152 (Book 2.23); idem, *Sachsenspiegel, mit vil newen addicion* (Augsburg, 1517), O1ʳ. A copy of the 1517 edition and a manuscript copy were available to Luther in the Wittenberg University library.

18. Eike von Repgau, *Sachsenspiegel, mit vil newen addicion*, O1ʳ.

19. Ibid., O2ʳ.

20. Bigamy is outlawed in the Bamberg Criminal Code at §146 and in the Imperial Criminal Code at §127. See *Die peinliche Gerichtsordnung Kaiser Karls V. nebst der Bamberger und der Brandenburger Halsgerichtsordnung*, ed. Heinrich Zoepfl (Leipzig, 1883), 102.

21. Bigamy is forbidden in D.26 C.3 of the *Decretals*. See *Corpus Iuris Canonici*, ed. Emil Friedberg, 2 vols. (Graz, 1959), vol. 1, 96–97. For a discussion of bigamy in medieval law, see G.W. Bartholomew, "Origin and Development of the Law of Bigamy," *Law Quarterly Review* 74 (1958): 259–71; and James A. Brundage, *Law, Sex, and Christian Society in Medieval Europe* (Chicago, 1987).

22. Martin Luther, "The Babylonian Captivity of the Church" (1520), LW, vol. 36, 3–127. Many scholars focus their attention on the single sentence in which he writes that he prefers bigamy to divorce (LW, vol. 36, 105). However, this sentence comes in the middle of his critique of divorce and has all the hallmarks of a literary device.

23. Luther, "Babylonian Captivity," LW, vol. 36, 103.

24. Peter Lombard, *Sentences*, trans. Giulio Silano (Toronto, 2010), 4.34.2.

25. Three other letters from this period deal with bigamous marriages among Anabaptists. In each, Luther rejects bigamy. See Luther to Philipp of Hesse, 28 November 1526, WA BR, vol. 4, 140 (no. 1056); Letter to Joseph Levin Metzsch, 9 December 1526, WA BR, vol. 4, 141–42 (no. 1057); Letter to Clemens Ursinus, 21 March 1527, WA BR, vol. 4, 177–78 (no. 1089). The letter to Philipp of Hesse is often cited as Philipp's first attempt at securing a bigamous marriage for himself. A more likely scenario is that Hesse and Metzsch heard of instances of bigamy and adult baptism during either the Diet of Speyer or the Synod of Homburg and sought Luther's opinion about these matters.

26. Letter to Gregor Brück, 13 January 1524, WA BR, vol. 3, 230–31 (no. 702). It is likely that the letter cited by Audin and others as Karlstadt's reply back to Luther in which he supposedly writes, "let us be bigamists, trigamists, as many wives as we can support," is actually from Jan of Leiden; see Jean Marie Vincent Audin, *History of the Life, Writings, & Doctrines of Luther*, 2 vols. (London, 1854), vol. 2, 185.

27. For an excellent in-depth analysis of Kramer's marriages, see Marjorie Elizabeth Plummer, "'The Much Married Michael Kramer': Evangelical Clergy and Bigamy in Ernestine Saxony, 1522–1524," in *Ideas and Cultural Margins in Early Modern Germany: Essays in Honor of H.C. Erik Midelfort*, ed. Marjorie Elizabeth Plummer and Robin B. Barnes (Aldershot, UK, 2009), 99–116. The chronology of events described depends on William W. Rockwell, *Die Doppelehe, des Landgrafen Philipp von Hessen* (Marburg, 1904), 89–90.

28. Martin Luther, "Das siebente Kapitel St. Pauli zu den Corinthern" (1523), WA, vol. 12, 95–142, here 123–24; "Commentary on 1 Corinthians 17," LW, vol. 28, 1–56, here 36.

29. Luther, "Das siebente Kapitel," WA, vol. 12, 125.

30. By 1523 Luther had already ensured Karlstadt's removal from Wittenberg, and in 1524 he actively campaigned for his exile from all of Saxony, which was commanded by Frederick the Wise in September. Luther's justification of his actions regarding Karlstadt's exile are in the treatise "Wider die himmlischen Propheten, von den Bildern und Sakrament" (1525), WA, vol. 18, 62–125; "Against the Heavenly Prophets in the Matter of Images and Sacraments," LW, vol. 40, 73–223.

31. The Protestant princes of Germany understood the embassy from London could have very positive implications for their political situation within the Holy Roman Empire. Though formal negotiations between the king and the Schmalkaldic League had not

yet begun, all the parties clearly saw the advantages of winning the English crown to the Protestant cause. To that end, Philipp of Hesse wrote to Wittenberg hoping for a positive answer to the king's request. Philipp's letter was written sometime at the end of September. Unfortunately for Philipp, Luther had already submitted his opinion earlier in the month. On Luther and the king's "great matter," see Preserved Smith, "Luther and Henry VIII," *English Historical Review* 25 (1910): 656–69 ; and Erwin Doernberg, *Henry VIII and Luther: An Account of Their Personal Relations* (Stanford, 1961).

32. Letter from Ambassador Chapuis to Charles V, 22 January 1532, in *Letters and Papers, Foreign and Domestic, Henry VIII,* ed. J.S. Brewer, 21 vols. (London, 1864–1920), vol. 5, 737.
33. Martin Luther to Thomas Barnes, 3 September 1531, LW, vol. 50, 27–40.
34. Luther, "Von Ehesachen," WA, vol. 30/III, 246; LW, vol. 46, 316.
35. Luther to Barnes, LW, vol. 50, 27.
36. Martin Luther to Georg Brück, May 1531?, WA BR, vol. 6, 107–17, here 115 (no. 1822).
37. Luther to Barnes, LW, vol. 50, 27.
38. The possibility of a second wife had already been raised by, for example, Erasmus (Letter to Vives, 2 September 1528; Desiderius Erasmus, *Erasmi Epistolae,* ed. P.S. Allen, 12 vols. (Oxford, 1906-55), vol. 7, no. 2040), "I should prefer that he [Henry] should take two Junos rather than put away one."
39. Martin Luther, "The Persons Related by Consanguinity and Affinity Who are Forbidden to Marry According to the Scriptures, Leviticus 18" (1522), LW, vol. 45, 7.
40. Justus Jonas, Martin Luther, and Philipp Melanchthon to Leonhard Beyer, 18 January 1535, WA BR, vol. 7, 152–53 (no. 2171).
41. Luther wrote to the city council and to Bernhard Rothmann in 1532 and continued to allude to Münster for years after, but the prefaces are the only two writings specifically on the Anabaptist kingdom. Examples of his desire to keep informed about the happenings in Münster can be seen in his letters to Friedrich Myconius on 5 July 1534 (WA BR, vol. 7, 86 [no. 2127]) and to Jacob Probst (WA BR, vol. 7, 239 [no. 2226]), in which he calls the events in Münster a "great scandal" caused by "lust."
42. Martin Luther, "Vorrede zu Urbanus Rhegius, Widerlegung des Bekenntnisses" (1535), WA, vol. 38, 338–40.
43. *Newe Zeitung von den wider Teuffern zu Münster* (Nuremberg, 1535), A4^r. Even in the sixteenth century, forcing twelve-year-old girls to marry would have shocked people. Most jurisdictions prohibited marriages before eighteen, with a few allowing them at sixteen; see Harrington, *Reordering Marriage,* 188, note 64.
44. Martin Luther, "Vorrede zur Neuen Zeitung von den Wiedertäufern zu Münster," WA, vol. 38, 347–350, here 348.
45. Ibid., 350.
46. Martin Bucer, Oecolampadius, Bullinger, and even Menno Simons all condemned the city. The best discussion of reactions to Münster is Sigrun Haude, *In the Shadow of "Savage Wolves": Anabaptist Münster and the German Reformation during the 1530s* (Boston, 2000).
47. Hans Formschneider published the *Newe Zeitung* with Luther's preface and the Melanchton's two tracts all in one pamphlet.
48. Philip Melanchthon, *Corpus Reformatorum. Philippi Melanchthonis Opera Quae Supersunt Omnia,* ed. C.G. Bretschneider and H.E. Bindseil (Braunschweig and Halle, 1834–1860), vol. 2: 526.

49. Philipp Melanchthon, *Etliche Propositiones witer die lehr der widerteuffer* ([Wittenberg], 1535), A4ʳ.

50. Ibid., A4ᵛ.

51. "Was Doctor Marthinus Bucerus an D. Marthinum Lutherum…werben soll" (December 1539), WA BR, vol. 8, 631.

52. See Rockwell, *Doppelehe*, 3–6.

53. All of the evidence used to support the argument that he had long considered bigamy come from after he met Margarete. He never claimed until after he met her, for example, that he had refrained from taking the sacrament since the "peasants' feud" (i.e., 1525 and thus fourteen years earlier). That claim is first made in 1540 in a letter to Luther (WA BR, vol. 9, 13–14; 5 April 1540).

54. Her list of demands is reprinted in Rockwell, *Doppelehe*, 316–17. He did secure the support of Lutheran clergy, specifically Luther and Melanchthon, but did not alert Maurice, his father Henry, nor the elector.

55. See Luther's letter to Elector John Frederick, 10 June 1540, WA BR, vol. 9, 131–35 (no. 3493).

56. See Polybius, *The Histories*, trans. William Roger Paton, 6 vols. (New York, 1922), vol. 4, 346–47. There are also stories of medieval monks being relieved of their vows to chastity because of triorchidism. See James Russell, *Observations on the Testicles* (Edinburgh, 1883), 8–10.

57. See Nicholas Remy, *Daemonolatriae libri tres* (Frankfurt, 1596), 44. The coat of arms can be seen on the base of his statue in Venice.

58. Philipp's physician retorted that his abnormal growth had been present from birth and that his father had even commented upon it when Philipp was an infant; see Hans Glagau, ed., *Hessische Landtagsakten: 1508–1521* (Marburg, 1901), 254 (March 1514). An autopsy performed after his death confirmed Philipp's condition; see Jacques-Auguste de Thou, *Iac. Augusti Thuani Historiarum sui temporis libri CXXV,* 11 vols. (Paris, 1609), vol. 1, 352–53.

59. Martin Luther to Elector Johann Friedrich, 10 June 1540, WA BR, vol. 9, 131–35 (no. 3493).

60. Martin Luther and Philipp Melanchthon to Landgrave Philipp, 10 December 1539, WA BR, vol. 8, 638–43 (no. 3423).

61. Luther to Elector Johann Friedrich, 10 June 1540, WA BR, vol. 9, 131–35 (no. 3493). The letter is not included in the LW. An English translation can be found in *Luther: Letters of Spiritual Counsel*, trans. Theodore G Tappert (Louisville, 1955), 288–91.

62. Martin Luther to Elector Johann, 16 June 1531, WA BR, vol. 6, 122–24 (no. 1826); Tappert, ed., *Letters of Spiritual Counsel*, 279–81.

63. For a discussion of the acrimony between Luther and Metzsch, see Martin Brecht, *Martin Luther*, trans. James Schaff, 3 vols. (Philadelphia, 1985–93), vol. 2, 436–38.

64. Though their relationship was certainly strained in the late 1520s because of the so-called Pack Affair, by the 1540s Philipp was counted among the most important and influential of Protestant princes.

65. Cochlaeus to Pirkheimer, 30 June 1528, quoted in Gustav Kawerau, "Der Nürnberger Streit über die zweite Ehe der Geistlichen," *Beiträge zur bayerischen Kirchengeschichte* 10 (1904), 119–29, here 121.

66. Luther, "Von Ehesachen," WA, vol. 30/III, 247; LW, vol. 46, 317. For an excellent study of Luther's attitude toward the law and the conscience, see James Estes, "Luther's Attitude toward the Legal Traditions of His Time," *Lutherjahrbuch* 58 (2010): 77–110.

CHAPTER 2

~: :~

Celibacy—Marriage—Unmarriage
The Controversy over Celibacy and Clerical Marriage in the Early Reformation

WOLFGANG BREUL

In December 1523 the council of the town of Hersfeld in eastern Hesse issued a mandate, threatening those who lived in "unmarriage" (*Unehe*)—that is, unmarried persons living as couples together, also referred to as concubinage—with banishment unless they married within the space of fourteen days. Those who refused to do so were to be punished physically.[1] I do not know of any other case in the entire area of Hesse and Thuringia in which, at least before the Peasants' Revolt of 1525, the authorities tried to use such radical means to combat concubinage. Although the Hersfeld mandate putatively addressed all inhabitants of the town who lived in concubinage, it was really directed mostly, perhaps exclusively, at priests.

The mandate itself tells us nothing about its background. However, we do know that one of the two Protestant preachers in Hersfeld, Heinrich Fuchs, was already married in May 1521. Indeed, Martin Luther reports on the case in one of his letters from the Wartburg castle.[2] He had gotten to know the pastor a few weeks before, on his way back from the Imperial Diet in Worms, where the reformer had famously refused to renounce his writings. Wartburg was roughly a two-day-trip from Hersfeld and this proximity meant that the news of the priest's marriage had already spread quite widely throughout the region. Heinrich Fuchs, therefore, was one of the first priests who broke the vows of celibacy by marrying.[3]

It is noteworthy that Hersfeld's overlord did not interfere in the marriage of Heinrich Fuchs. Certainly, the abbot had ample reason to do so: Hersfeld, after all, was the administrative seat of a medium-sized ecclesiastical territory—the Imperial Abbey of Hersfeld.[4] As the reigning prince in Hersfeld and peer of the empire, the abbot was responsible for upholding both the secular and ecclesiastical laws of his realm—including the canonical ban against clerical marriage. His motives for allowing the priest's marriage to proceed may well have been theological. For reasons we cannot reconstruct, the abbot, Krafft Myle von Hungen, sympathized with the Reformation movement—so much so in fact that he showed hospitality toward Luther himself when he passed through Hersfeld in May 1521. On that occasion Abbot Krafft extended an honorable welcome to Luther, urged him to spend the night in his residence, and invited him to preach the following morning.[5]

Whatever the abbot's motivations, the marriage of Heinrich Fuchs aroused little public indignation, let alone official censure—at least in 1521. In stark contrast to the extreme measures taken against married priests taken in territories nearby, Hersfeld remained calm. The fate of married priests in nearby Saxony illustrates the contrast. In May 1521—about the time Luther was passing through Hersfeld—a priest named Jakob Seidel, who sympathized with Luther's cause, married his cook. Duke Georg of Saxony had Seidel arrested for his crime, then transferred him to the bishop of Meissen.[6] A similar case emerged in June 1521 after the marriage of Balthasar Zeiger, the priest in a village subject to the count of Mansfeld. The count denounced him to Archbishop Albrecht of Mainz and delivered into his custody.[7] In contrast to the county of Mansfeld, there are no reports of any such interventions in the Imperial Abbey of Hersfeld, either by Abbot Krafft as secular overlord or by the archbishop of Mainz as the abbot's metropolitan.[8] We cannot attribute this silence and inaction to ignorance: As we have seen, news of Heinrich Fuchs's marriage reached Luther's ears in the Wartburg castle. It is also reasonable to assume that Fuchs's repudiation of celibacy and his violation of the ban against clerical marriage attracted attention among supporters of the Reformation in Hersfeld.

Criticism of Concubinage in the Early Reformation

The mandate of Hersfeld marks concubinage as unmarriage, the moral opposite of matrimony.[9] There had been criticism of the clerical practice of concubinage before, but only in the discussion of the early Reformation was the distinction drawn this sharply. In the later Middle Ages the concubinage of priests became a matter of course in many regions. In some places clerics could even appear in public with their wives and children.[10] Because clandestine marriage remained widespread long into the sixteenth century, moreover, a sharp distinction between marriage and concubinage was not always possible. This was so despite a series of canonical prohibitions beginning with the Fourth Lateran Council in 1215, as well as diocesan bans against the practice.[11] Only in the aftermath of the Council of Trent were the first effective efforts to eradicate clandestine matrimony implemented.[12]

The criticism of clerical celibacy and concubinage in the early Reformation had two main sources: one derived from a new departure in theological anthropology that held a more positive view of human sexuality, and the other rested on the idea of the priesthood of all believers. Starting in May 1519 Luther began to move away from the idea that sexuality within matrimony is per se impure, "dirt," "stench," as he wrote for the first time in his *Sermon on Married Life* (Sermon vom ehelichen Stande).[13] Luther fleshed out these cautious approaches in his great writings of 1520. In his open letter *To the Christian Nobility of the German Nation* (An den christlichen Adel deutscher Nation), for example, he attacks clerical celibacy as "devilish tyranny" (*teuffelisch tyranney*).[14] Not only did he reject the ban against clerical marriage under canon law, but also Luther justified the marriage of priests on scriptural grounds. His argumentation also extended the new understanding of human sexuality he had begun to develop in 1519: a man intending to become a priest could not promise chastity because the weakness of the human constitution (*fragilitas humana*) would not allow that. Sexual abstinence for priests could not be demanded, just as the renunciation of other natural needs cannot be called for. Thus the pope should "not have the power to prohibit [this], just as he does not have the power to prohibit eating, drinking, natural secretion or becoming fat."[15]

Underlying these statements were a fundamental, anthropological shift and a new understanding of the physical needs of human beings: the ability to live in abstinence is a grace given only to very few people. Thus, all others need to marry to avoid sin. This is a God-given human order, and only a few extraordinary individuals are rid of it. Luther continued to reevaluate the importance of conjugal sexuality in his sacramental writing *On the Babylonian Captivity of the Church* (De captivitate Babylonica ecclesiae). Here he disputes the sacramental character of marriage, calling it a "worldly thing" that Christians generally share with all human beings. Luther's suggestion that a woman whose husband is impotent may have an extramarital affair results from this view.

Both in *To the German Nobility* and *On the Babylonian Captivity*, Luther established lines of argumentation that would appear fully developed in his first major treatise devoted entirely to marriage and sexuality, *On Married Life* (Vom ehelichen Leben), published in 1522.[16] The two sexes and matrimonial fertility, as part of God's good creation, are the reason for marriage, sexuality, and the responsibility for children. This writing further developed his description of conjugal life and sexuality in opposition to the claim that monks, nuns, and priests led morally superior lives because they were sexually abstinent. Sexual abstinence, like abstinence in general from the needs of the flesh, was, according to Luther, a great gift that only very few possessed.[17] All others who are physically capable of conjugal sexuality must marry if they do not want to find themselves in a sinful existence. Whoever is not impotent or endowed by God with chastity "should only consider marriage, for nothing else remains for him. You will not remain righteous; that is impossible" (*der dencke nur tzum ehlichen leben, denn da wirt nicht anders auß, du bleybst nicht frum, das ist unmuglich*).[18] Luther's decisive statements stem from the fight of the early Reformation against clerical celibacy and monastic vows of chastity. At the same time, in *On Married Life*, Luther attempts to extensively formulate the basis and sense of conjugal community in a positive way for the first time. He states that human beings are created with two sexes and that man and woman are destined to help one another.

A new understanding of priesthood was the second source for Luther's critique of clerical celibacy and concubinage. In *To the Christian Nobility* Luther also developed an idea of the general priesthood—a concept he derived from his critique of the Roman Church's claim to spiritual authority.[19] Specifically, he sought to tear down what he called the "three walls of the Romanists": first, the claim to an overarching authority over the secular authorities; second, the claim to an exclusive monopoly over interpretation of Scripture; and third, the claim that papal authority was superior to that of a general church council. Luther attacked the first wall with his idea of a priesthood of all believers, which for spiritual purposes eliminated the distinction between clergy and laity. But his interpretation also represented a fundamental break with the hierarchy of the Church. In baptism, he argued, every Christian became priest, bishop, or pope. Therefore, priests had the same rights and responsibilities as all Christians and were allowed to marry. Among Christians, he argued, there are generally no differences in spiritual terms: all are baptized, all live under the same law, and all have the same authority at their disposal, including the authority to interpret Scripture. In view of this equality, the claim that specific ethical codes pertained to priests, monks, and nuns was in Luther's opinion no longer tenable, and could be justified only as a voluntary commitment.

By removing spiritual distinctions between priests and laymen, therefore, Luther desacralized the special status of priests, monks and nuns.[20] Luther's acknowledgement of the value and sanctity of conjugal sexuality compelled him to apply to priests and monastics the same moral expectations held for, and by, the rest of the population. These two—the desacralization of priesthood and Luther's desire to normalize the priestly estate—formed the central, social tenets of early Reformation propaganda. But what drove the change was the widespread criticism of the immoral practice of concubinage and the popular demand that priests marry.

Controversy over the Celibacy of Priests in Hersfeld

Public debate over clerical celibacy reached its climax in 1523, and once again the Imperial Abbey of Hersfeld was at the center of attention.[21] In fact the town council's mandate of that year represented the culmination of a much broader development. By the spring of 1523 several unnamed priests had married in the area around Eisenach, some fifty kilometers to the east of Hersfeld.[22] In a sermon delivered on 10 May 1523, Jakob Strauss, the well-known evangelical preacher in Eisenach, used these incidents to argue for the right for priests to marry.[23] In his homily Strauss portrayed marriage as God's irresistible commandment for all human beings.[24] This argument sharpened considerably Luther's statements published the preceding year. According to Strauss, the celibacy of priests was "a horrible, tyrannical command" (*grawsam / tirannisch gepott*), which tried to replace God's word by human invention. At the same time, he warned priests not to use marriage to satisfy "fleshly lusts" (*Wollust des Leibes*). He further criticized those priests who celebrated their wedding with "gluttony, carousing, drinking, dancing, leaping, and other work of the devil" (*Schlemmen, Prassen, Völlen, Tanzen und Springen und anderem Teufelswerk*).[25] Jakob Strauss himself married sometime in 1523.[26]

There were more cases of clerical marriage in the Imperial Abbey of Fulda, a territory that bordered on the Imperial Abbey of Hersfeld. In July 1523 the priest Georg Witzel addressed his overlord, the coadjutor Johann von Henneberg, requesting permission to marry.[27] It was well known in Vacha, where Georg Witzel preached, that he had been living with his intended bride for some time already.[28] Witzel's embrace of Luther's ideas was related to his quest for a legally valid marriage.[29] In retrospect, Witzel also ascribed his desire for marriage to the persuasion of like-minded Protestants in nearby Thuringia. But he received no answer from Johann von Henneberg, his overlord. For that reason he left the Imperial Abbey of Fulda, moved to the nearby town of Eisenach, married a daughter of a well-to-do-citizen there, and joined Jakob Strauss's program of evangelical reform.[30] A short time later Balthasar Raidt, a vicar resident in Fulda and a supporter of the Reformation, also asked for permission to marry. He was expelled from the territory.

In the same year, the case of two high-ranking clerics attracted even more public attention in the nearby diocese of Würzburg. When in 1523 the prince-bishop of Würzburg, Konrad von Thüngen, resolved to publish a mandate against concubinage, he learned that two high-ranking clerics, Johann Apel and Friedrich Fischer, both canons at the collegiate monastry (*Stift*) of Neumünster, were living in marriage-like relationships. In a face-to-face meeting, Bishop von Thüngen tried to convince Johann Apel to give up his marriage. But Apel, a well-known humanist and adviser of the bishop, was not open to persuasion. Like Luther at the Imperial Diet of Worms in 1521, Johann Apel stood on conscience, which, he said, bound him to the Gospel. In his *Defensio pro suo coniugio*, an apologetic tract that appeared in the summer of 1523 with a preface by Martin Luther, Apel emphasized that his concerns were not merely personal, but that after his own marriage became known he also supported the right of priests to marry publicly; he sought deliberately to provoke a dispute with his lord, Bishop von Thüngen, in the matter.[31] Subsequently, Bishop von Thüngen had both Apel and Fischer arrested. Their wives were able to flee in time because another canon, the humanist Jacob Fuchs the Younger, had warned them in advance.[32] In an open letter to Bishop von Thüngen, Jakob Fuchs the Elder, a humanist canon in Würzburg, also intervened on behalf of the two arrested colleagues.[33] As a result, both the Elder and the Younger Fuchs were compelled to leave the bishopric of Würzburg. Since all the clerics involved came from well-respected families and enjoyed good reputations in the empire-spanning network of highly placed humanists, the Würzburg case became a political affair. Relatives of Johann Apel petitioned his case to the Imperial Governing Board (*Reichsregiment*) seated in Würzburg, requesting the release of both detainees.[34] The Board accepted their plea and wrote to Konrad von Thüngen, reminding the prince-bishop of a resolution of the imperial diet, which von Thüngen had helped craft, which "has mandated a certain sanction and penalty for those mentioned and others" (*Hast du dich wol zuberichten, daß es dem Abschied auff unserm Reichstage, den du selbst mit hast helffen berathschlagen, und beschliessen in dem fall, vnd mit solcher scherpff, vnd straff gegen obgenandten und andern zuhandeln entgegen wer*).[35] After long hesitation, Bishop Konrad finally bowed to the political pressure and, after they had taken an oath of obedience (*Urfehde*), released Apel and Fischer in August 1523. Both, however, lost their benefices and were exiled from the territories subject to the prince-bishop's rule.[36]

Since both Apel and Fischer were famous humanists, it is most likely that the Protestant preachers of Fulda and Hersfeld learned quickly of the events in Würzburg.[37] Taken together with contemporaneous events in Hersfeld and Eisenach, these incidents offer four insights into the whole question of clerical marriage in the early Reformation. The first is simply public interest in the topic of clerical celibacy; the marriage of priests reached a climax in 1523. This was the same year in which the production of pamphlets advocating ecclesiastical reform achieved its zenith.[38] Second, all the clerics who were accused of breaking with celibacy also sympathized with the Reformation movement. Third, due to its relevance in ecclesiastic law, the subject of the marriage of priests worked well to provoke a conflict. This is particularly clear with the controversies in Eisenach and Fulda. Prior to 1523, by contrast, the marriage of priests seems to have attracted relatively little attention. Johann Apel and Friedrich Fischer, presumably, did not initially intend to make their marriages public. Once their marriages had become public knowledge, however, controversy flared. Fourth and finally, in Fulda and Würzburg the marriages of priests or their desire to marry led to reactions of the clerical sovereign. While the dismissal of Protestant priests in Fulda was accepted in the end without any recognizable public conflict, a public and even legal argument arose in Würzburg.

Municipal against Ecclesiastical Competence

These regional findings confirm the general trend identified long ago by Bernd Moeller: "The public marriage of a priest was a scandal which brought together a coalition of entirely heterogeneous interests: to the actors, it brought about the opportunity for an effective demonstration and explanation of their new conviction; to the bishops, it allowed a disciplinary-juridical intervention against Lutherans usually hardly to be arrested; to secular authorities, it offered the opportunity to fight for the protection of their jurisdiction or even, under quite new conditions and circumstances, to fight for its expansion."[39] Moeller rightly suggests that conflicts over ecclesiastical jurisdiction exacerbated conflicts between priests who wished to marry and bishops who reacted by disciplining them. This is certainly true of the Hersfeld case. For about two centuries prior to the Hersfeld affair, jurisdictional conflicts had flared time and again between the town and its ecclesiastical overlord.[40] These had calmed down during the years before the Reformation with the coming into power of the first non-noble abbot in the history of the imperial abbey—the very same Krafft Myle von Hungen, elected in 1516, whom we encountered at the beginning of this chapter. But a new situation arose when the first Reformation sermons were preached in Hersfeld, which had the effect of reviving the old jurisdictional conflict.[41] Initially, the town council and the imperial abbot agreed in their sympathy with the Reformation movement. Tensions increased, however, when evangelical preaching led to ruptures with the status quo. The source of tension was a new preacher, Melchior Rinck (c. 1493–c. 1550), who later became a leader of the Anabaptist movement.[42] After Rinck became vicar in Hersfeld in May 1523, a clear increase of the conflicts can be registered. Increasingly, the townspeople refused to make ecclesiastical contributions. The Eucharist and crucifix were subjected to mockery. On both sides there were also sporadic breaches of the peace.[43] The mandate of the town council passed in December 1523 marked the climax of this escalation of conflict about the Reformation movement.[44]

By decreeing its mandate against concubinage, municipal authorities intruded on the sphere of competence that properly belonged to the abbot of Hersfeld as the ecclesiastical authority over the city and to the archbishop of Mainz as bishop of the diocese. The mandate denied the authority of the ecclesiastical powers:

> [T]he Word of God, according to the rules of the Old and New Testaments, condemns very strongly and does not tolerate whoredom and those who live in concubinage [*Uneheliche*], but rather it seeks to harry them from the land—be they clergy or laity. Similarly, no public sin which is against the commandment of

God shall be tolerated, like blasphemy in word and deed, the shameful and dis-
graceful drunkards who daily lie about publicly in the taverns and do not work.
Accordingly, the secular authorities must act according to God's command, for
they must answer to God for the damage to the souls. This was the opinion of
many and the majority of the council. They wanted that public vice be opposed
and not tolerated. They mandated that a statement be composed which pastors
should be required to promulgate on the third Sunday of Advent of the year
1523.[45]

Besides prostitution and *Unehe*, the mandate also condemns blasphemy in
word and deed, as well as drunkards and layabouts. The majority of the council
considered the concubinage of priests, as much as alcoholism and unwillingness to work, as violating good public order (*Polizey*). Thus, the city council
attempted to integrate clerics into the secular legal system of the town.

Of course, not everyone in the council agreed with the wording or the intention of the mandate. A report on the debate that had led up to its promulgation
gives a vivid account of individual opinions for and against the mandate. One
opponent of the mandate found it personally embarrassing because people living in concubinage worked for him, combing wool and spinning. Because of
this, he would not want to participate in their expulsion.[46] Another argued that
concubinage was a long-established practice that the council could not abol-
ish.[47] A further member of the council agreed, mentioning that concubinage
was also common practice in the towns of Erfurt, Nuremberg, and Frankfurt.
In these places, a man could live righteously, with wife and children, in a recognized form of concubinage.[48] Such dissension within the Hersfeld council
demonstrates how widespread and accepted the concubinage of priests had become in the decades prior to Reformation.

Those who supported the mandate refused to accept such arguments, however, insisting that whoever could not do without woman and children should
marry. As an outlet for sexual desires, prostitution should not be tolerated. It
is noteworthy that the disagreement corresponded with social divisions within
the town. The report notes that "the top people and big shots" (*die obersten und
großen hanßen*) opposed the mandate.[49] As the voting shows, opponents of the
mandate were cloth manufacturers and wholesalers. As in many other towns of
Hersfeld's size and function, their guilds to which the opponents belonged—
the merchants' guild and the wool manufacturers' guild—constituted the socio-
economic and political elite in Hersfeld. By the same token, it therefore seems
likely that those who supported the mandate represented the less-well-to-do
guilds, perhaps also the nonguilded citizens. These men, often from artisan
backgrounds, believed in a strict code of ethics that should, they thought, apply
to all citizens indiscriminately. For them, the mandate was meant to absorb
clergy into the artisans' code of honor and probity.

End of the Marriage Conflict in Hersfeld

After the majority of the Hersfeld council had voted to promulgate the mandate, Heinrich Fuchs was ordered to proclaim it from the pulpit of the town church on the third Sunday of Advent 1523. Once this decision became known to the affected priests, they appealed to Abbot Krafft, who forbade Hersfeld's four mayors to publish the decree.[50] Abbot Krafft rightly saw the mandate as a challenge to his ecclesiastical jurisdiction and reacted by abandoning the friendly, tolerant stance toward the Reformation movement that he had held earlier. One day after nullifying the council's decision, Abbot Krafft decreed a "mandate and plaint" against the Heinrich Fuchs and Melchior Rinck. The priest and the vicar were ordered to leave the town within two weeks.[51]

Abbot Krafft allowed both priests one final, farewell sermon, to be held on 27 December. Heinrich Fuchs and Melchior Rinck, however, were not willing to go quietly and accept their banishment without protest. Their first maneuver was one that had already led to Reformation in several German cities—to call for a public disputation on points of religious controversy.[52] Facing the "doctors and educated people" (*doctores und gelert luthe*), Fuchs and Rinck wanted to take public responsibility for the content of their sermons.[53] The sole basis of doctrine, they proposed to argue, should be the word of the Holy Scripture. But the governing elite in Hersfeld did not react favorably to this proposal. This may have been because the council had not yet published its decree against the concubinage, nor had the priests' dismissal been made public.

Tensions escalated when the two Protestant preachers announced to the parish the abbot's decision. During the early mass on 17 December 1523, the pastor and the chaplain ascended the pulpit, one after the other, and announced that they had been forced to leave Hersfeld. They added that they had been dismissed without legal consultation.[54] It is unlikely that either preacher failed to reveal that the council's order against concubinage was the reason for their dismissal. This announcement greatly angered the followers of the Reformation movement in the city, who in reaction stormed the office of the chancellor of the imperial monastery and destroyed it. After that, the citizenry gathered before the wall surrounding the monastery within the town. Prevented from entering the monastery's precincts, they moved into the town to destroy the houses of priests who lived in concubinage.

Despite the considerable excitement and strong emotions expressed in these violent actions, the Hersfeld supporters of Protestant sermons did not act blindly. The main reason for the turmoil was—as the Hersfeld report says— "that the Word of God would be denied and driven from the populace" (*das das gots wort dem folgke solt ßo genomen und verjhaget warden*) if they did not intervene.[55] Accordingly, the crowd demanded that Abbot Krafft to retract the dismissal of Heinrich Fuchs and Melchior Rinck and reinstate them.[56] But the wrath of the crowd tapped deeper sources of resentment. Looking back on the episode, the wives of Hersfeld citizens arrested in the confrontation described a conflict fueled by anger against the immorality of unmarriage: the "whole common crowd," they recalled, "descended on the houses of several priests, who lived together openly with disreputable women, and punished them" (*der ganze gemeine Haufen etzlicher pfaffen hewser, dy mit bosen Weybern vffenlich zu hawß sytzen, visitirtt vnd gestrafft*).[57] The citizenry, in other words, had intervened to overthrow the abbot's authority and to execute the council's mandate against concubinage.

Conclusion

The events in eastern Hesse, western Thuringia, and northern Franconia illustrate the prominence of conflicts over clerical marriage during the early years of the Reformation. Few demands flowed so easily from Luther's concept of the priesthood of all believers as did the elimination of moral and legal distinctions between clergy and laity, including the ban against clerical marriage. With the abolition of priestly celibacy and the ban against concubinage, Protestant laity desacralized and normalized the clergy, assimilating them into the ranks of the regular citizenry. The events in Hersfeld also reveal that the demand for a normalization of the priests' estate emanated mainly from the socially and economically less prominent members of the town. The interests of the wealthier and more substantial citizens were closely entwined with those of the ecclesiastical dignitaries, and thus they were unwilling to support a mandate that attacked clerical concubinage.

Notes

1. *Staatsarchiv Marburg, Politisches Archiv des Landgrafen Philipp des Großmütigen*, no. 1961 [hereafter StAM], Best. 3, no. 1961, "Anzeigung," fol. 2ʳ.
2. Martin Luther to Philipp Melanchton, 25 May 1521, WA BR, vol. 2, 346–52 (no. 413), here 349.
3. In January 1523 Luther had been informed that the Hersfeld pastor had married a second time after the death of his first wife. This information came again from a source at the Wartburg: "Insuper hospes meus speculativus scribit . . . Pastorem Hisfeldiensem defuncta uxore prima super duxisse secundam"; see Luther to Georg Spalatin, 2 January 1523, WA BR, vol. 3, 1–4; and Luther to Spalatin, January 1523, WA BR, vol. 3, 24–26. In addition to Heinrich Fuchs, other pastors also married during this time, among them Jakob Seidel (Glashütte) and Bartholomäus Bernhardi (Kemberg); Martin Brecht, *Martin Luther*, 3 vols. (Stuttgart, 1986), vol. 2, 30–31.

4. On the ecclesiastical territories of the Holy Roman Empire, see Peter Moraw and Volker Press, "Fürstentümer, Geistliche," in Horst Robert Balz et al., *Theologische Realenzyklopädie*, 36 vols. (Berlin, 1876–2007), vol. 11, 711–19. As in most ecclesiastical territories, power was shared between the abbot and the chapter of the monastery—a relation that in Hersfeld was often strained; see Wolfgang Breul, *Herrschaftskrise und Reformation: Die Reichsabteien Fulda und Hersfeld ca. 1500–1525* (Gütersloh, 2000), 53–59; Kurt-Ulrich Jäschke, "Ein Hersfelder Stadtbuch aus dem Jahre 1431 als Quelle zur Geschichte von Stift und Stadt Hersfeld im 1. Drittel des 15. Jahrhunderts," *Archiv für Diplomatik* 13 (1967): 313–457; and Heinrich Butte, *Stift und Stadt Hersfeld im 14. Jahrhundert mit einem Anhang: Die Stadt Hersfeld bis zum Beginn des 15. Jahrhunderts* (Marburg, 1911).

5. Whereas the trip to Worms had had the character of a triumphal procession, offering Luther accommodation on his furtive return trip was a political risk. Luther presumably spent 1–3 May 1521 in Hersfeld. See Michael Fleck, "Luther in Hersfeld: Zur Chronologie der letzten Tage von Luthers Rückreise vom Wormser Reichstag," *Zeitschrift des Vereins für Hessische Geschichte und Landeskunde* 102 (1997): 7–14; Breul, *Herrschaftskrise*, 177–78. Luther enthusiastically reported about the impressive hospitality extended to him by the local lord in Hersfeld; see Luther to Spalatin, 14 May 1521, WA BR, vol. 2, 337–38. During this visit Luther presumably also met Heinrich Fuchs.

6. Temporarily released, Seidel was rearrested after he persisted in maintaining the matrimonial relationship; see Ulrich Bubenheimer, "Streit um das Bischofsamt in der Wittenberger Reformation 1521/22: Von der Auseinandersetzung mit den Bischöfen um Priesterehen und den Ablaß in Halle zum Modell des evangelischen Gemeindebischofs: Teil I," *Zeitschrift der Savigny-Stiftung für Rechtsgeschichte. Kanonistische Abteilung* 73 (1987): 155–209, here 166–70.

7. Numerous petitions on behalf of Zeiger, and perhaps even Albrecht's own uncertainty on the matter of clerical marriage, led to Zeiger's release on the condition that he swear an oath of obedience (*Urfehde*); Bubenheimer, "Bischofsamt," 190–96.

8. See Breul, *Herrschaftskrise*, 180–86.

9. See Jacob Grimm and Wilhelm Grimm, *Deutsches Wörterbuch*, 32 vols. (Leipzig, 1854–1961), vol. 24, 449–50.

10. See Oskar Vasella, "Über das Konkubinat des Klerus im Spätmittelalter," in *Mélanges d'histoire et de litterature offerts à Charles Gilliard* (Lausanne, 1944), 269–83.

11. "De poena contrabentium clandestina matrimonia," in Norman P. Tanner, ed., *Decrees of the Ecumenical Councils*, 2 vols. (London, 1990), vol. 1, 258. See also Schmugge, *Die Supplikenregister*, 68–71, 82–83; Hans Erich Feine, *Kirchliche Rechtsgeschichte: Die katholische Kirche* (Cologne, 1964), 381–82; and Emil Friedberg, *Das Recht der Eheschliessung in seiner geschichtlichen Entwicklung* (Leipzig, 1865), 78–93.

12. Tanner, *Decrees*, vol. 2, 755–57 (11 November 1563).

13. "Eyn Sermon vom Elichen Standt" (1519), WA, vol. 2, 166–71; WA, vol. 9, 213–19.

14. Martin Luther, "An den Christlichen Adel deutscher Nation" (1520), WA, vol. 6, 404–69, here 441.

15. The pope has "solchs nit macht . . . zupietten / als wenig er macht hat zuuorpieten / essen / trincken / vnd den naturlichenn auszgang / odder feyst werdenn"; WA, vol. 6, 442.

16. Martin Luther, "Vom ehelichen Leben" (1522), WA, vol. 10/II, 267–304. This writing appeared for a concrete reason. The bishop of Meissen had tried to enforce the rules of

canon law concerning confirmation and marriage more stringently. He was primarily concerned about the observance of canonical obstacles. Before addressing the question of marriage more thoroughly, Luther wrote a flyer in which he reduced the canonical restrictions on matrimony due to blood relations and intermarriage. See "Welche Personen verboten sind zu ehelichen" (1522), WA 10/II, 261–66. See also Brecht, *Luther,* vol. 2, 95–96.

17. Luther, "Vom ehelichen Leben," WA, vol. 10/II, 279.
18. Ibid., 277.
19. Luther, "An den Christlichen Adel," WA, vol. 6, here 407–10. See also Thomas Kaufmann, *An den christlichen Adel deutscher Nation von des christlichen Standes Besserung* (Tübingen, 2014).
20. See Bernd Moeller, "Kleriker als Bürger," in Bernd Moeller, *Die Reformation und das Mittelalter: Kirchenhistorische Aufsätze,* ed. Johannes Schilling (Göttingen, 1991), 35–52.
21. Stephen E. Buckwalter, *Die Priesterehe in Flugschriften der frühen Reformation* (Gütersloh, 1998), 291.
22. This information is based on a passage from a sermon by Jakob Strauss in which he called on priests to conduct their marriages in such a way as to provide a role model for the laity: "wie dan etlich hie gethan habe[n]. . . . Dargege[n] aber habe[n]tz aber nun etlich mehr als weltlich angehaben/ wie neuwelich hie beschehen/ das vmb den vnselige[n] freuedigen ta[n]tz/ das goettlich wort zur gebrechlicher stu[n]dt/ yn eins pfaffen hochzeyt nidergelegt wart"; Jakob Strauss, *Eyn Sermon in der deutlich angezeigt und gelert ist die pfaffen Ee / yn Euangelischer leer nitt zu der freiheyt des fleischs / vnd zu bekrefftygen den allten Adam / wie ettlich fleischlich Pfaffen das Elich wesen mi taller pomp / hofart vnd ander teuffels wreck anheben / gefundiert* (Erfurt, 1523), B 3ʳ.
23. See Hermann Barge, *Jakob Strauss: Ein Kämpfer für das Evangelium in Tirol, Thüringen und Süddeutschland* (Leipzig, 1937); Joachim Rogge, *Der Beitrag des Predigers Jakob Strauss zur frühen Reformationsgeschichte* (Berlin, 1957); Stephen E. Buckwalter, "Strauss, Jakob," *Theologische Realenzyklopädie* vol. 32, 246–49. Strauss was friends with the Kemberg provost Bartholomäus Bernhardi, whose marriage in the spring of 1521 was highly publicized. Bernhardi came from Tirol, where Strauss had previously preached the Reformation message before he was driven out. The Wittenberg theologians had publicly defended Bernhardi's marriage. On Bernhardi see Bubenheimer, "Bischofsamt," 170–90; Buckwalter, *Priesterehe,* 94–96, 133–34; Dorothea McEwan, *Das Wirken des Vorarlberger Reformators Bartholomäus Bernhardi: Der Lutherfreund und einer der ersten verheirateten Priester der Lutheraner kommen zu Wort* (Dornbirn, 1986), and Marjorie Elizabeth Plummer's contribution to this volume.
24. Only God's miraculous intervention can validate an exception in this command to procreate (Gen. 2:18), which is evident through all of creation; Jakob Strauss, *Eyn Sermon.*
25. Ibid., A 2ʳ, B 3ʳ, A 2ᵛ.
26. The exact date of his marriage is not known. Luther sent greetings to his wife and child on 18 October 1523 (Luther to Spalatin, WA BR, vol. 3, 179–80 [no. 675]) and on 25 April 1524 (Luther to Jakob Strauß, WA BR, vol. 3, 275-278, [no. 733], here 278). See also Buckwalter, *Priesterehe,* 266.
27. On the dating of this document, see Breul, *Herrschaftskrise,* 237, note 188.
28. Catholic as well as Reformation sources report that Georg Witzel lived with a woman soon after his ordination to the priesthood. See Günter Franz, "Ein Gutachten über Georg Witzel und seine Lehre," in *Festschrift zum 60. Geburtstag von Karl-August Eck-*

hardt, ed. Otto Perst (Marburg, 1961), 155–68, here 159; Justus Jonas, *Wilch die rechte Kirche / vnd dagegen wilch die falsche Kirch ist / Christlich antwort vnd tr[oe]stliche vnterricht / Widder das Pharisaisch gewesch Georgij Witzels* (Wittenberg, 1534), N 3ʳ–N 4ʳ.

29. After 1530 Georg Witzel rejected the Reformation program, but the marriage he made in 1524 remained valid. His status as a married priest and theologian limited severely his effectiveness within the Roman Church. See Werner Kathrein, Karlheinz Diez, Barbara Henze, Cornelius Roth eds., *Im Dienst um die Einheit und die Reform der Kirche: Zum Leben und Werk Georg Witzels* (Frankfurt, 2003); Barbara Henze, *Aus Liebe zur Kirche Reform: Die Bemühungen Georg Witzels um die Kircheneinheit* (Münster, 1995); and Remigius Bäumer, "Georg Witzel," *Katholische Theologen der Reformationszeit*, ed. Remigius Bäumer, Erwin Iserloh, and Thomas Berger, 2nd ed., 6 vols. (Münster, 1984–2004), vol. 1, 125–32.

30. Breul, *Herrschaftskrise*, 238.

31. Johann Apel, *Defensio Iohannis Apelli ad Episcopum Herbipolensem pro suo coniugio* (Wittenberg, 1523).

32. See August Amrhein, *Reformationsgeschichtliche Mitteilungen aus dem Bistum Würzburg 1517–1573* (Münster, 1923), 17–18; and Hans-Christoph Rublack, *Gescheiterte Reformation: Frühreformatorische und protestantische Bewegungen in süd- und westdeutschen geistlichen Residenzen* (Stuttgart, 1978), 25–26.

33. Jakob Fuchs, *Eyn Missiue an Bischoff von Wirtzburg / von herr Jacob Fuchß / den Eltern Thumbherrn außgangen* (Erfurt, 1523); Melchior Goldast, *Politische Reichshandel: Das ist / Allerhand gemeine Acten / Regimentssachen / und Weltliche Discursen; Das gantze heilige Römische Reich / die Keyserliche und Königliche Majestäten / den Stul zu Rom/ die gemeine Stände deß Reichs / insonderheit aber das geliebte Vatterlandt Teutscher Nation betreffendt* (Frankfurt, 1614), 783–84; Buckwalter, *Priesterehe*, 212–14.

34. Jakob Fuchs the Elder was able to return to the bishopric due to an intervention of the *Reichsregiment*; Amrhein, *Reformationsgeschichtliche Mitteilungen*, 28–31. The *Reichsregiment* was a government demanded by the German princes in 1521 and that was authorized to govern within limits during the long periods of Emperor Charles V's absence from the empire. Charles dissolved the unpopular body in 1531. See Horst Rabe, *Reich und Glaubensspaltung: Deutschland 1500–1600* (Munich, 1989).

35. Goldast, *Politische Reichshandel*, 788. An imperial mandate of 6 March 1523 stipulated that clergy who broke their vow of celibacy should be punished only with the penalties set by canon law, namely the loss of their positions; *Deutsche Reichstagsakten: Jüngere Reihe: Deutsche Reichstagsakten unter Kaiser Karl V.* [hereafter RTA JR], vol. 3: *Der Reichstag zu Nürnberg*, ed. Adolf Wrede (Gotha, 1901), 447–52, here 451; and Paul Hinschius, *System des katholischen Kirchenrechts mit besonderer Rücksicht auf Deutschland*, 5 vols. (Berlin, 1869), vol. 1, 157.

36. An extensive description is found in Goldast, *Politische Reichshandel*, 787–95.

37. On Apel's humanistic contacts, especially in Fulda, see Breul, *Herrschaftskrise*, 240–41.

38. See Buckwalter, *Priesterehe*, 287–92. See also Hans-Joachim Köhler, "Erste Schritte zu einem Meinungsprofil der frühen Reformationszeit," in *Martin Luther: Probleme seiner Zeit*, ed. Volker Press and Dieter Stievermann (Stuttgart, 1986), 244–81.

39. Bernd Moeller, "Die Brautwerbung Martin Bucers für Wolfgang Capito," in Schilling, ed., *Die Reformation und das Mittelalter*, 151–60, here 154.

40. See Breul, *Herrschaftskrise*, 53–59, 90–114.

41. The priest Heinrich Fuchs started preaching the teachings of Luther near the end of 1520 or beginning of 1521; Breul, *Herrschaftskrise*, 170–80.

42. After his expulsion from Hersfeld, Rinck was active around Eisenach in the circle around Jakob Strauss and took part as a preacher in the Peasants' War of 1525 in central Germany. Rinck survived the defeat of the peasants in the Battle of Franken-hausen (where Heinrich Fuchs died) and later turned to Anabaptism. He became the most important Anabaptist preacher in eastern Hesse and western Thuringia. After being repeatedly arrested and expelled from Hesse, Rinck was finally and permanently imprisoned by Landgrave Philip of Hesse in November 1531. The landgrave was reluctant to impose the death penalty for questions of religion and thus refused to comply with Saxon demands to execute the obstinate Anabaptist leader. On Rinck see most recently Wolfgang Breul, "Vom Humanismus zum Täufertum: Das Studium des hessischen Täuferführers Melchior Rinck an der Leipziger Artistenfakultät," *Archiv für Reformationsgeschichte* 93 (2002): 26–42; idem, "Anfänge moderner Toleranz? Philipp und die religiösen Minderheiten," in *Landgraf Philipp der Grossmütige (1504–1567). Hessen im Zentrum der Reform*, ed. Ursula Braasch-Schwersmann, Hans Schneider, and Wilhelm Ernst Winterhager (Marburg, 2004), 105–12.
43. Breul, *Herrschaftskrise*, 186–89.
44. See ibid., xxx.
45. StAM, Best. 3, no. 1961, fol. 1ᵛ, "Anzeigung wo durch sich die auffrur der pfaffen halber hier zu hirsfelt erhaben hadt geschehen vff donnerstag nach lucie v[ir]ginis Anno etc. xxiij."
46. "One said, he would be ashamed in front of these people, for they had spun and combed his wool. The other said he did not want to help to drive them out" (Sagt[en] eyner erhett sich solch[er] luthe mussen generenn, hett[en] ime syn woln gespon[e]n vnd gekameth, der ander sagt Ich will er nicht helff[en] v[er]trieb[en]); StAM, Best. 3 no. 1961, fol. 2ʳ.
47. "It has been this way since the beginning; one cannot do without their work" (i.e., the work of those living in concubinage) (Er [es] ist von anbegin gewest, Man kan er nit enpheren); ibid.
48. "The third said, it is so in Erfurt, Nürnberg, and everywhere. One has to have them, in this way a respectable man maintains his wife and children" (Der dritt sagt, Er ist zu Erffort zu Nornb[er]g zu frangfurt vnd an allen end[en], man muß sie auch haben, ßo blibt ein[em] from man sein frawen vnd kinder); ibid.
49. StAM, Best. 3, no. 1961, fol. 2ᵛ˙
50. See StAM, Best. 3, no. 1961, fol. 3ʳ.
51. "Fünf Hersfelder Bürger und Bürgerinnen an Landgraf Philipp [early January 1524]," StAM, Best. 3, no. 1961, fol. 11ʳ.
52. StAM, Best. 3 no. 1961, fol. 3ᵛ. See also Bernd Moeller, "Zwinglis Disputationen," *Zeitschrift der Savigny-Stiftung für Rechtsgeschichte. Kanonistische Abteilung* 86 (1970): 275–324; 91 (1974): 213–364.
53. StAM, Best. 3 no. 1961, fol. 3ᵛ.
54. See StAM, Best. 3 no. 1961, fol. 4ʳ.
55. StAM, Best. 3 no. 1961, fol. 4ᵛ.
56. "Protokoll der Verhandlungen zwischen Abt und Gemeinde zu Hersfeld vor dem hessischen Landgrafen Philipp, 11–12 February 1524," in StAM, Best. 3 no. 1961, fol. 26ʳ.
57. StAM, Best. 3, no. 1961, Fünf Hersfelder Bürger und Bürgerinnen an Landgraf Philipp [January 1524], fol. 11ʳ.

~:~

CHAPTER 3

"Nothing More than Common Whores and Knaves"
Married Nuns and Monks in the Early German Reformation

MARJORIE ELIZABETH PLUMMER

In early 1523 Hans von der Planitz reported a rumor circulating in Nuremberg about a Carthusian monk who had kidnapped a nun from her convent, dressed her as a man, and taken her to Wittenberg where she then married both the Carthusian monk and an Augustinian monk.[1] Despite declaring his source unreliable, Planitz felt enough uncertainty to ask Frederick the Wise to confirm that the story was not true, which Frederick did, hinting the gossip possibly stemmed from a Fastnacht prank.[2] Even though the rumor was false, this episode illustrates the perception that clerical marriages, especially of monks and nuns, were certainly immoral and inherently absurd. The flagrant disregard for social rules present in the rumored kidnapping, cross-dressing, and bigamy point to a fear of the disorder caused when monastics married, a fear that would continue long after the legalization of clerical marriage. Such apprehension of married monastics' potential to damage the institution of marriage, and by extension the community, undermined attempts to make marriage an accepted norm for clergy, and entrenched the initial assessment of such unions as transgressive.

Secular and regular clergy who married during the early Reformation crossed the boundary of celibacy that had always separated clergy from the laity. Monastics broke an additional boundary to marry: the cloister wall. During the Middle Ages the regular violation of the vow of stability that bound monastics to their cloister was met with equally regular condemnation by authorities and communities. Even the exceptional cases in which monastics left the cloister with official permission to attend university or take up secular clerical positions generated suspicion and the monastics taking these positions suffered repeated accusations of immorality or impiety.[3] Ecclesiastical authorities responded to unsanctioned attempts at more permanent abandonment of vows by returning the runaway to the cloister and demanding that the delinquent monk or nun repent.[4] Imperial, canon, and civic laws judged the few married monastics as apostates and heretics for violating their vow of stability, and as bigamists for forsaking their vows of celibacy. In the late fifteenth century, German monastic reform movements sought to solidify the boundary between the cloister and the secular world by discouraging even minimal social and economic interaction between laity and monastics.[5]

Most studies on clerical marriage have focused on priestly marriage as a significant experience only to those monks and priests who formed the core of the new Lutheran clergy, or they have explored exclusively the theological and published polemical debate on celibacy by the reform leaders, or they have dealt with clerical marriage as a uniform experience.[6] These approaches certainly illustrate the important and varied theological discussions of clerical celibacy, but do obscure the unique experiences of male and female religious, disregard the different obstacles regular and secular clergy faced in marrying, and ignore the important exchanges between ideas and individual reception.[7] Most studies also miss the social significance of the deep-rooted resistance that monastics met from neighbors and family when entering the community as married men and women in the early Reformation. Married monks and nuns forced all levels of society to consider a radically new definition of marriage, religious practice, and institutional organization, and not everyone was immediately willing to accept the social change this implied, even when they favored the theological shifts and alterations in religious ritual. Many individuals, families, and communities treated married former monastics as outsiders and considered them deviant and untrustworthy for their oath breaking, which made their marriages a significant contrast to the usual social inclusion that marriage signaled. Traditional definitions of social roles, rituals of social inclusion and honorable behavior, and residual distinctions between religious and laity often complicated a straightforward redefinition of marriage to include the clergy, especially former monastics.

Debating Monastic Marriages

In the early Reformation, theologians distinguished clerical types when discussing celibacy or priestly marriage. On the matter of monks, theologians' initial focus concerned monks leaving their cloisters; marriage of those monks was unthinkable, even to those advocating monastic reform.[8] The voluntary nature of the monks' personal oaths made them indissoluble, unlike the forced celibacy vow required for priestly consecration, as Martin Luther and many other theologians argued in the early 1520s. The complexity of the theological issues surrounding monastic vows led Luther, even as he gradually came to support immediate marriage of priests, to caution against supporting the marriage of monks and to advise waiting for the decision of a future ecumenical council. The reformers' recommendations concerning the marriage of nuns was even less forthcoming. In his first work on monastic vows, Luther mentions nuns merely once, and only in passing.[9] Andreas Karlstadt considered nuns, only stipulating that their vows must be made with the permission of parent or husband.[10] With the rare exceptions, theologians provided no framework to justify monastic marriage.

Silence on monastic marriage ended abruptly in early 1521 with the first clerical marriage, that of Bartholomew Bernhardi, an Augustinian monk and provost in Kemberg. But Bernhardi's marriage by no means dispelled the reformer's ambivalence about clerical marriage, and opened new questions about married monks. The issue of female monastic marriage was raised soon thereafter when the former monk, Martin Bucer, married a nun, Elisabeth Silberstein, in 1522. These decisive steps were not always matched by decisive pronouncements. Even after Bernhardi's marriage, Luther expressed skepticism to Philipp Melanchthon about whether monks ever could renounce celibacy and marry.[11] When Karlstadt and Melanchthon supported the marriage of monks as well as priests,[12] Luther wrote to Georg Spalatin: "Good Lord! Will our people at Wittenberg give wives even to monks? They will not push a wife on me!"[13] The response of the imperial council was to dismiss such cases as isolated and localized and to distinguish between the marriage of monastics and the expected sexual misconduct of priests and monks. Their mandate commanded bishops to punish marrying priests and return runaway monks to their cloister.[14] None of these responses took seriously the idea that clerical marriage, especially that of monks or nuns, would be a significant concern or require any subsequent discussion.

It quickly became impossible to discuss clerical marriage as an isolated and localized issue, however. By 1524 more than seventy-five priests, forty-six monks, and thirty-three nuns had married. These early monastic marriages by their very existence generated a discourse that provoked many other monastics to consider whether they, too, wished to stay or leave their convents and marry. They also compelled rulers to develop a cohesive response to those who did choose to marry, and forced communities to decide whether to welcome these newly laicized ex-monks and ex-nuns into their households, guilds, and communities. In the end, ambivalence about whether monastics could ever truly retract their monastic vows heightened the transgressive nature of monastic marriage even as it was legalized.

Given the uncertainty the Reformed leadership expressed about monastic marriage, it is not surprising that the first unequivocal support for monastic marriage came from monks and nuns themselves as they fought to justify why their marriages were not only valid, but also a necessary moral step for them personally and for the community generally. Many former monastics argued they should be allowed to leave the cloister and marry because their vows, including those of celibacy, were not valid and thus did not represent any legal or moral issues of oath breaking, apostasy, or heresy. They contrasted the immoral celibate life in the cloister with the moral married life outside the convent, thereby inverting traditional spiritual functions of cloister and household. Many monks and nuns also emphasized marriage as a vital step in establishing normalcy in their lives outside the convent. Those clergy who opposed monastic marriage also seized on the issues of stability and sexual behavior presenting the lasciviousness of married clergy taking such a step as a significant danger to the community and contrasting it to the unparalleled spirituality and morality of cloistered monastics.

In keeping with their social isolation, monastics initially did not conduct their marriages as public events, and thus their appeals for support took the form of polemic pamphlets after they had married or as letters appealing to secular authorities for protection and permission to marry. In some of the earliest published pamphlets on monastic marriage, former monks interwove their own experiences, and especially the spiritual dangers of the cloister, with scripturally based theological arguments about vows and celibacy. In justifying their marriages, monastics, mostly male, focused on the moral need to marry. They emphasized their personal inability to observe the vow of celibacy and stressed the extent of immorality in the convent including various forms of sexual misconduct. Bucer defended the legality and morality of his marriage to a former nun by arguing that their individual experiences demonstrated the sinfulness of cloistered life that went against godly law and endangered their souls.[15] In 1524 Aegidius Mechler explained leaving his monastery and his intent to marry "a virtuous maiden" as being made necessary by the "monastic lack of chastity" found in the convents and monasteries.[16] This theme of the immorality of the monastery and about the need to include monks and nuns, as well as priests, in any discussion of clerical marriage soon was mirrored in the works of Lutheran polemicists. Johann Eberlin called on families to remove nuns from the convent "while they still have their honor and can come home to . . . a husband with honor."[17] Simon Reuter, for instance, sarcastically pointed out in 1523 that clerical marriage would resolve the problems of concubinage and illegitimate children of priests, monks, or nuns.[18]

Despite such efforts by newly married monastics to demonstrate the necessity and morality of their marriages, reform critics within the cloisters and Catholic preachers highlighted the deviant behavior and complete disregard of tradition and law exhibited by so-called runaway monks and nuns in order to expose the basic immorality of monastic marriage. In 1523 Johannes Dietenberger, prior of the Dominican monastery in Frankfurt, condemned Luther as having misled monastics to become "servants of the devil" through his slandering of the "cloistered life."[19] He criticized Luther for tempting the nine nuns out of Nimbschen, saying, "the poor, runaway, cloisterless nuns . . . are now with your help, breakers of oaths before God . . . perfidious before mankind, and aggravating to their friends and relatives . . . as they have gone from an honorable estate to a dishonorable one."[20] The ensuing polemic discussion thus increased popular distrust of married monastics by making explicit the immorality of monks and nuns who left their cloister by calling them perjurous, self-indulgent, and unable to control themselves physically and sexually.

Such remonstrations had an impact, and not only on critics of reform. Some monks and nuns, having left the cloister, hesitated to cross the line to full laicization through marriage, and condemned such hasty or lust-driven marriages as setting dangerous precedents. They disassociated leaving the convent from marriage, viewing the latter as a secondary, incidental effect of laicization, possible only when their abandonment of the convent was legalized and they had become fully integrated into the community. In a 1523 pamphlet defending his right to leave the monastery, Ambrosius Blarer pointed out specifically that the need to marry had not prompted his decision. He noted "it was the general cry on the streets that monks and nuns leave the convents . . . to enter a fleshly life."[21] Sophia Buchner, a former nun from Eisleben, responded to a demand from the duke of Albertine Saxony that former nuns return to the convent by disconnecting her leaving the cloister from any desire to abandon celibacy. She wrote that she had left her convent at the peril of her "body and soul" when it was stormed during the Peasants' War and was rescued by her brother. As evidence of her continued spiritual compliance with her monastic vows outside the convent, Buchner offered the fact that she was living now as a celibate in Leipzig with her elderly mother and a female servant.[22] Some reluctance to marry was prompted by awareness that although many were ready to support monastics leaving convents, monastic marriage was still unimaginable to most people. These two examples also show an emerging difference in how nuns and monks approached justifying their actions. Former monks usually cited spiritual reasons for leaving or a desire to work, but former nuns defended their decision to leave the convent by highlighting their continued celibacy and the support of their family.

Public rejections of the binding nature of monastic vows, debates over the immoral climate of the cloister, and personal justifications by former monastics all drew considerable attention, positive and negative, to monastic marriage, as did the increasing number of such marriages. Such actions and discussions found a receptive audience among monks and nuns as the growing exodus from the cloisters by 1525 indicates. Nonetheless, many monastics were reluctant to link leaving the cloister directly with marriage. Monastic marriage also gained more uniform support among the evangelical leadership, as indicated by the willingness of Luther to marry Katharina von Bora, a former nun, in 1525. Nonetheless, reformed-minded leaders and individuals continued to view clerical marriages as transgressive even after Luther's marriage. Monks and nuns often exited the convent at night without official permission from the abbot or abbess, further highlighting the sense of deviance. Because most monks and nuns found little enthusiastic support beyond their immediate family and remained less willing than priests to marry publicly, the earliest monastic marriages remained covert. This desire of married monks and nuns for secrecy added to the impression that there was something illicit about these unions.

Legalizing Monastic Marriage

From the very beginning, monastic marriage received a mixed response from territorial, civic, and ecclesiastical leaders. The residual ambiguity about whether earlier imperial prohibitions against clerical marriage included monks was resolved in 1523 when the emperor issued a mandate requiring all territorial rulers to uphold imperial and ecclesiastical policy forbidding the repudiation of monastic vows and proscribing the clerical marriage of "priests, monks, and nuns."[23] Nevertheless, many secular authorities displayed ambivalence and inconsistency in dealing with newly married monastics throughout the 1520s, hesitating about allowing them to remain in the community or wavering on accepting their marriages as legitimate. Monastics quickly exploited this indecisiveness to their advantage when seeking official support for their actions. They turned to territorial princes and city councils for support and willingly gave up a part of their autonomy in the decision to marry in return for assistance and official confirmation of the legitimacy of their marriages.

In lieu of supportive congregations and in the face of mounting disapproval of monastic marriage, monastics increasingly sought permission to marry from their secular rulers and pressured temporal authorities to confirm their union's legitimacy by issuing mandates or public sanctions legalizing them. In Magdeburg four former monks published a pamphlet containing their response to eighteen articles, including several on the validity of monastic vows and marriage, in preparation for a formal disputation with the local cathedral clergy and monks.[24] This and other such appeals hinged on the argument that the monastic was entering a normal, orderly life and that the civic authorities should assist this move because it promoted civic morality. "Those called religious, who enter into marriage," they exclaimed, "are not erring by marrying . . . but, to indulge in fornication, adultery, and other unnameable sins [in the convent] is wrong and against God's command."[25] With the city council's approval all four married between October 1524 and February 1525. The Peasants' War accelerated this process as more monks and nuns were involuntarily, but permanently, displaced from their convent or presented with a rare chance to escape. In 1525 three Franciscan monks asked the Rothenburg city council for support in leaving the cloister, arguing they could lead "a good Christian life" more easily as artisans and married men than as monks.[26] They exploited civic concerns by arguing sanctioning monastic marriage would create good citizens and prevent immorality in the convents from spreading.[27]

The lack of resources most monastics faced and the uncertain atmosphere of the 1520s heightened the generalized trend toward imputing former monastics with a reputation for illicit activities. Some leaders unequivocally treated the act of monastic marriage as illegal, the monks and nuns who left their convents to marry as personally immoral, and the very existence of a married monastic as a threat to marriage and the fabric of society. Duke Georg of Albertine Saxony, commenting on Luther and Melanchthon's teachings on monastic vows, asked, "Where in the gospel is it written that either a monk or a nun who has vowed celibacy, may leave the cloister and marry?" He then made clear the immorality such moves represented: "How many of these pious former monks and nuns have become nothing more than common whores and knaves."[28] The assembly of southern German bishops held at Regensburg in 1524 called on bishops to strengthen regulation of monastic institutions and improve moral standards of all clergy.[29] Papal legate Lorenzo Campeggio noted a consensus by the bishops that "no monastic . . . should be allowed to live outside their cloister, and that no exemptions . . . be allowed."[30] The bishops also agreed not "to tolerate or allow in any way the runaway male and female monastics" and to punish all violators.[31] Opponents of reform called on bishops and the Church to strengthen the current definitions of spiritual life dividing the monastics from the laity through enclosure and insisting on stricter adherence to celibacy.

Catholic authorities certainly renewed their efforts to ensure that monastic rules were obeyed strictly. The same impulse emerges from their public and private statements on the problem of monastic marriages. As he dealt with a nun attempting to marry, Hugo, bishop of Constance, stated his intention not let any nuns or monks leave their cloister and to force those who did back into the cloister as outlined in the Regensburg agreement.[32] Duke Georg mandated that all "religious or lay" found guilty of transgressions of the Nuremberg or Regensburg mandates be punished.[33] Yet neither the duke nor the bishop successfully achieved full compliance from monastics, nor did civic leaders under their jurisdictions fully support them. Local resistance and the ambivalence of civic leaders about the reform movement undermined efforts at effectively discouraging additional runaway and marrying monks and nuns.

Even ostensibly neutral civic and territorial authorities did not coordinate their efforts or fully execute imperial or episcopal policies they considered impossible to enforce. At a 1524 meeting of the Swabian League, the Memmingen representative brought up the rebellion in the male and female Augustinian convents after one of the nuns married a monk from Buxheim.[34] The League members expressed concern that the presence of evangelical-leaning monks might lead to a general exodus from the cloisters and cited the marriage of the nun as an example of how far things had deteriorated. After finding that the city council "had been diligent" in its actions, however, the League advised that the city to leave runaway monastics to their own fate.[35] In other words, the cities gathered in Ulm decided not to intervene in what appeared to them to be an ecclesiastical matter and advised Memmingen to do the same.

Even those individuals most committed to the evangelical reforms were divided on the implementation of so broad-ranging a social transformation as monastic marriage. This resistance to concrete changes stemmed from a variety of social, political, legal, and economic causes. Although by 1523 Luther agreed that monastic marriage was justified theologically, he found the practical implications worrisome. Many newly married monks and nuns, unprotected by a supportive congregation as the parish priests often were, fled to the relative safety of Wittenberg.[36] As he wrote to Spalatin, "I am growing to hate the sight of these renegade monks . . . what annoys me most is that they wish to marry at once, though they are of no use for anything. I am seeking a means to put an end to it."[37] Their desire to marry immediately meant that Luther had not only to defend their leaving the convent, but also to protect them from prosecution and provide them an income. Yet Luther also exclaimed that if his opponents had any idea of the stories he heard every day from monastics of the sinful lives and torments they suffered while in the monasteries and convents, "they would help me storm the cloisters tomorrow."[38] Others shared Luther's recognition of the social and legal problems monastic marriages raised and the discomfort he felt.

Initially, most temporal rulers were reluctant to challenge the emperor directly or to deal with the social and economic consequence of reintegrating monastics into lay society. In 1523, after discovering a married former monk and nun had been granted citizenship, a de facto acceptance of the marriage, the Nuremberg city council quickly withdrew the citizenship and returned the citizenship fee.[39] Instead of turning them over to the bishop, the council banished the couple, which had the dual effect of assisting them in the abandonment of their vow of stability and of relieving the city of any direct responsibility for overseeing their integration into lay society. However, in using banishment in this particular instance, Nuremburg also effectively treated the couple exactly like they would any other foreign couple accused of sexual misconduct, and thus confirmed their laicization, without further disrupting the community or gaining undue imperial attention.[40]

This designation of monastic marriage as merely a new form of sexual misconduct was echoed in legal action in areas where the reform had made less progress. Rulers in these regions cited the need to protect the community from the immorality introduced by the settling of runaway, married monastics. Their deviance seemed adequate justification for banishment. Thus Duke Georg commanded the city council of Sangerhausen in 1525 to allow any monks or nuns "who had not married" to return to their cloisters, but to banish those who had married.[41] This policy became official in 1528, when Emperor Ferdinand dispatched a mandate to all territorial princes stipulating that "all former or married monks, priests, or nuns" who had broken with the rules of the church were to be banished. Married runaway monks and nuns were to be punished unfailingly within a month after the publication of the mandate.[42] These two policies (return and banishment) emerged as the dominant secular official forms of dealing with runaway and marrying monastics.

As the reform movement progressed, however, many rulers sought to evade both alternatives by claiming that monastics who had already left their monasteries and convents were no longer suitable for monastic life because circumstances had laicized them. Already in 1525, the elector John of Saxony stated that he did not intend to allow any monastics to return because of the "godless lives" they had lived outside the cloister during the rebellion of that year.[43] Thus, under the guise of protecting the cloister's enclosure, John effectively reduced the number of monks and nuns under his jurisdiction, and allowed monastic marriages within Saxony, without directly challenging imperial authority. Philip of Hesse reported that the "common word" was that John intended to drive the monastics out of the cloister without compensation, keeping the wealth of the cloisters for himself, thus forcing them to become nothing better than "whores and knaves."[44] Others claimed that because the clergy were now independent, whether to return monks and nuns to their monasteries was no longer a matter for the secular authorities to decide. Despite an order from the Swabian League, the Heilbronn city council refused to assist the abbot of the Carmelite Order in returning his monks to the monastery.[45] The city council defended their action saying that they would not intervene in an issue of personal "conscience, oath and duty" and that each monk should decide for himself whether he wished to reenter the monastery, or marry.[46] Accepting the idea that the former monastics could make their own decisions effectively recognized that their monastic vows no longer bound them.

Such moves eventually allowed cities and territories to begin the formal process of closing monasteries with justifications drawn directly from initial clerical defenses of monastic marriage. The Nuremberg city council closed its convents in 1525, defaming them as hotbeds of immorality, that nurtured unchristian lives and condoned the sexual misconduct on the part of monks and nuns.[47] As the Augsburg city council debated closing convents in 1534, it sought advice from a variety of theologians and legal experts on how to deal with monastic marriages. One anonymous correspondent commented that, while it was nearly impossible for monks to remain chaste and free of sin, the danger was even greater for nuns because "women are much weaker . . . in spirit and body" and that whatever sins one finds in the monastery are found "a thousand times over in the convent."[48] Some convents and monasteries in Augsburg closed and monastics obtained the right to marry, but other cloisters remained open albeit under closer scrutiny.

Official support of the reform movement did not stop other clergy from criticizing monastic marriage, casting doubt on its legitimacy, and slandering those who married and those who did not condemn their nuptials. Such opposition was particularly intense when the new husbands did not become Lutheran pastors. Caritas Pirckheimer commented that chaos reigned after the closing of the Nuremberg monasteries as the monks indulged in a "wild life and held no order."[49] In 1528 the newly reformed congregation of Geilsheim complained to Margrave Georg of Brandenburg-Ansbach about the content of the Good Friday sermons of their priest, Johannes Siebentail, including the statement that "all monks who take wives are nothing but faithless rascals" and that their children were nothing better than "whores' children."[50] Siebentail's sermon, the existence of those who supported and reported on him, and the official stance of the territory allowing monastic marriage demonstrate how difficult it was to effect a change in attitude about monastic marriage. Ultimately, the decision of secular authorities to legalize monastic marriage had only a limited influence on popular attitudes toward monastic marriage.

Popular Responses

The polemic engaged in by the reformers, critics, monastics, and rulers raised new questions for the laity about the monastics in their communities and helped underscore a continuing belief that monastic marriage was irregular at best and deviant at worse. Competing predictions of imminent disaster and the destruction of social values played out before a public seeking to determine its own standards of socially acceptable behavior. Some doubted the validity of marriages their own state authorities had sanctioned. They remained concerned that these unions represented a new form of clerical sexual misconduct and that married monks and nuns truly were just "whores and knaves." Others questioned whether monastics who broke their vows could even enter into another "marital" bond since this would make them bigamous and cast a shadow on the reliability of any oaths they might take as laypeople in social and economic interactions. Because of the long-range social and economic implications it bore for families and communities, even those who did not oppose the reform movement or even supported the closure of cloisters hesitated to accept monastic marriage. These unions also undermined the stability of existing gender relations and family dynamics because monks and nuns who married assumed traditional gender roles that they had previously forsworn and demanded legal inclusion in inheritance and property agreements.

To be sure, some individuals, families, and lay groups actively supported monastics in their flight from convents and pushed for their re-integration into lay society during the early reform movement even before authorities issued official mandates supporting either clerical marriage or the closure of the cloisters. The Peasants' War exacerbated lay tendency to present monastic marriage as an absolutely necessary part of the peasants' larger social programs. In one dramatic event in Salza, a peasant mob from Mühlhausen forced monks and nuns to leave their cloisters in the middle of the night. The next day the mob leaders informed the monastics at a meeting at the city hall that they now were expected to marry and become citizens.[51] Most often in the case of nuns, concerned family members sought to remove them from the convent using arguments clearly influenced by polemical pamphlets. Thus Ursula Tetzel petitioned the Nuremberg city council to let her remove her daughter from the Poor Clares convent, because she had learned "through God's word and merciful reports" that the cloister endangered her daughter's "body and soul."[52] Relatives of the Poor Clares in Esslingen petitioned the city council for permission to remove their daughters from the cloister, stating that only God could decide whether they "could hold chastity or should marry."[53] Clearly, arguments about the moral dangers presented to nuns in cloistered life had persuaded some. This assistance, often extended at great personal risk, indicated personal willingness to accept nuns back into the family specifically for the nun's spiritual and physical well-being and for the sake of family honor.

Even more striking, however, was the unwillingness of laypeople to recognize monastic marriage until its status had been clarified by law. To do otherwise was to risk exposing one's self unnecessarily to social censure, perhaps even criminal prosecution. At an individual level, many refused to consider marriage to former monastics, avoided social contact with married monks and nuns, engaged in circulating rumors or used defamatory language about married monastics, or refused to accept sacraments or listen to the sermons of married former monks. Popular distrust expressed itself in the failure of marriage to convey normal social rights automatically. In 1525 authorities questioned Georg Crucinger about the presence of his daughter and his daughter-in-law, both former nuns, at the marriage of another daughter at Leipzig. Crucinger claimed that his daughter-in-law, Elizabeth von Meseritz, had not danced at the wedding "because it was not allowed her as a former nun," although she had taken part in the celebration at the inn.[54] Secular society did not always accept monks as members of their community either, and married monastics faced obstacles in gaining citizenship and guild membership. In Augsburg, for example, the weavers' guild decided to exclude Johann Schmid, a former monk who had married into the guild, even though they had previously granted membership to illegitimate children.[55] Since his wife was the daughter of a guild member and a citizen, failure to grant him guild membership signaled that the guild did not recognize the legitimacy of the marriage; rumors circulated that the city council intended to force Schmid to give up his wife.[56] The subsequent rebellion in support of the monk demonstrates that at least some were willing to support the union against the council's prohibition.[57] Some reactions were clearly determined by confessional differences as individuals disagreed about larger reform issues.

Things became more complicated, however, when officials published mandates directing the closure of the convents and allowing monks and nuns in those convents remaining open the freedom to leave and to marry. Within reformed territories this next, more nuanced, stage shifted the spectrum of opinion away from complete rejection, toward limited acceptance of married monastics into society, and finally to full acceptance of clerical marriage. In a few cases it is possible to document this shift in sentiments of individual people. In 1525 Heinrich Vogel removed his daughter from her convent in Gotha and took her home during the Peasants' War when Elector John closed the convents, yet he intended that she continue as a nun. Three years later, he wrote that he now understood that convent life lacked all spiritual value. This realization led him to conclude that he now wanted his daughter to marry rather than to be a nun. Moreover, he wished her to be compensated as other "honorable maidens" had been.[58] Others expressed greater doubt about whether such a shift was possible. Dr. Johann Rechlinger, a member of the Imperial Chamber Court (*Reichskammergericht*), successfully advocated keeping at least some convents open in Augsburg; his argument rested on his observation of previous reactions among the elite. He contended that the uncontrolled exodus from the monasteries had led former nuns to "dishonorable vice, unseemly unchastity, and other sins" and brought about much discord among families who refused to take back their children. He also expressed concern that many nuns were marrying dishonorably: "I still never have seen that a nun given in marriage to a high, prominent or rich man or a monk to a rich maiden. The elite and propertied people would participate if marriage to a monk or nuns were such godly work."[59] Over time, after the establishment of laws allowing monastic marriage, a general acceptance of monastic marriage emerged in those communities where the Reformation prevailed. So, too, did a small, but often vocal and radicalized, opposition movement among the laity.

Families reacted in many ways when faced with a decision whether to support their son or daughter in the choice to leave a convent and marry against the express order of local officials. A direct confrontation with a governmental official, especially an imperial one, often forced parents to make a public statement as to their beliefs, which they might have avoided without close outside scrutiny. In 1528 Anna Grab was accused of leaving the Dominican convent in Binsdorf to "live in sin." Hans von Stotzingen, a noble imperial representative and reform opponent, arrested Grab, and forced her to swear to live a "like a nun should" and not forget "the vow she made when she entered the convent," threatening to banish her from convent and village if she did not. Her father, in a separate agreement, confirmed his acceptance of these provisions, stating neither he nor anyone else in the family would interfere with any punishments.[60] Other families supported nuns who married. In 1528 the Brunn city council intervened when former nun Barbara Hemler tried to marry a local citizen, claiming that she was too poor to marry and that she was a "runaway, abjuring, and uncompleted" nun who had left her convent without her parents' permission. Hemler countered with a response showing her parents accepted her decision to leave and to marry.[61] The importance of social networks in establishing the former monastic in the community meant that ambivalence on the part of families left a monk or nun unprotected against official actions, or left him or her socially and economically vulnerable.

Even evangelical families balked when faced by the practical implication of the marriages of the monks and nuns. Many monks married women of lower social status, but the social disparity for the patrician and noble nuns, who often married artisan or lower-middle-class men, provoked the greatest outcry from families. Johann Eberlin's call for a husband with honor was often complicated by the social transgression, noted by Rechlinger, of nuns marrying significantly down in social status. Katharina von Kertzsch, a former nun from Nimbschen, was able to marry a citizen from Torgau in 1533 with the full support of her family, but her sister Margaretha ran into problems with their brother in 1532 when she became engaged to the convent baker. The brother blocked the marriage and Margaretha was only able to marry another man, a citizen from Borna, after the convent finally was dissolved.[62] Some families defended their honor by removing female relatives from a convent and supporting their marriages, but others acted only when such a marriage was considered appropriate to the overall family status. Transgression of social expectations could lead to disputes within the family.

Arguably the most complicated conflicts that emerged as monastics left the convents and entered secular life revolved around property. Some families refused to accept a nun back into the household, withheld inheritance from former nuns, or denied the payment of a dowry to married nuns.[63] These conflicts based on differing opinions on the validity of clerical marriage led some married former nuns and monks to seek out the imperial court system for resolution of such disputed inheritance or property claims against parents or convents. These complicated cases often forced imperial lawyers to confront a clear transgression of imperial law forbidding monastic marriage while dealing with controversial property issues. In 1537, for instance, the Imperial Chamber Court dismissed the case of Barbara Zerweck, a former nun from Sirnau married to an Esslingen citizen, against her brother Hans Lemblin, a citizen of Öhringen, over her claim on parental inheritance. The case had run on for four years in various civic and territorial courts. Lemblin's lawyers argued that under imperial law Zerweck had no standing to inherit because she had been excommunicated and condemned as an apostate for having abandoned her convent. The court agreed and declared Zerweck a persona non grata who had no right to use the imperial court system.[64] In this case, as in many others, former monastics found that in leaving the cloister and marrying they achieved little financial security, gained the distrust of their family and community as oath-breakers, suffered considerable public ridicule and social snubbing, and risked significant denial of their legal rights and restriction of individual autonomy. Battles over finances became important not only to the former nun and her husband and interfamily dynamics, but also to the civic, territorial, and religious leaders supporting her decision to leave. By refusing to pay the dowry or not recognizing the children or inheritance rights of a former nun or monk, families made their nonrecognition or disapproval of the marriage clear and weakened chances that the newly married couple would receive communal recognition that was even more significant than the finances involved.

Legal support from officials did not mean that former monastics thrived professionally in their new positions or that suspicions about their morality or social status disappeared. The many petitions for additional financial support from monks and nuns pleading poverty indicate a notable, and widespread, lack of financial success. Many former monastics painstakingly chronicled varied unsuccessful attempts to secure permanent occupations and pointed to residual prejudice and marginalization directed against their relatives. The ex-monk Georg Raute, despite serving as a Lutheran pastor and author, appealed for a return of money he brought into the cloister from his parental inheritance, in order to secure the future of his foreign wife and children, who he worried would be unable to survive without the money.[65] The state could diminish a former monk or nun's social position by presenting financial compensation as charity. This proved the case in 1527 when the Zwickau city council awarded a married monk his severance or pension (*Abfertigung*) in the form of charity, even as the council was issuing mandates against beggars.[66] Numerous other locations followed this approach, awarding financial compensation as charity rather than as a standard payment for services in the cloister or a repayment of money brought in, which served to marginalize former monastics further.

Even years later former nuns and monks were forced to prove that they had left the cloister for the proper reasons and that they continued to live an honorable life, before any funding could be given. In his letter of support for a former nun, Jörg von Folge, administrator of the Ichtershausen convent, carefully pointed out that when Katharine Gebhardt left the convent during the

Peasants' War she did not do so "secretly or silently" but with the permission of her parents, with whom she resided until she married honorably. Since that time, she had lived as pious housewife, took her children to catechism regularly, and attended church services with her family faithfully.[67] In this she, like many others, attempted to show that the institution of marriage had not suffered because of her entry into it.

Conclusion

Nuns and monks who left monasteries in the 1520s and 1530s defied imperial and ecclesiastical law in order to marry. In the opening years of the German Reformation, growing numbers of monastics left convents simultaneously and united this step with their marriages to make the abandonment permanent. While celibacy was expected of all clergy and they made a clear vow of chastity, the vows made by the monastics, male and female, were held as more binding because of the separation of the monks and nuns from the rest of society. It became a more complicated argument to explain why they should leave the convent and even more so why they should marry.

The impact of that decision was to be felt, however, even years later as the initial struggle to leave the cloister turned to an often unending struggle to reintegrate into society and to survive suspicion and financial hardship. Monks and nuns typically entered lay society in ways that priests did not, assuming non-spiritual functions as citizens and artisans and as husbands and wives within a traditional household. This transition was not fully successful; many former monastics fell into poverty or suffered social marginalization. The situation was further complicated by the fact that many former nuns and monks married spouses generally not of their social class. These new positions often necessitated initial financial support from families and localities since most monks and nuns needed funds to marry, enter guilds, and set up households, and such support was not always forthcoming.

The ambivalence often displayed by leading reformers and secular authorities recognized that even if the majority tacitly accepted monastic marriage, some would never accept married monastics in their families or communities. Many others remained ambivalent about whether they personally believed that monastic marriage was honorable or fit their spiritual or personal definitions of marriage. The popular opinion that such marriages were transgressive remained evident in subtle ways, but was mitigated by the force of the legal and institutional support of those marriages. It is in this atmosphere that rumors about the marriages and families of former monastics similar to the one noted at the beginning of this chapter could be imagined and circulated with a certain level of credibility long after the reform movement was accepted.

Notes

1. Letter from Hans von der Planitz to Frederick the Wise, 24 February 1523; Hans von der Planitz, *Bericht aus dem Reichsregiment in Nürnberg, 1521–1523*, eds. Ernst Wülcker and Hans Virck (Leipzig, 1899), 378.
2. Planitz, *Bericht*, 399.
3. F. Donald Logan, *Runaway Religious in Medieval England, C.1240–1540* (Cambridge, UK, 1996), 42–65, 78–79; Alison I. Beach, *Women as Scribes: Book Production and Monastic Reform in Twelfth-Century Bavaria* (Cambridge, UK, 2004), 19.
4. Logan, *Runaway Religious*, 122.
5. Marie-Luise Ehrenschwendtner, "Virtual Pilgrimages? Enclosure and the Practice of Piety at St. Katherine's Convent, Augsburg," *Journal of Ecclesiastical History* 60 (2009): 45–73; Helmut Zschoch, *Klosterreform und monastische Spiritualität im 15. Jahrhundert* (Tübingen, 1988), 204–30; Anne Winston-Allen, *Women Writing About Women and Reform in the Late Middle Ages* (University Park, 2004), 84–86; Felician Gess, *Die Klostervisitationen des Herzog Georg von Sachsen nach ungedruckten Quellen dargestellt* (Leipzig, 1888), 14–15.
6. Buckwalter, *Priesterehe*; Waldemar Kawerau, *Die Reformation und die Ehe: Ein Beitrag zur Kulturgeschichte des sechzehnten Jahrhunderts* (Halle, 1892), 12–40; August Franzen, *Zölibat und Priesterehe, in der Auseinandersetzung der Reformationszeit und der katholischen Reformation des 16. Jahrhundert* (Münster, 1971); Bernhard Lohse, *Luthers Theologie in ihrer historischen Entwicklung und in ihrem systematischen Zusammenhang* (Göttingen, 1995), 156.
7. Some exceptions include Barbara Steinke, *Paradiesgarten oder Gefängnis?: Das Nürnberger Katharinenkloster zwischen Klosterreform und Reformation* (Tübingen, 2006); Leonard, *Nails in the Wall*; Johannes Schilling, *Klöster und Mönche in der hessischen Reformation* (Gütersloh, 1997).
8. Lohse, *Luthers Theologie*, 154–61; Franzen, *Zölibat*, 22–27.
9. Martin Luther, *Kurtz schluszrede von den gelobdten vnnd geystlichen leben der closter* (Erfurt, 1521); "The Judgment of Martin Luther on Monastic Vows," LW 35: 305.
10. Andreas Karlstadt, *Von gelubden vnterrichtung . . . Das Pfaffen, Monche, vñ Nonnen, mit gutem gewissem, vnd gottlichem willen, sich mogen vnd sollen vermelen, vnd yn eelichen stand begeben. . . . vnd ynn ein recht Christlich leben tretten* (Wittenberg, 1521), Gi^r–Hiv^v.
11. "Letter to Philip Melanchthon, Wartburg, 3 August 1521," LW 48: 285.
12. Jens-Martin Kruse, *Universitätstheologie und Kirchenreform. Die Anfänge der Reformation in Wittenberg 1516–1522* (Mainz, 2002), 293–94; Karlstadt, *Von gelubden vnterrichtung,* Hiv^v.
13. Martin Luther to Georg Spalatin, 6 August 1521, LW, vol. 48, 290; WA BR, vol. 2, 377–79 (no. 426).
14. Hauptstaatarchiv Dresden [hereafter SächsHStADres] 10024 Geheimer Rat, Loc. 10300/1, 148–51, Ferdinand to George, 20 January 1522.
15. Martin Bucer, *Verantwortug M. Butzers uff das jm seine widerwertigen . . . züm ärgsten zümessen. Mit begebung in alle leibs straff, so er mit seinem leben, oder leer nach Götlichem gesatz straffbar erfunden würt.* (Strasbourg, 1523), Di^v.
16. Aegidius Mechler, *Apologia oder schutzrede Egidy Mechlery . . . . Jn welcher wyrt grund vnd vrsach ertzelt seynes weyb nemens* (Erfurt, 1523), Aii^{r-v}.

17. Johann Eberlin, *Eyn freundtlichs zuschreyben an alle stendt teutscher nation, daryn sie vermanet werden, nit widerstandt zuthun den geystlichen so auß klostern oder pfaffenstandt gehen wöllen* (Erfurt, 1521), Aivʳ.

18. Simon Reuter, *Ein Christliche frage Simonis Reuters vonn Schlaytz, an alle Bischoffe . . . Warumb sy doch: an priestern: vnnd andern geistlich geferbten leutte, den eelichen standt nicht mügenn leyden* (Bamberg, 1523), Aiiᵛ.

19. Johannes Dietenberger, *Antwort das Jungfrawen die klöster vnd klösterliche gelübt nümner götlich verlassen möge* (Strasbourg, 1523), Aiiʳ.

20. Dietenberger, *Antwort*, Aiiiᵛ; Johannes Dietenberger, *Doctor Johan. Dietenberger. Widerlegung des Lutherischen büchlins, da er schreibt von menschen leren zumeiden rc.* (Strasbourg, 1524), Aiiʳ–Aiiiᵛ.

21. Ambrosius Blarer, *Wahrhafft verantwortnng Ambrosij Blauerer, . . ., warub er auß dem Kloster gewichen, vnd mit was geding er sich widerumb, hynein begeben wöl* (Augsburg, 1523), Aiiʳ.

22. SächsHStADres, 10024 Geheimer Rat, Loc. 10300/2, 251–52, 6 January 1534.

23. Planitz, *Bericht*, 67–69; SächsHStADres, 10024 Geheimer Rat, Loc. 10300/1, 148v; Gess, *Klostervisitationen*, 16–18; Staatsarchiv Augsburg [hereafter StAA], Rst. Nördlingen, Bd. 35, 11, 6 March 1523.

24. Melchior Mirisch, Eberhard Weidensee, and Johannes Fritzhans, *Doctor Melchior Mirisch . . . Erbithen sich diese nach gedruckte Artickell, vor eyner gantzen gemeyn mit gegrunter schrifft tzu erhalten, widder alle Papisten Alhye tzu Maydeburgk* (Magdeburg, 1524).

25. Eberhard Weidensee and Johannes Fritzhans, *Ein erklerung der achzeen artikel, durch die prediger zu Magdeburg außgangen erkleret* (Eilenburg, 1524), Biiiʳ.

26. Stadtarchiv Rothenburg ob der Tauber, A1519, 76r–82v; Staatsarchiv Nuremberg [hereafter StAN], Rst. Ro. Rep. 200I Rst. Rothenburg, Urkunden und Akten, no. 331, 26–28; Paul Schattenmann, *Die Einführung der Reformation in der ehemaligen Reichsstadt Rothenburg ob der Tauber (1520–1580)* (Munich, 1928), 53–55.

27. Johannes Lang, *Von gehorsam der Weltlichen oberkait, vnd den außgangen klosterleuten, ain schutzred* (Augsburg, 1523), Biiᵛ.

28. Gess, *Akten*, vol. 2, 54.

29. Christoph Volkmar, *Reform statt Reformation: Die Kirchenpolitik Herzog Georgs von Sachsen, 1488–1525* (Tübingen, 2008), 606–9; Klaus Unterburger, *Das Bayerische Konkordat von 1583* (Stuttgart, 2006), 114–19.

30. Lorenzo Campeggio, *Ordnung und Reformation zu abstellung der Mißbreuch, . . . durch Bäbstlicher haylikait Legate rc: zu Regenspurg aufgericht* (Augsburg, 1524), Biᵛ.

31. *Entschliesung der hierin benannten Fürsten, . . . zu Regenspurg versamlet, zu handthabung Christenlichs glaubens, vnd euangelischer leere* (Augsburg, 1524), Aiiiʳ.

32. Alfred Vögeli, ed., *Jörg Vögeli: Schriften zur Reformation in Konstanz, 1519–1538*, 2 vols. (Tübingen, 1972–73), vol. 1, 233.

33. *Hierin findest du Das Kaiserlich Mandat zu Nurenberg außgangen. . . . Item Hertzog Georgen tzu Sachsen . . . Mandat und Execution* (Dresden, 1524), Diiiʳ.

34. Stadtarchiv Memmingen [hereafter StadtAMm], Rst. Memm. Akten, A298, 291ᵛ–293ʳ, 17 June 1524.

35. StAA, Rst. Nördlingen, Schwäbisch Bund, no. 924.

36. See, for example, the marriage of Nicolaus Demuth to a former nun: RTA JR 3, 452; Gess, *Akten*, vol. 1, 448.

37. Martin Luther to Georg Spalatin, 11 July 1523, WA BR, vol. 3, 109–10 (no. 633).
38. Johann Georg Walch, ed., *Martin Luthers Sämmtliche Schriften* (St. Louis, 1899), vol. 15, 2213.
39. On the same day, the city council banished another former monk who was serving as a tailor's apprentice for his advances on his master's wife. StAN, Ratsbuch no. 12, 201^r; RTA JR IV, no. 155, 624; Hauptstaatsarchiv Stuttgart [hereafter HStAS], A44, U1850, 16 May 1528.
40. Jason P. Coy, *Strangers and Misfits: Banishment, Social Control, and Authority in Early Modern Germany* (Leiden, 2008), 67.
41. Gess, *Akten*, vol. 2, 283–84.
42. StAN, Rep. 111 Ansbach Religionsakten, Tom. XI, no. 74, 327r, 1 August 1528.
43. Ibid., Tom. IV Supp., fasz. 5, 60^{r-v}, 12 October 1525.
44. Gess, *Akten*, vol. 2, 554.
45. StadtAA, Schwabische Bund, Bd. 9, 27 July 1526.
46. StadtAA, Literaliensammlung 1528, 19 March 1528.
47. StAN, Rep. 61a/b Briefbücher, no. 89, 70^v, 1 April 1525.
48. StadtAA, Literaliensammlung 1534, Nachtrag no. 24, 26^v–27^r, 28^r.
49. Josef Pfanner, ed., *Die "Denkwürdigkeiten" der Caritas Pirckheimer (aus den Jahren 1524–1528)* (Landshut, 1962), 66.
50. Landeskirchliche Archiv der Evangelisch-Lutherischen Kirche in Bayern MKA, spez. 343, 2r, 24 July 1528; C. Scott Dixon, *The Reformation and Rural Society: The Parishes of Brandenburg-Ansbach-Kulmbach, 1528–1603* (Cambridge, UK, 1996), 39–41.
51. SächsHStADres, 10024 Geheimer Rat Loc. 9134/10, 15 May 1525.
52. Gerhard Pfeiffer, ed., *Quellen zur Nürnberger Reformationsgeschichte. Von der Duldung liturgischer Änderungen bis zur Ausübung des Kirchenregiments durch den Rat (Juni 1524—Juni 1525)* (Nuremberg, 1968), 209; Pfanner, *Denkwürdigkeiten*, 20–21, 96.
53. Stadtarchiv Esslingen, Bestand Reichsstadt, Fasz. 204, no. 49a.
54. Gess, *Akten*, vol. 2, 451.
55. StadtAA, Urgichten, no. 5, 11 September 1524.
56. StadtAA, EWA 480, 3^r.
57. Lyndal Roper, *The Holy Household: Woman and Morals in Reformation Augsburg* (Oxford, 1989), 132.
58. Thüringisches Hauptstaatsarchiv Weimar, Ernestinisches Gesamtarchiv [hereafter ThHStAW, EGA], Reg. Ji 282.
59. StadtAA, Literaliensammlung 1534, Nachtrag no. 21, 14^r–15^v.
60. Staatsarchiv Sigmaringen, Dep. 38 T1, no. 911, 21 April 1528.
61. StAN, Rep. 61a/b, Briefbücher, no. 97, 171^v–172^r, 13 June 1528.
62. ThHStAW, EGA, Reg. Oo 1022, no. 22; Anne-Katrin Köhler, *Geschichte des Klosters Nimbschen. Von der Gründung 1243 bis zu seinem Ende 1536/1542* (Leipzig, 2003), 131.
63. WABR 3, no. 929, 585.
64. HStAS C3 Reichskammergericht, no. 2586, Doc. 8, 19 March 1537.
65. ThHStW EGA, Reg. Oo pag. 792, no. 689, 30 June 1535.
66. Stadtarchiv Zwickau, III.x, no. 62, RP 1525–1529, 105, 23 September 1527.
67. ThStAW EGA, Reg. Oo pag. 792, no. 484, 18 October 1540.

CHAPTER 4

~:~

Transgressive Unions and Concepts of Honor in Early Modern Defamation Lawsuits

RALF-PETER FUCHS

The scene of the marriage between Johan Bruns, mayor of Korbach, and Maria von Viermund, a Westphalian noblewoman, was one of peace, appropriate to feelings of love and affection between groom and bride. The two were wed in an orchard near Korbach on Sunday Jubilatis, 1 May 1547. Because this ceremony, like every wedding, established a legal relationship, it was attended by witnesses: three men, a chaplain among them, and a woman called the *Grevesche*.[1]

Initially, the groom addressed himself to his bride's kinfolk: "Dear Mary," asked Bruns, "are you sure that your cousin, the Bailiff of Dringenberg, and your kinfolk agree to our marriage?"[2] The mayor accepted Maria's answer: she never would have approached him had her kin objected. Only after the bride and groom had established the propriety of their union to family and kin did they turn to their own will. Johan Brun's next question reads as follows: "Dear Mary, is it your wish and desire to take me as your husband? If this is your wish so it is mine to take, to have, and to hold you as my married wife and homekeeper."[3] Afterwards both partners exchanged presents. Johan Bruns gave Maria von Viermund a gold coin and received a Joachimsthaler from his bride in return. The next day Johan Bruns confirmed his marriage in the presence of another member of the noble family, Berndt von Viermund, and a further high-born witness, Heinrich van Twiste, a canon of the cathedral in Paderborn.

Yet the marriage was never consummated. The reason did not lie in the bride's noble kinship but in the bridegroom's social network. The members of the magistracy in Korbach prevented Johann Bruns from meeting his bride again because they feared that his goods could be inherited by people who were not members of the community.[4] Had things gone according to plan, Bruns should have received Maria von Viermund some days later in a town nearby to consummate the union. But we are told that he was forbidden to do this and was verbally threatened if he defied the magistrates' decision. His fellow citizens extorted an oath from him not to approach Maria von Viermund. There are reports that the citizens of Korbach actually compelled Bruns to marry a ninety-year-old woman, although they later stoutly denied it. Be that as it may, when Johan Bruns died a few months later, Maria von Viermund lodged a complaint against the magistracy of Korbach, claiming a widow's share of Bruns's inheritance. She also asserted that her honor had been violated. Because the magistracy prevented her from consummating her marriage, there had been a great deal of gossip, mockery, and scoffing at her expense.

Why did Maria von Viermund think that her honor had been damaged? Her sense of injury prompts us to ask how the process of matchmaking and wedlock itself affected individual honor in the early modern period. There can be no question that a relationship existed between Maria and Johan. Matchmaking, however, was always a difficult social and economic transaction that generated many lawsuits, some of which were litigated all the way up the appellate ladder to the Imperial Chamber Court, the highest court in the empire. To show how and why marriage and honor were related, this chapter examines a set of lawsuits that arose when, for one reason or another, a marriage generated words or gestures of defamation. All came before the Imperial Chamber Court between 1525 and 1805; some were prompted by verbal allegations of theft of witchcraft (*iniuria verbalis*), by humiliating and violating actions such as flogging (*iniuria realis*), or by pasquils (*iniuria scriptis*).[5] The defamations that triggered these lawsuits often impugned sexual morality. The most frequent invective against women was, "Whore!" At various points in the legal proceedings, each party was given the chance to clarify his or her actions and intentions. In the process, defamers sometimes articulated their reasons for hurling slanders. While it would be naïve to take their stories at face value, these narratives offer a guide to the social norms that defined honorable and dishonorable behavior. Like all discourse, the stories told in a judicial setting reflected the norms and values of the society in which they were embedded. As we will see, these norms also defined what made transgressive unions dishonorable.

What is Honor?

What is honor? Since the 1980s an ever-growing number of scholars have studied the concept and its evolution over time. One of the first was the ethnologist, Karl-Sigismund Kramer, who argued that the concept of honor belonged not only to elites, but infused the social attitudes of peasants and townsfolk as well.[6] His work also reflected the rediscovery of everyday life and the men-talities of ordinary people as objects of historical research. Broadly speaking, historians developed three major approaches to honor and its social logic in early modern Europe. Each approach brings us closer to defining more clearly the relationship among transgressive unions, honor, and dishonor.

First, historians of crime have shown that honor was capable of generating violence in premodern societies.[7] Affronts to honor often resulted in armed combat and even manslaughter. Conflicts over honor also generated slander and lawsuits for libel; the fine rolls and similar serial data that such trials pro-duced have enabled historians to determine what words were perceived as in-jurious.[8] Historians of crime have also shown how profoundly status honor could affect the manner in which a delinquent was punished. These practices of punishment formed part of broader concepts, led to more flexible means of criminal prosecution, and created opportunities to sharpen punishments or to show mercy.[9]

In the second approach, historians of gender have attempted to show how honor functioned in the construction of gender and sexual identities, mascu-line as well as feminine.[10] As Barbara Krug-Richter has shown, for example, university students and journeymen engaged in armed fights with one another as a means for both sides to demonstrate their masculinity.[11] On the feminine side, historians have emphasized a strong connection between female honor and sexual discipline. Susanna Burghartz, for example, has shown how con-cepts of virginity served to shape specifically female construction of honor in the fifteenth and sixteenth centuries.[12] Others have asked how far women were able to expand their autonomy and exercise power within the constraints of gendered expectations. Claudia Ulbrich, for example, shows how women de-ployed gossip and manipulated clichéd gender stereotypes as a means to influ-ence power relations in village society.[13] These findings transfer to early modern towns as well: the stereotype of the nattering market woman as a dangerous source of troubles offers a distorted mirror of similar practices in an urban setting.[14]

In this connection, it is worth emphasizing that gossip and tattle about the honor of neighbors were not solely feminine modes of communication. Re-cently Barbara Groß analyzed social functions of male and female gossip in the Westphalian town of Minden and showed how suspicion of witchcraft could emerge from this form of communication.[15] The importance of honor for witchcraft trials has been discussed in historical research for quite some time. In the early 1990s, Rainer Walz, in his study of agonistic communication in the villages subject to the count of Lippe, characterized honor as a binary pat-tern of perception that distinguish between people who were thought honest and people who were thought dishonest.[16] Villagers resorted to accusations of witchcraft as a means to violate the honor of neighbors with whom they were feuding. For judges and magistrates, too, honor played an important role in the evaluation of evidence in trials for witchcraft. From their point of view, only dishonorable men and women were capable of entering into the most abhorrent sort of transgressive union imaginable: a sexual relationship with the devil. The honor and reputation of the accused were therefore crucial to the determination of guilt or innocence.[17]

A third historical approach to concepts of honor emerges from the study of symbolic communication.[18] In early modern Europe, social rank, status, and honor were communicated principally by visual, symbolic enactments. Parishioners, for example, acted out social hierarchies by fighting over the right to occupy church pews located closest to the altar; similar conflicts demonstrated status relations among university faculty.[19] As Barbara Stollberg-Rilinger has shown, symbolic conflicts over rank and status often became the objects of litigation in which competitors continued the struggle for honor by legal means.[20]

As these three approaches show, honor has become a central object of study, especially to cultural historians interested in mentalities and communication practices in the premodern era; their work has greatly enriched our knowledge of social norms and the manner in which early modern communities distinguished between honorable and dishonorable ways of living. Still the discourses this research has uncovered were multifaceted and shot through with paradox; for this reason honor resists precise definition.[21] This difficulty has led to a tendency to describe honor as a pattern of communication and to abandon attempts to give it an explicit and concrete definition. Thus, Martin Dinges recommends characterizing struggles over honor (*Ehrenhändel*) simply as a "communicative genre" (*kommunikative Gattung*).[22]

A more fruitful approach, I argue, derives more directly from Pierre Bourdieu's concept of honor as habitus.[23] In his reflections about honor as symbolic capital, Bourdieu builds on Max Weber's concepts of the estate-status position (*ständische Lage*) and class situation (*Klassenlage*). Bourdieu thus conceives of honor as a secondary form of capital that symbolizes class structures. As symbolic capital it affects status hierarchies just as economic capital affects class structures.[24] Bourdieu suggests that honor can be accumulated just as economic capital is built up in markets and production, and that both forms of capital, symbolic and economic, influence one another. So honor is also deployed socially in the struggle to acquire economic capital. However, while it is doubtful that both economic and symbolic capital were as convertible in early modern times as Bourdieu argued, his concept can help us nonetheless to detect strategies behind human actions, even when those strategies are denied insistently and consciously.[25]

Bourdieu developed a special theory of social practices that attempted to weigh the influence of societal structures, both on the perceptions of people living within them as well as on their attempts to conceive creative strategies and to manage everyday problems. At the core of this theory was the concept of habitus, which he hoped would dissolve the dichotomy between what he named an objectivistic and a subjectivistic theory of social action. Bourdieu defines habitus as a system of internalized societal attitudes and patterns of behavior that in a given situation guide social actors toward concrete decisions.[26] It is grounded in social knowledge communicated by members of the society, especially members of the actor's own class. Class experience is therefore the basis for any individual's orientation within the societies' norm systems. In this sense, habitus does not determine individual action, but rather forms and shapes it. According to Bourdieu, it is the actor's task to adjust internalized norms to concrete situations. The actor's sense for honor motivates him or her to respond to provocations or challenges to honor in a manner compatible with social norms.[27]

Bourdieu's concept of habitus brings us closer to a working definition of honor. In this connection, it is useful to recall the meaning of the Middle High German term *êre* which, as the linguist Hans Wellmann argues, is best translated with the modern term "identity."[28] Bearing in mind that identity in early modern times was linked with to social norms, we can define honor as an attribution of identity based on social norms. This definition has the advantage of integrating Bourdieu's concept of habitus as a "system of societal structures which are internalized" with early modern understandings of honor.[29]

It also enables us to set honor apart from forms of identity based on individualistic and socially defiant patterns of behavior, which almost by definition are associated with forms of identity that emerged after the early modern period. Generally, societal norms were not questioned in early modern times. People whose honor had been impugned had therefore to demonstrate that their identity was consistent with social norms. Consequently they often argued that honor-impugning allegations were the products of rogue calumniators; the aim was to shift dishonor from the target of the slander to its perpetrator. The aim of fights over honor was to demonstrate good and bad identities. Conceived of in this way, honor does not rule out the complex strategies that underlay these behaviors. People doubtless fought for their interests. But they also wanted to express their views on social norms and their own identity.

Honor and Matchmaking

If we transfer this concept of honor to the early modern practice of matchmaking, we see more clearly the profound implications marriage had on the honor of brides and grooms. Their marriage created a new social unit, the seed from which a new family must develop. New role expectations emerged, binding the newlywed husband and wife. Both also experienced the increase in social status associated with entry into the estate of marriage (*Ehestand*). Indeed, in some social contexts the expectation that an adult should marry was so strong that unmarried adults often felt compelled to defend themselves against the suggestion that their status was somehow disreputable. Thus, in 1614 the jurist Conrad Wippermann teased his colleague, Dr. Heinrich Worth, over the fact that he had long been unmarried. In his own defense, Worth published a lampoon of Wippermann; a lawsuit ensued.[30]

Perhaps the most important precondition for successful matchmaking was that the marriage conform to prevalent social norms and expectations. This was necessary because marriage was the principal means by which society reproduced itself; its aims were primarily biological reproduction and the creation of an economic foundation for offspring and descendants.[31] Yet marriage also had to secure the reproduction of social structures and norms. From this systemic point of view, a marriage only made sense if it reinforced those structures and norms. Referring to marriage customs among the Kabyles of Algeria in the 1950s, Bourdieu concluded that every marriage has a "tendency to reproduce those conditions which lead to it."[32] For the Kabyles, the aim of reproduction was mainly to secure economic and symbolic capital through marriage. Marriage was therefore construed as a kind of barter, practiced by the marriage parties standing behind each member of the bridal pair. They brought the bride and groom together and established close ties between themselves by this means. The success or failure of the exchange depended on complex marriage negotiations to ensure that neither party to the marriage would experience a loss of economic and symbolic capital as a result of the transaction.[33]

This kind of societal supervision over matchmaking occurred in the early modern world as well, as the marriage negotiations between Maria von Viermund and Johan Bruns show. It is discernible, for example, in the liturgy of their wedding, into which the groom inserted a question after the consent of the bride's family. At a formal confirmation of the marriage on the following day, Maria's family seems again to have acknowledged their acceptance of the fact that Maria von Viermund was wedding a man of lower social rank. There is no doubt that the bailiff of Dringenberg, Maria von Viermund's most important relative, consented to the project. In his case, the reason was presumably that the prospective groom would contribute a considerable amount of property. The marriage, in other words, was combined with prospect of increased economic capital.

Their marriage demonstrates that members of high-ranking status groups in early modern society sometimes were willing to allow family members to marry persons with less symbolic capital, under certain circumstances. Because early modern society was highly stratified, this fact may seem astonishing. Though certain basic values applied to all, each status group was distinguished by its own values, norms, and roles.[34] Even more: social differentiation itself was a basic value and early modern Europeans made every effort to ensure that such distinctions were guarded and reproduced. Even so, several studies have shown that noble families often acceded to matches with partners having a lower status when they presented an opportunity to forge links with families that could command considerable financial resources.[35]

In Maria von Viermund's case the problem clearly lay on the other side. Ultimately, the marriage was opposed not only by her kin, but also by her husband's status group. This, it seems, was an important reason why Maria von Viermund complained that her honor had been violated: by giving herself in marriage to a bridegroom who was not of noble descent, Maria von Viermund and her family had offered Johann Bruns a gift. His fellow citizens had rejected and devalued this offering. In her view, they had disregarded her superior social identity; their actions had turned proper social hierarchies upside down. She therefore feared that if others learned of the affair they, too, would similarly reject and devalue her honor. It is likely, moreover, that the honor of her family and kin had been affected, too. Unfortunately, the sources do not reveal whether the bailiff of Dringenberg fought to defend the honor of his family. We only know that Maria von Viermund applied to the church court in Paderborn, which sequestered the disputed goods. The magistrate of Korbach afterward appealed to the Imperial Chamber Court, protesting this intervention. The appeal was rejected in 1556.[36]

As defamation lawsuits from the late sixteenth and early seventeenth centuries show, matchmaking in general came to be perceived and organized as a transboundary procedure: the two marriage parties tried to establish a connection. Here we discern a dialectic of closure and disclosure. On the one hand, both parties confronted each other as different families. But on the other hand, in order to make alliance possible they had to present themselves to each other. Moreover they had to allow the opposite parties to validate their economic as well as their symbolic capital.

This leads to a second important observation: matchmaking was increasingly associated with risk; failure could damage honor and give rise to conflict. The danger was greatest when one party rejected the other. We therefore can find families devising strategies that were intended to minimize those risks. Many noble families, for example, narrowed the circle of eligible marriage partners in order to facilitate socially endogamous unions. This strategy, however, created a different set of hazards, especially in Catholic territories. The need to marry among coreligionists likewise encouraged the opening of marriage circles. As Stephanie Marra has shown, even protestant noble families in Westphalia reopened their marriage circles in order to prevent marriages within the forbidden degrees of consanguinity (*Verwandschaftsehen*) in the second half of the sixteenth century. Other families wanted simply to improve their fortunes by marrying up the social hierarchy.[37]

Matchmaking involved high risk for non-nobles as well. A defamation suit carried out in the early seventeenth century shows that even higher-ranking burgher families (officials and jurists) had to fear such problems. A dispute that arose between the family of Johann Reich, son of the mayor of Hanover, and the family of Anna Leiffart, the daughter of Anna Woltersdorf, a widow living in Minden, illustrates clearly that non-nobles, too, ran elevated risk of conflicts over honor. This particular dispute began in 1608, after negotiations to join Johann and Anna failed.[38] The project had come to a sudden end when Anna Leiffart gave birth to a child fathered by another man. Her family insisted that the pregnancy had been caused by rape and offered Johann Anna's sister, Walburga, as a substitute bride. But Johann Reich rejected this proposal. Bitter recriminations ensued, followed by suits and countersuits. Both families used legal writs to insult each other. The family of Anna Leiffart complained that these diatribes had dishonored their whole lineage ("*ihre gantze geschlechte*").[39] With the help of their attorney, himself a member of the clan, the Leiffart family filed suit to determine "which family had been stigmatized" by the affair (*ob diese oder jenne familia dadurch ein brandtmal ubir sich getzogen*).[40]

Astonishingly, the Leiffart family succeeded in marrying Anna off to another man, a high-ranking district magistrate (*Amtmann*) in the county of Lippe. Anna's prenuptial pregnancy, it seems, had not in fact extinguished her eligibility for marriage, even into elevated social circles. To be sure, the Leiffart family lamented the loss of Anna's sister Walburga, who, they claimed, had died of out of fear "that she would no longer be eligible to marry" (*keiner heyrath mehr deuchtig [zu] sein*).[41] Nevertheless, the case reminds us that all violations of honor that formed the subject of litigation did not inevitably lead to social isolation nor did they necessarily destroy the future marriage prospects of either bride or groom.

Even though their status was comparable, the lawsuit had prompted both families to draw firm boundaries between them. The case also brought to light the dysfunctional aspects of early modern defamation suits. As the litigation wore on, both parties exchanged harsh words about honor and rank of their adversaries. Each side interpreted the other's writs as the work of rogue calumniators. Thus Anna Leiffart's family, invoking the fact that gossip had emerged in Minden, Hanover, Hildesheim, and elsewhere, demanded that the Reichs repudiate the rumors publicly and pay 4000 *Reichstaler* in compensation. Johann Reich's family retaliated with a counterclaim, demanding 8000 *Reichstaler* in damages from the Leiffarts. In the end, neither party prevailed; the litigation was still pending in 1623.[42]

So the failed match created a mess for both families. An attempt to establish a social bond between them had yielded enmity instead. In the end, even the cordialities and gifts that had been exchanged at the beginning of the matchmaking became sources of bitter reproaches. Thus Anna Leiffart's family demanded that the Reichs return some golden chains she had received as a token of the engagement.[43] Most likely the Leiffarts were angry that gifts bound to their marriage project now were in the possession of the so-called wrong people. Ritualized approaches that in the game of matchmaking had been meant to communicate honorable intentions were now unmasked as evidence of duplicity. Both parties, consequently, drew the conclusion that the adversary family was without honor.

Marion Lischka has pointed out that in the seventeenth century the risks involved in matchmaking were great even for peasants.[44] As her study of villagers in the county of Lippe shows, ritualization normally minimized those risks: young men had to court prospective brides while their fathers negotiated to preserve the economic and symbolic capital on both sides.[45] To secure economic capital, for example, farmstead holders were careful to a size up a bride's dowry against her family's ability to pay it. In addition to the parents, the agreement of the nearest kin was often required for a successful match. If they disagreed with a marriage project, kin typically signaled their rejection early in the process so as to minimize the risk of dishonor to either side. Likewise neighbors exerted great influence in marriage markets. They initiated relationships between young men and women and then kept them under close scrutiny. Neighbors sometimes even became mediators to facilitate contacts between the marriage parties and their own candidates.[46]

The approach of a young man to a prospective bride followed a scripted pattern of verbal interaction. First he gave signals indicating interest. When the time was right, the bridegroom gave the bride his promise of marriage, often affirmed by handshake. Sometimes young men tried to establish trust by "conditional cursing" themselves, declaring that they should be delivered to the devil if they should later refuse to honor the marriage agreement.[47] Gifts between groom and bride served as tokens for truthfulness and honest intentions. Handkerchiefs, socks, shirts, scarves, and, above all, money served as proof of the promise. The ritual by which these fidelity gifts were presented was integral to the creation of a new social entity. The gifts were also material symbols to make actions of communication in intimate togetherness recordable.[48] When marriage negotiations failed and litigation ensued, rejected brides often cited betrothal gifts as judicial evidence of a promise to marry.[49]

Yet in spite of all these ritual safeguards, some negotiations failed. Why? If we look at the defamation suits it seems probable that the danger of failure increased with the widening of marriage circles. The larger the pool of potential mates, the more young people dared to consider unions that transgressed the barriers of social rank. The example of Johan Bruns and Maria von Viermund demonstrated that sometimes matchmaking was projected across the all-important social divide between nobles and non-noble urban citizens. Similarly, the match between Anna Leiffart and Johann Reich shows what could go wrong when families transgressed the boundaries of local marriage markets and sought out appropriate candidates in towns far away. As the failure of that negotiation showed, the initial game of opening and closing could lead suddenly to great disappointment when more exact information about the other party came to light. In such cases, the disappointment was exacerbated by the fact that both parties had displayed familiarity and willingness to form an alliance through marriage. In the rural world, too, we can discern a tendency to widen circles of marriage and to move beyond the immediate social environment. In the county of Lippe during the seventeenth century, marriage projects often collapsed when one party discovered a more promising candidate in a more distant region. In such cases, money was often the decisive factor: the more-distant candidate's wealth, typically, trumped his or her local competitor.[50]

The problem of failed matches and the honor conflicts they spawned, therefore, was related to the increasing complexity of early modern European society. Social interactions between people of different rank, as well as personal contacts beyond local environments, were increasingly common in early modern society. Related to these trends was a phenomenon described by Filippo Ranieri—that people tended ever more frequently to carry out their conflicts before judicial tribunals.[51] For Ranieri, the most important cause for increasing litigation lay in the intensification and differentiation of economic activities. Throughout the sixteenth and early seventeenth centuries, as Ranieri shows, many European societies experienced pronounced differentiation, and with it growth in the sheer volume of potential points of conflict. All this coincided with increasing pressure from state authorities to resolve conflict within legal systems that were themselves also becoming more differentiated.

Confessionalization and Transgressive Unions

Our final example leads us again to peasant circles in Westphalia and confronts us with a new ingredient in matchmaking: religion. In 1572 Catharina von Dahlhausen, a resident of the county of Mark, brought suit against the peasant farmer Eberhard unter den Eichen, the man she had intended to marry several years earlier.[52] Catharina sought reparations from the farmer, who, she claimed, had called her a "priest's whore" (*pfaffenn hoir*). She also claimed that Eberhard unter den Eichen had sired her child, which he denied. The farmer claimed, rather, that Catharina had had sexual relationships with a Catholic priest named Robert Loer and one other person. After twenty-nine years of litigation, the defendant, Eberhard unter den Eichen, was found to be at fault and was required to recant publicly his statements against Catharina von Dahlhausen.

As the briefs and counterbriefs in this case show, prenuptial sex was common in the county of Mark, a territory where subjects of different confessions lived together even in the mid-sixteenth century. Like many other women before her, Catharina von Dahlhausen had tried to legitimate a sexual relationship through a subsequent marriage with the priest. At a hearing in November 1569 several witnesses testified that the priest Robert Loer had been willing to take Catharina von Dahlhausen as his wife and to acknowledge her child as his own.[53] They testified that Loer had expressed his wish that "if he should get the child he should also get the mother as well" (*wannehr hie dat kyndt hedde, wolde hy oick die moder woll kriegenn*).[54] These statements testify both to the ubiquity of prenuptial sex in sixteenth-century rural society and to the possibilities for legitimizing those relationships.[55] As the witnesses' statements show, Westphalian villagers did not even rule out the possibility that marriage could legitimate prenuptial sex with a Catholic priest.

On the other hand, this lawsuit played out against the backdrop of efforts by church and state to enforce sexual discipline. From a different set of records we know that Loer was prosecuted, found guilty, and in 1580 punished for "proven crimes against [decrees of the] Council of Trent" (*excessibus contra conc. Tridentinum factis declaratus*).[56] In all likelihood, his prosecution had its origins in Catharina von Dahlhausen's lawsuit. The writs of her defamation process show that refuting Eberhard unter den Eichen's charge that she had had sexual intercourse with a priest was central to her case. In order to preserve her honor, Catharina aimed to make clear to anyone that she was no "whore of priests and other people" (*pfaffenn und ander leutte hoir*).[57] Clearly, she had learned that sexual intercourse with a priest was transgressive. She also declared that the accusation of sex with a priest had caused great reproach and scorn to be heaped upon her; the defamation suit against Eberhard unter den Eichen was a fight for survival. Ultimately, Catharina von Dahlhausen gained a favorable judgment, but she paid a heavy price. Her last surviving statement on the matter, given as an old woman in 1600, hints strongly that the stain to her reputation had forced her to remain unmarried.[58]

From other lawsuits we know that sexual relationships between Catholic clergymen and laywomen were widespread and debated in a variety of contexts. In 1587, for example, the provost of the Premonstratensian monastery of Cappenberg, Wennemar von Hoete, and several of his fellow monks reacted with a defamation suit alleging sexual misconduct.[59] Specifically, it was charged that the monks had maintained concubines. One of the accusers, Johann Horstorff, himself now charged with slander, reinforced his allegations by characterizing the monks' behavior as a sin that had brought down God's wrath on all the people. According to Horstorff, this sin had caused a fire in Werne, a town in the prince-bishopric of Münster, in which thirty-seven houses were destroyed. In his brief against the monks, Horstorff indicated that the provost referred to his concubine as "dear heart" (*Hertzlieb*) and that he had provided her with a horse and coach. Wennemar von Hoete was also said to have bestowed houses on her.[60]

Sexual discipline and the matter of transgressive unions were also at the center of another quarrel that arose in the small protestant Westphalian town of Lügde, between Detmold and Hameln. In 1610 Gottschalk Knedteisen filed a suit against his neighbor, Arndt Kannengießer. Knedteisen had learned that Kannengießer was spreading the rumor that he had broken the incest taboo.[61] As the testimony of witnesses made clear, this allegation was false: not Knedteisen but his son had had sexual intercourse, in a stable, with his kinswoman.[62]

The lawsuit shows that, by 1600, rulers' measures to achieve sexual discipline had made a deep impression on the subjects. Arndt Kannengießer's allegation had been inspired by an actual shaming ritual that another neighbor had been forced to perform some time before. The neighbor, Evert Strohschneider, had been paraded through the town, dressed in a penitential white robe and carrying a rod and a burning candle, both as punishment for adultery and as a condition for his grandchild's baptism.[63] Witnesses of this event remembered that his robe had borne letters, but recalled their meaning differently: some said that they were "Hebrew letters" (*judden buchstabe*), while others recalled only that the letters had been written in red.[64] In any case, shortly after this shaming ritual Arndt Kannengießer informed his neighbors of his own wish that his archenemy, Knedteisen, should also be forced to wear such a robe on account of his incest.[65]

Knedteisen's testimony suggests that subjects discussed intensely the spectacles of punishment that authorities staged to establish their concepts of morality and piety. The lawsuit also shows that official pressure to conform in matters of religious doctrine and practice tended to sharpen the boundary between permissible and forbidden forms of sexual behavior. As subjects internalized that boundary, they criminalized alleged or real behavior that had once been regarded as permissible and used these violations to challenge the honor of those who misbehaved. This was the experience of Johann Pollmann, a peasant living in the county of Ravensberg. In 1583 a neighbor challenged his honor after he had been fined for indecent sexual behavior. Because he was rumored to have tolerated "frivolous women" (*leichtfertige weiber*) as guests and watched whoring (*hurereien*) in his house, Pollmann was also said to have neglected his duties as a father.[66]

Conclusion

By way of conclusion I would like to call attention to an area of tension between discourse and reality in the writs I have analyzed. In general, the litigants in defamation lawsuits accentuated rank and awareness of honor. They also drew sharp boundaries between status groups; sometimes they even erected walls between members of the same status group. On the other hand, the rigidity of these discourses contrasted with practices that were considerably more flexible. In any given situation, historical actors often found creative pathways around moral strictures imposed from above. Members of the lower classes found ways to circumvent rigid rules of sexual discipline and social barriers to matchmaking. To a certain extent, such possibilities also existed within higher classes. Now and then, members of different status groups formed unions across the lines of social division. Even in a society that enshrined hierarchy, the quest for economic capital could lead to unions that transgressed seemingly impermeable social boundaries.

Each case analyzed here originated in a complaint against the violation of honor. They make evident the risks of matchmaking in a society of orders. Within higher-ranking status groups, matchmaking was especially fraught because, time and again, failure resulted in damage to honor. Failed matchmaking inevitably brought social imbalance into focus; a marriage party repelled appeared as a party deficient in weight. Anxiety was especially keen among the bride's family; her rejection would impugn the whole family's prestige and diminish ever after her prospects of making a good match.

To minimize these risks, families developed elaborate procedures of marital approach and nuptial negotiation. Within the framework of these procedures, men and women sought out opportunities for contact that initially obscured their main purpose, then intensified them gradually to the point of marriage. As society became more complex and marriage markets widened, however, matchmaking was combined with ever-greater risks. Complexity and growing social differentiation meant that more and more marriage negotiations would fail. Conflicts over honor thus often resulted.

Sexual disciplining exacerbated this trend. The efforts of secular and ecclesiastical authorities to enforce religious orthodoxy and orthopraxy strengthened greatly during the second half of the sixteenth century and exerted profound influence on the subjects' everyday lives as well as on their conceptions of norms of sexual behavior. These measures also reshaped popular definitions of what constituted a transgressive relationship. The more subjects internalized official norms of sexual propriety, the greater the role they played in the to-and-fro of everyday life. In essence, the new norms gave everyone new tools to defend their interests against troublesome neighbors, whose honor could be damaged by accusations of sexual misbehavior. Although men as well as women confronted such reproaches, the potential consequences for women were especially dire.

What, then, motivated so many to take their grievances to courts of law? For women, their family members, and their legal representatives, the most common reason for legal recourse was that defamation had reduced or eliminated opportunities to marry. To make the point in Pierre Bourdieu's terms, defamation threatened to diminish the symbolic capital available to a prospective bride. That said, a diminution of this form of capital was not the inevitable outcome of a failed marriage negotiation, whether a defamation lawsuit resulted from it. Certainly, a marriage party might sue for strategic reasons—to to restore their reputation, for example, and in so doing to improve their chances on marriage markets. Yet this, too, was risky business: time and again, the lawsuits themselves generated further defamations and broadcast such allegations to a larger audience.

Despite all these potential pitfalls, the plaintiffs demonstrated confidence, persistence, and self-esteem in order to retain control of their own reputation. To go to law was to demonstrate one's sense of honor. Nonetheless, we should not conclude from this that feelings of honor and injury were false. Plaintiffs stressed that the violation of honor had touched their hearts, and we have every reason to take them at their word. For them, the defense of honor by legal means was a matter of self-esteem; we should not doubt the plaintiffs' assertions that they perceived honor both as an outward status and a state of being. By defending their honor in court, they communicated identity.

Notes

1. Landesarchiv Nordrhein-Westfalen, Abteilung Westfalen (hereafter LAV NRW W), Reichskammergerichtsakten (hereafter RKG) C 762, vol. 2, fol. 6 f.
2. LAV NRW W, RKG C 762, vol. 2, fol. 5.
3. Ibid., fol. 6.
4. Ibid., fol. 6ff.
5. Ralf-Peter Fuchs, *Um die Ehre: Westfälische Beleidigungsprozesse vor dem Reichskammergericht 1525—1805* (Paderborn, 1999).
6. See, for example, Karl-Sigismund Kramer, "Würzburger Volk des 16. Jahrhunderts vor Gericht," *Bayerisches Jahrbuch für Volkskunde* (1955): 141–56; idem, *Grundriß einer rechtlichen Volkskunde* (Göttingen 1974); and idem, "Hohnsprake, Wrakworte, Nachschnack und Ungebühr: Ehrenhändel in holsteinischen Quellen," *Kieler Blätter zur Volkskunde* 16 (1984): 49–85.
7. See, for example, Gerd Schwerhoff, *Köln im Kreuzverhör: Kriminalität, Herrschaft und Gesellschaft in einer frühneuzeitlichen Stadt* (Bonn, 1991); Susanna Burghartz, *Leib, Ehre und Gut: Delinquenz in Zürich Ende des 14. Jahrhunderts* (Zurich, 1990); Michael Frank, "Ehre und Gewalt im Dorf der Frühen Neuzeit: Das Beispiel Heiden (Grafschaft Lippe) im 17. und 18. Jahrhundert," in Klaus Schreinder and Gerd Schwerhoff, eds., *Verletzte Ehre: Ehrkonflikte in Gesellschaften des Mittelalters und der Frühen Neuzeit* (Cologne, 1995), 320–38.
8. Frank, "Ehre und Gewalt," 338. See also Mark Häberlein, "Tod auf der Herrenstube: Ehre und Gewalt in der Augsburger Führungsschicht (1500–1620)," in *Ehrkonzepte in der Frühen Neuzeit: Identitäten und Abgrenzungen*, ed Sibylle Backmann, Hans-Jörg Künast, and Sabine Ullmann (Berlin, 1998), 148–69.
9. Gerd Schwerhoff, "Kriminalitätsgeschichte im deutschen Sprachraum: Zum Profil eines 'verspäteten' Forschungszweiges," in *Kriminalitätsgeschichte: Beiträge zur Sozial- und Kulturgeschichte der Vormoderne*, ed. Andreas Blauert and Gerd Schwerhoff (Konstanz, 2000), 21–68, here 31.

10. Gitta Benker, "'Ehre und Schande': Voreheliche Sexualität auf dem Lande im ausgehenden 18. Jahrhundert," in *Frauenkörper, Medizin, Sexualität: Auf dem Wege zu einer neuen Sexualmoral,* ed. Johanna Geyer-Kordesch and Annette Kuhn (Düsseldorf, 1986); Lyndal Roper, "'Wille' und 'Ehre': Sexualität, Sprache und Macht in Augsburger Kriminalprozessen," in *Wandel der Geschlechterbeziehungen zu Beginn der Neuzeit,* ed. Heide Wunder and Christina Vanja (Frankfurt, 1991), 180–97. See also Martin Dinges, "'Weiblichkeit' in 'Männlichkeitsritualen'? Zu weiblichen Taktiken im Ehrenhandel in Paris im 18. Jahrhundert," *Francia* 18 (1991): 71–98.

11. Barbara Krug-Richter, "'Du Bacchant, quid est grammatica?': Konflikte zwischen Studenten und Bürgern im frühneuzeitlichen Freiburg/Br.," in *Praktiken des Konfliktaustrags in der Frühen Neuzeit,* ed. Barbara Krug-Richter and Ruth-Elisabeth Mohrmann (Münster, 2004), 79–104.

12. Susanna Burghartz, "Jungfräulichkeit oder Reinheit? Zur Änderung von Argumentationsmustern vor dem Basler Ehegericht im 16. und 17. Jahrhundert," in *Dynamik der Tradition,* ed. Richard van Dülmen (Frankfurt, 1992), 13–40.

13. See Claudia Ulbrich, "Unartige Weiber: Präsenz und Renitenz von Frauen im frühneuzeitlichen Deutschland," in *Arbeit, Frömmigkeit und Eigensinn,* ed. Richard van Dülmen (Frankfurt, 1990), 13–42, here 41. See also Regina Schulte, "Bevor das Gerede zum Tratsch wird," *Journal für Geschichte* 2 (1985): 16–21.

14. See Pia Holenstein and Norbert Schindler, "Geschwätzgeschichte(n): Ein kulturhistorisches Plädoyer für die Rehabilitierung der unkontrollierten Rede," in van Dülmen, *Dynamik der Tradition,* 41–108.

15. Barbara Groß, *Hexerei in Minden: Zur sozialen Logik von Hexereiverdächtigungen und Hexenprozessen (1584–1684)* (Münster, 2009).

16. Rainer Walz, "Der Hexenwahn im Alltag: Der Umgang mit verdächtigen Frauen," *Geschichte in Wissenschaft und Unterricht* 43 (1992): 157–68; and idem., *Hexenglaube und magische Kommunikation im Dorf der Frühen Neuzeit: Die Verfolgungen in der Grafschaft Lippe* (Paderborn, 1993).

17. Rainer Walz, "Das Hexengerücht im Dorf und bei den Gebildeten," in *Kloster-Stadt-Region: Festschrift für Heinrich Rüthing,* ed. Johannes Altenbehrend (Bielefeld, 2002), 315–34. See also Ralf-Peter Fuchs, *Hexerei und Zauberei vor dem Reichskammergericht: Nichtigkeiten und Injurien* (Wetzlar, 1994), 40–45.

18. See Barbara Stollberg-Rilinger, "Symbolische Kommunikation in der Vormoderne: Begriffe-Thesen-Forschungsperspektiven," *Zeitschrift für historische Forschung* 31 (2004): 489–527.

19. On fights over pews, see Thomas Weller, "'Ius subselliorum templorum': Kirchenstuhlstreitigkeiten in der frühneuzeitlichen Stadt zwischen symbolischer Praxis und Recht," in *Raum und Konflikt: Zur symbolischen Konstituierung gesellschaftlicher Ordnung in Mittelalter und Früher Neuzeit,* ed. Christoph Dartmann, Marian Füssel, and Stefanie Rüther (Münster, 2004), 199–224. On battles over space in universities, see Marian Füssel, "Rang und Raum: Gesellschaftliche Kartographie und die soziale Logik des Raumes an der vormodernen Universität," in ibid., 175–98.

20. Barbara Stollberg-Rilinger, "Rang vor Gericht: Zur Verrechtlichung sozialer Rangunterschiede in der frühen Neuzeit, *Zeitschrift für Historische Forschung* 28 (2001): 385–418.

21. See Walz, *Hexenglaube und magische Kommunikation,* 423–24.

22. Martin Dinges, *Der Maurermeister und der Finanzrichter: Ehre, Geld und soziale Kontrolle im Paris des 18. Jahrhunderts* (Göttingen, 1994), 412–13. See also idem, "Die

Ehre als Thema der historischen Anthropologie: Bemerkungen zur Wissenschaftsges-chichte und zur Konzeptualisierung," in Klaus Schreiner and Gerd Schwerhoff, *Verletzte Ehre*, 29–62, esp. 52–55.

23. Pierre Bourdieu, *Entwurf einer Theorie der Praxis auf der ethnologischen Grundlage der kabylischen Gesellschaft* (Frankfurt, 1979).

24. Max Weber, *Wirtschaft und Gesellschaft. Grundriß der verstehenden Soziologie*, 5th rev. ed. (Tübingen, 1976), 179.

25. Martin Dinges "Die Ehre als Thema der Stadtgeschichte: Eine Semantik im Über-gang vom Ancien Régime zur Moderne, *Zeitschrift für historische Forschung* 16 (1989): 409–40, here 420.

26. See Beate Krais' interpretation of Bourdieu's theory in her "Soziales Feld, Macht und kulturelle Praxis: Die Untersuchungen Bourdieus über die verschiedenen Fraktionen der 'herrschenden Klasse' in Frankreich," in Klaus Eder, ed., *Klassenlage, Lebensstil und kulturelle Praxis: Theoretische und empirische Beiträge zur Auseinandersetzung mit Pierre Bourdieus Klassentheorie* (Frankfurt, 1989), 47–70, here 53.

27. Bourdieu, *Entwurf einer Theorie der Praxis*, 50.

28. Hans Wellmann, "Der historische Begriff der 'Ehre'—sprachwissenschaftlich unter-sucht," in *Ehrkonzepte in der Frühen Neuzeit*, 27–39, here 38.

29. Bourdieu, *Entwurf einer Theorie der Praxis*, 188.

30. LAV NRW W, RKG W 1649, vol. 1, fol. 34.

31. See also Bourdieu, *Entwurf einer Theorie der Praxis*, 122–24.

32. Ibid., 135.

33. Ibid., 130–32.

34. See Münch's article about this topic: Paul Münch, "Grundwerte der frühneuzeitlichen Ständegesellschaft? Aufriß einer vernachlässigten Thematik," in *Ständische Gesellschaft und soziale Mobilität*, ed. Winfried Schulze (Munich, 1988), 53–72.

35. See, for example, Karl-Heinz Spieß, *Familie und Verwandtschaft im deutschen Hochadel des Spätmittelalters. 13. bis 16. Jahrhundert* (Stuttgart, 1993), 349–50.

36. LAV NRW W, RKG C 762, vol. 1, fol. 3.

37. Stephanie Marra, *Allianzen des Adels: Dynastisches Handeln im Grafenhaus Bentheim im 16. und 17. Jahrhundert* (Cologne, 2007).

38. LAV NRW W, RKG R 377.

39. LAV NRW W, RKG L 24, fol. 39.

40. Ibid., fol. 14.

41. Ibid., fol. 62.

42. See my article about this case: Ralf-Peter Fuchs, "Schmähschriften unter Männern: Ein Blick auf den Kampfstil eines frühneuzeitlichen Juristen," in *MannBilder: Ein Lese- und Quellenbuch zur historischen Männerforschung*, ed. Wolfgang Schmale (Berlin, 1998), 57–77, here 71–72.

43. Fuchs, "Schmähschriften unter Männern," 77.

44. Marion Lischka, *Liebe als Ritual: Eheanbahnung und Brautwerbung in der frühneuzeitli-chen Grafschaft Lippe* (Paderborn, 2006).

45. Lischka, *Liebe als Ritual*, 149–51.

46. Ibid., 154–56.

47. Ibid., 156.

48. About this function, see Marcel Mauss, *Die Gabe: Form und Funktion des Austausches in archaischen Gesellschaften* (Frankfurt, 1990).

49. Lischka, *Liebe als Ritual*, 245.

50. Ibid., 149–50.
51. Filippo Ranieri, *Recht und Gesellschaft im Zeitalter der Rezeption: Eine rechts- und sozial-geschichtliche Analyse der Judikatur des Reichskammergerichts im 16. Jahrhundert*, 2 vols. (Cologne, 1985), vol. 1, 149–51.
52. LAV NRW W, RKG E 160.
53. See LAV NRW W, RKG E 160, vol. 1, fol. 48–50.
54. Ibid., fol. 61.
55. See, for example, Stefan Breit, *"Leichtfertigkeit" und ländliche Gesellschaft: Voreheliche Sexualität in der frühen Neuzeit* (Munich,1991).
56. Landesarchiv Nordrhein-Westfalen, Abteilung Rheinland (hereafter LAV NRW R), Stift Rellinghausen, Akten 11, fol. 13.
57. LAV NRW W, RKG E 160, vol. 1, fol. 115.
58. Ibid., fol. 266.
59. LAV NRW W, RKG H 1790.
60. Ibid., fol. 48ff.
61. LAV NRW W, RKG K 81, vol. 2, fol. 99.
62. Ibid., fol. 675.
63. Ibid., fol. 607.
64. LAV NRW W, RKG K 81, vol. 1, fol. 99.
65. Ibid., fol. 30.
66. LAV NRW W, RKG H 270, fol. 92–93.

CHAPTER 5

~:·:~

Negotiating Rank in Early Modern Marital Mismatches

MICHAEL SIKORA

There is no need to stress that the differences between the social orders in the societies of the early modern period were of crucial importance for how these societies functioned. The concept of inequality formed the basis for the unequal distribution not only of reputation, but also of rights and privileges. These included authorities connected with lordship over people and land as well as sovereign rule, and determined how one could profit from agricultural production and trade. In the framework of orders, nobles enjoyed the most far-reaching privileges and therefore profited most from this particular social structure.

From the nobles' point of view, the idea of inequality also legitimated their position, which rested on the assumption that nobles shared exclusive traditions and virtues that enabled them to handle the special duties inherent in their privileged status.[1] This self-confidence was, at least for the older nobility, integrally linked with the heritability of status and virtue. Accordingly, heritability reinforced legitimation because it accumulated noble virtues and exclusivity over generations. It was also the essential tool nobles deployed to maintain social exclusivity and uphold their monopoly over the claim to virtue, as well as the privileges they and their equally-ranked peers enjoyed. This held particularly true for the higher nobility of the Holy Roman Empire.

In order to maintain high status, it was necessary to preserve the existing distance from lower ranks. It also meant actualizing one's own reputation and distinction in everyday life. Many symbolic means existed for expressing status: salutations and gestures, clothes and jewelry, life style and elaborate interiors, and social interactions with people of equal rank. Most important, however, was the choice of a spouse, since rank and its inheritance depended not only on the patrilinear descent, but also on the rank of the mothers.[2] This criterion could easily be used as a tool for excluding rivals whose ancestry was questionable or who had only recently been ennobled. Tests of noble lineage, the so-called *Ahnenproben*, were established to facilitate this exclusion, most often in territories where nobles enjoyed certain privileges collectively as a legally-defined status group. In ecclesiastical states, for example, lineage tests limited access to membership in the cathedral chapter or noble convents. Sometimes they were also used to control the membership of noble benches of provincial estates.[3] Typically, the number of these barriers tended to increase during the early modern period, resulting in requirements for as many as sixteen or even thirty-two noble ancestors.

This situation reflected the fact that the system of orders, although seemingly fixed and immutable, underwent constant change that facilitated social mobility.[4] In the Holy Roman Empire in particular, the process of political institutionalization and state building contributed to a growing diversification and specification of noble ranks, each with its own mode for participating in the imperial diet and provincial estates.[5] On the other hand, the expansion of government and the exigencies of war generated groups of social climbers, often in the shape of civil servants who were rewarded for their diligence with noble status. Loyalty often elevated low-ranking nobles into a higher stratum.[6] In return, the old elites attempted to strengthen their distinctiveness from upcoming rivals, so that on every level the nobility additionally divided itself into old and new families.

This chapter deals with a very special form of social mobility: marital unions that transgressed the social barriers on which noble status depended. Misalliances, certainly, were not common, nor were they a major factor in social mobility. Rather, their special importance lies in the fact that every misalliance required all parties involved to deal with a transgression that should not have been possible. As such, misalliances touched every possible aspect of social rank and status differentiation. The special focus of this chapter is on the effect that discrepancies of social rank had on the married life of an unequal couple—whether and in what way differences of rank between the spouses in a misalliance persisted or changed over time, and to what extent those changes altered the transgression itself.

The cases examined here come from the highest nobility.[7] This stratum included the ruling families of the empire's territories, who were also members of the imperial diet. In fact the high nobility comprised two ranks—the princes, who bore titles like duke (*Herzog*), prince (*Fürst*), margrave (*Markgraf*), or landgrave (*Landgraf*); and a lower rank, consisting of the imperial counts. Neither group even considered members of the territorial nobilities their equals. Therefore, dealing with the high nobility provides a maximum of social distance between the partners. It is doubtful that misalliances could have seriously eroded the status of these high-ranked families. Nevertheless, the requirements of noble identity and collective memory obliged them to defend the most important privileges and the oldest pedigrees.[8] This chapter is therefore based on the assumption that the deepest insights into social distinction, how it was discussed, defended, or even diminished, can best be obtained in cases that displayed them most dramatically.

However, the importance of social distinction depended on the legal form of the relationship. Of course, the crucial factor was marriage. While most nobles avoided marrying partners from lower ranks, the opposite is true of concubinage. Many male nobles entered into extramarital partnerships that took place more or less in public, were more or less official, and coexisted with a marriage to a person of equal rank.[9] Extramarital partnerships of this type would have ruined the honor and reputation of a woman from the high nobility. Consequently the concubines inevitably stemmed from the lower ranks. In this sense, it was precisely the social difference between the male prince and his female partner that made such relationships possible; in these cases, there was no need to deal with the problem of inequality.

The consequences of unconventional partnerships were differently distributed according to gender. While an extramarital partnership might well call the moral principles of a prince into question, it definitely did not damage his rank or status. In contrast, female nobles who engaged in similar liaisons risked repudiation by their husbands or their families. Obviously this is why very little information about such relationships exists in the documentary record. But we cannot deduce from the paucity of evidence that such relationships did not occur.[10]

Many women apparently considered a relationship with a higher-ranking male partner as offering certain advantages. However, these extramarital relationships involved no legal commitments, therefore the women not only ran the danger of moral censure, but also remained totally dependent on the benevolence of their partner. This configuration did not prevent some nobles from honoring their female partners with gifts, privileges, and other signs of regard. Such acts of respect could include conferring a noble title on a non-noble woman. There was, in other words, some latitude in the way these partnerships were arranged; sometimes they almost seem like a marriage.[11]

Rank, certainly, could be changed more easily than sex or skin color, but it was not easy to do. Normally, within the empire, only the emperor had the right to raise one's rank. Because most princes in the empire could not elevate anyone in rank, the practice of true ennoblement remained infrequent, although a variety of other practices existed.[12] Sometimes non-noble women received noble-sounding names. One must, however, examine each particular case carefully in order to clarify whether the woman had actually received formal noble rank, whether the name was simply a usage by her partner and her entourage, or whether it derived from manors she had received as gifts.

Obviously, ascribing noble rank was the easiest and most widely used method for princes to reward and distinguish their nonmarital partners. Symbolically, status ascription allowed these women to approach the rank of their partners, and perhaps made them more acceptable within the court society. Nonetheless, they never achieved coequal rank.

There were also cases in which princes did not content themselves with elevating the social status of their partners. In some cases, they wished to marry their partner, perhaps out of concern for their moral status. But to do so was to alter fundamentally the framework of the relationship. A prince could not combine such a marriage with an already-existing union to a woman of his equal rank. This assertion may sound self-evident and trivial, but in fact several princes actually pursued this option.

In 1540, while already wed to a woman of princely rank, Landgrave Philipp of Hessen asked the most prominent Protestant theologians to allow him a second marriage to Margarete von der Saale.[13] He admitted that he committed adultery throughout his first marriage and argued that he could calm his conscience only by marrying one of his concubines.[14] Thus he aimed at something like extramarital monogamy. The records reveal that this was not only a question of Philipp's conscience: it was also a matter of conscience for the mother of the desired bride, a member of the territorial nobility, who insisted on maximizing the amount of legitimacy involved in the union before she would allow her daughter to enter into such a dubious partnership.[15] As David Whitford relates in his contribution to this volume, the theologians Philipp consulted were concerned about the impact the misalliance would have on his political influence and therefore allowed him the bigamous marriage only on the condition that he keep it strictly secret.[16] However, it came to light soon after the wedding and caused a public scandal that made clear that bigamy was unacceptable and an unequal marriage could not be combined with an equal marriage.[17] It was no accident that this experiment took place just at the moment when the new reformed churches were replacing the Roman faith in northern Germany, and it reveals a great deal about the consequences of the Reformation for gender relations. Although the Reformation opened space for rethinking tradition, in the long run its main result was to strengthen norms and the exclusive legitimacy of marriage, even for the high nobility. This had several indirect, but crucial consequences for those who had entered into unequal relationships.

Another major change that resulted from legitimating concubinage through marriage had important legal ramifications: the very act of marriage conferred at least some indisputable rights on the wife. According to ecclesiastical law, the validity of a marriage did not depend on equal rank, but on maintaining certain formalities.[18] Ecclesiastical law as well as Roman law prescribed that the bride entered the household of the groom and thenceforth participated in his rank and rights.[19] Those privileges included rights of inheritance for their future offspring. In theory, at least, the pure fact of marriage should abrogate differences in rank.

Obviously, this provision contradicted the interests and the self-image of noble houses. To resolve the tension between judicial norms and noble traditions, the legal institution of morganatic marriage was introduced during the last decades of the sixteenth century within the empire. It stemmed from a Lombard collection of feudal laws, composed in the thirteenth century.[20] The morganatic form of marriage excluded a woman from the lower ranks (and any children of that union) from participation in the rank, rights, and inheritance of her husband (and their father), although she was married according to ecclesiastical law and her children were legitimate.

One example nicely illustrates the process by which this institution was introduced within the empire. Some years after Landgrave Philipp's bigamy became publicly known, Count Anton of Isenburg-Büdingen married a non-noble bride, Katharina Gumpel.[21] Unlike Philipp, Count Anton was a widower. Like Philipp, he wished to avoid living in concubinage, not only because of his own qualms of conscience, but also because his pastor, his family, and the friends of Katharina exerted considerable pressure on him. Furthermore, Count Anton expressed no intention of treating Katharina as a wife of equal rank. This position, too, corresponds to Philipp's attitude toward his second wife. In addition to the ecclesiastical ceremony, Count Anton assured his wife an income and presented her with gifts. These benefits, fixed in a formal deed, perfectly paralleled similar agreements frequently found in nonmarital relationships. Although generous, the provisions made for her clearly indicated that Katharina was not a princely wife in the conventional sense. The jurist who composed the document was somewhat puzzled by the task of defining the conditions of a marriage without naming the wife a wife, as the count had ordered. Therefore, the legal character of this relationship hung in abeyance.[22] Thus, even in the early 1550s the option of a morganatic marriage was not yet established in the empire.

However, the marriage worked for Anton and Katharina, who had three children before they died a few years later. A serious conflict did not emerge until many years after, when their only son, Hans Otto, became discontent with his living conditions and the way in which his uncles treated him. He soon claimed a greater portion of the paternal inheritance and underlined his demands by adopting the title of count. This action suggested that he considered himself socially equal to a son of an imperial count and entitled to all the inheritance and succession attached to that status. The struggle between Hans Otto and his uncles continued for many decades, even beyond the son's lifetime, and was not settled until the beginning of the eighteenth century.[23] The complex details of this case need not detain us here. Suffice it to say that the sheer duration of the conflict illustrates the risks attendant on such situations.

The case is revealing for many reasons. First, several jurists, including members of an imperial commission, who tried to mediate the conflict after Count Anton's son had appealed to the Imperial Aulic Council in 1598, discussed whether the marriage of Count Anton and Katharina could be considered morganatic.[24] Although the parties involved had different reasons for not accepting this interpretation, the fact that a morganatic marriage was suggested at all established a legal fiction as a solution to exactly these sorts of problems.

Second, the involvement of one of the two supreme courts of the empire demonstrates that political institutionalization had serious implications for the family strategies of even the highest-ranking nobility. The offspring of marital mismatches could call upon these courts to confirm their rights and to challenge noble houses, which in turn were forced to transform their traditional values into juridical arguments.

Third, the offspring of unequal couples typically initiated legal challenges. Dealing with social distance was hard enough for unequal husbands and wives, but the situation was far worse for their children, who were born into a kind of no-man's land. They had to be placed somewhere in this framework, but finding a satisfactory place for them was far from easy.

Fourth, the problem of rank was inseparably linked to the question of whether the wife and her offspring would enter the princely family as members with equal rights. In the case of Count Anton's son, this problem merged with those of inheritance and succession and therefore could provoke serious resistance from agnates who must have feared a setback to their social ambitions.

Even the legal construct of morganatic marriage could not always resolve such difficulties, at least in its early days. In 1637, for example, Prince Georg Aribert of Anhalt-Dessau married a woman from the lower nobility. To pacify his brother and cousins who objected to the union, Georg Aribert drew up a contract with them.[25] According to this document, they would accept the marriage as lawful if the wife and all future children retained the former rank of the bride. In addition, the offspring would forfeit all rights of succession and would be barred from employing any marks of princely rank, including the family name and coat of arms. At least, however, the children received one small but subtle sign of their origin: the contract allowed them the right to call themselves "by the name von Aribert." Thus, in contrast to Count Anton's marriage, the new paradigm of morganatic marriage definitely shaped this union.

As in Count Anton's case, Georg Aribert's son, Christian Aribert, protested the contract in 1660, long after his father's death. Once again quarrels about the inheritance seemingly impelled Christian Aribert to question the contract. Apparently, while staying at the imperial court in Vienna, fellow aristocrats had encouraged Christian Aribert to claim equal rights. His arguments exactly targeted the weak point of the morganatic marriage: that it was a legally recognized partnership and therefore enjoyed full legality.[26] On this point, Christian Aribert tried to have the restrictions specified in the contract abolished. He insisted on being counted a legitimate and fully entitled descendant of his princely father. He even explicitly declared that he would not be worthy of being a son of a prince of Anhalt if he did not claim his rights.

It would have been interesting to see how jurists and judges would have solved this dilemma, but they never got the chance. The agnates avoided a formal trial and, after about a decade, consented to a major compromise.[27] In contrast to Count Anton's son, who continued to take the title of count but whose pretensions were never approved nor even finally determined, the compromise here precisely defined Christian Aribert's status. He, his sisters, and their descendants were allowed the rank of count and countesses; they thus attained a higher rank of nobility than their mother had enjoyed. They were even allowed to represent themselves as the legitimate children of Prince Georg Aribert of Anhalt, but they did not become equal in rank to other members of the princely house. Thus their new title was not combined with the name "Anhalt"; rather, they adopted the name "von Bäringen," which at least evoked the mythical ancestors of the house of Anhalt and also the bear, as a well-known element in its coat of arms. On the one hand the social distance was reduced, as the parties met each other halfway. Nonetheless, the agreement excluded the offspring from the house of Anhalt and they could claim no rights of succession. Thus, their existence did not tarnish the pedigree of the princes. In a certain sense, as will be discussed below, this constituted a progressive solution.

Of course, morganatic marriages did not inevitably end in conflict, especially when they produced no children. It was an adequate option, therefore, for ruling widowers who wanted to avoid the costs of another equal partnership or for younger brothers who had difficulties finding a partner of equal rank at all. In fact, an unequal marriage in the morganatic mode could well serve the interests of a noble house. So there were many morganatic marriages that apparently caused no further trouble.

Nonetheless, morganatic marriage remained a rather rare exception in the high nobility of the Holy Roman Empire, especially in comparison to the countless nonmarital concubinages that existed. Approximately 5 percent of princely marriages—not including the marriages of counts—transgressed the border of the order.[28] This statistic includes all morganatic marriages that, according to their legal implications and the intentions of the spousal parties, can be counted as marital unions in a narrow sense. However, it is very important to note that not all transgressive marriages were morganatic unions. Of the aforementioned 5 percent of all marriages, approximately one third were not morganatic. It is not possible to give exact figures because one has to assume that there might have been secret partnerships.

Another source of uncertainty is the fact that opponents of those legal marriages often considered them to be morganatic in principle, as have many historians since then. Therefore we should be somewhat cautious about taking these assertions at face value. It is quite difficult to get anything like conclusive evidence about this because non-morganatic marriages were not distinguished by a contract with restrictive conditions. Non-morganatic marriages were distinguished, so to speak, only by the lack of such evidence. There certainly existed a number of cases, however, in which a male member of the high nobility intentionally entered into a fully valid, unrestricted marriage with a partner from the lower ranks. Their motives cannot be discussed here, but of course the difference in rank was addressed in another, special way.

This difference in social rank became obvious almost immediately. A marriage between members of the high nobility normally constituted one high point of court culture; it was celebrated with all imaginable pomp and circumstance for weeks.[29] The crucial importance of such an event was readily apparent, not least because it guaranteed the perpetuation of the ruling dynasty; it also generated new familial alliances and confirmed others. Therefore marriages represented important political occasions. Moreover, two equally ranked families thus demonstrated their own importance and honored each other in exchanging marriage partners. They thereby increased the reputation of both sides. The marriage ceremony made all these things public while, at the same time, presenting an opportunity for the nobility to accept and acknowledge the union through their physical presence at the wedding. None of this could be said of a marriage between unequals. In that event, public recognition was simply unimaginable. Furthermore, the couple had to fear the resistance of their own family members. Typically, therefore, unequal marriages were celebrated with only a few people present: a priest, of course, and a small number of familiar officials at the most. In many cases, the ceremonies took place in secret and sometimes under rather strange circumstances. In several cases we cannot even determine the precise date of the marriage—one such example being the well-known union between the Habsburg Duke Ferdinand of Tyrol and Philippine Welser in the sixteenth century.[30] The ceremony itself corresponded to the rank of the lesser party, so to speak, and in this respect there was nothing to choose between morganatic and non-morganatic marriages. Here, too, the decisive factor was difference of rank.

Some evidence suggests that this difference carried over into the everyday life of the couple. Usually one can only find some isolated notes in the sources, but a unique document from the end of the sixteenth century provides insight into such practices. These are records of several interrogations made some forty years after the fact in order to clarify the status of the marriage between Count Anton of Isenburg and the commoner, Katharina Gumpel. The testimonies painted a vivid but ambivalent picture.[31] The witnesses remembered that Katharina wore fine clothing appropriate for a countess, that she entered the castle like a countess, and that she remained at the castle when other counts visited.

Accordingly, it seems that she enjoyed the rights and reputable position of her husband. On the other hand, her house was located in the village outside the castle and she was also not allowed to take her meal at the same table as other counts and countesses. Obviously, in this regard, she was not a wife of equal rank and rights.

These observations are significant for two reasons. First, they show the way in which differences in rank left their traces in everyday life. Even in mundane settings, clothes and placement within a room symbolized differences of rank. Second, these symbols could not, however, be decoded unambiguously. Obviously, Count Anton attached importance to the difference, but the ambiguity also reflected the differences between ecclesiastical law and noble tradition in a period when morganatic marriage was still unknown in the empire. The volume and wealth of evidence we have about the relationship between Count Anton and Katharina are exceptional, but similar practices also pertain in other cases. In one, for example, a bride from the territorial nobility was compelled to pledge in her marriage contract that she would defer to all other female members of her husband's family.[32]

Obviously, princes who intentionally refused morganatic marriage even after the option became well-known wished to treat their nonequal-ranked wives and possibly their children similarly to a partner of equal rank. The limits of possibility were definitely tested at their maximum in the well-known case of Prince Leopold of Anhalt-Dessau (1676–1747).[33] As a ruling prince, his first and only spouse was Anna Luise Föse, the daughter of a common druggist. In 1701, shortly after the marriage, he managed to obtain a deed from the emperor that immediately raised his wife to the rank of princess.[34] While it was not unthinkable, such elevations were rare, nor did families and kin readily accept the beneficiaries of such rapid advancement as equals. Normally, it took several generations for acceptance to become general.[35] Anna Luise's shift in status was exceptional in the extreme, the more so because her children also bore princely rank with all the rights and pretensions the status conferred.

Three remarks are necessary to contextualize this episode properly. First, even Prince Leopold needed to obtain permission from the emperor for his wife to be considered a fully entitled member of the house of Anhalt. To put the point another way, Leopold could not simply assume that an unrestricted marriage endowed his bride with rank, even though the letter of Roman law so stipulated. Although there was a considerable amount of disagreement about whether princes had the right to elevate commoners into the ranks of territorial nobility, it was universally agreed that only the emperor could elevate someone into the highest noble rank, that of counts and princes. After all, this was one of the emperor's very few exclusive rights (the so called *iura reservata*).[36] As we will see, this legal fact bore many consequences for the unequal couples, their families, and even for the emperor himself.

Second, the main precondition for Leopold's success was the undoubted strength of his position. Leopold's father was dead by the time he married Anna Luise. He was already the ruling prince and thus no one could overrule his decision, he had no brothers who possibly could have intervened, and Leopold's political and military accomplishments assured him the sympathy and support not only from the emperor, but also from his powerful neighbor, the king of Prussia.[37] So while it seems that his mother deeply disagreed with this match, no opponent had enough power to thwart Leopold's plan.[38]

Nonetheless, even Leopold had to consider the reputation of his house. Obviously this was why he excluded his eldest son from the succession. This son was married to a non-noble woman, like Leopold himself. It seems that one irregular union was enough in the family and Leopold arranged to have his territories and title transferred to his second son.[39] Obviously, Leopold had no difficulty with the idea that he should be succeeded by someone whose mother was a commoner. What he could not abide, however, was that his heir would further dilute the lineage by marrying a non-noble woman, as he had done.

Leopold's second son was not the only example of an heir of mixed parentage. Still, the descendents of unequal couples who actually succeeded to the throne of a princely territory can be counted on the fingers of one hand; in the other cases the succession did not proceed as smoothly as in Anhalt-Dessau. An intricate but instructive example is that of Duke Georg Wilhelm of Braunschweig-Lüneburg (1624–1705). It is not easy to outline his convoluted story. Georg Wilhelm was the second of four brothers and was slated to marry the daughter of the prince elector of the Palatine. But he refused to do so and instead, in 1658, persuaded his youngest brother, Ernst August, to marry her. As compensation, Georg Wilhelm promised his brother that he would never marry, so that his portion of the inheritance and his rights of succession would fall to Ernst August and his offspring.

In the early 1660s, however, he fell in love with a young court lady from France, Eleonore d'Olbreuse, who stemmed from the provincial nobility of the Poitou and therefore could not be considered his equal in rank.[40] While Georg Wilhelm and Eleonore intended to shape their relationship as honorably as possible, Ernst August and his wife jealously insisted that Georg Wilhelm keep his promise never to marry. Ernst August agreed to some improvement of Eleonore's status but strongly resisted any attempts to let her participate in the house's rank, name, and dignity. The implications of Eleonore's exclusion became apparent when the two remaining brothers of Georg Wilhelm and Ernst August passed away without leaving a male heir, so that now Georg Wilhelm's promise permitted the future reunification of all the inherited territories in the hands of Ernst August. Things became even more complicated when Eleonore gave birth to a daughter whose future spouse could threaten to upset all these intricate arrangements.

In the end, Ernst August and his wife decided that the best way to secure their lineage was to marry their son and heir to Georg Wilhelm's daughter, Sophie Dorothea. For Ernst August, this implied a complete change of strategy, because it required elevating the daughter of a mixed marriage to princely rank. Georg Wilhelm facilitated this turnabout by consenting to an extraordinary dowry. As a result, Sophie Dorothea became the wife of the future prince elector of Braunschweig-Lüneburg, who in 1714 was crowned king of England. Sophie Dorothea was also the stepmother of the Prussian king, Frederick William I, and thus the grandmother of Frederick the Great. High rank did not, however, bring happiness. Unlike her parents' union, Sophie Dorothea's marriage was by all accounts miserable.[41]

The mother, Eleonore, also profited from the elevation of her daughter. Unusually, she had passed through each stage of unequal partnership. She started off like many others as a concubine, with nothing more than acknowledged gifts and promises from Georg Wilhelm. During subsequent years, however, she formally married Georg Wilhelm and became an imperial countess, just like a morganatic bride. In the end she was accepted as a prince's wife and as a princess of equal rank to her spouse.

Two aspects of this confusing story are worth emphasizing in respect to the subject of transgressive unions. First, it illustrates the importance of family constellations and dynastic strategies, which in this case overruled the principles of rank and reputation. In fact, the example shows that even under these circumstances the logic of rank and reputation served the strategic interests of the high nobility and could be adapted to new situations, albeit with a heavy heart. Second, the story shows that in many cases the adjustment of the wife's rank was not an isolated act, but rather was the outcome of a longer process composed of many stages that varied according to conditions and attitudes. This reflects the uncertainties of such a constellation as well as its remarkable dependence on external influences.

The case of Prince Karl Friedrich of Anhalt-Bernburg provides further insights into the ways in which misalliances developed.[42] As a widower he married the daughter of a high-ranking and esteemed, but non-noble, civil servant. His first marriage had been to an imperial countess, with whom he sired several children, including his future successor. Karl Friedrich's father, who was still alive at the time of his second marriage, strongly opposed the union. In a sense, the fate of this relationship went through even more stages and configurations than in the example of Georg Wilhelm and Eleonore.

As in other cases, the conflicts focused on Karl Friedrich's and Wilhelmina Charlotte's ambition to achieve complete approval for her sons as fully entitled heirs and successors. Several changes gave the case a very special shape. First, Karl Friedrich had to deal with his father's reproaches and the obstructions he threw up to the union. After his father's death, Karl Friedrich, however, survived only a short time. His widow was forced to contend with the disdain of her stepson (the ruling prince), and her brother-in-law, who was Karl Friedrich's younger brother. After the latter's death, his son (and Wilhelmina Charlotte's nephew by marriage) opposed the widow's claims even more aggressively. The ruling prince distanced himself from his cousin and started to support his stepmother. After her death the sons continued to fight for their rights and the conflict continued for almost three decades.

In the short time that he was married before his death, Karl Friedrich took three decisive steps on behalf of his wife and their two sons. First, in 1719 Karl-Friedrich obtained the elevation of his wife to the rank of an imperial countess with the name "von Ballenstedt."[43] This act consolidated the practice of partial elevation, in which the unequal wives of princes were elevated into the high nobility, but not to equal rank with their husbands. Thus the wives were still kept at a distance, and allowed to approach their husbands only half-way, so to speak. Importantly, the document making Wilhelmina Charlotte a countess did not mention her sons. The omission was probably intentional in order to leave open the possibility that they might one day be considered princes of Anhalt.

Opponents to these arrangements quickly took this point as an opening to express their discontent. After Karl Friedrich's death, the widow insisted that she should be treated as a prince's widow and her sons as princes of Anhalt. Paradoxically, her stepson and her brother-in-law who opposed her elevation seemed to intercede in Vienna in favor of her sons. Their aim, however, was to preserve for them the combination of proximity and distance to the house of Anhalt that had characterized their mother's status. In fact they succeeded in raising the sons to the rank of imperial counts with the name "von Bärenfeld."[44] It was an elegant solution. Fixing the rank of Karl Friedrich's sons forestalled further pretensions on their part. Making them counts, it was hoped, would prevent them from pretending to be princes, while their new names made it clear that they were not members of the house of Anhalt.

As an aside, it is worth noting that the ruling prince of Anhalt and his uncle considered that rank of lower nobility would have sufficed. It was the emperor and the Imperial Aulic Council that insisted on making the sons counts. In doing so the emperor demonstrated that he alone claimed the right to determine the rules of ennoblement and once again confirmed what started to become a usage. Last but not least, the fees he would collect for making them counts were much higher.

This decision, however, did not end the story. In 1742 the sons, supported by their stepbrother, actually managed to obtain further elevation.[45] To accomplish this they exploited the crisis brought on by the extinction in 1740 of the direct male line in the Habsburg dynasty, which resulted in the election of a member of the house of Wittelsbach as emperor. Cut off from the archives and the resources of the court of Vienna, the new emperor, Charles VII, was favorably disposed to meet the requests of every potential supporter. He granted the sons of Karl Friedrich their wish to be raised to the rank of princes. The draft of the deed still cautiously named them "princes of Bernburg," but they eventually succeeded in having the decisive words added to their title: "of Anhalt-Bernburg."

The thrill of victory did not last long. The emperor soon died and was succeeded by Franz Stephan von Habsburg-Lorraine, who slightly but decisively revised the elevation by renaming the sons yet again. Under the revised deed, Karl Friedrich's sons retained the rank of prince, but lost the right to bear the name "Anhalt." Instead, they were to content themselves with the name Bären-feld.[46] The sons now enjoyed equal rank in a formal sense, but still were excluded from all rights connected to the ruling house of Anhalt. Although the distance in rank had been abolished, the difference in names backed the last wall to keep them out. Unlike the children of Leopold and Anna Luise and the offspring of Georg Wilhelm and Eleonore, the descendants of Karl Friedrich's mixed marriage were barred from the succession.

The revision of an imperial act was a rather unusual event that cannot be understood unless we look at one last example. In 1713 Duke Anton Ulrich of Saxony-Meiningen married a woman from a non-noble family of officers and civil servants.[47] The couple had several children. For several years after their marriage, they lived abroad and their relationship attracted no special attention. In 1717, however, the agnates indicated their disfavor by signing a pact against marital mismatches.[48] Not only the dukes of the diverse lines of the Ernestine Saxony, but also the princes of Anhalt-Bernburg and Anhalt-Zerbst added their signatures. The document expressed the fear that misalliances might seriously weaken the reputation of the princely houses in the empire and further recommended that such mismatches be avoided or at least undertaken only as morganatic marriages. In no way, they insisted, should morganatic wives or their children be treated as princesses and princes. This pact can be interpreted as the essential commonsense position of the smaller princes in the empire in regard to the challenge posed by misalliances. This pact called on Anton Ulrich to act accordingly. Anton Ulrich, however, who was already involved in several quarrels with his brothers, refused to comply with the pact's provisions.[49] On the contrary, he petitioned to obtain the elevation of his wife and children at the imperial court. He succeeded in 1727 when Charles VI raised his wife and children to princely rank and explicitly granted his children the right of succession. This act was even more comprehensive than the elevation of Prince Leopold's wife, and intentionally ignored the objections of the other princes. It was probably helpful that Anton Ulrich was related to the empress. Nonetheless, it also seems possible that the emperor or his advisers wanted to demonstrate that he would not allow a pact of princes to constrain his *ius reservatum*.[50]

The Saxon princes' protests were ignored at first, but the princes continued to protest this decision until the dynastic crisis of 1740 broke. In this case, the opponents of the misalliance profited from the election of the new emperor from the house of Wittelsbach. With the support of the prince-elector of Saxony, a new paragraph was inserted in the electoral capitulation (*Wahlkapitulation*) that Charles VII was obliged to sign as a condition of his election as emperor. The capitulation already contained some regulations restricting the emperor's ability to raise someone's rank. The new paragraph stipulated that the emperor would not be allowed to bestow the title and honors of the paternal family on the children of a misalliance.[51] Referring to the clauses in this document, the Saxon princes demanded a revision of the elevation of 1727. In 1744 the emperor deprived Anton Ulrich's wife and his children of their titles and right of succession. This also formed the basis for revision in the case of Karl Friedrich of Anhalt-Bernburg.[52]

Now it was Anton Ulrich's desperate protests that went unheard. As if to add insult to injury, his wife died only a few weeks later. Nonetheless he continued to struggle on behalf of his sons, the more so as the death of his brothers and his nephews made him the only ruling prince of Saxony-Meiningen. In 1750 he strengthened his position by entering into an equal marriage with a Hessian princess who was forty years his junior. The couple had several sons and daughters, and therefore one could anticipate that the fate of Anton Ulrich's children from his first marriage would be decided after their father's demise.

Anton Ulrich's death in 1763 caused a dramatic showdown. The princes from the other branches of the house of Saxony tried to occupy the territory of Meiningen, denying the validity of Anton Ulrich's arrangements to install the elder sons as his successors. In the end, his widow (and the elder sons' stepmother) managed to settle the confrontation by abandoning the succession of the elder sons but securing the succession of her own underage sons. The offspring of Anton Ulrich's misalliance lived a discontented life as a barely tolerated presence in their rooms under the roof of Meiningen castle.

The previous four examples dealt with princes and wives who tried to obliterate the distance of rank and to transform non-nobles or nobles of low rank into members of princely families. As the examples from Anhalt-Dessau and Braunschweig-Lüneburg prove, this was indeed possible. Yet, as the examples from Anhalt-Bernburg and Saxony-Meiningen demonstrate, there was nothing certain or self-evident about the results.

Obviously, misalliances created a social vacuum that needed to be filled, but resisted regulation that satisfied all affected parties. The matrix of social expectations was such that the unequal wife's status did not necessarily require adjustment, although the fact that in so many cases the distance of rank at least was reduced reflects the widespread conviction that close proximity to the prince would justify, if not actually require, elevation to at least noble rank.

However, the need to determine precisely the rank of the children was critical. The usual practice of according them a rank somewhere between that of
their parents symbolized their ambiguous and mixed status. The disputes over
children of misalliances also made clear that their intermediate status held out
the possibility that they might indeed enter into the high nobility, if not into a
princely family. Though such halfway elevations made them coequal in a formal
sense they remained, at least in most cases, unequal in relation to the rights of
their uncles, stepbrothers, brothers-in-law, cousins, and nephews. At this point
no room for compromise existed. Although issues of inheritance rights allowed
some room for compromise, the question of the succession could only be answered with yes or no.[53]

While the vast majority of princes and counts seem to have accepted the
compromise solution as commonsensical and workable, the cases described in
this chapter also demonstrate that there were no fixed rules for dealing with
misalliances. The difficulties involved emerged from different sources. Different power and relational constellations within families played a major role.
Probably the most important factors were external moral and legal norms, the
newly introduced exclusivity of marriage, and increased institutional backing
for individual rights. The more conflicts over noble status became subject to the
arbitration of the emperor and the imperial courts of law, the weaker became
the autonomy of noble families in dealing with misalliances internally and as
they saw fit. Consequently they tried to restrict the emperor's power through
litigation, but that in turn subjected noble autonomy itself to judicial arbitration. The process was inevitable, but norms and trials determined only a part
of social reality. While the noble community could not dissuade some individuals from transgressing the rules about marriage choices, rank and reputation
remained subject to the judgment of peers. Ultimately, nobles could not be
forced to accept spouses of minor rank.[54] Thus even Prince Leopold of Anhalt-
Dessau was not able to celebrate his wedding in a princely manner. In everyday
life, low-ranking wives suffered endless indignities and real disadvantages for
themselves and their children.

Social acceptance also impinged, finally, on the marriage options available to
the offspring of misalliances. Normally, the children married within their rank
which, as we have seen, was usually below that of their fathers. Where rank
was disputed, marriage presented a potentially decisive opportunity for assert-
ing pretensions to princely status. As the example of Duke Georg Wilhelm's
daughter demonstrates, dynastic interests could at times enable the formal integration of mixed offspring into the rank and family of their father. The sons
of Prince Karl Friedrich of Anhalt, on the other hand, never married; in all
likelihood they probably were unable to find a partner with whom they would
be able to uphold their claims to status.

And what about the eight surviving children of Prince Leopold? As mentioned above, his eldest son also entered into a misalliance; this prompted Leopold to transfer the succession to his second son. This younger brother, in turn, married a princess of Anhalt-Köthen, a member of the same dynasty, but who was herself the product of a misalliance, since her grandmother stemmed from the lower nobility. This partnership, however, was of sufficiently high rank to preserve the princely reputation for the next generation. A daughter of Leopold married the prince of Anhalt-Bernburg—that is, the son of Prince Karl Friedrich from his first coequal marriage—who at the time still opposed his stepmother and stepbrothers. Another daughter of Leopold married a margrave of Brandenburg-Schwedt and was thus the only child who married outside the house of Anhalt. None of the other children married, although Leopold's youngest daughter bore an illegitimate child with a non-noble partner.[55] So the strategic outcome of Prince Leopold's offspring was, shall we say, mixed.

Notes

1. On the defining aspects of nobility, see *Europäischer Adel 1750–1950*, ed. Hans-Ulrich Wehler (Göttingen, 1990); on the legitimation of nobility, see Klaus Bleeck and Jörn Garber, "Nobilitas: Standes- und Privilegienlegitimation in deutschen Adelstheorien des 16. und 17. Jahrhunderts," *Daphnis* 11 (1982): 49–114. For a general introduction from a pan-European perspective, see Ronald G. Asch, *Nobilities in Transition 1550–1700* (London, 2003); idem, *Europäischer Adel in der Frühen Neuzeit* (Cologne, 2008). For an overview that focuses on German nobility, see Michael Sikora, *Der Adel in der Frühen Neuzeit* (Darmstadt, 2009).

2. Recent studies on marriage strategies in the high nobility of the Holy Roman Empire include Anne-Simone Knöfel, *Dynastie und Prestige: Die Heiratspolitik der Wettiner* (Cologne, 2009); Marra, *Allianzen des Adels*; Judith J. Hurwich, *Noble Strategies: Marriage and Sexuality in the Zimmern Chronicle* (Kirksville, 2006); idem, "Marriage Strategy among the German Nobility, 1400–1699," *Journal of Interdisciplinary History* 29 (1998): 169–95; and Thomas Mutschler, *Haus, Ordnung, Familie: Wetterauer Hochadel im 17. Jahrhundert am Beispiel des Hauses Ysenburg-Büdingen* (Darmstadt, 2004). Still inspiring is Evelin Oberhammer, "Gesegnet sei dies Band: Eheprojekte, Heiratspakten und Hochzeit im fürstlichen Haus," in *Der ganzen Welt ein Lob und Spiegel: Das Fürstenhaus Liechtenstein in der frühen Neuzeit*, ed. Evelin Oberhammer (Vienna, 1990), 182–203.

3. For a short discussion of this practice, see Ronald G. Asch, "Das monarchische Nobilitierungsrecht und die soziale Identität des Adels im 17. und 18. Jahrhundert," in *Die frühneuzeitliche Monarchie in Europa und ihr Erbe: Festschrift für Heinz Duchhardt zum 60. Geburtstag*, ed. Ronald G. Asch, Johannes Arndt, and Matthias Schnettger (Münster, 2003), 91–107, here 99–102. With regard to cathedral chapters in general, see Ute Küppers-Braun, *Frauen des hohen Adels im kaiserlich-freiweltlichen Damenstift Essen (1605–1803)* (Münster, 1997), 52–59, 275–301; on provincial estates, see Elizabeth Harding, "Warum der Adel seine Ahnen über die Schwelle trägt: Zur Symbolik rit-

terschaftlicher Aufschwörungen," in *Symbolik in Zeiten von Krise und gesellschaftlichem Umbruch*, ed. Elizabeth Harding and Natalie Krentz (Münster, 2011), 131–52; and Friedrich von Klocke, *Justus Möser und die deutsche Ahnenprobe des 18. Jahrhunderts* (Leipzig, 1941).

4. This aspect is highlighted in *Ständische Gesellschaft und soziale Mobilität*, ed. Winfried Schulze (Munich, 1988).

5. On the importance of the membership in the diet for the imperial counts, see Barbara Stollberg-Rilinger, "Der Grafenstand in der Reichspublizistik," in *Dynastie und Herrschaftssicherung in der Frühen Neuzeit*, ed. Heide Wunder (Berlin, 2002), 29–53.

6. See Karin J. MacHardy, *War, Religion and Court Patronage in Habsburg Austria: The Social and Cultural Dimensions of Political Interaction, 1521–1622* (Basingstoke, 2003). For typical careers, see Thomas Winkelbauer, *Fürst und Fürstendiener: Gundaker von Liechtenstein, ein österreichischer Aristokrat des konfessionellen Zeitalters* (Vienna, 1999); and Erwin Riedenauer, "Zur Entstehung und Ausformung des landesfürstlichen Briefadels in Bayern," *Zeitschrift für Bayerische Landesgeschichte* 47 (1984): 609–73. On the composition of government councils, see, among others, Bernd Wunder, "Die Sozialstruktur der Geheimratskollegien in den süddeutschen protestantischen Fürstentümern (1660–1720)," *Vierteljahrschrift für Sozial- und Wirtschaftsgeschichte* 58 (1971): 145–220. On general aspects of ennoblement in a European context, see Asch, "Das monarchische Nobilitierungsrecht."

7. For a brief overview of the German nobility's rank system, see Sikora, *Adel*, 12–16.

8. The culture of memory has attracted a lot of research during the last two decades, including *Zwischen Schande und Ehre: Erinnerungsbrüche und die Kontinuität des Hauses: Legitimationsmuster und Traditionsverständnis des frühneuzeitlichen Adels in Umbruch und Krise*, ed. Martin Wrede and Horst Carl (Mainz, 2007); Thomas Fuchs, *Traditionsstiftung und Erinnerungspolitik: Geschichtsschreibung in Hessen in der Frühen Neuzeit* (Kassel, 2002); Kilian Heck, *Genealogie als Monument und Argument* (Munich, 2002); and *Adelige und bürgerliche Erinnerungskulturen des Spätmittelalters und der Frühen Neuzeit*, ed. Werner Rösener (Göttingen, 2000).

9. For some case studies at the beginning of the early modern era, see "*. . . wir wollen der Liebe Raum geben*": *Konkubinate geistlicher und weltlicher Fürsten um 1500*, ed. Andreas Tacke (Göttingen, 2006). On the phenomenon of concubinage in general, see Paul-Joachim Heinig, "Fürstenkonkubinat um 1500 zwischen Usus und Devianz," in ibid., 11–37; idem., "'Omnia vincit amor': Das fürstliche Konkubinat im 15./16. Jahrhundert," in *Principes: Dynastien und Höfe im späten Mittelalter*, ed. Cordula Nolte, Karl-Heinz Spiess, and Ralf-Gunnar Werlich, eds. (Stuttgart, 2002), 277–314. For a probing study of an eighteenth-century German mistress, see Sybille Oßwald-Bargende, *Die Mätresse, der Fürst und die Macht: Christina Wilhelmina von Grävenitz und die höfische Gesellschaft* (Frankfurt, 2000).

10. For a complicated but striking example, see Hans Kruse, "Wilhelm von Oranien und Anna von Sachsen: Eine fürstliche Ehetragödie des 16. Jahrhunderts," *Nassauische Annalen* 54 (1934): 1–184.

11. See Michael Sikora, "Ungleiche Verbindlichkeiten: Gestaltungsspielräume standesverschiedener Partnerschaften im deutschen Hochadel der Frühen Neuzeit," in *zeitenblicke* 4, 2005, no. 3 (13 December 2005), http://www.zeitenblicke.de/2005/3/Sikora/index_html, sections 9–13.

12. See the brief remarks in Sikora, *Adel*, 132–34. The emperors' right to raise individuals into the imperial nobility is discussed in Jürgen Arndt, "Zur Entwicklung des kai-

serlichen Hofpfalzgrafenamtes von 1355–1806," idem, *Hofpfalzgrafen-Register*, vol. 1 (Neustadt a. d. Aisch, 1964), x–xxiv.

13. Still essential is Rockwell, *Doppelehe*. For more discussion of this critical event, see Stephan Buchholz, "Rechtsgeschichte und Literatur: Die Doppelehe Philipps des Großmütigen," in *Landgraf Philipp der Großmütige von Hessen und seine Residenz Kassel*, ed. Heide Wunder, Christina Vanja, and Berthold Hinz (Marburg, 2004), 57–73; Kerstin Merkel, "Ein Fall von Bigamie: Landgraf Philipp von Hessen, seine beiden Frauen und deren drei Grabdenkmäler," in *Grabmäler: Tendenzen der Forschung an Beispielen aus Mittelalter und früher Neuzeit*, ed. Wilhelm Maier, Wolfgang Schmid, and Michael Viktor Schwarz (Berlin, 2000), 103–26; Michael Sikora, "'. . . so muß man doch dem Kindt ainen Nahmen geben': Wahrnehmungsweisen einer unstandesgemäßen Beziehung im 16. Jahrhundert," in *Adel in Hessen: Herrschaft, Selbstverständnis und Lebensführung vom 15. bis ins 20. Jahrhundert*, ed. Eckart Conze, Alexander Jendorff, and Heide Wunder (Marburg, 2010), 571–93; and the contribution of David Whitford in this volume.

14. "Memorial, was der Herr M. Bucerus bei D. M. Luthero und M. Philippo Melanchthone ausrichten soll," in *Philippi Melanchthonis Opera quae supersunt omnia*, ed. Karl Gottlieb Bretschneider and Heinrich Ernst Bindseil, 28 vols. (Halle, 1834–1860), vol. 3, cols. 851–56.

15. See the notes Landgrave Philipp made on the matter, probably written in fall 1539, reprinted in Rockwell, *Doppelehe*, 316–17.

16. See the so-called "Wittenberger Ratschlag," of 10 December 1539, in *Philippi Melanchthonis Opera*, vol. 3, cols. 856–63.

17. The polemics are broadly summed up in Rockwell, *Doppelehe*, 101–36.

18. See Karl Michaelis, *Das abendländische Eherecht im Übergang vom späten Mittelalter zur Neuzeit* (Göttingen, 1989); Paul Mikat, "Ehe," in *Handwörterbuch zur deutschen Rechtsgeschichte* (Berlin, 1971), vol. 1, cols. 809–33; and Dieterich, *Das protestantische Eherecht*. There were some differences between Protestant and Catholic norms, but as far as I can see they did not have consequences in regard to the misalliances. For a useful introduction, see Barbara Henze, "Kontinuität und Wandel des Eheverständnisses im Gefolge von Reformation und katholischer Reform," in *"In christo ist weder man noch weyb": Frauen in der Zeit der Reformation und der katholischen Reform*, ed. Anne Conrad (Münster, 1999), 129–51.

19. As outlined in Dietmar Willoweit, *Standesungleiche Ehen des regierenden hohen Adels in der neuzeitlichen deutschen Rechtsgeschichte* (Munich, 2004), 103–6.

20. See Albert Boenicke, *Die Ehe zur linken Hand* (Berlin, 1915), 29.

21. I have discussed this case in detail in Sikora, "Wahrnehmungsweisen"; see also Jürgen Ackermann, "'Graf Antons zu Ysenburg-Kelsterbach Mißheurath hat seiner Gräflichen Familie vilen Unlust verursachet,'" in *Sammlungen zur Geschichte von Wächtersbach*, 41 (January 2003), no. 265, 1–12.

22. See Sikora, "Wahrnehmungsweisen," 580; the title of this essay is a quotation from a 1554 letter of the jurist who unsuccessfully insisted on a clear definition of the relationship.

23. See also Jürgen Ackermann, *Verschuldung, Reichsdebitverwaltung, Mediatisierung: Eine Studie zu den Finanzproblemen der mindermächtigen Stände im Alten Reich: Das Beispiel der Grafschaft Ysenburg-Büdingen 1687–1806* (Marburg, 2002), 65–82.

24. For some quotations, the earliest from the 1580s, see Sikora, "Wahrnehmungsweisen," 588–89; and idem, "Verbindlichkeiten," sections 22–23. For another example of the re-

ception of morganatic marriage during just these years, see August Meininghaus, "Von der morganatischen Ehe des niederen westfälischen Adels," *Westfälische Zeitschrift* 95 (1939): 194–212.

25. The document has been printed in Johann Christian Lünig, *Teutsches Reichs-Archiv*, 14 vols. (Leipzig, 1710–21), vol. 10, part IV, section 13, no. 39, 240–47; for some commentary on this story, see Michael Sikora, "Über den Umgang mit Ungleichheit: Bewältigungsstrategien für Mesalliancen im deutschen Hochadel der Frühen Neuzeit—das Haus Anhalt als Beispiel," in *Zwischen Schande und Ehre*, 97–124, here 102–7.

26. See Johann Christoff Beckmann, *Historie des Fürstenthums Anhalt* (Zerbst, 1710; reprint Dessau, 1993–98), 2: 242–43.

27. Beckmann, *Historie*, 2: 244–45; see also Michael Rohrschneider, *Johann Georg II. von Anhalt-Dessau (1627–1693): Eine politische Biographie* (Berlin, 1998), 91–93.

28. This figure is my own estimate, based for the most part on data found in Detlev Schwennicke, *Europäische Stammtafeln*, new series (Frankfurt, 1997–[2011]).

29. See, for example, Vinzenz Czech, *Legitimation und Repräsentation: Zum Selbstverständnis thüringisch-sächsischer Reichsgrafen in der frühen Neuzeit* (Berlin, 2003), 186–211; Myriam Franke, "Die höfische Hochzeit," in *Erdengötter: Fürst und Hofstatt in der Frühen Neuzeit im Spiegel von Marburger Bibliohteks- und Archivbeständen*, ed. Jörg-Jochen Berns, Frank Druffner, Ulrich Schütte, and Brigitte Walbe (Marburg, 1997), 327–48; Andrea Sommer-Mathis, *"Tu felix Austria nube": Hochzeitsfeste der Habsburger im 18. Jahrhundert* (Vienna, 1994); Karl Vocelka, *Habsburgische Hochzeiten 1550–1600* (Vienna, 1976).

30. The only document is found in Johann Michael von Welser, *Die Welser* (Nuremberg, 1917), vol. 2, 150–51.

31. See Sikora, "Wahrnehmungsweisen," 588.

32. The woman in question was Gisela Agnes von Rath, who married Prince Emanuel Lebrecht of Anhalt-Köthen. See Sikora, "Bewältigungsstrategien," 109.

33. A recent discussion can be found in ibid., 112–16.

34. The deed is printed in Lünig, *Teutsches Reichs-Archiv*, vol 11, part 4 ("Supplementa ulteriora zu einigen Fürstlichen Häusern"), no. 1, 93–95.

35. About elevations into the rank of princes, good information and insights are provided by Thomas Klein, "Die Erhebungen in den weltlichen Reichsfürstenstand 1550–1806," *Blätter für deutsche Landesgeschichte*, 122 (1986): 137–92; and Harry Schlip, "Die neuen Fürsten," in *Liechtenstein: Fürstliches Haus und staatliche Ordnung*, ed. Volker Press and Dietmar Willoweit (Munich, 1987), 249–92. Gert Kollmer relates an extraordinary story in *Die Familie Palm: Soziale Mobilität in ständischer Gesellschaft* (Ostfildern, 1983).

36. For a very useful, systematic introduction to the Holy Roman Empire's constitution, see Helmut Neuhaus, *Das Reich in der Frühen Neuzeit*, 2d ed. (Munich, 2003), here 17.

37. Recent contributions on Leopold include Michael Rohrschneider, "Leopold I. von Anhalt-Dessau, die oranische Heeresreform und die Reorganisation der preußischen Armee unter Friedrich Wilhelm I.," in *Die preussische Armee zwischen Ancien Régime und Reichsgründung*, ed. Peter Baumgart, Bernhard R. Kroener, and Heinz Stübig (Paderborn, 2008), 45–71; *Fürst Leopold I. von Anhalt-Dessau 1676–1747 "Der alte Dessauer,"* (Dessau, 1997); and Rohrschneider, *Johann Georg II.*

38. Joachim Arenkow, *Geschichte und Thaten Sr. Hochfürstl. Durchl. Leopoldi, Fürstens von Anhalt-Dessau etc., als eines wahrhafften Heldens unserer Zeit* . . . (Dessau, 1742), 180.

39. See Paul Herre, *Die geheime Ehe des Erbprinzen Wilhelm Gustav von Anhalt-Dessau und die Reichsgrafen von Anhalt* (Zerbst, 1933; reprint Dessau, 2006).

40. For more details, see Michael Sikora, "Eleonore d'Olbreuse—die Herzogin auf Raten," in *mächtig—verlockend: Frauen der Welfen* (Celle, 2010), 17–43. There are several other instructive contributions on Eleonore in this volume. See also an earlier version of my essay: Michael Sikora, "Dynastie und Eigensinn: Herzog Georg Wilhelm von Celle, Eleonore d'Olbreuse und die Spielregeln des Fürstenstandes," in *Hof und Medien im Spannungsfeld von dynastischer Tradition und politischer Innovation zwischen 1648 und 1714*, ed. Heiko Laß (Munich, 2008), 19–30.

41. See Ulrike Weiß, "'Gefährliche Liebschaften': Die Affäre—Mittel der Karriere oder Katastrophe?," in *Mächtig—verlockend*, 132–65; Frauke Geyken, "'Ohne seiner frau todt witwer zu werden, ist doch etwas rares': Folgen des ehelichen Ungehorsams— Sophie Dorotheas Verbannung nach Ahlden," in ibid., 167–85; Georg Schnath, *Sophie Dorothea und Königsmarck: Die Ehetragödie der Kurprinzessin von Hannover* (Hildesheim, 1979).

42. A more detailed treatment of this example can be found in Michael Sikora, "Eine Miss-heirat im Hause Anhalt: Zur sozialen Praxis der ständischen Gesellschaft in der ersten Hälfte des 18. Jahrhundert," in *Die Fürsten von Anhalt*, ed. Werner Freitag and Michael Hecht (Halle, 2003), 248–65. For a short summary, see Sikora, "Bewältigungsstrate-gien," 117–120.

43. The deed was edited by Samuel Lentz, *Becmannus enucleatus, suppletus et continuatus* . . . (Köthen, 1757), 756–58.

44. See ibid., 766–67.

45. See ibid., 768–69.

46. See *Selecta Juris Publici Novissima*, ed. Johann Carl König, 48 vols. (Frankfurt, 1740– 66), vol. 31, 112–13.

47. The year of the marriage has been revealed by Stefanie Walther: *Die (Un-)Ordnung der Ehe. Normen und Praxis ernestinischer Fürstenehen in der Frühen Neuzeit*, (Munich, 2011), 255. For more details on this case, see pp. 250–326.

48. See Bernhard von Hellfeld, *Beiträge zum Staats-Recht und der Geschichte von Sachsen* 3 vols. (Eisenach, 1785-90), vol. 1, 289–90.

49. Michael Sikora discusses some aspects of the pact in "Ein kleiner Erbfolgekrieg: Die sachsen-meiningische Sukzessionskrise 1763 und das Problem der Ebenbürtigkeit," in Helmut Neuhaus and Barbara Stollberg-Rilinger, eds., *Menschen und Strukturen in der Geschichte Alteuropas* (Berlin, 2002), 319–39.

50. See ibid., 329–30.

51. Johann Jacob Moser, *Ihro Römisch-Kayserlichen Majestät Carls des Siebenden Wahl-Ca-pitulation* . . . , Erster Theil (Frankfurt, 1742), 74; see also Fritz Georg Iwand, *Die Wahlkapitulationen des 17. und 18. Jahrhunderts und ihr Einfluß auf die Entwicklung des Ebenbürtigkeits- und Prädikatsrechts des deutschen hohen Adels* (Biberach, 1919), esp. 20–25.

52. See some of the documents collected in *Abgemüßigte Vorstellung, welche [Anton Ulrich] An Eine Hochlöbliche und Hochansehnliche Reichs-Versammlung . . . überreichen lassen* (n.p., 1744); also in *Des Gesamten Fürstlichen Hauses Sachsen gründlicher Bericht . . .* (n.p., 1745), no. 33.

53. In several cases one can identify a characteristic compromise. While the sons from a misalliance were excluded from the succession according to the usual order, it was

stipulated that they or their offspring could succeed to the throne in the event that no fully entitled male heir was available. The sons of morganatic marriages, therefore, functioned as something like a dynastic reserve to be called upon to avoid the extinction of the house.

54. It should be remembered, as mentioned above, that marital mismatches could, under certain circumstances, accord with family interests.

55. See Walther Schmidt, *Prinzessin Henriette Amalie von Anhalt-Dessau, die Begründerin der Fürstlichen Amalienstiftung in Dessau (1720–1793): Ein Lebensbild aus der Zeit des Rokoko* (Dessau, 1937; reprint Dessau-Roßlau, 2009). For further details, especially concerning some remarkable information on her art collection, see *Sammlerin und Stifterin: Henriette Amalie von Anhalt-Dessau und ihr Frankfurter Exil*, ed Manfred Großkinsky (Frankfurt, 2002).

CHAPTER 6

~:~

Between Conscience and Coercion
Mixed Marriages, Church, Secular Authority, and Family

DAGMAR FREIST

On 16 Feburary 1609, Cordes von Amelunxen, a Catholic, married the Lutheran Catharina von Borchorst. Only a few years later, Catharina fled to a convent in order to escape the physical abuse of her husband. Her brother sued for divorce on her behalf, and when Amelunxen received notice from his brother-in-law, Amelunxen rejected any suggestion that "the misunderstanding between he and me [has] resulted from the provocations of wicked people."[1] On the contrary, at the root of the problem were Catharina's religious attitudes and her interference in his affairs. He had had "sufficient cause . . . to slap her on the neck on one or two occasions," which in his opinion was "no great sin" and certainly no justification for divorce. The charges—that he had "treated her badly, hit her, beat her, threatened to stab her with bare knives" and that "in my presence her life had been in danger"—parodied the truth. Friends who had attempted to mediate their difference soon recognized that "not I, but she, my wife, had caused every misunderstanding." In their marriage contract, the couple had reached a clear understanding about their future lives together, an agreement that Catharina had never kept. Amelunxen recalled that "my wife pledged in good faith to accept my Catholic religion [and] that she would subordinate herself to me and obey me, as befits a loyal woman." Yet, he went on, not only had she refused Catholicism, but she had also, in fact, "cursed it in the strongest terms, kept her religious books, and read them daily in defiance of me." Amelunxen could only contemplate continuing the marriage if his wife "would hereafter accept my religion, according to her pledge and promise, and show obedience toward me as her husband, according to God's command as a loyal wife ought and should." With the support of her brother, Catharina insisted on and received an amicable court hearing and eventually reconciled with her husband in 1603.[2]

Mixed marriages surely rank among the most impressive manifestations of inter-confessional and religious coexistence. In the early modern period, mixed marriages could be found everywhere various confessions and religious groups existed side by side. But the theological, social, political, and familial acceptance of mixed marriages cannot be forced into a scheme of continuity and change in the early modern era. Rather, the manner in which people dealt with mixed marriages depended on the attitude of the parties involved, on the behavior of the confessions toward such unions, on each confession's particular position within the region and the territory, on legal parameters, and finally on the politics of religion in the territory in question. Throughout the early modern period, mixed matches were fundamentally at odds with the intolerant attitude of most princes toward religious minorities, with existing theologies of marriage, and with state policies aimed at creating a religiously homogenous subject population. As the following examples show, confessional interests continued to influence the policies of territories and policies toward religious minorities long after the Peace of Westphalia.

Marriage contracts that guaranteed freedom of conscience between future spouses and prescribed how children would be raised testify to the willingness of betrothed couples to organize confessionally mixed families on the basis of tolerance and compromise. At the same time, however, these contracts also demonstrate that couples were aware of the dangers mixed marriages seemed to pose and that they hoped to use prenuptial contracts to prevent outside interference with the family's religious life. Territories that stipulated a particular form for marriage contracts, as the Rhine Palatinate did, usually invoked as justifications the conflicts over religion and coercion of conscience (*Gewissenszwang*) that often resulted from such unions.[3]

The polarity between conscience and coercion lies at the heart of this chapter. It generated political conflicts well into the late eighteenth century and these, as opposed to the subjective experience of living in a mixed marriage, form the primary focus. Moreover, once the Peace of Westphalia guaranteed freedom of conscience, conflicts over mixed marriages acquired a potent diplomatic and juridical dimension: from then on, ordinary Protestant subjects could present grievances over violations of their freedom of conscience in mixed marriage to the formal Protestant caucus of the imperial diet (*corpus evangelicorum*) for arbitration by the empire's supreme deliberative body.

Gender relations played a central role in the quest for tranquil, bi-confessional coexistence; likewise the conduct of children influenced profoundly the question of freedom of conscience. Marriage contracts often stipulated the right, or more often the obligation, of both parties to recognize each other's freedom of conscience and to structure the religious education of offspring on the basis of mutual consent. Typically this arrangement meant that girls would be raised in their mother's religion and boys in their father's faith. This in turn casts new light on patriarchal authority—*patria potestas* (the power of fathers to determine the religion of their children).[4] As the story of Cordes von Amelunxen and Catharina von Borchorst suggests, conflicts that inevitably arose in the everyday religious life of mixed households set patriarchal authority against the religious conscience of wife and children. This constellation of tensions was reproduced at the level of the territorial state, if and when conflicts arising from confessionally mixed families touched on the question of whether patriarchal authority or the official state religion could or should determine the religion of the children. From the year 1672 the consistories in Leipzig and Wittenberg were preoccupied with the question of "whether fathers who have changed their religion have capacity on the basis of patriarchal authority [*ex capite patria potestatis*] to require the conversion of children in his household who were born into and wish to remain in the evangelical religion, and also whether children must be required to follow their fathers."[5] As this statement suggests, mixed marriages remained in tension with theological positions, confessional policies, freedom of religion, and ideas about good conscience long after 1648. Insofar as mixed marriages united the conjugal pair in body but not in spirit, and in the event conflicts over conscience dissolved the subordination of wife to husband, these unions also ruptured societal norms that defined the peaceable Christian household.

The problem of mixed marriages therefore presents itself as a socioreligious prism through which complex questions of religious freedom and the confessional settlements of 1648 were refracted. Was domestic tranquility in mixed marriages sacrificed for individual freedom, one might ask, or purchased at the price of relinquishing one's own religious inclinations?[6] How did interests of the great confessional blocs shape mixed marriages, and what role did they play in conflicts over educating the young? After 1648 religious conscience and confessionally specific marriage law continued to challenge the confessionally neutral imperial law, which "in the matter of mixed marriages was recognized and exploited as an institutional guarantee of interconfessional peace."[7] But as Stephan Buchholz notes, "each of the religious blocs made the toleration of *matrimonium mixtum* dependent on the willingness of the married couple to declare that they would promote the victory of the *vera verae religionis cognitio et professio*—the one true religion."[8] Thus everyday religious observance, territorial confessionalization, and imperial law were intertwined and collided when conflicts arose.

This chapter first surveys the phenomenon of mixed marriages in Germany and analyzes it from the standpoint of theology, politics, and the experience of everyday life. The chapter then explores the relationship between freedom of conscience, religious coercion, and imperial law on the basis of cases taken from the prince-bishopric of Osnabrück, a bi-confessional territory in the northwest corner of the empire. The evidentiary basis for my analysis rests on early modern treatises, laws and regulations, the opinions of university faculties, the records of judicial conflicts over mixed marriages, and finally grievenaces presented to the *corpus evangelicorum* protesting the exercise of religious coercion in violation of the Peace of Westphalia.

Mixed Marriages in Theology, Politics, and Everyday Life: An Overview

Both testaments of the Bible warn against marrying persons of different religions, a warning that was incorporated, albeit with varying degrees of severity, into Jewish and Christian teachings. The original positions of the pre-Reformation church addressed marriages between Jews and heretics (*disparitas cultus*), and were based overwhelmingly on the Old Testament. As with Judaism, the central concern of the church was to protect and secure the purity of Christianity. Mixed marriages posed a threat to the Christian faith and violated the command of God, who had forbidden his people to mix with alien tribes. The prayer of Ezra, for example, protests that the people of Israel "have taken some of their daughters as wives for themselves and for their sons, so that the holy race has intermingled with the peoples of the lands."[9] For the Catholic church, unbelief constituted a barrier to marriage and so-called spiritual divorce, in the event one partner converted, presented grave difficulties. Marriage with Jews was forbidden categorically. In this sense marriage law abandoned the hope, articulated by Paul in his first letter to the Corinthians, for conversion of the unfaithful and therefore toleration of mixed marriage.[10]

A new situation emerged with the Reformation, inasmuch as it introduced the problem of marriages among Christians of different confessions and religious groupings (the *diversitas religionis*). A great many theologians in all the major camps addressed themselves to this question, theological faculties were solicited for opinions on mixed marriage and the question of religious freedom, and dozens of law dissertations concerned themselves with the problem.

In all the controversies of the sixteenth through eighteenth centuries, within and between the confessional blocs, all the major participants either rejected mixed marriage categorically or tolerated it only on the condition of conversion and the children being raised in the so-called true faith. This division also came to characterize Catholic teaching on marriage. Mixed marriages were forbidden, although a marital dispensation was possible if the non-Catholic party declared him- or herself willing to convert and promised to raise their children as Catholics.

Martin Luther, for his part, invoked Paul to argue in his essay, "On Marriage," against unbelief as an impediment to marriage. But he also criticized mixed marriage in his exegesis on Deuteronomy:

[W]e too live in dangerous times. For behold! There are a great many who would deny the Gospel for the sake of princes, godless bishops and tyrants, solely to obtain favor and grace among men. And many among them now take wives not for the sake of a godly and pious life, but solely for riches, power, and friendship, and no one even asks whether the woman or the man is a Christian.[11]

Concerns over the preservation of right belief and a good conscience in mixed marriages were also expressed in positions taken by theologians, casuists, and legal referees on the question "whether one should take to wed persons who are not of the pure faith."[12] At a minimum, the major confessions seem to have agreed with the maxim that on the basis of the Word of God, a Christian should not marry one of an alien religion. Yet even here a closer examination of the evidence reveals a profound diversity of opinion and ambivalence, most of it arising from weight that was given to religious toleration and to the dictates of conscience. In 1689 the Lutheran jurist and philosopher, Christian Thomasius, endorsed mixed marriages with an essay entitled *A Lawful Examination of the Question of Conscience in Marriage, Whether Two Princely Persons in the Holy Roman Empire, of Whom the Man is a Lutheran and the Woman Reformed, Can in Good Conscience Marry.*[13] Thomasius was prompted to publish this text by the protests of orthodox Lutheran theologians in electoral Saxony against the planned marriage between the Lutheran duke of Saxony-Zeitz and the Reformed sister of Elector Friedrich III of Brandenburg. As late as 1735 the jurist Friedrich Benedikt Carpzov sharply condemned mixed marriages, arguing that the couple would face a choice between religious indifference or perpetual discord—an assessment in which Carpzov was not alone.

The Lutheran theologian Philipp Müller provided dramatic insight into the everyday travails that contemporaries feared mixed marriages would cause. In a treatise entitled *The Dividend of Noble Life through Marriage with One of Alien Faith,* Müller joined opponents to the planned marriage between the Lutheran duke of Saxony-Zeitz and the Reformed daughter of Friedrich III.[14] He based his qualms primarily on the disharmony expected among married partners of different confessions, and anticipated the constraints on conscience and the inevitable loss of patriarchal authority. Like many contemporaries, Müller located the source of conflict in the incompatibility of spirit and body in mixed marriages. The ideal of a Christian marriage was predicated on a Christian household under the guidance of a morally exemplary housefather. Harmony, love, mutual respect, the raising of children, and the instruction of servants were demanded of both partners in marriage. Concord in faith constituted the decisive precondition for harmonious marriage and a peaceful and well-ordered family life.[15] Among the biblical passages cited most frequently in support of this ideal—which, ironically, has nothing to do with marriage—was from the letter of Paul to the Ephesians: "one Lord, one faith, one baptism, one God and Father of all."[16] Mixed marriage could not satisfy the mandate to unity in spirit: "How can such contempt of doctrine and danger to conscience subsist in a community of love?"[17]

Müller painted an alarming picture of everyday difficulties in a confessionally mixed household:

> The one seeks God here, the other there: children should be led to the good by their dear mother, like chicklets to the sun and food; this she cannot do; and the father's teaching and will is hindered. The father would guide the children toward holiness; but the mother follows her heart no less than he, and speaks differently to them. What the husband calls God's blessing is to the wife accursed. So each servant chooses the religion he fancies . . . and society is debased.[18]

To the question "whether one should take to wed persons who are not of the pure faith," the Lutheran theologian answered predictably, speaking of the "various things [that] cause . . . untold hurt." Moreover, he continued, such a union lacked "true and heartfelt love" as well as warm companionship. None of the desiderata of a real marriage, such as the proper education of children, mutual respect, common prayer, and patience, could possibly exist in such a situation.[19] In 1616 the theological faculty at Rostock endorsed a published sermon that condemned mixed marriage as incapable of fulfilling its ultimate purpose, to honor God. "How can God be honored in marriage when the spouses are not united in faith," the text asks. "Indeed, in such a marriage, one party must listen in silence as the other blasphemes and dishonors God. The sort of love that can exist in such circumstances may easily be imagined."[20]

These treatises on mixed marriage do not confine themselves to the question of disunity of belief, its consequences for marital harmony, and education of offspring. They also grapple with the implications for hierarchies of gender within the household and family: "Every single Christian wife should honor the Lord. But how can she serve two masters, Christ and a heathen husband?"[21] Müller describes the hazardous consequences for everyday life:

> Certainly, she cannot as a rule do the Lord justice, for she has the Devil's servant at her side. . . . When she should accompany her husband to church, she tells him she will go to the baths instead: when she should be fasting, her husband puts on a feast: when she should going on processions, that is when there is most to do at home.[22]

The problem of obedience was bound up closely with the question of whether a woman could venture outside the home—to visit the sick, say—without damaging her good name. Should the husband give and receive the kiss of Christian greeting, which was customarily given to women as well as men? Christian women in marriages with heretics were encouraged by their churches to remain steadfast in faith and seek to convert their husbands. In the seventeenth century, for example, the consistory in Dresden permitted the marriage of a Lutheran woman to a Catholic man in recognition of the fact that she was unshakeable in her religion and would raise the children as Lutherans, confident that there was little danger of her converting.[23]

In light of these anxieties and controversies, how were mixed marriages treated politically and as an object of ecclesiastical jurisprudence in the various territories of the empire? What effects did these often contradictory positions have on everyday life in confessionally mixed families? From the sixteenth through the eighteenth centuries, the majority of Lutheran, Calvinist, and Catholic theologians and jurists rejected mixed marriages as a violation of God's command to unity of faith in marriage and warned about the dangers of marital discord and the threat of conversion. This attitude left its stamp on ecclesiastical ordinances, synodal decrees, sermons, and memoranda of university faculties, and in the behavior of parish clergy. Protestant pastors were obliged to educate their flocks about the dangers of mixed marriages. Thus the Ecclesiastical Ordinance of Essen, promulgated in 1705, enjoined ministers "frequently and expressly to dissuade their parishioners [from such mixed unions] by presenting the most important and comprehensible arguments in sermons and private visitations." In the case that couples failed to heed such warnings, they were to be summoned before the consistory, punished, and "cautioned to remain true to their faith." Those already living in mixed marriages "should be admonished with all sincerity, diligence, and meekness to hold constant to their religion," to educate their children in that religion, and to labor constantly to convert "the false-believing spouse."[24]

Officially, the Catholic Church forbade mixed marriages, but issued dispensations under certain conditions. In an undated sermon against mixed marriages, a Lutheran pastor substantiated his warnings citing the dangers of conversion, violation of God's command, and the threat of domestic conflict over household devotion and the children's religious upbringing: "If the father is a papist, he takes his sons to Mass, while the mother takes her daughters to the pure church. Either there is no true love here, or the spouses have little regard for religion, and pursue an epicurean existence."[25]

In addition to these public warnings and private efforts to separate prospective marriage partners on the basis of confessional difference, territorial law regulated ecclesiastical jurisdiction over the civic functions of religion (marriage, baptism, divorce) as well as education. Over the course of the seventeenth and eighteenth centuries, virtually all sovereign territories and imperial cities crafted laws to govern mixed marriages and the religious upbringing of their offspring: mandates requiring that the children be educated in the official religion of the territory, in conjunction with conversion of the dissenting spouse; or that all children be raised in the religion of the father, based on the *patria potestas*; or that religious upbringing align with the sex of the child, that is, daughters in the religion of the mother and sons in the religion of the father; or that marriage contracts should stipulate the terms of each union individually. By the eighteenth century, electoral Saxony, for example, had developed a formal judicial review process that "was entrusted with securing the primacy of the state religion and extended from the parish pastor to the district consistory, from there to the Superintendent and the Supreme Consistory of the territorial prince."[26] Mixed couples were obliged to negotiate this system to obtain permission to marry and secure a dispensation if they wished to educate their children in a manner other than that prescribed by territorial law.

Territorial ordinances and marriage contracts that determined the religion of the children, however, did not typically conform with the positions of the Protestant and, even more so, the Catholic churches. Jurisdictional conflicts and attempts to exert influence over mixed marriages often resulted. To take one example: the mandate under canon law that Catholic partners in mixed marriages raise their children in the Roman faith contradicted with the majority of Protestant territorial codes, to say nothing of private marriage contracts that departed from this requirement, and opened the gates to all sorts of circumvention and subterfuge. The formation of a mixed marriage, as well as the exercise of religion within a mixed household, was not simply the product of personal decision-making, but was always a matter of politics and church law as well. Conflicts between territorial law and the biddings of theology extended into the domestic sphere, weakened the rule of law, undercut the validity of marriage contracts, provoked domestic violence, and encouraged the abduction of children. Confessionally motivated kidnappings by relatives, fathers, mothers, or even by clergy and state officials were facts of life long after 1648. On the Catholic side, the canonical obligation to educate children in the true faith seemed to justify the practice, yet they remained controversial.[27] Now and again clergymen or secular officials tried to win dissenting parents and children for their own religion; under such pressure spouses often found themselves in violation of marriage contracts. In ambiguous cases the children might be interrogated about their religious beliefs. In 1742, for example, the legal guardians of children from a mixed marriage in Quackenbrück filed suit against their surviving parent, Adelheit Clasing. According to the marriage contract, sons were to have been raised Lutheran, like the father, and the daughters Catholic. Clasing, according to the plaintiffs, had violated her marriage contract by raising her son Catholic. To settle the matter, the privy council in Osnabrück instructed the lower court in Quackenbrück to interrogate the boy *ad protocollum* as to how he had been compelled.[28]

As a result of such pressures, contractual instruments that were originally intended to guarantee reciprocal freedom of religion and irenic, inter-confessional coexistence often became forms of coercion against conscience in everyday life. Family and neighbors were not solely responsible for these conflicts.

The confessional interests of princes and state churches also bore a share of responsibility. The final section of this chapter deals with everyday conflicts within mixed marriages, the question of conscience, and the role played by imperial laws that guaranteed freedom of religion.

Imperial Law in Everyday Life

Typically, the arbitrary exercise of sovereign territorial authority could be arrested only after long-winded petitioning and negotiations at the imperial diet. Oral and written grievances presented in 1748 to the electors of Cologne and Mainz by representatives of King George II of England, in his capacity as elector of Hanover, provide good illustrations. At the heart of these grievances was a charge against Catholic authorities, spiritual and ecclesiastic, in the prince-bishopric of Osnabrück. These, it was alleged, had abducted underage children who, according to marriage contracts, were to have been raised Lutheran. The children had been taken away from the surviving parent by force or in secret when he or she had refused to surrender them as the Lutheran authorities had demanded "under the perfectly reasonable pretext that children should be able to enjoy freedom of conscience" despite the fact that they were minors.[29]

The king's delegates demanded a mutually agreeable determination of the so-called age of majority (*annorum discretionis*), and forbade that all attempts to convert underage children. A legislative submission to the imperial diet in that same year bore the title "Provisional Grievances in Matters of Religion delivered in Regensburg 1748, *Protensum Regulativum Annorum Discretionis* of Children, Who Were Born *ex matrimonii mixta religionis*."[30] Members of the Catholic caucus (*corpus catholicorum*) rejected this demand on the grounds that the Peace of Westphalia had made no determination on this matter. In their opinion, accepting the Catholic faith should be possible at any time, because even underage children had the capacity for freedom of religion. The Protestant estates rejected the suggestion that underage children could exercise their own freedom of religion and demanded that the age of majority be set at fourteen. The Catholic side in turn rejected this position. Unless the *annorum discretionis* for changing religion in a mixed marriage were fixed, according to a report on the imperial diet in 1752, the "thorough-going equality [of religions] inscribed in the Peace of Westphalia, so piously invoked by both sides, would be destroyed at its foundations and go down to utter annihilation."[31] In the same year a corresponding grievance was presented to the emperor.

What had prompted the Osnabrück Affair, which had evidently so agitated the nobility of that prince-bishopric that its members found it necessary to assemble a petition, gather support for it among the Protestant estates of the realm, and present it to their territorial overlord, Clemens August, bishop of Osnabrück and archbishop of Cologne, to the *corpus evangelicorum* at the imperial diet in Regensburg, and finally to the emperor in Vienna?

According to the Protestants, Catholic nobles had compelled orphans and the children of bonded widows to convert, without regard for the terms of their parents' marriage contracts. Their grievance also charged that Catholic parents, relatives, guardians, clergy, and officials abducted children as a means to resolve conflicts over religious upbringing. Such actions violated both freedom of conscience and the terms of marriage contracts that remained binding for the life of both parents. When the father died, conflicts flared mainly over a widow's right to continue the children's religious upbringing. Here, the wishes of the widowed mother collided with the interests of other guardians, parish clergy, and relatives. Quite often in such cases, the women took their children across a territorial boundary in order to escape the grasp of secular authorities and to prevent separation from her children. Like many women in her situation, the widow Appelbaum had considered fleeing with her children into the neighboring prince-bishopric of Münster, a Catholic territory (her deceased husband had been Lutheran). Protestant clergy and officials anticipated this and sought to prevent it. Their observations shed light on legal realities involved, typical for the Holy Roman Empire, when for whatever reason a person sought to move from one zone of jurisdiction into another. They argued that because she had little property and lived near a border, it would be very easy for her, especially with the help of her better-off relatives, to flee one jurisdiction for another.[32]

These conflicts, which preoccupied the *corpus evangelicorum*, threatened to undermine the legal parity of the two confessions and clashed with legal custom and practice in Osnabrück. In mixed-marriage cases, one often stumbles across references to "the principle ... accepted by both sides" that children of either sex had to be raised in the father's religion "unless he determines otherwise or has entered into a marriage contract."[33] An entry in the *Codex Constitutionem Osnabrugensem* of 1738 notes that "all imperial estates of both religions" recognized the principle of *patria potestas* in the absence of a marriage contract.[34] This maxim, in turn, derived from a resolution of the commission charged with implementing the Peace of Westphalia, dated 14 September 1650. A complaint over the treatment of orphans had generated a series of legal questions. One concerned the problem of religious education in confessionally mixed households and considered several fraught situations: when the parents differed in religion, when no prenuptial contract existed, and when law did not specifically decree the manner of education. "How [then] shall children be treated? According to the *patria potestas* alone? Or should ... orphaned sons follow the father, the daughters the mother?"[35]

Legal opinions were solicited to answer these complex questions. The commission gave its provisional endorsement to the principle of *patria potestas*, finding that because the principal obligation for raising, nourishing, and instructing children fell principally to the father, the children are "subject to his disposition in ecclesiastical and secular matters." Yet this opinion also "prudently conceded" that the clauses of preexisting marriage contracts had to be taken into consideration and even observed.[36] Accordingly, in Osnabrück the maxim held "that the under-age children . . . must be educated in the religion with which the father was affiliated, if he had not agreed otherwise."[37]

The same ruling also provided that, at the request of legal guardians, widows were obligated to surrender all children of a different faith so that their instruction in the father's religion could continue. Yet mothers still had to provide sustenance for children that had been transferred to guardians against her will.[38] Did ordinary people know about these laws and act on them in their villages and farmsteads? Members of the consistory dealt with this question in February 1777, when they were confronted with the case of the Catholic widow Appelbaum. They felt certain that she knew of the rule because it had become custom in the territory and "is now everywhere heard from the mouth of the common man that sons follow the father and daughters the mother." Thus she had launched her plan in full cognizance of this maxim.[39]

In the legal record explicit references to this custom are at least as widespread as the position founded on *patria potestatis*. Marriage contracts, which had to be concluded in the presence of witnesses, formed the basis for sex-specific religious education. Only private, oral agreements lacked the necessary evidence. When conflicts arose in such cases, the courts took recourse to codified law: the education of all children must follow the father's religion. This was now demanded of the widow Appelbaum, albeit with the concession that she "was permitted under the customary practice of rural people in this territory" to raise her daughters in her own faith. She must surrender her son, however, to a Lutheran affinal kinsman, to be raised in the faith of his father.[40] A shepherd named Schadwinkel had already volunteered to assume the task. At an interrogation in Melle on 18 February 1778, however, the widow protested this decision, referring to the agreement that she had reached with her husband before their marriage in which he stipulated that "should God give them heirs," they would raise them as Catholics. Unfortunately, there was no written record of this accord.[41] But she was able to name one Lutheran and two Catholic witnesses present at the time who could attest to the family's religious practices. Despite the widow's statement, however, the tribunal found against her and ordered her to surrender her son to Schadwinkel to be raised in his father's religion.[42]

All seemed settled, but then the case took an unanticipated turn. When the time came to depose witnesses, the former man- and maidservant in the Appelbaum household both affirmed that the father had never been especially interested in the religious instruction of his children. Apparently an oral agreement had in fact existed, that the children would be raised in their mother's religion. The jurisprudential process in this case is revealing: first the case was decided on the basis of law, then custom, and only finally was it concluded on the evidence of practices in everyday life.

Apparently the rural population was conversant with more than custom and territorial law governing the resolution of conflicts over mixed marriage. References to freedom of religion in the period after 1648 were frequent, and husbands and wives based their claims on the demands of conscience and the constitutional right to free exercise of religion. The familial life of the confessionally mixed Fischer household in Osnabrück reflects the tension between freedom of religion and coercion of conscience, which spawned an escalation of conflicts so great they could no longer be resolved outside of court. Ultimately, imperial law determined the case. Here we return to the question posed at the beginning of this chapter concerning the everyday realities of family life in a confessionally mixed household. When Wilhelmina Steinmeyer, a Lutheran, and the Catholic Conrad Fischer had decided to marry, neither was prepared to adopt the other's religion. On 18 November 1766 the pair signed a marriage contract, in the presence of witnesses, "made necessary by caution" so that the couple "could live in a pleasant marriage ... considering that the groom and his future bride are not of the same religion." With regard to future children, the couple stipulated terms for the exercise of religion. They resolved that, "according to the customs of this territory," their daughters would follow Wilhelmina's religion, the sons Conrad's, and that "neither ... would ever interfere in any way with the other." Moreover, the couple "promised and pledged ... never to hinder each other in the exercise of religion, but to encourage one another, as the circumstances permit."[43]

In a bi-confessional territory like Osnabrück, this agreement would not seem to present problems. The Peace of Westphalia established the principle of parity in the prince-bishopric and divided the ecclesiastical properties on the basis of the so-called normative year (1 January 1624). A supplementary treaty, the *capitulatio perpetua*, stipulated that the office of prince-bishop should alternate between a Catholic occupant and a Protestant, who would be a member of the house of Braunschweig-Lüneburg.[44] A high degree of hybridity characterized everyday religious practice. In 1624 an episcopal visitor, Albert Lucenius, noted with disgust that Catholic parishioners in Iburg recited the *paternoster* in the Lutheran manner, with the addition "for thine is the kingdom, and the power, and the glory."[45]

In several parishes, the population divided evenly between the two confessions. In the village of Hunteburg, where Wilhelmina and Conrad Fischer lived, 60 percent were Catholic and 40 percent Lutheran.[46] The village had only a Catholic church, but the Lutherans were permitted to attend church in neighboring villages. Similarly, in Bohmte, where Wilhelmina had grown up, there was only a Catholic church, even though Protestants formed a majority. Private Lutheran services were held on the neighboring Arenhorst manor, although the Catholic prince-bishop was determined to stop this. Similar arrangements characterized the educational system: private Lutheran schools in Catholic parishes were tolerated when the prince-bishop was Lutheran, but restricted when a Catholic occupied the throne.[47] It was not uncommon for Lutherans to be allowed to attend Catholic services in their village, provided they paid the appropriate fee (*taxa stola*). The Catholic priest even performed baptisms, marriages, and funerals for Lutherans. The situation differed for Catholics, however, who segregated themselves more thoroughly and who were forbidden to attend any services except the Catholic mass.

Most studies of bi-confessionality in Osnabrück paint a picture of religious irenicism after 1648, marred by only a few clashes.[48] As proof of this, historians point to the participation of Protestants in Catholic processions, attendance at mass, as well as baptisms, marriages, and funerals conducted by ministers of a different religion. Even mixed marriages, which in the seventeenth and eighteenth centuries made up as many as 20 percent, serve as evidence of peaceable coexistence between the confessions. But the volume of grievances presented by Catholics and Protestants against interference with religious practice, as well as the records of investigations into conflicts over mixed marriage, call this interpretation into doubt. Confessional identity did not depend primarily on church attendance and official categorizations, but was predicated also on a private component, consisting of domestic instruction in religion and doctrine. Nevertheless, in cases of conflict over domestic instruction these were often played out in public, with the aid of relatives and coreligionists. In 1715 a district magistrate (*Amtmann*), who had been assigned the task of seizing children from their widowed Lutheran mother, complained that the children's grandmother, accompanied by a large throng of people, had accosted him on his doorstep. She said, "and I quote, [that] she would rather go to the market square with her grandson, whom she had raised, and have her [own] head chopped off than allow him to become Catholic." She then threw the order down on the ground and she and her daughter shouted "it's a dog's business, I shit on it!"[49]

In conflicts over mixed marriage, the criteria of confessional belonging, frequently brought into discussion by the parties themselves, repeatedly turn on questions of religious instruction. Take prayers, for instance. Was the "Our Father" prayer to be recited in the Catholic or the Lutheran form? What catechisms and devotional books should the household possess? In short, these matters touched on the whole range of religious practices in the family. The decisive criterion for determining confessional belonging, however, was first communion, which put on display the individual's official, confessional status and fixed it permanently. Even though everyday religious practice produced hybrid forms that diverged from theological standards of purity, strong confessional identities nevertheless formed among the population. These cannot be comprehended solely as a form of popular religiosity: they depended in large measure on the confessional criteria of the state churches.

In the everyday reality of confessionally mixed coexistence, toleration of those who believed differently presented a difficult task. Despite the noble intentions that Wilhelmina and Conrad Fischer set down in their contract, a bitter conflict ignited between them eleven years later over the education of their daughter, and prompted the wife to seek the aid of the territorial government. "Having been insulted for her conscience" she was compelled to watch "as her daughters, in flat contradiction of the marriage contract, were to be raised in the Catholic religion." When she attempted to intervene "to soothe her conscience," "discontent in the household" welled up. Indeed her husband even threatened "secretly to abduct the children, [an action] for which there are plenty of available examples."[50] In distress, Wilhelmina took refuge for a time with her brother. She then appealed to the government as "paternal protector" to intervene "so that, to the relief of her conscience and [in fulfillment] of the marriage contract, her daughters may be raised without hindrance in the Evangelical Religion." The conflict escalated: the husband brutally beat the wife on several occasions and temporarily abducted the daughters.

The Catholic priest in Hunteberg supported the husband and rejected all Wilhelmina's charges, referring to her as a woman of dubious "public reputation." The privy councilors in Osnabrück ordered compliance with the marriage contract and required the couple to reconcile themselves in the presence of the district fiscal officer for Wittlage and Hunteberg. But the peace did not last. Owing to "his evil disposition," the husband was incapable of improvement. A memorandum on the case from 1777 assigned guilt to Conrad:

> [T]he husband wants to convert his wife with a cudgel and force her to send the children to the Catholic school; he has pursued this mission for several years already and because the wife believed that their marriage contract supported her position and would be troubled in conscience if she acted against it, the wrath of the husband grew so great that in a few years she was obliged to flee from him.

In fact, outsiders had fueled the conflict. Conrad Fischer received frequent nocturnal visits from a Dominican monk, who was staying with the priest in Hunteberg. This monk "made Fischer believe that he was not obligated to adhere to the contract, God only knows for what evilly made-up reason, all of which Fischer explained to the priest personally." Evidently the Dominican had instigated other spouses in mixed marriages to adopt similarly defiant attitudes. In violation of the contract, Fischer forced his daughters to attend the Catholic school. Finally, in 1777 the privy council insisted that the monk be recalled to his monastery because he "had disrupted communal peace with the aim of depriving the children of these marriages of rights guaranteed to them under the imperial constitution." Only after he had been summoned to the district court and threatened with punishment did Fischer accede to the Lutheran education of his daughters. To the bitter end, he strove to raise at least one daughter a Catholic.

Thus Fischer forfeited his right as housefather to determine the religious education of his children. Although he belonged to the religious majority in his village, he was now a minority in his family. The marriage contract, which was originally inspired by the idea of toleration and the constitutionally guaranteed parity of religions, undermined his patriarchal authority. Fischer's situation was doubly grim because he had no sons, whom he might have raised in his own religion. The only avenue left to Fischer was the use of force, supported by the Catholic priest and a few officials. Even the privy council refused at first to hear his wife's complaint: "In this matter the wife should be instructed no longer to disrupt the domestic peace and to interpret a lawful castigation [by her husband] as religious persecution."[51] Despite her weakened position as a woman of ill repute, as an immigrant from another village, and as a member of a religious minority, Wilhelmina felt certain of her rights and believed herself justified by conscience and her marriage contract. Eventually, by invoking a valid marriage contract, peace was restored.

Not all familial relationships were founded on the obligation of wife and children to subordinate themselves to the *patria potestas* of the father. Wilhelmina Fischer resisted the demands of her husband by appealing to conscience and the terms of her marriage contract. When the *patria potestas* of the father and husband over his wife and children could be undermined by means of territorial law, marriage contracts, and the intervention of church and state officials, the impact on the internal organization of the family and the function of the family itself as an organizing element of the social structure was great. What were the implications in everyday life for the traditional hierarchy of gender, if a wife and mother, as in the case of the Fischer family, became responsible for the religious upbringing of children and servants? Conrad Fischer's reputation as a housefather must have been damaged terribly by this loss of authority.

Conclusion

The archives of bi-confessional territories yield up many similar cases from the seventeenth and eighteenth centuries, where tensions within confessionally mixed marriages erupted into open conflict. Individual conscience, marriage contracts, and claims to religious freedom guaranteed under imperial law formed the constant themes in these disputes, even when the particular instances varied widely. Unfortunately, while the surviving evidence often documents discord, it rarely allows more than a glimpse into the inner life of mixed marriages characterized by reciprocal toleration.

Treatises on mixed marriage before and after 1648, as well as the evidence of family life in confessionally blended households, offer insight into contradictions of religious pluralization. Individualization of religious convictions in the early modern period appealed to religious conscience and freedom of religion. It also had a limited emancipatory effect on gender relations and also affected church and state. That said, individualization cannot be equated with the privatization of religiosity or with secularization. On the contrary, the confessionalization of politics and society clearly persisted well into the eighteenth century, despite variations from one region to the next, and encumbered interactions with people of different faiths in everyday life. With regard to gender relations, it appears that women could undermine the patriarchal authority of their husbands by appealing to conscience, a marriage contract, or to the freedom of religion codified by the Peace of Westphalia.

A glance at secular legislation on mixed marriages in the nineteenth century shows a pronounced retreat from confessional considerations in favor of a concern with questions of political order. Rationalized as a means to counter the constant conflict in mixed marriages arising from questions about the religious education of children, virtually all German states adopted the principle of *patria potestas*. With few exceptions, among them Bavaria and Württemberg, marriage contracts that assigned confessional identity by gender or that allowed education in the mother's faith were now forbidden.

Notes

This chapter was translated by David M. Luebke.

1. Staatsarchiv Osnabrück [hereafter StAOS], Dep. 6 b 9/25 (1609–1612).
2. Carl Stüve, *Geschichte des Hochstifts Osnabrück von 1508–1623*, 3 vols. (Osnabrück, 1970), vol. 2, 668.
3. Freist, "One Body, Two Confessions."
4. Dagmar Freist, "Der Fall von Albini: Rechtsstreitigkeiten um die väterliche Gewalt in konfessionell gemischten Ehen," in Siegrid Westphal, ed., *In eigener Sache: Frauen vor den höchsten Gerichten des Alten Reiches*, ed. Siegrid Westphal (Cologne, 2005), 245–70.
5. Sächsisches Hauptstaatsarchiv Dresden [hereafter HStAD], Loc. 10333.
6. Ronald G. Asch, "'Denn es sind ja die Deutschen . . . ein frey Volk': Die Glaubensfreiheit als Problem der westfälischen Friedensverhandlungen," *Westfälische Zeitschrift* 148 (1998): 113–37.
7. Buchholz, *Recht, Religion und Ehe*, 352.
8. Ibid., 353.
9. Ezra 9:1–2. See also Gen. 24:3; Ex. 34:16; Deut. 7:3, 4; Jos. 23:12.
10. 1 Cor. 7:12–13.

11. Cited in Friedrich Benedikt Carpzov, *Dissertatio altera . . . de eo, quod consultum est, in nuptiis personarum diversae religionis* (Wittenberg, 1735), 68.

12. Georg Dedeken, *Thesauri consiliorum et decisionum*, 3 vols. (Jena, 1671), vol. 3, 172–74.

13. Christian Thomasius, *Rechtmäßige Erörterung der Ehe- und Gewissens Frage Ob zwei fürstliche Personen im Römischen Reich deren eine der Lutherischen die andere der Reformierten Religion zugetan ist einander mit gutem Gewissen heirathen können* (Halle, 1689).

14. Philipp Müller, *Der Fang des edlen Lebens durch frembde Glaubens-Ehe* (n.p., 1689).

15. Martin Luther, "Ein Sermon von dem ehlichen Stand," in WA, vol. 2, 166–71; idem, "Eine Predigt vom Ehestand," in ibid., vol. 17/I, 22–29. The rights and obligations of marriage partners were thoroughly discussed in the so-called "housefather literature"; see Julius Hoffmann, *Die "Hausväterliteratur" und die "Predigten über den christlichen Hausstand": Lehre vom Hause und Bildung für das häusliche Leben im 16., 17., und 18. Jahrhundert* (Weinheim, 1959).

16. Eph. 4:5–6.

17. Müller, *Der Fang des edlen Lebens*, 99.

18. Ibid., 68–69.

19. Dedeken, *Thesauri consiliorum*, vol. 3, 173.

20. Ibid., vol. 3, 175.

21. Müller, *Der Fang des edlen Lebens*, 74.

22. Ibid., 75.

23. Friedrich Kunstmann, *Die gemischten Ehen unter den christlichen Konfessionen Teutschlands* (Regensburg, 1839), 57.

24. Quoted in Carpzov, *Dissertatio altera*, 70.

25. Dedeken, *Thesauri consiliorum et decisionum*, vol. 3, 174–75.

26. Buchholz, *Recht, Religion, und Ehe*, 354; Carpzov, *Dissertatio altera*, 63.

27. Cited in Müller, *Der Fang des edlen Lebens*, 129 (referring to the Council of Trent, canon IV.c.59).

28. StAOS Rep. 100 374, 12 (1742), fol. 27.

29. HStAD Loc. 30231 (*Conclusum Corporis Evangelicorum de dato 12 Aprilis*, 1752). See also StAOS Rep. 100 374, 12 (1748–52).

30. StAOS Rep. 100 374, 12 (1748–52), fol. 1.

31. Ibid..

32. StAOS Rep. 100 374, 22 (1778), fos. 2–3.

33. Ibid.

34. *Codex Constitutionem Osnabrugensem*, 2 parts (Osnabrück, 1800), part 1, vol. 2, 1090-1091; Aegidius Kloentrup, Art. "Religions-Zustand," in idem, *Alphabetisches Handbuch der besonderen Rechte und Gewohnheiten des Hochstifts Osnabrück mit Rücksicht auf die benachbarten westfälischen Provinzen*, 3 vols. (Osnabrück, 1798–1800), vol. 3, 110–17, here 111–12.

35. Session of the *Friedensexecutionsdeputation* in Nuremberg, 10/20 August 1650, in Johann Gottfried Meiern, ed., *Acta Pacis Publicationis Publica: Oder, Westphälische Friedens-Handlungen und Geschichte*, 6 vols. (Hanover, 1734–36), 2, Book 12, § 12.

36. Karl Schmidt, *Die Confession der Kinder nach den Landesrechten im deutschen Reiche* (Freiburg, 1890), 33.

37. *Codex Constitutionem Osnabrugensem*, part 1, vol. 2, 1090–91.

38. Ibid., 1091.

39. StAOS Rep. 100 374, 22 (1778), fols. 2–3.

40. Ibid., fol. 8.

41. Ibid., fol. 13.
42. Ibid., fol. 26.
43. StAOS Rep. 100 374, 20 (1766).
44. For the *capitulatio perpetua* of 1650, see *Codex Constitutionis Osnabrugensis*, part 1, 2, 1635–60. See also Gerd Steinwascher, "Die konfessionellen Folgen des Westfälischen Friedens für das Fürstbistum Osnabrück," *Niedersächsisches Jahrbuch für Landesgeschichte* 71 (1999): 51–80.
45. Cited in Anton Schindling, "Reformation, Gegenreformation und Katholische Reform im Osnabrücker Land und im Emsland," *Osnabrücker Mitteilungen* 94 (1989): 35–60, here 49.
46. The following account relies on Hermann Hoberg, *Die Gemeinschaft der Bekenntnisse in kirchlichen Dingen: Rechtszustände im Fürstentum Osnabrück vom Westfälischen Frieden bis zum Anfang des 19. Jahrhundert* (Osnabrück, 1939).
47. The proper religious education of children was an important order to inculcate true belief in them. There was a Lutheran private school mentioned in Hunteberg in 1720.
48. See Steinwascher, "Die konfessionellen Folgen."
49. StAOS Rep 100 374, 1 (1715). Translator's note: "dog's business" is a loose rendering of the untranslatable original, *Hasenputzerei*.
50. StAOS Rep. 100 374, 20 (1775–77). Unless otherwise indicated, the following quotations are from this source.
51. StAOS Rep. 150 Wit no. 1691.

CHAPTER 7

~:~

The Rhetoric of Difference
The Marriage Negotiations between Queen Christina of Sweden and Elector Friedrich Wilhelm of Brandenburg

DANIEL RICHES

The suggestion of a potential match between Queen Christina of Sweden (1626–1689) and Elector Friedrich Wilhelm of Brandenburg (1620–1688) was debated over the course of fifteen years but never came to be. An acute consciousness of difference between the prospective partners stood at the center of the rhetoric surrounding the marriage plan. Interestingly, both opponents *and* proponents of the Brandenburg–Swedish match seized on this developed sense of difference as an organizing principle of their countervailing positions. Marriage supporters in particular highlighted the potential of a union between significantly different partners to function (in Victor Turner's terms) as a liminal moment that would entail the reexamination (and perhaps reconfiguration) of assumptions of difference themselves, with auspicious results for political and confessional harmony in the Protestant North. The nature of this rhetoric highlights the propensity of the issue of marriage to lead to a fixation on matters of difference in the early modern world, as well as the symbolic power that the combination of marriage and difference could wield in an early modern context.

The basic parameters of the marriage talks have attracted prior scholarly attention and need only quick review here.[1] The precise genesis of the idea for a marriage alliance between Christina and Friedrich Wilhelm is not entirely clear, although it appears to have originated with Christina's father Gustav Adolf in 1631, when the prospective couple were still children and heirs to the thrones they would eventually occupy.[2] Christina herself was the issue of a Brandenburg–Swedish match, her mother Maria Eleonora being a Brandenburg princess by birth and the aunt of Friedrich Wilhelm. By 1632, high-level—although secretive—discussions regarding the marriage were taking place, and they continued off and on until 1636, when Brandenburg accepted the Peace of Prague and joined the ranks of Sweden's enemies in the ongoing Thirty Years' War.[3] Talks resumed shortly after Friedrich Wilhelm came to power in 1640 and withdrew Brandenburg from the imperial alliance. But no agreement could be reached: the negotiations dragged on inconclusively until the increasingly impatient elector permanently slammed the door shut to a Swedish marriage by marrying Luise Henrietta of Orange in 1646.[4]

Factions in favor of and opposed to the marriage were present in both Sweden and Brandenburg, indeed throughout Europe, and nearly all involved engaged in the discussion of difference. The use of arguments based on difference by opponents of the marriage is not surprising, and their contentions are more straightforward and a good deal less interesting than those advanced by the marriage's supporters. The opponents' arguments were rooted in the premise that the marriage partners and the states they represented were so fundamentally different that a match between them would be unworkable. This claim can be broken down into four components. The first dealt with rank. Christina was heiress to a kingdom that without much exaggeration could be considered a rising empire, whereas Brandenburg was a mere electorate whose inability to project power or even to defend the integrity of its own territory was made plain by the ongoing events of the Thirty Years' War. Opponents of the match stressed to the Swedes that they would be marrying down in the world, and to the Brandenburgers that the ambitious Friedrich Wilhelm would be confined perpetually to the role of junior partner if the marriage were to occur. Maria Eleonora herself expressed the desire that her daughter marry someone of higher station than her own brother's son.[5]

Related to arguments of rank was a second set of arguments that stressed differences in nationality and political culture. Those opposed to the marriage plan in Sweden raised the specter of importing a foreign lord and feared that the hordes of foreign officials who would accompany him would threaten Swedish national independence. The Swedish Council of the Realm, for example, raised concerns in 1633 that Friedrich Wilhelm "was not raised in our Swedish customs, and one can fear many great changes in our Fatherland under foreign rule," adding that "his rule is so much more to be feared since he … could easily make encroachments on our freedoms."[6] No less an observer than Samuel Pufendorf, who had lived and served in both Sweden and Brandenburg in the course of his career, noted that Chancellor Axel Oxenstierna and others in Sweden worried over Friedrich Wilhelm's ability to negotiate with the Swedish Estates and guarantee them their liberties in the appropriate Swedish fashion.[7] In this light it should come as no surprise that even those Swedish proposals in favor of the marriage insisted from the outset that Friedrich Wilhelm be brought to Sweden and steeped in Swedish language and customs. Only if he transformed himself into a Swede, in other words, would Friedrich Wilhelm make an acceptable partner for Christina.[8] It should equally come as no surprise that many Brandenburgers, including supporters of the match, responded negatively to the perceived need to reprogram their prince before the plan could proceed. The perception of a mismatch in national and political culture was a significant hurdle over which the champions of the marriage needed to find a way to navigate.

The third group of arguments offered by marriage opponents focused not on differences between the prospective pair, but rather on differences between Christina and the prevailing gender conventions of the day, and the consequences these differences could pose to Friedrich Wilhelm. In what can only be taken as an effort to scare the elector off, Axel Oxenstierna went out of his way to describe the young queen to Brandenburg diplomats sent to negotiate on the marriage issue as a headstrong, independent-minded intellectual.[9] Given the image of the ideal wife extolled in countless Protestant sermons and marriage manuals that centered on her dutiful submission to the authority of the male partner, Oxenstierna's description of Christina could hardly have painted the picture of the kind of woman a seventeenth-century German Protestant man would want to take as wife, especially if she outranked him to boot.[10] Oxenstierna may here have been playing off of the *Siemann*—or "she-man"—trope, in which a "domineering wife" runs roughshod over her "humiliated, henpecked husband" to his universal derision.[11]

Lurking behind these claims about Christina's character was the even more damning suggestion of transgressive sexuality. Heterosexual activity for the purpose of producing an heir had always been a fundamental expectation in dynastic marriage negotiations. Along with this came the Reformation redefinition of marriage as an estimable institution designed to grant legitimate (and controlled) expression to the natural, God-given sexual desire that only a miniscule fraction of individuals could wholly resist.[12] Sexual relations between husband and wife therefore stood at the center of Protestant understandings of marriage and "[f]ailure to observe this conjugal responsibility . . . contradicted the very purpose of marriage."[13] Opponents of the marriage sent out signals that the queen may not have been inclined to fulfill this crucial sexual role. Rumors of lesbianism had swirled around Christina since she was still a teenager. Johan Oxenstierna, the son of Axel Oxenstierna and one of the lead Swedish negotiators at Westphalia, declared in a moment of alcohol-assisted candor and with what a contemporary source pointedly describes as a laugh that questions of Christina's marriage were mute, since the queen had resolved never to marry anyone.[14] Other highly placed Swedes who opposed the marriage plan showed more decorum in spreading the message that Christina was not the sort to marry.[15]

While arguments like those discussed above made a powerful case, the fourth and by far most important point of difference raised by opponents of the marriage dealt with religion: Friedrich Wilhelm was Reformed; Christina from staunchly and almost uniformly Lutheran Sweden. Virtually everyone— regardless of whether they wanted the marriage to take place or not—identi- fied the religious issue as the most substantial obstacle standing in its way.[16] The antipathy with which members of the two main Protestant denomina- tions frequently regarded one another resonates with Freud's concept of the "narcissism of small differences," in which generally similar groups "construe … nuance of difference in oppositional terms" for the purpose of constructing and strengthening their own group identity.[17] As Dagmar Freist's contribu- tion to this volume shows, all confessionally mixed marriages sharpened this effect because they raised the charged question of religious upbringing for the children.[18] Dynastic mixed marriages were even more fraught because of their potential impact on the entire polity. This was certainly a concern in Sweden, where anti-Calvinism had broad and deep roots and talk of a potential mar- riage between Christina and a Reformed prince was bound to stir up popular resistance. One set of Brandenburg diplomats wrote in the context of the mar- riage talks that "the clergy and common man in Sweden fear Calvinists more than Papists," while another diplomat in Stockholm negotiating on the matter reported that the sentiment on the street was that "if one religion is practiced in the city, but a different one in the palace, then secret Calvinists could make an appearance, which would change the whole land."[19] King Gustav Adolf's solution to this dilemma was simple and firm: Friedrich Wilhelm's relocation to Sweden would include his conversion to Lutheranism.[20] Brandenburg's Re- formed councilors, in turn, argued against any thoughts of buying a crown at the price of the elector's conscience. And Christina herself—ironically, in light of her subsequent conversion to Catholicism—rejected the idea that Friedrich Wilhelm should convert, declaring with some vehemence that "others should not place their faith in those who disown their God."[21] One of the prospective partners would face tough decisions on the religious front if the marriage plan were to be made to work.

Opponents of the marriage argued that the differences they described were irreconcilable, and that the barrier they posed to a successful match was insur- mountable. These arguments appear to have been internalized by one of the marriage plan's most ardent and consistent supporters who stood to be most directly affected by its outcome, Friedrich Wilhelm himself. When in 1646 he gave order to his diplomats to finally give up on pursuing the match, the elector listed a litany of reasons that could have been taken straight from the mouths of the plan's detractors: the confessional difference was fundamental and de- fied solution; Christina herself viewed the match as unworkable; even if the marriage were to occur his children would be viewed forever as foreigners in

Sweden; and it would be shameful "if I had to wait upon the Queen as a mere chamberlain."[22] So it appears the arguments of difference had won, not only in helping see to it that the marriage never took place, but also even in winning over some of the opposing side to their logic.[23]

This, however, is only half of the story, since working against the marriage was only one direction in which the rhetoric of difference could be employed. The deeper connections between marriage and difference begin to emerge only when one examines how those in favor of the marriage pointed to some of the same differences as the greatest *attractions* of the proposed match and the strongest reasons why it should take place. The key to understanding this attractive side of difference lies in the special status and symbolic power that the institution of marriage enjoyed in early modern Europe. That dynastic marriages could serve as tangible markers of good intentions between ruling houses that were otherwise antagonistic toward one another is well understood. To those whose aims were not limited to the idiom of traditional high politics, however, the Brandenburg–Swedish marriage plan held a much richer symbolic value. For them, this marriage between significantly different partners held the potential to radically reshape their world across a much broader and deeper array of issues, ranging from the bitter territorial dispute over Pomerania to more transcendent matters of Lutheran-Calvinist union.

As Joel Harrington and others have shown, marriage was seen as a model for, and constitutive element of, nearly all early modern understandings of social and political order.[24] Protestants in particular saw marriage as "the cornerstone of society, the institution on which all other institutions were based."[25] It was, as Isabel Hull has noted, "the institution where the divine and the human meet," where "God's order for individuals and society becomes fully congruent" and "God's plan for human destiny" were fulfilled.[26] Added to this was the supercharged, multivocal symbolic overload of any issue related to sexuality, a symbolism that often reached into the realm of the transcendent.[27] Early modern marriage thus held a real potential to resonate on multiple levels, and to build connections between diverse matters of fundamental importance.

In this respect marriage holds similarities to the organizing concept of this chapter: difference. The literary critic Mark Currie has written that "the concept of difference has a rather unusual power to link the realms of social identity, philosophy, political power and the nature of language."[28] In doing so, difference—like marriage—participates in the construction of the relationships and codes of meaning through which people understand themselves and the world around them. The connection between early modern marriage and difference, however, went beyond the merely analogous. David Sabean and Simon Teuscher have recently shown that early modern marriage patterns often aimed at seeking out the dissimilar as marriage partners, those so-called strangers notably different from each other, in contrast to the pronounced modern preference for marriages amongst the familiar that developed from the middle of the eighteenth century.[29] Susan Karant-Nunn has noted how early modern German communities drew upon the symbolic power of the marriage ritual to create conditions for "social perdurance" between "persons and groups with genuine differences."[30] In her study of marriage and violence in early modern English texts, Frances Dolan has gone even further to suggest that there is something intrinsic to marriage in the West that involves joining together the incompatible or even irreconcilable.[31]

Early modern marriage, then, brought symbolic richness into contact with a focus on the negotiation of difference. To link this combination back to the proposed match between Christina and Friedrich Wilhelm, let us turn to Victor Turner's concept of liminality, a move inspired by Abby Zanger's interesting study of the imagery surrounding Louis XIV's marriage to the Spanish princess María Teresa.[32] Turner wrote at length on the ritual process, and in particular on rites of passage—those transformative, ritual moments that move their participants from one state of being into another. The middle stage in this ritual process is liminality, where initiates are suspended between their previous state and that toward which they are moving without truly being part of either, where they are in Turner's famous phrase "betwixt and between" in an "interstructural phase in social dynamics" where the symbolism of ambiguity is made intelligible and given positive valence. Much like early modern marriage, the liminal "stood in close connection with deity or with superhuman power."[33]

Two aspects of Turner's theory of liminality are of special value for looking at the appeal of the Brandenburg–Swedish marriage plan. The first is *communitas*, the particular bonds of unity and the elision of structural gradations that arise among those who find themselves together in a liminal state. Turner referred to this group as a "community or comity of comrades and not a structure of hierarchically arrayed positions" where distinctions of rank, age, kinship and the like are replaced by the spirit of "[e]ach for all, and all for each."[34] Even more powerful than the ability of liminality to produce *communitas* was its capacity to reconfigure structure itself. Turner described liminality as the "realm of pure possibility whence novel configurations of ideas and relations may arise," adding that "[l]iminality . . . breaks, as it were, the cake of custom and enfranchises speculation."[35] Those passing through this process "are withdrawn from their structural positions and consequently from the values, norms, sentiments, and techniques associated with those positions. They are also divested of their previous habits of thought, feeling, and action. During the liminal period, neophytes are alternately forced and encouraged to think about their society, their cosmos, and the powers that generate and sustain them."[36]

The liminal element of ritual action could be especially potent with regard to linguistically constructed categories such as difference. Currie notes that the very concept of difference arises from the repeated, habitual, taken-for-granted aspects of naming via language, with our sense of difference between two entities becoming more powerful the more automatically the process of naming them runs.[37] Ritual action, on the other hand, has the power to communicate outside the confines of language, to "give access to emotional states that resist expression in language [and] convey complex messages without saying a single word."[38] Symbolic events such as a marriage can operate beyond the limits of rational modes of political activity and thus strive to accomplish different kinds of work.[39]

In transcending language, the liminal not only opens up new realms of possibility and action, but also exposes the constructed-ness of traditional categories such as difference. Turner wrote that those experiencing liminality are pushed "into thinking hard about the elements and basic building blocks of symbolic complexes they had hitherto taken for granted as 'natural' units."[40] Once the categories of difference are thus denaturalized, the strength of their pull on our understanding wanes. Those sharing in *communitas* are liberated from the "encumbrances . . . of role, status, reputation, class, caste, sex or other structural niche."[41] These and other social structures of difference are exposed as arbitrary, while the underlying common ground shared amongst individuals and groups but normally concealed beneath categorical divisions is revealed.[42]

Once freed from obligation to defer to prevailing conceptions of difference, participants in liminality can engage in radical rethinking and creative experimentation. Turner wrote of the play of liminality in which the fundamental elements of social structure can be examined "from a liminal or antistructural distance [and] reflected upon, isolated, rearranged, assigned new meaning, rejected, approved, given new weight, depreciated, and attached to new symbols."[43] Under these conditions, new categories of understanding can be created, new modes of being explored, new shared identities crafted.[44]

For many of the diplomats, political advisers, and irenic theologians who supported the Brandenburg–Swedish marriage, the proposed match carried precisely this transformative, creative potential to rethink and reconfigure their world and bring resolution to seemingly irreconcilable dilemmas that appeared impervious to political solution. It had the power to do so *because of*, rather than in spite of, the myriad differences between the prospective partners and their states. In fact, preserving an awareness of difference between the parties was required if supporters of the marriage were to be able to harness the full symbolic force of *communitas* to help bring a new order into being.[45] It seems likely that the original impetus for the marriage plan grew out of the recognition—and this could indeed have been foreseen as early as 1631—that Brandenburg's and Sweden's competing claims to Pomerania would lock the two into a cycle of animosity that neither could afford unless a creative and unexpected solution could be found. Supporters of the marriage in both Brandenburg and Sweden stressed to the very end that the marriage presented the best, and perhaps only, mutually acceptable solution to the Pomeranian issue.[46] There was surely an element of salesmanship here in attempting to sell the merits of the plan to the powers that be, but this was coupled with the legitimate belief that marriage across lines of difference could create the space for conflict resolution in ways that traditional political exertion could not.[47]

In fact, supporters of the match claimed that the plan would not only untie the Pomeranian knot, but also would more fundamentally produce a political combination of an entirely new kind. A French supporter of the plan told a skeptical Swedish diplomat that the marriage would produce "a power of the sort there has not been in Europe," referring I believe not only to the scope of power a Brandenburg–Swedish combination would wield, but also to its unique nature.[48] The idea implicit here of dramatic or even revolutionary political recombination—of a scrambling of political structures—would have resonated with Swedish plans for creating a new political constellation to challenge the Reich in the North that would unite both German and non-German, those living within the confines of the Reich and those without, those oriented toward the sea and those tied to land.[49] The energy and potency of the new creation would have been accentuated rather than hindered by a consciousness of its novel combination of difference.

The greatest attraction of the plan for many of its champions, however, was the prospect that its symbolic negotiation of difference could drive fundamental change in the realm of religion. Talk of a union between Lutheran and Reformed dynasties sent a dramatic burst of energy through irenic circles, which in turn provided many of the plan's staunchest advocates. Individuals such as Sigismund von Götze and Johann Bergius in Brandenburg, and Johan Adler Salvius in Sweden, saw the marriage plan as an opportunity sent by God to fulfill His desire of reunifying His Protestant church. Götze, for instance, wrote to Axel Oxenstierna that the advent of the marriage plan "must be considered a certain sign of Divine providence," words that fit perfectly with early modern theories of marriage as the location where God carries out His plan for man.[50] The marriage talks were a motor that rattled the foundations of confessional antipathy and set in motion sustained efforts to seek agreement between the faiths that would not only allow the marriage to go forward, but also would more importantly have profound and lasting ramifications for the Protestant world. Gustav Adolf told Brandenburg diplomats that a solution to the religious aspects of the marriage should be sought through a formal, interconfessional reconciliation (*Konfessionsausgleich*) of the sort Bergius advocated at the Leipzig Colloquy of 1631.[51] The transformative potential of this proposed mixed match was such that it could even move a leader as risk-and-change averse as the cautious Georg Wilhelm to call repeatedly for a synod of Lutheran and Reformed theologians to iron out the differences between their faiths, efforts that were continued with gusto by his son in the 1640s.[52] Here again, the consciousness of difference between the prospective marriage partners was a creative rather than restrictive force, invigorating those working to reconfigure their world.

Many of the supporters of the Brandenburg–Swedish marriage therefore embraced the fact that the match would bring together partners from polities and confessions broadly recognized as significantly different, in the belief that through the ritual of coming together in marriage the very bases of these categories of difference would be undermined and the energy thus released would be harnessed as a vehicle for fundamental change. The marriage of Christina and Friedrich Wilhelm could lead the way in remaking the political and religious constellation of early modern northern Europe, and could itself serve as a model of change for the broader world to follow.[53]

An examination of the rhetoric of difference associated with the Brandenburg–Swedish marriage plan gives rise to questions of broader scope for those interested in the study of diplomatic interaction. First, for those movements that seek the fundamental reconfiguration of boundaries and structures, might the maintenance of a sense of difference from one's negotiating partner rather than a narrow fixation on accentuating pieces of common ground not be such a bad thing, at least insofar as one wishes to mobilize the energy of symbolic action to challenge the status quo?[54] Or to phrase things slightly differently, do we require a symbolic vehicle built from a sense of difference in order to enter into the liminal; to, as Turner would say, "break the cake of custom" in a way that more rationally driven efforts, no matter how earnest and persistent, cannot; to find that elusive "realm of pure possibility" where fundamental change is truly possible? Perhaps, ironically, success in things like irenic movements might hinge more on preserving a consciousness of difference between the groups than on its elision, at least until the transformative power of liminality has had a chance to breed some *communitas*.[55]

Finally, the focus in this chapter on a *rhetoric* of difference that flowed freely between Brandenburgers and Swedes (and others as well) makes one wonder whether those seeking to understand the semiotics of early modern diplomacy would be well served in shifting our focus away from more culturally bounded notions of political culture and toward the more fluid concept of discourses which, like early modern diplomatic life itself, paid scant heed to state or national borders?

Acknowledgments

The author would like to acknowledge the generous support of the University of Alabama's Research Grants Committee for helping fund research for this chapter.

Notes

1. Most general works on seventeenth-century Brandenburg or Swedish history discuss the basics of the marriage plan. More extended, if dated, treatments include Richard Schulze, *Das Project der Vermählung Friedrich Wilhelms von Brandenburg mit Christina von Schweden* (Halle, 1898); Oscar Malmström, I. *Änkedrottning Maria Eleonora och hennes Flykt till Danmark. II. Underhandlingarna om ett Giftermål mellan Kristina af Sverige och Friedrich Wilhelm af Brandenburg* (Helsingborg, 1895); and Richard Armstedt, *Der schwedische Heiratsplan des Grossen Kurfürsten* (Königsberg, 1896).

2. The king likely raised the issue during a discussion with Brandenburg chancellor Sigismund von Götze at Bärwalde in January 1631; see Malmström, *Änkedrottning*, xii; Johannes Kretzschmar, "Die Allianzverhandlungen Gustav Adolfs mit Kurbrandenburg im Mai und Juni 1631," *Forschungen zur Brandenburgischen und Preußischen Geschichte* 17 (1904): 341–82, here 380; Michael Roberts, *Gustavus Adolphus: A History of Sweden 1611–1632*, 2 vols. (London, 1953–58), vol. 2, 512. The claim that the impetus for the marriage plan came from Gustav Adolf himself is supported by a seventeenth-century annotated index of documents relating to Swedish–Brandenburg relations found in the Svenska Riksarkiv and entitled "Notitia Actorum inter Potentissimos Reges Sueciæ et Serenissimos Electores Brandeburgicos, a tempore Regis Gustavi Adolphi." Under the section for 1631 it reads, "wid denna tyden att drifwa på ett gifftermåhl emellan hennes Kl: Mtt: drottning Christina och ChurPrintzen. Salig Kl. Mtt. hade sielf forst gifwit anledning dertill, och jämwal begynet derom att tractera; så mycket mehra syntes det nu Regeringen att wara nyttigt . . . som det Kgl: och Churfurstl: huset . . . belfwa dergenom narmare förbunden"; Svenska Riksarkiv [hereafter RA], Diplomatica, Brandenburgico-Borussica, vol. 206.

3. Talks took place in 1632 at Frankfurt between Swedish Chancellor Axel Oxenstierna, Götze, and Gerhard Romilian von Kalcheim, genannt Leuchtmar. By April 1632 Götze and Leuchtmar were sounding cautiously optimistic about the chances for success in the marriage issue. See Sigismund von Götze to von dem Knesebeck, Frankfurt/Main, 17 April 1632. Geheimes Staatsarchiv, Preußischer Kulturbesitz [hereafter GStA PK], I. HA, Rep. 24c., no. 4, fasc. 3, 24r–31v, here 29v. On the deterioration of Brandenburg–Swedish relations in the years after Gustav Adolf's death in 1632, leading to the full break in 1636, see Torgny Höjer, "Brandenburgs Brytning med Sverige Efter Gustav Adolfs Död," *Historisk Tidskrift* 68 (1948): 197–238. See also Malmström, *Änkedrottning*, xiv.

4. By spring 1641 Leuchtmar, who was in Sweden to negotiate a Brandenburg–Swedish armistice, was being encouraged to raise the marriage issue; see Samuel von Winterfeld to [Sigismund von Götze], Hamburg, 19/29 May 1641. *Urkunden und Actenstücke zur Geschichte des Kurfürsten Friedrich Wilhelm von Brandenburg* [hereafter UA], 23 vols. (Berlin, 1864–1930), vol. 1, 538–42, here 539. Leuchtmar discussed the matter with Johan Oxenstierna at Stralsund and Stettin in January 1642, and the following month Johan Adler Salvius wrote to Axel Oxenstierna that the elector seemed poised to pursue the marriage with Christina publicly, whereas everything had been done indirectly and in secret before; see Johan Adler Salvius to Axel Oxenstierna, Hamburg, 5 [15] February 1642, UA, vol. 23, 19. On the discussions in January 1642, see Malmström, *Änkedrottning*, xiv. Friedrich Wilhelm himself wrote to Axel Oxenstierna in July 1642 asking for his support in the marriage negotiations. Friedrich Wilhelm to Axel Oxenstierna, Königsberg, 27 July 1642, UA, vol. 23, 33. Several historians have pointed out

that Friedrich Wilhelm turned to the Orange match only after concluding that the Swedes were stringing him along on the marriage issue. Ferdinand Schevill wrote that "at length he [Friedrich Wilhelm] could no longer blind himself to the fact that the Swedes were making sport of him." See his *The Great Elector* (Chicago, 1947), 117. Derek McKay added that "by the end of 1645 Frederick William accepted he had been led a dance"; McKay, *The Great Elector* (Harlow, 2001), 30.

5. For concerns about the discrepancy in rank, see Schulze, *Project der Vermählung*, 14; Reinhold Koser, *Geschichte der brandenburgischen Politik bis zum Westfälischen Frieden von 1648* (Stuttgart, 1913), 490–92; Ulrich Kober, *Eine Karriere im Krieg: Graf Adam von Schwarzenberg und die kurbrandenburgische Politik von 1619 bis 1641* (Berlin, 2004), 294. For Elector Georg Wilhelm's sensitivity to such arguments and efforts to counter them, see Georg Wilhelm to Kurt Bertram von Pfuel, Cöln an der Spree, 28 June 1633, GStA PK, I. HA, Rep. 11, no. 247I Schweden, fasc. 7, 1r–36r.

6. "2) Där han ock icke blefve i våra svenske seder uppfödd, skulle man många stora förändringer, som för detta under främmande herrskap i vårt fädernesland äro förorsakade, hafva att befara. 3) Och vore hans härskande så mycket mera att frukta, som han är själf mäktig och oss lätteligen skall kunna i våra friheter göra intrång"; Rådets memorial till Axel Oxenstierna, Stockholm, 29 Mach 1633, printed in full in Malmström, *Änkedrottning*, xii–xxiv. It is important to note that the council balanced these concerns against other factors and eventually arrived at a qualified and cautious approval of at least exploring the marriage plans further.

7. "Cancellarii tamen Oxenstiernæ mens erat, id connubium Sueciæ non expedire. Nam præter discrepantiam circa sacra, Principem eum pervicaci videri ingenio, cui cum splendidum patrimonium sit, Sueciam minus cordi fore. Extaneis Regibus solitum Sueciam opibus exhaurire, easque cum præcipuis muneribus in populares suos transferre. Nec suevisse eum cum Ordinibus tractare, & eorum libertatem ferre. Fortasse & ipsum amitæ exemplo cœlum, solumque Sueciæ fastiditurum"; Samuel Pufendorf, *Commentariorum de Rebus Suecicis Libri XXVI. Ab expeditione Gustavi Adolfi Regis in Germaniam ad abdicationem usque Christinæ* (Utrecht, 1686), 493.

8. Michael Roberts wrote of Gustav Adolf's plans for the marriage in 1632 that the king viewed it as "an essential condition that the Prince be brought up as a Swede in Sweden": Roberts, *Gustavus Adolphus*, vol. 2, 645–46. See also Malmström, *Änkedrottning*, xiii; Schulze, *Project der Vermählung*, 3–5; and Pufendorf, *Rebus Suecicis*, 101–2.

9. See Leuchtmar's diary for his 1642 mission to Sweden, excerpts of which are printed in UA, vol. 1, 591–95. See also Schulze, *Project der Vermählung*, 27.

10. McKay notes that Friedrich Wilhelm pursued marriage with Christina "despite her reputation as a headstrong bluestocking"; see his *Great Elector*, 30. On early modern German Protestant concepts of the ideal husband and wife, see Harrington, *Reordering Marriage*, esp. 71–82; Ozment, *When Fathers Ruled*, esp. ch. 2; and Susan Karant-Nunn, *Reformation of Ritual: An Interpretation of Early Modern Germany* (London, 1997), 6–42. For a selection of documents expressing Luther's own views, see Susan C. Karant-Nunn and Merry E. Wiesner-Hanks, eds., *Luther on Women: A Sourcebook* (Cambridge, UK, 2003), 88–136.

11. Harrington, *Reordering Marriage*, 79–80.

12. On Protestant attitudes toward sexuality and marriage, see Merry E. Wiesner-Hanks, *Christianity and Sexuality in the Early Modern World* (London, 2000), 63–67; Harrington, *Reordering Marriage*, 59–68; Isabel V. Hull, *Sexuality, State, and Civil Society in Germany, 1700–1815* (Ithaca, 1996), 17–24; Lyndal Roper, "Luther: Sex, Marriage

and Motherhood," *History Today* 33, no. 12 (December 1983): 33–38. For Luther's own writings on sexuality, see Karant-Nunn and Wiesner-Hanks, *Luther on Women*, 137–70.

13. Thomas Max Safley, *Let No Man Put Asunder: The Control of Marriage in the German Southwest: A Comparative Study, 1550–1600* (Kirksville, 1984), 33–34. Wiesner-Hanks adds that in Protestant thought "marriages in which it [sexual desire] could not be satisfied . . . were not truly marriages"; see her *Christianity and Sexuality*, 63.

14. "Darüber hätte *Oxenstjerna* gelacht, wäre sehr trunken gewesen und hätte selbsten von der Königin zu reden angefangen und gesagt, es wäre nun gar in andern Terminis, als es vor diesem gewesen; die Königin in Schweden hätte sich nun anders resolvirt, und würde nimmer heiraten"; Brandenburg Gesandten in Osnabrück to Friedrich Wilhelm, Osnabrück, 9 [19] February 1646, UA, vol. 4, 424–25, here 425.

15. See Leuchtmar's diary for his 1642 mission to Sweden, UA, vol. 1, 591–95, here 595.

16. One was Chancellor Axel Oxenstierna; see Leuchtmar's diary, UA, vol. 1, 591–95, here 593. For more on Oxenstierna's identification of the confessional issue as a great challenge facing the marriage plans, see Sigismund von Götze to Georg Wilhelm, Mainz, 15 January 1635. GStA PK, I. HA, Rep. 24c., no. 9, fasc. 3; Schulze, *Project der Vermählung*, 24–25; and Höjer, "Brandenburgs Brytning," 203.

17. Mark Currie, *Difference* (London, 2004), 18, 86. Freud discussed the "narcissism of small differences" in *Das Unbehagen in der Kultur* (Vienna, 1930), 85. See also Freud's *Group Psychology and the Analysis of the Ego*, tr. and ed. James Strachey (New York, 1989), 42.

18. On the importance of the issue of the children's religious education in conflicts surrounding interconfessional marriages in early modern Germany, see Dagmar Freist's contribution to this volume; and her "One Body, Two Confessions."

19. "Dass sich die Pfaffen und der gemeine Mann in Schweden mehr vor den Calvinisten als Papisten fürchteten"; Brandenburg Gesandten in Osnabrück to Friedrich Wilhelm, Osnabrück, 24 November [4 December] 1645, UA, vol. 4, 413; "ty, om i staden utöfvandes en religion, men på slottet en annan, vid hvilken de hemliga kalvinisterna kunde infinna sig, så skulle sådant alterera hela landet"; cited in Malmström, *Änkedrottning*, xx.

20. See Roberts, *Gustavus Adolphus*, vol. 2, 645–46; and Malmström, *Änkedrottning*, xiii.

21. "Däruppå svarades med sådana ord och med tämlig ifver: Den människa, som förnekar sin Gud, bör icke sättas någon tro till af andra. Och indrog H.Mt. detta exempel och sade: Det gick alt väl i Sverige, till dess konung *Johan* tog sig en papistisk drottning; sedan gick det aldrig väl"; Åke Axelsson (Natt och Dag) to Axel Oxenstierna, Örebro, 2 [12] September 1642, UA, vol. 23, 37–38, here 38. On the resistance of Brandenburg's *Geheime Räte* to talk of Friedrich Wilhelm's conversion, see Armstedt, *Der schwedische Heiratsplan*, 6; and Malmström, *Änkedrottning*, xiii.

22. "Wenn Wir der Königin bloss als etwan ein Kämmerer sollten aufwarten"; Friedrich Wilhelm to Brandenburg delegation at Westphalia, Berlin, 22 June [2 July] 1646; UA, vol. 4, 446–47.

23. Historians writing about the marriage plan sometimes embrace the language of inevitable failure through predetermined irreconcilable difference cast as identity. Schevill, for example, writes that a realistic appraisal (in this case Axel Oxenstierna's) of the plan's chances dismissed "the notion that the hunter and his quarry could ever be divested of their fated respective roles" (Schevill, *Great Elector*, 117).

24. Harrington, *Reordering Marriage*, 26–27.

25. Wiesner-Hanks, *Christianity and Sexuality*, 64.

26. Hull, *Sexuality, State, and Civil Society*, 19.

27. "[T]he body and its sexual possibilities bore enormous symbolic weight; they became saturated with meanings belonging to systems of faith, of order and hierarchy in a Christian community, of signs revealing eternity"; Hull, *Sexuality, State, and Civil Society*, 10.

28. Currie, *Difference*, 18.

29. "During the early modern period, marriage alliances were sought with 'strangers,' frequently cemented long-term clientage relations, and created complex patterns of circulation among different political and corporate groups (*Stände, ceti, ordres*) and wealth strata. From the mid eighteenth century onwards, marriages became more endogamous, both in terms of class and milieu and among consanguineal kin: marriage partners sought out the 'familiar.' These innovations are intimately related to the formation of social classes and a differentiation of new gender roles within property-holding groups from the late eighteenth century onwards. And they also reflect reconfigurations in political institutions, state service, property rights, and the circulation of capital"; see David Warren Sabean and Simon Teuscher, "Kinship in Europe: A New Approach to Long-Term Development," in David Warren Sabean, Simon Teuscher, and Jon Mathieu, eds., *Kinship in Europe: Approaches to Long-Term Development (1300–1900)* (New York, 2007), 1–32, here 3.

30. Karant-Nunn, *Reformation of Ritual*, 38–39.

31. Frances E. Dolan, *Marriage and Violence: The Early Modern Legacy* (Philadelphia, 2008).

32. Abby E. Zanger, *Scenes from the Marriage of Louis XIV: Nuptial Fictions and the Making of Absolutist Power* (Stanford, 1997), 3–4. Karant-Nunn also makes use of Turner in analyzing early modern marriage ceremonies in her *Reformation of Ritual*.

33. Turner, "Betwixt and Between," 98.

34. Ibid., 100–101.

35. Ibid., 97 ("realm"), 105 ("liminality").

36. Ibid., 105.

37. Currie, *Difference*, 3–5.

38. Edward Muir, *Ritual in Early Modern Europe*, 2nd ed. (Cambridge, U.K. , 2005), 2; and Lisa Schirch, *Ritual and Symbol in Peacebuilding* (Bloomfield, 2005), 4. Turner himself wrote that some consider the structures of liminality to be "metalanguages" that "transcen[d] the languages in which members of societies transact their daily business" (*Blazing the Trail: Way Marks in the Exploration of Symbols* [Tucson, 1992], 136).

39. "Rational political methods alone cannot bring about transformation of society from a less to a more just condition, because they cannot fuse the visionary with the actual (the absent with the present) as rituals do, thus profoundly affecting the moral life" (Tom F. Driver, *Liberating Rites: Understanding the Transformative Power of Ritual* [Boulder, 1998], 184).

40. Turner, *Blazing the Trail*, 50.

41. Bobby C. Alexander, *Victor Turner Revisited: Ritual as Social Change* (Atlanta, 1991), 35.

42. See ibid., 36, 43, 63.

43. Turner, *Blazing the Trail*, 151.

44. Schirch, *Ritual and Symbol*, 84, 129; and Alexander, *Victor Turner Revisited*, 29.

45. Zanger notes, "Marriage, also a ritual of transition or passage, joins two bodies or two nation-states, absorbing difference, which it cannot erase. To do so would defeat the purpose of the symbolic event. Maintaining a trace of difference offers a reminder that there has been an exchange of kin, an interaction between two groups" (*Scenes from the Marriage*, 8).

46. See Schering Rosenhane to Johan Oxenstierna and Johan Adler Salvius, Münster, 25 October [4 November] 1645, UA, vol. 23, 73–74; and Brandenburg delegation in Osnabrück to Friedrich Wilhelm, Osnabrück, 26 October [5 November] 1646, UA, vol. 4, 464–65. See also Pufendorf, *Rebus Suecicis*, 596; Armstedt, *Der schwedische Heiratsplan*, 3–4; Schulze, *Project der Vermählung*, 1–2, 16–18; and Roberts, *Gustavus Adolphus*, vol. 2, 643–45.

47. Schevill wrote that the side of the marriage plan that appealed to Axel Oxenstierna was that it offered hopes for "the whole cantankerous quarrel [over Pomerania] to be in this manner magically put to sleep" (Schevill, *Great Elector*, 117).

48. "Önskades för allting, H. Mt. måtte låta sig behaga Churf. af Brandeburg, hvilket vore det säkraste medlet, att komma utur de besvär, som nu förestå. Och kunde man alltså i stället för Pommern, som dock blifve Cronans, begära ett stycke annat land, och blefve utaf den coniunctionen en sådan puissance, som dess like inte vore i Europa" (Schering Rosenhane to Swedish delegation in Osnabrück, Münster, 20 February [2 March] 1646, UA, vol. 23, 84–85, here 85). The French diplomat quoted here was the Duc du Longueville. Rhetoric surrounding the Franco–Spanish dynastic marriages of the seventeenth century included similar excitement over the mighty political power to be wrought by the union of fundamentally different realms. Antoine de Brunel wrote that "on peut assurer que de la promptitude des François et de la lenteur des Espagnols, il se peut faire un admirable composé pour la conqueste du monde et pour le gouvernement des Estats"; Brunel, *Voyage d'Espagne curieux, historique et politique* (Paris, 1655), cited in Alexandra Testino-Zafiropoulos, "Les alliances royales franco-espagnoles au XVIIᵉ siècle: Propagande et raison d'état," in Richard Crescenzo, Marie Roig-Miranda, and Véronique Zaercher, eds., *Le mariage dans l'Europe des XVIᵉ et XVIIᵉ siècles: Réalités et représentations*, 2 vols. (Nancy, 2003), vol. 1, 175–90, here 182.

49. The prominent Swedish historian Nils Ahnlund wrote of Gustav Adolf's vision of the marriage plan being formed in conjunction with "the dream of a great Swedish-German State under a common ruler"; Ahnlund, *Gustav Adolf the Great*, tr. Michael Roberts (Princeton, 1940), 93.

50. "Dieweilen wir [Götze and Gustaf Adolf] uns der Zeit auch die geringste Gedanken nicht machen können, als haben wir, indem wir dabei erwogen, wie nahe der Allerhoheste die status beider Reiche und Lande zusammen gefüget, dieses billig vor ein sicheres argumentum der göttlichen . . . Vorsehung halten müssen"; Sigismund von Götze to Axel Oxenstierna, Berlin, 7 [17] February 1644, UA, vol. 23, 68–70, here 68. Similarly Götze reported to Georg Wilhelm on a conversation he had with Oxenstierna in 1635 in which he replied to Oxenstierna's discussion of the challenges facing the marriage plan, and in particular the issue of confessional difference, by stating "Hierauf wuste Ich weiterß nichts zuantworten, dann daß es d providentz Gottes an heim zu geben." Sigismund von Götze to Georg Wilhelm, Mainz, 15 January 1635. GStA PK, I. HA, Rep. 24c., no. 9, fasc. 3, 1r-7v, here 3r.

51. Schulze, *Project der Vermählung*, 3. On Bergius' irenic strivings, see the essays collected in Bodo Nischan, *Lutherans and Calvinists in the Age of Confessionalism* (Aldershot, 1999).

52. The amount of evidence connecting irenic efforts to the marriage plan is substantial. See, for example, documents in GStA PK, I. HA, Rep. 11, no. 247I, fasc. 7; GStA PK, I. HA, Rep. 24c., no. 7, fasc. 2; GStA PK, I. HA, Rep. 24c., no. 9, fasc. 3; GStA PK, VI. HA, Nl Arnheim, fasc. 4, 1–6, esp. 3; RA, Diplomatica, Brandenburgico-Borussica, vol. 2; UA, vol. 4, 407; and UA, vol. 23, 60–61, 68–70, 73–74. See also Pufendorf, *Rebus Suecicis*, 73; Malmström, *Änkedrottning*, xiii, xvi; Schulze, *Project der Vermählung*, 3, 7, 19–22; Roberts, *Gustavus Adolphus*, vol. 2, 646.

53. On ritual action as a model for broader processes of change, see Don Handelman, *Models and Mirrors: Towards an Anthropology of Public Events* (New York, 1990), 23–31. Handelman notes that "an event-that-models has built into itself incompatible, contradictory or conflicting states of existence, and in the course of its working it must overcome, synthesize, or otherwise solve these." When successful, the event "indexes or pre-views a hypothetical future condition that will be brought into being, and it provides procedures that will actualize this act of imagination"; *Models and Mirrors*, 28, 30. See also Muir, *Ritual in Early Modern Europe*, 4–5.

54. A handshake between rivals, for instance, carries symbolic value only when the participants (and those observing them) acknowledge the animosity that has marked their relationship.

55. The appreciation of *communitas* implies an awareness of the structural divisions that prevail in its absence. Turner thus claimed that "communitas can be grasped only in some relation to structure"; cited in Driver, *Liberating Rites*, 163.

CHAPTER 8

~:~

Mixed Matches and Inter-Confessional Dialogue

The Hanoverian Succession and the Protestant Dynasties of Europe in the Early Eighteenth Century

ALEXANDER SCHUNKA

Europe in the early eighteenth century witnessed a number of significant changes that are usually said to explain the transition from a confessional age to an era of enlightenment. To draw out those changes, the present chapter examines several cross-confessional dynastic marriages during the years around 1700. Four closely related trends intersected here. One was the growing significance of discussions surrounding royal succession, monarchical stability, and the continuity of Europe's ruling houses.[1] Another was the evolution of a new, more stable, and more professional system of political interaction following the peace negotiations of Westphalia (1648) and usually connected to an evolving balance of power in Europe.[2] A third trend concerned the role of confessional affiliations in politics and society, specifically the rise of voices that questioned the presumed superiority of religion over more worldly matters, resulting in increased interreligious debates about toleration and irenicism.[3] Finally, a fourth factor accompanied these developments, namely the evolution of a new system of communication and media, consisting of newspapers and periodicals, and backed by close personal ties among scholars, journalists, politicians, and ecclesiastics, all of whom formed part of a republic of letters and spent a significant amount of their lives engaged in scholarly networking and exchange.[4]

Dynastic marriages that crossed confessional lines muddled boundaries between the spheres of dynasty, politics, religion, and communication. This blurring sometimes caused political or confessional troubles, even as it stimulated public discussions among eager journalists. On the other hand, cross-confessional marriages also linked different Christian denominations, various courts and dynasties, and formerly distinct political camps.[5]

This chapter shows how these unions affected religious, political, and dynastic interactions at the courts of London, Hanover, and Berlin. All three courts were closely connected to one another, yet in each a different Protestant confession prevailed—Anglican, Lutheran, and Calvinist, respectively. At the same time, attempts to foster Protestant politics, to open a dialogue across confessional lines, or even to unify the Lutheran and Calvinist denominations of Europe emanated—sometimes jointly—from Berlin, Hanover, and London, and were often closely connected with the respective rulers and politicians. These irenic efforts derived as much from dynastic necessities as from theological or political considerations.

Historians have largely overlooked the relationship among the courts of Berlin, Hanover, and London in terms of mixed-confessional matches and European confessional politics. This chapter addresses the shared and interlinked practices of dealing with plural confessions at court in the early eighteenth century. It highlights the connections between dynastic decisions and Protestant politics in the transitional period of the early Enlightenment, between an "international Calvinism" and an evolving "Protestant interest."[6] The chapter begins with a brief overview of the Protestant setting including the links between dynastic marriage decisions, politics, and efforts at theological reconciliation in the early eighteenth century, and then outlines the confessional and political interactions among the Hohenzollern, Stuart, and Hanoverian courts before and after the Hanoverian succession of 1714. It concludes with a case study of King George's two confessional identities: the Church of England and the Lutheran faith.

Irenic Hopes and Dynastic Affairs

Choosing a royal marriage partner who belonged to a different confessional denomination was by no means new in the eighteenth century. Such mixed matches can be found throughout the age of confessionalism, albeit not as frequently as in the later period treated here. Earlier examples include Friedrich V of the Palatinate, a Calvinist who married Elizabeth Stuart, the Anglican daughter of James I.[7] The number of mixed marriages at court or of conversions preceding the wedding grew significantly around 1700. The reasons can be found in the lack of adequate marriage partners of the same faith, in political necessities, and in the wish of dynasties of lesser importance to advance into the sphere of major European ruling houses. Perhaps even love-matches played a substantial role, although these are hard to document.

Because of increased coverage in the contemporary media, knowledge of these liaisons was widespread among European observers, and it was no surprise that a number of interest groups tried to capitalize on these relationships. Irenicist theologians, for example, placed high expectations on cross-confessional marriages, which they hoped could build a broader constituency for their quest for religious compromise, or perhaps even foster a pan-European Protestant dialogue. In 1719, for example, the Calvinist Prussian court preacher and renowned irenicist, Daniel Ernst Jablonski, wrote to the archbishop of Canterbury, William Wake, stressing the feasibility and necessity of a Protestant reconciliation. According to Jablonski, who had long advocated a closer dialogue between the Protestant churches of Europe, several Protestant princes belonged to more than one confession. King George I, for example, was a member of the Church of England when he was in Britain, but he adhered to his Lutheran faith when as elector of Hanover he visited his hereditary lands in Germany. Similarly, the prince of Hesse-Kassel and future king of Sweden was a Calvinist in Germany, but a Lutheran in Scandinavia. Why, Jablonski asked, should the people not follow the example of their rulers? Why not grant everybody in the country what seemed to be common practice for the territorial princes?[8]

Jablonski could have easily added more examples of the several inter-confessional marriages among Protestant monarchs. King Friedrich Wilhelm I of Prussia, a Calvinist, had married a Lutheran princess from Hanover in 1706; Queen Anne of Britain, the predecessor of King George and a staunch Anglican, had been married to Prince George of Denmark, a Lutheran, since 1683; and, finally, the wife of the Lutheran prince, Friedrich Ludwig of Württemberg, descended from the Calvinist Hohenzollerns of Brandenburg-Schwedt.[9]

These marriages remained bi-confessional, with the result that a number of clerical and lay dignitaries of the spouse's faith usually made their way into formerly mono-confessional courts. Under these circumstances it was no great step to begin challenging the doctrinal and ecclesiological differences of Protestant beliefs and practices converging at the ruler's court as well as their implications for the country. Court preachers and other theologians close to the ruling dynasties or to the country's universities most often conducted these discussions. It is therefore no coincidence that royal marriages raised the possibility of Protestant unity, or at least contemporaries, in London, Hanover, and Berlin might have so perceived it.

Historians of confessional dialogue and reconciliation have not paid much attention to the impact of these mixed dynastic unions on cross-confessional dialogue. That is beginning to change. Long overshadowed by a larger interest in questions of toleration or secularization, the topic of confessional reconciliation has begun to attract the interest not just of theologians, but also of historians. Irenicism was undoubtedly a major topic among Protestant ecclesiastics in the early modern era. Theologians, understandably, have approached early modern irenicism from the standpoint of doctrine and ecclesiology.[10] Historians have tended to focus on the political dimensions of an evolving "Protestant interest" in Europe.[11] What both groups have neglected is the link between these two spheres. Considering the dynastic aspects of confessional unity underscores the very pragmatic dimension of theological irenicism and highlights the connections between religion and politics in the early Enlightenment.

With the benefit of hindsight, it seems easy to deduce from the ultimate failure of confessional reconciliation that these efforts were insignificant or misguided. However, the question of inter-confessional dialogue resulted in thousands of printed treatises, in political actions, and in a remarkably profuse correspondence between major European intellectuals. What all Protestants could agree with was the unsatisfactory situation of the division between Lutherans and Calvinists, a fissure that obviously weakened the Reformation and its accomplishments. In addition, it was hotly debated whether or how confessional reconciliation should take place—that is, how the contesting groups could compromise on matters they considered nonnegotiable religious truths. For many years the idea of predestination and the doctrinal differences concerning the Lord's Supper formed the main points of contention between Lutheran and Calvinist theologians. Irenicists sought solutions by concentrating on liturgical issues, on early Christianity, or on defining which aspects were absolutely essential or fundamental for salvation.[12]

It was also debated whether irenicism was a theological problem that could be solved among theologians, or if it were a worldly matter best handled politically. Some ecclesiastics remained skeptical when it came to the influence of politicians and rulers in the debate. Lutheran opponents of irenicism, in particular, dismissed the whole problem as secular, emanating from the political interests of certain states such as Brandenburg-Prussia. Indeed, many proponents of confessional dialogue and unity were closely connected to or paid by their courts. This was certainly true in Prussia for the court preacher, Jablonski, the high-ranking diplomat Ezechiel von Spanheim, or the politician Marquard Ludwig von Printzen. The links to the ruling elites were equally obvious in Hanover, where the philosopher and court councilor (*Hofrat*), Gottfried Wilhelm Leibniz, engaged in reconciliation talks with members of the state university of Helmstedt. In Britain the situation seemed only slightly more pluralistic, with some archbishops and bishops, professors, clerical or lay members of the so-called religious societies, as well as politicians or embassy chaplains who fostered dialogue with continental Protestants. To their adversaries, these ties underscored the charge that irenicist theologians mingled religious truths with worldly affairs. However, when Jablonski stressed the importance for territorial rulers to overcome confessional differences he was not simply neglecting his duties as a theologian to seek religious truth: his dedication to Protestant unity was the work of his lifetime as a pastor. Jablonski was fully aware that theological treatises and pamphlets were useless unless they enjoyed the support of worldly rulers and politicians.[13]

The Protestant discussions across Europe materialized in printed books and treatises, but more so in extensive correspondence networks. Jablonski and Wake were connected to one another as well as to hundreds of other correspondents in this way. The court preacher and the archbishop had met personally at least once and had known each other for many years. During his career from 1693 to 1741, Jablonski served three different Prussian rulers. Wake became archbishop of Canterbury and head of the Church of England right after the Lutheran king George I had come to power in Great Britain. At various times in their lives, both Jablonski and Wake were important advisers to their rulers.[14] Both shared the conviction that the unity of European Protestants was necessary to withstand an increasing Roman Catholic threat in Europe and to save the achievements of the Reformation from possible adversaries.

The royal courts in London and Berlin had not been strictly mono-confessional for quite some time: Britain's ruler George I was born a Lutheran, his predecessor Queen Anne had a Lutheran husband, and both Anne and the Hanoverian king George, paid to support a Lutheran court chapel in St James's Palace. Berlin, however, was the capital of a Lutheran territory governed by Reformed elites, and King Frederick William I of Prussia was a Calvinist married to a Lutheran; in this he had followed the example of his father.[15] Under these circumstances, a certain amount of inter-confessional cooperation and dialogue was unavoidable, even necessary.

In conjunction with the Hanoverian Succession in Great Britain, Jablonski advocated Protestant intercommunion as a first step toward unity; he considered King George's accession in Britain the right moment to put Protestant union into practice. Like his Anglican correspondent Wake, Jablonski recognized that confessional reconciliation mattered as much to secular rulers as to their theologians, whose task it was to lay the doctrinal and ecclesiological foundations for unity. It was thus no coincidence that after a period of silence the irenicist talks between Prussians and Britons resumed when George of Hanover had finally ascended the throne in 1714, and after he had installed the irenicist Wake as archbishop of Canterbury.[16]

The Impact of the Hanoverian Succession

In order fully to grasp the significance of the Hanoverian Succession (or Protestant Succession, as it was called by contemporaries) in regard to dynastic interaction and irenicism, we need to look at its prehistory.[17] Many years before it actually took place, irenicists had vested great hopes in the succession scheme and its potential to generate interconfessional dialogue among Protestants. Irenicist efforts in Germany had already been under way for some years when in 1701 Parliament chose the Hanoverians to succeed the Stuarts as British monarchs. The Prussian court preacher Jablonski was part of a discussion network consisting of, among others, the Hanoverians Gerard Wolter Molanus and, most notably, Leibniz. All these scholars were discussing possibilities for mutual toleration and liturgical unity between Lutherans and Calvinists, possibly under the umbrella of the Anglican Church, which was considered by a number of irenicists the appropriate *via media* between the rival confessions. In order to propagate Anglican thought in Europe, Jablonski also engaged in translations of theological and devotional treatises from English into Latin and German. In addition, the Prussian monarchy installed the renowned irenicist scholar, Ezechiel von Spanheim, as its ambassador in London in summer 1701, only few months after the Act of Settlement had passed.[18]

The purpose of the Act of Settlement was to secure the Protestant succession and exclude the Catholic Stuarts from the British monarchy. As the youngest daughter of the so-called "Winter King," Friedrich V of the Palatinate and Elizabeth Stuart, the Hanoverian electress Sophia was the closest Protestant relative among all possible heirs to the throne. She was also the widow of elector Ernst August of Hanover and mother of the current Hanoverian ruler Georg Ludwig. Sophia was therefore the offspring of a mixed marriage between a Calvinist and an Anglican and had a Lutheran husband. Although she retained the opportunity to visit Calvinist services occasionally even after her marriage, her children were raised as Lutherans. Her only daughter, Sophia Charlotte, married the Calvinist Friedrich III (I) of Prussia. The cross-confessional links between England, Prussia, and Hanover could therefore build on a strong dynastic tradition.[19]

Preparing the British for the succession of a German Lutheran who was not even a proper member of the Church of England presented no small challenge. It fell into the hands of particular interest groups in England (notably the Whigs) as well as councilors such as Leibniz in Germany. Neither the lengthy parliamentary negotiations in London—known as the *invitation crisis*—on the problem whether the future queen should be invited from Hanover to England in 1705 (which Parliament finally dismissed), nor the fact that a civil parliament granted its prospective monarch Sophia and her family British naturalization in 1706, added to Georg Ludwig's eagerness to succeed to the throne by grace of Parliament. Leibniz himself saw the succession not only as a chance to raise Hanoverian dynastic prestige, but also to preserve and promote Christian unity. His support of the Hanoverians, however, had some rather unfortunate results.[20]

Because of their dynastic links and political alliances, the Hohenzollern dynasty in Prussia watched the Hanoverian succession with great interest. One reason was that the naturalization of the Hanoverians and their offspring as British citizens in 1706 made the Hohenzollern prince (and future so-called "Soldier King") Friedrich Wilhelm a potential heir to the British throne: he was the son of Sophia Charlotte and the grandson of Sophia of Hanover, the prospective queen of Britain. In addition, 1706 saw the lengthy preparations for the marriage of Friedrich Wilhelm to Sophie Dorothea, daughter of Georg Ludwig, the ruling elector of Hanover and therefore another of Sophia's grandchildren. This wedding was supposed to tie the two dynasties even more closely together. Yet the union was difficult to accomplish because the proposed marriage was again a mixed match. The groom belonged to the Calvinist faith, and his bride was Lutheran.[21]

Several Protestant theologians debated about using this marriage to promote Protestant unity. The question was whether the bride would have to renounce her Lutheran faith officially or if the Prussian court should allow her to continue Lutheran worship. Jablonski's correspondent Leibniz suggested adopting the British court's practice, referring to the fact that Britain was then ruled by a queen, Anne, whose husband belonged to a different faith. In fact, the cross-confessional match between Anne Stuart and her Lutheran husband, George of Denmark, became a significant problem only when Anne succeeded to the throne after her brother-in-law, King William III, had died in 1702. Now the royal consort was awarded with the office of high admiral.[22] The Test and Corporation Acts, however, required those who held a public office to participate in the Anglican communion. Therefore the Lutheran prince George had to attend Anglican services and communion on official occasions, similar to the so-called occasional conformity many Protestant dissenters practiced in analogous situations.

Still, on a much more regular basis George attended the services of his private Lutheran court chapel. This congregation was headed by Anton Wilhelm Boehme, a German Lutheran Pietist with close relations to the charitable foundations of August Hermann Francke in Halle. Boehme thus acted as the London outpost of Francke's world-encompassing plans to spread Pietism. On the one hand, the German Pietist leader cherished Boehme's proximity to the ruling elites of the British Empire. On the other hand, the famous theologian in Halle was a devout Lutheran when it came to doctrinal and ecclesiastical issues, opposing everything that seemed like an amalgamation of different beliefs. Francke therefore despised Prince George's practice of occasional conformity that he considered a dangerous confessional indifference, and he also arranged that the Pietist chaplain Boehme could only conduct religious services for Prince George of Denmark, but not administer the sacraments.[23]

George of Denmark's confessional practices at the London court provoked great controversy among orthodox Lutherans as well as among dedicated Calvinists and Anglicans. Supporters of irenicism, however, could easily pin their hopes on such cross-confessional practices. This is why the Hanoverian councilor Leibniz suggested a similar occasional conformity for the Hanoverian princess Sophie Dorothea after she wed Friedrich Wilhelm of Prussia. According to the councilor, she could be Calvinist on official occasions while following Lutheran rites in private.[24] Unfortunately, Leibniz's proposal was not regarded with much favor. His correspondent Jablonski immediately communicated the letter from Hanover to a number of authorities at the Prussian court who reacted with shock and disgust. Eventually King Friedrich of Prussia ordered his court preacher to terminate this "indecent correspondence" with Leibniz on irenic matters. The Hanoverian elector, Georg Ludwig, followed suit and likewise ordered Leibniz to suspend his correspondence with Jablonski. One result was that the Hanoverian councilor was highly offended by what he understood as Jablonski's indiscretions and broke off correspondence with the Prussian court preacher completely. For several subsequent years irenic talks between Hanover and Berlin remained at a standstill. The wedding between Sophie Dorothea and Friedrich Wilhelm took place as scheduled in the autumn 1706, but a secret agreement between the courts of Hanover and Prussia allowed the princess to remain Lutheran.[25]

This episode illustrates the fragile character of inter-confessional dialogue, especially when courts and politics were concerned. In this case, neither Hanover nor Prussia could risk being seen as indifferent toward doctrinal or ecclesiastical issues because this could have led to dangerous political consequences. Therefore, inter-confessional exchange had to be fostered in a very subtle manner; it needed the political skills that some theologians sorely lacked.

The ties between Berlin, Hanover, and London on the eve of the Hanoverian succession in Britain continued to be close but frail, as the problem of confessional unity indicates. Whereas the Prussian–Hanoverian wedding affair was merely a crisis between two German states, another incident at roughly the same time almost halted the Hanoverian succession in England and inflicted further damage on the talks about confessional unification. Here, another mixed match was involved. The granddaughter of the ruling duke of Brunswick-Wolfenbüttel, a close relative of the Hanoverian elector, was marrying the future Habsburg emperor Charles. In order to preempt the possible scandal of a Lutheran princess marrying a Roman Catholic, the bride was persuaded to convert from the Lutheran to the Catholic faith, following a number of secret expert opinions of renowned Lutheran theologians on the issue of whether the bride could still expect to gain eternal salvation even after defecting to the Papists. Most opinions supported the conversion, but only one, written by a

Hanoverian ecclesiastic, was published; it immediately caused a major uproar in the Holy Roman Empire as well as in Britain. What British observers disliked most was the assumption that German Lutherans thought so little of their religion. How could a (formerly Lutheran) king of England (and a close relative of the convert in question) be trusted as the future defender of the Anglican faith and a stronghold against the Roman Catholics if he acquiesced in such an abomination? Defusing the affair required a massive effort of pro-Hanoverian circles in Britain and also of Jablonski in Berlin. On the eve of the Hanoverian succession however, this scandal further discredited Lutheranism in Britain and pan-Protestant dialogue in general.[26]

Considering all these troubles with inter-confessional relations, it comes as no surprise that plans to unify the Christian faiths proceeded rather badly. When the Hanoverian succession finally came into being in 1714, it was not Electress Sophia, who died shortly before Queen Anne, but her son, Georg Ludwig, who ascended the British throne. At first it might seem that Realpolitik had won over the irenic reveries of a coterie of theologians. However, the Lutheran succession in England neither ended the cross-confessional troubles nor did it terminate the hopes of irenicists for pragmatic arrangements across frontiers of faith.

Between Anglicanism and Lutheranism: George I

In 1714 Queen Anne and her expected successor, Sophia of Hanover, both died within weeks of each other. When Sophia's son was crowned George I more than a decade had gone by since Parliament had passed the Act of Settlement. At the time of his accession to the British throne, the Hanoverian ruler had to become a member of the Church of England. A Prussian diplomat reported that the king immediately began attending Anglican services every Sunday, even though he did not understand a word of the English language.[27]

Even if feelings toward the new ruler were generally mixed, the succession went hand in hand with a slowly growing English interest in his hereditary lands. A few years before 1714 a few committed supporters of the Church of England had already tried to prepare the German inhabitants of Hanover for the Protestant Succession by popularizing the Anglican faith, propagating Anglican services, and distributing copies of the Book of Common Prayer.[28] These initiatives do not seem to have been particularly successful. Thus, after George's succession in Britain, the electorate of Hanover remained a Lutheran territory, and its administration worked almost fully separated from British politics. George brought a so-called German chancery to London that dealt with Hanoverian affairs. At the same time, a ruling council in the city of Hanover debated the local politics of his hereditary country, where a painting of George replaced the absent monarch.[29] Whereas religious issues are almost completely absent in Hanoverian documents concerning the personal union, a number of publications in Britain addressed questions of the new ruler's confessional affiliations and loyalties.[30]

In irenicist circles George's accession to the British throne immediately sparked new hopes for Protestant unity. Now a Lutheran ruled Britain as an Anglican, while Friedrich Wilhelm (who meanwhile had become king of Prussia in 1713) was married to the king of Britain's daughter. Furthermore, the renowned irenicist Wake had become archbishop of Canterbury and, as such, a leading figure of the Anglican Church. In this situation Jablonski intensified his contacts with Wake, hoping that the examples of multi-confessional rulers and courts would inspire theologians and politicians to extend interconfessional practices to their territories. Jablonski also traveled to Hanover in 1716 where he expected to meet King George in person and to propagate his plans for confessional unity, but the king happened to be hunting and was not to be disturbed. Leibniz died soon after Jablonski's visit, depriving irenicism of one of its major advocates.[31]

The fact that George I was the ruler of a Lutheran territory in Germany while at the same time king of the British Empire and the nominal head of the Church of England continued to excite irenicists, especially in regard to royal religious practices and the monarch's everyday life. George quite regularly visited his Hanoverian lands in summer, fulfilling his duties as a Lutheran elector (*Kurfürst*) of the Holy Roman Empire. To complicate matters, as king of Britain he was accompanied by Anglican clergy while traveling abroad. On his 1716 journey his entourage included Lancelot Blackburne, later archbishop of York. Blackburne had been nominated as George's Anglican chaplain only after the intervention of Wake, the archbishop of Canterbury.[32] It is more than likely that Wake's choice of Blackburne had something to do with his own irenic intentions. Blackburne's letters to Wake are particularly telling about the practical chances and failures of inter-confessional dialogue at Hanover following the succession, and, for this reason, it is worth looking more closely at them.

While George took the waters at the Pyrmont spa, his chaplain was already in the city of Hanover, where he administered Anglican services for the British entourage in the royal bedchamber, as there was apparently no other space available. When a leading Hanoverian politician arranged for him to use a Lutheran church, the chaplain was shocked by the crucifix on the altar and the images in the church. Blackburne considered this lack of Hanoverian cooperation dangerous latitude, and primarily a political and not an ecclesiastical matter. He eventually managed to administer services in the local Reformed church, apparently with great success and a large audience. The Anglican chaplain commented that both the Lutheran majority and the Reformed minority in the capital lived "tolerably wel [sic] together, tho' they can hardly forbear complaining of one another."[33]

The chaplain continued his services in the Reformed church while George had already arrived at his castle in Herrenhausen close to Hanover. Rumor had it that the king had immediately started to worship according to Lutheran rites.[34] Blackburne became increasingly fed up with continental Protestantism and with his personal situation at Hanover. He wrote to Wake,

> But in good Truth the Emulation between the Lutherans & the Reform'd here is so great . . . that one must take everything they say of one another with many grams of allowance before one swallows it. They lay claim on both sides to the Church of England, & attempt to draw me into an allowance of their claims Respectively: But they get nothing from me, but wishes of a General Union of all Protestants as the only means of withstanding the great Torrent of Popery, & that they cannot find a better Method for it than the Moderation which Our Church has us'd.[35]

This, in a nutshell, described the position of many High Church Englishmen: Protestant unity would be an expedient way to fight popery, but only as long as no damage to the Church of England resulted. What happened if people went too far in their irenic beliefs and practices, Blackburne noticed when he learned about the reputation of Leibniz: "Both the Lutherans & Calvinists here look on Mr Leibnitz as an unbeleiver, the Lay-men also of the Court tel [sic] me he has his Religion to choose & was ready to turn Roman Catholic. . . . But this is the Common fate of Men that have more Learning, or a larger mind, than Others!"[36]

Exasperated by confessional quarrels and royal disinterest, Blackburne left Hanover for England after the king had set off on a hunting trip. Still, the chaplain's journey turned out to be a major success if not for confessional irenicism but for Blackburne himself who was soon promoted by the king to the Episcopal See of Exeter.[37]

Like the Hanoverian Succession, the story of Lancelot Blackburne in Lutheran Hanover reveals the pragmatic, sometimes trivial, and often fruitless dimensions of confessional compromise. In the following years it seems that Britain accommodated the Lutheran, continental background of her king or at least tried to downplay its importance in regard to an overarching Protestantism.[38] Prussia and its theologians and politicians slowly moved from the center of inter-confessional dialogue to the periphery, not least because the political climate changed. Hopes still existed that another clever match with a British (i.e., Hanoverian) princess would solve irenic quarrels for good—Jablonski in a letter to an English irenicist observer expected the marriage plan of Prince Frederick of Prussia (later to become Frederick the Great) in 1730 with a daughter of George II of Britain as a decisive turn.[39] However this liaison did not come into being, in contrast to the marriage of the Lutheran princess Augusta of Saxe-Gotha with Friedrich Ludwig (Frederick Lewis), Prince of

Wales, in 1736. This new match was hailed as truly irenic and most valuable not only for the achievements of the Reformation, but also for the well-being of international Protestantism, and the fight against Popery.[40] It seems that in the field of politics and confessions the denominational ruptures among Protestant groups slowly faded in favor of an international Protestantism—the earlier rallying cry of a Protestant interest had now left the political and reached the religious sphere, which made Protestant irenicism of earlier decades increasingly obsolete.

In his justly famous study, *The King's Two Bodies*, Ernst H. Kantorowicz showed how medieval and early modern Europeans distinguished between the corporeal person of the king and a spiritual body that was undying and that passed unbroken from one temporary occupant of the throne to his successor. In the case of George I, we would have to multiply the usual two to six: temporal and spiritual, but also British and Hanoverian, Anglican, and Lutheran.[41] The bi-confessional character of his rule did not change. In England he remained an Anglican, disregarding his Lutheran background. The electorate of Hanover, however, did not turn Anglican but stayed solidly attached to Lutheranism, just as the king did while he was on the continent. What needs to be stressed in the context of the Hanoverian Succession and the confessional links between Berlin, Hanover, and London, is the degree to which contemporaries explored the possibilities of cross-confessional co-operation, and the extent to which they used royal examples.

For adherents of all faiths, a fine line separated inter-confessional dialogue from dangerous syncretism and religious indecencies. Cross-confessional marriages illustrate the hopes and the chances as well as the limits of dynastic influence on the confessional framework of a country. In this respect, public reactions and discussions about bi-confessional courts and rulers and the influence of these courts must be more fully analyzed in order to unite theological approaches to confessional unity with the political and dynastic dimensions. Once done, these studies will lead us to a more thorough understanding of the relationship between religion and politics in the early eighteenth century.

Notes

I am grateful to Kelly and Charles Whitmer for valuable corrections and comments.

1. Marriages and questions of dynastic identity formation among the nobility are treated rather peripherally in Ronald G. Asch, *Europäischer Adel in der Frühen Neuzeit: Eine Einführung* (Cologne, 2008), 103–6; and Sikora, *Adel*, 116–38. A number of chapters in Wrede and Carl, eds., *Zwischen Schande und Ehre*, 97–124 touch on issues of dynastic identity.

2. Heinz Duchhardt, *Balance of Power und Pentarchie: Internationale Beziehungen 1700–1785*, vol. 4 of *Handbuch der Geschichte der internationalen Beziehungen* (Paderborn, 1997).

3. See, for instance, Benjamin J. Kaplan, *Divided by Faith: Religious Conflict and the Practice of Toleration in Early Modern Europe* (Cambridge, MA, 2007), 333–58. An excellent overview on early modern Irenicism is found in Howard Hotson, "Irenicism in the Confessional Age: The Holy Roman Empire, 1563–1648," in *Conciliation and Confession: The Struggle for Unity in the Age of Reform, 1415–1648*, ed. Howard P. Louthan and Randall C. Zachman (Notre Dame, 2004), 228–85.

4. On the practices of the republic of letters, see Anne Goldgar, *Impolite Learning: Conduct and Community in the Republic of Letters, 1680–1750* (New Haven, 1995). On the development of the media in the early modern era, see Andreas Würgler, *Medien in der Frühen Neuzeit*, vol. 85 of *Enzyklopädie deutscher Geschichte* (Munich, 2009), 43–64.

5. Whereas marriages across confessional boundaries among early modern nonelites have been topics of recent research, the situation differs with regard to the aristocracy and ruling dynasties. On cross-confessional marriages among ordinary people, see Dagmar Freist, "Crossing Religious Borders: The Experience of Religious Difference and its Impact on Mixed Marriages in Eighteenth-Century Germany," in *Living with Religious Diversity in Early Modern Europe*, ed. Dagmar Freist, C. Scott Dixon, and Mark Greengrass (Aldershot, 2009), 203–24. On migration and cross-confessional family identities, see Alexander Schunka, "Konfessionelle Liminalität: Kryptokatholiken im lutherischen Kursachsen des 17. Jahrhunderts," in *Migration und kirchliche Praxis: Das religiöse Leben frühneuzeitlicher Glaubensflüchtlinge in alltagsgeschichtlicher Perspektive*, ed. Joachim Bahlcke and Rainer Bendel (Cologne, 2008), 113–31.

6. Menna Prestwich, *International Calvinism 1541–1715* (Oxford, 1985); Andrew Thompson, *Britain, Hanover and the Protestant Interest: 1688–1756* (Woodbridge, UK, 2006).

7. Christof Ginzel, *Poetry, Politics and Promises of Empire: Prophetic Rhetoric in the English and Neo-Latin Epithalamia on the Occasion of the Palatine Marriage in 1613* (Göttingen, 2009).

8. Christ Church College Library (Oxford) [hereafter ChCh], William Wake Letters 25, no.129: Daniel Ernst Jablonski to William Wake, Berlin 28 March, 1719. On Hesse-Kassel, see *Friedrich, König von Schweden, Landgraf von Hessen-Kassel: Studien zu Leben und Wirken eines umstrittenen Fürsten (1676–1751)*, ed. Helmut Burmeister (Hofgeismar, Germany, 2003).

9. On Württemberg, see Samantha Owens, "Und mancher grosser Fürst kann ein Apollo seyn: Erbprinz Friedrich Ludwig von Württemberg (1698–1731)," *Musik in Baden-Württemberg* 10 (2003): 177–90.

10. Christoph Böttigheimer, *Zwischen Polemik und Irenik: Die Theologie der einen Kirche bei Georg Calixt* (Münster, 1996); Martin I. Klauber, *Between Reformed Scholasticism and Pan-Protestantism: Jean-Alphonse Turretin (1671–1737) and Enlightened Orthodoxy at the Academy of Geneva* (Selinsgrove, 1994); Wolf-Friedrich Schäufele, *Christoph Matthäus Pfaff und die Kirchenunionsbestrebungen des Corpus Evangelicorum 1717–1726* (Mainz, 1998).

11. See, for instance, Simon L. Adams, "'The Protestant Cause: Religious Alliance with the West European Calvinist Communities as a Political Issue in England, 1585–1630," PhD diss., Oxford University, 1973; William B. Patterson, *King James VI and I and the Reunion of Christendom* (Cambridge, UK, 1997); Thompson, *Britain, Hanover, and the Protestant Interest*.

12. Alexander Schunka, "Union, Reunion, or Toleration? Reconciliatory Attempts among Eighteenth-Century Protestants," in *Diversity and Dissent: Negotiating Religious Differ-*

ence in *Central Europe, 1500–1800,* ed. Howard Louthan, Gary B. Cohen, and Franz A. J. Szabo (New York, 2011), 309–34.

13. See relevant chapters in *Daniel Ernst Jablonski: Religion, Wissenschaft und Politik um 1700,* ed. Joachim Bahlcke and Werner Korthaase (Wiesbaden, 2008).

14. Hermann Dalton, *Daniel Ernst Jablonski. Eine preußische Hofpredigergestalt in Berlin vor 200 Jahren* (Berlin, 1903); Norman Sykes, *William Wake Archbishop of Canterbury 1657–1737,* 2 vols. (Cambridge, UK, 1957).

15. On the Hohenzollern dynasty in the early eighteenth century, see Linda Frey and Marsha Frey, *Frederick I: The Man and His Times* (New York, 1984).

16. Sykes, *William Wake,* 1, 205–6; 2, 1–88.

17. Georg Schnath, *Georg Ludwigs Weg auf den englischen Thron: Die Vorgeschichte der Thronfolge 1698–1714,* vol. 4 of *Geschichte Hannovers im Zeitalter der neunten Kur und der englischen Sukzession 1674–1714* (Hildesheim, 1982); Edward Gregg, *The Protestant Succession in International Politics, 1710–1716* (New York, 1986).

18. Victor Loewe, *Ein Diplomat und Gelehrter: Ezechiel Spanheim (1629–1710). Mit Anhang: Aus dem Briefwechsel zwischen Spanheim und Leibniz* (Berlin, 1924); Alexander Schunka, "Brüderliche Korrespondenz, unanständige Korrespondenz. Konfession und Politik zwischen Brandenburg-Preußen, Hannover und England im Wendejahr 1706," in Bahlcke and Korthaase, eds., *Daniel Ernst Jablonski,* 123–50.

19. Adolphus William Ward, *The Electress Sophia and the Hanoverian Succession* (London, 1909), 109, 345–47.

20. Waltraut Fricke, *Leibniz und die englische Sukzession des Hauses Hannover* (Hildesheim, 1957); Nora Gädeke, "Die Rolle des Historikers: Gottfried Wilhelm Leibniz und der Aufstieg des Welfenhauses," in *Hannover und die englische Thronfolge,* ed. Heide Barmeyer (Bielefeld, 2005), 157–78; Schnath, *Georg Ludwigs Weg,* 99–171.

21. Otto Krauske, "Die Verlobung Friedrich Wilhelms I," in *Beiträge zur brandenburgischen und preußischen Geschichte: Festschrift zu Gustav Schmollers 70. Geburtstag* (Leipzig, 1908); Schunka, "Brüderliche Korrespondenz," 137–48.

22. On George of Denmark, see Charles Beem, "'I Am Her Majesty's Subject': Prince George of Denmark and the Transformation of the English Male Consort," *Canadian Journal of History* 39 (2004): 457–88.

23. He was not an ordained pastor; see Alexander Schunka, "Zwischen Kontigenz und Providenz. Frühe Englandkontakte der halleschen Pietisten und protestantische Irenik um 1700," *Pietismus und Neuzeit* 34 (2008): 103–4.

24. Gottfried Wilhelm Leibniz to Daniel Ernst Jablonski, Hanover, 25 June, 1706, in *Neue Beiträge zum Briefwechsel von D. E. Jablonsky und G. W. Leibniz,* ed. Johann Kvačala (Jurjew, 1899), 98, No. 130.

25. GStAPK, Brandenburg-Preußisches Hausarchiv, II. Hauptabteilung, Rep. 46, N 2, 24r; see also Schunka, *Brüderliche Korrespondenz,* 144–45.

26. More details can be found in Alexander Schunka, "Irenicism and the Challenges of Conversion in the Early Eighteenth Century," in *Conversion and the Politics of Religion in Early Modern Germany,* ed. David Luebke, Jared Poley, Daniel Ryan, and David Warren Sabean (New York, 2012), 101–18.

27. GStAPK, 1. Hauptabteilung, Rep 81 London no. 10, 21, Report of the Prussian Resident Bonnet, London 24 December/4 January 1714/5. George's knowledge of the English language is discussed in Ragnhild Hatton, *Georg I: Ein deutscher Kurfürst auf Englands Thron* (Frankfurt, 1982), 138–42.

28. British Library (London) [hereafter BL], Ms. Stowe 223, 258v, Robert Hales to Jean Robethon, Windsor 3 August, 1709; Staatsbibliothek Berlin preußischer Kulturbesitz, Nachlass August Hermann Francke, 11,2/17 No. 55, Daniel Ernst Jablonski to John Robinson, Berlin 8 September, 1711; BL, Add. Mss. 70022, 142r, Robert Hales to (?), Hamburg, 5 May, 1705.

29. Aubrey Newman, "Two Countries, One Monarch: The Union England/Hanover as the Ruler's Personal Problem," in *Die Personalunionen von Sachsen-Polen 1697–1763 und Hannover-England 1714–1837 Ein Vergleich*, ed. Rex Rexheuser (Wiesbaden, 2005), 360.

30. A famous British pamphlet was written by the archbishop of York: William Dawes, *An Exact Account of King George's Religion: With the Manner of His Majesty's Worship in the English and Lutheran Church. And the First Rise of the Lutheran Religion. Shewing also, The Difference between Them and the Church of England as by Law Establish'd, and the Protestant Dissenters Therefrom. With a New Prayer for His Majesty* (London, 1714). On British perceptions of King George being a Lutheran, see Frauke Geyken, *Gentlemen auf Reisen: Das britische Deutschlandbild im 18. Jahrhundert* (Frankfurt, 2002), 135–53; Bob Harris, "Hanover and the Public Sphere," in *The Hanoverian Dimension in British History, 1714–1837*, ed. Brendan Simms and Torsten Riotte (Cambridge, UK, 2007), 183–212. On the print production in Hanover, see Nicholas Harding, "Hanoverian Rulership and Dynastic Union with Britain, 1700–1760," in *Die Personalunionen*, 389–414. The absence of religious issues in many Hanoverian documents is striking, especially in the "Regierungs-Reglement" of 1714, printed in Ludwig Timotheus Spittler, *Geschichte des Fürstenthums Hannover: seit den Zeiten der Reformation bis zu Ende des siebenzehnten Jahrhunderts*, 2 vols. (Göttingen, 1786), vol. 2, Appendix, 120–32.

31. Jablonski's visit to Hanover is documented in GStAPK, 1. Hauptabteilung, Rep. 13, 19d Fasz. 21. Additionally, see Walter Delius, "Berliner kirchliche Unionsversuche im 17. und 18. Jahrhundert," *Blätter für Berlin-Brandenburgische Kirchengeschichte* 45 (1970): 71–73.

32. ChCh, William Wake Letters 20, 111–12, Lancelot Blackburne to William Wake, Hanover, 16/27 July, 1716. On Blackburne, see Andrew Starkie, "Blackburne, Lancelot (1658–1743)," *Oxford Dictionary of National Biography*, 60 vols. (Oxford, 2004), vol. 5, 936–38. On the practice under George II, see Uta Richter-Uhlig, *Hof und Politik unter den Bedingungen der Personalunion zwischen Hannover und England. Die Aufenthalte Georgs II. in Hannover zwischen 1729 und 1741* (Hanover, 1992), 38–39.

33. ChCh, William Wake Letters 20, 118–20, Lancelot Blackburne to William Wake, Hanover, 31 July/11 August 1716.

34. ChCh, William Wake Letters 20, 127r–127v, Lancelot Blackburne to William Wake, Hanover, 17/28 August 1716.

35. ChCh, William Wake Letters 20, 139r, Lancelot Blackburne to William Wake, Hanover, 28 August/8 September 1716.

36. ChCh, William Wake Letters 20, 139v, Lancelot Blackburne to William Wake, Hanover, 28 August/8 September 1716.

37. ChCh, William Wake Letters 20, 294v-295r, Lancelot Blackburne to William Wake, Exeter 31 December1716; see also Sykes, *William Wake*, 2, 111–12.

38. Andrew Thompson, "The Confessional Dimension," in *The Hanoverian Dimension*, 173–77.

39. Moravian Archives (Bethlehem), Jablonski Papers 7, No. 33, Daniel Ernst Jablonski to Robert Hales (Berlin) 14 August, 1730.

40. Among others, see Jenkin Thomas Philips, *The History of the Two Illustrious Brothers, Princes of Saxony . . . Ernestus the Pious, First Duke of Sax-Gotha, and Bernard the Great, Duke of Sax-Weimar . . .* (London, 1740). See also Hannah Smith, *Georgian Monarchy: Politics and Culture, 1714–1760* (Cambridge, UK, 2006), 45–47.

41. Ernst H. Kantorowicz, *The King's Two Bodies: A Study in Mediaeval Political Theology* (Princeton, 1957).

~:~

CHAPTER 9

Transethnic Unions
in Early Modern
German Travel Literature

ANTJE FLÜCHTER

In the second half of the seventeenth century, Johann Christian Hoffmann, originally from Bischhausen, a small town in Hessen, sailed with the Dutch East India Company (Vereenigde Oost-indische Compagnie; VOC) to India. His travel account describes at length life onboard a VOC ship: the harsh punishments, the illnesses, and the deaths as well as one marriage: On the ship, one of the officers—the quartermaster (*Speisemeister*) Jacob Janson de Nys, from Amsterdam—married a young woman, named Maria Zacharia, the daughter of a VOC sergeant. The relationship astonished and shocked Hoffmann: "Such an unequal pair I have not seen all the days of my life. He is a very comely, reasonable, and learned person. She on the other hand is especially ugly in form, ignorant, childish, and, moreover, sired by a Hollander on a black Bengal slave."[1] Obviously Hoffmann perceived this relationship between a rational attractive man and a brutish unattractive female as very unequal. And last but not least: he was white and she was what today we would call a person of mixed race.

Marriage is a social institution through which property and resources are distributed and passed down. Connubial circles reveal and represent social distinctions. Marriages and, moreover, socially acceptable marriages follow specific criteria of exclusion. Each particular cultural and historical context sets the boundaries or rules according to which who could marry whom is determined. All the chapters in this volume tackle one or another aspect of this social reality. The process of redefining or restructuring marriage circles, either allowing or excluding persons from the circle of acceptable mates, represented every process of change with the social system, its shifting hierarchies or its criteria for social distinction. The question of the suitability of marriage partners was always one place where social distinctions were negotiated, as Michael

Sikora's recent research on misalliances among the high nobility in the Holy Roman Empire has demonstrated.[2] Thus, marital relationships or less-formal unions always represent power relations; that is as true for the European context as it is for any colonial or transcultural context.

During the early modern period, encounters between Europeans and non-Europeans increased significantly, both in sheer numbers and duration. While no German state was a major player in the European expansion, Germans did travel as sailors and soldiers with all the many European trading companies. At least 500,000 German-speaking men signed on with the VOC. Their letters and stories brought Asia into German homes. Moreover, several wrote travelogues. Roelof van Gelder has counted 154 nonfictional travelogues in German, among them forty-seven written by VOC employees.[3] The travelogues are especially important as part of the German discourse on Asia because they were often produced by men who were not learned, but rather who sprang from social backgrounds that only rarely have left behind autobiographical texts.[4] Furthermore, they were often written for a local or regional readership and for the purpose of entertainment or amusement rather than instruction.[5]

In addition to depicting the hardships of early modern travel and describing the many astounding fruits, plants, and animals travelers encountered, travelogues also regularly discussed unions between Indians and Europeans and commented on the mixed populations found in Asian harbor towns. In these texts the relevance of marriage as a social institution entwined with descriptions and discussions of cultural and ethnic encounters and sexual mingling. These travel accounts and the 1702 novel *The Hot Indian Woman, or: An Interesting and Curious Description of East-Indian Women* (Die hitzige Indianerin, Oder artige und curieuse Beschreibung derer ost-indischen Frauens-personen) are the main sources of this chapter. The novel was probably written by the German-Transylvanian author Andreas Pinxner, and represents the contemporary perception of India.[6] This fictional text processed and tailored information about India to fit the mentalities of German readers.[7]

Discussions about ethnically mixed marriages from the colonial period included efforts to forbid them or at least to complicate the procedure of marrying.[8] By the mid- to late-nineteenth century the racial discourse had become crucial; it determined whether a union was socially accepted. In premodern times, however, the criteria determining social boundaries and social distinctions were still multifaceted; ethnic and social boundaries were very important, but so, too, were religious ones. Which factors decided whether transethnic unions were legitimate or transgressive in the premodern period? What issues were important before aspects of race as a biological category became dominant? What role did social, ethnic, religious, or financial considerations play, and what were the relationships among them? Did a hierarchy exist among the criteria?

The early modern era was a formative period in respect to many basic structures of modern life. Parallel to the evolution of the modern state and modern civil society there occurred an equally important paradigm shift in the fundamental ways in which people viewed and explained the world: a scientific and biological worldview replaced a religious one. The increasing influence of biology engendered two concepts crucial for understanding the attitudes toward the interethnic and interracial unions treated here: the modern concepts of gender roles and race. And the other way round: The way in which early modern Europeans represented interethnic unions and consequently the emerging of a transcultural social group offers an important way to analyze how old interpretation patterns, like religion, began to disappear and new ones, like biology, have evolved.[9]

The following pages analyze descriptions of Indian-European relations as they appeared in German early modern travelogues. European travelers to India were always impressed by the great diversity in the Indian population. The VOC servant Jürgen Andersen, for example described the many *Nationen* in the Indian harbor town Surat.[10] First, he mentioned the ones who traded here—the English, Dutch, Arabs, Persian, Turks, Armenian, and Jews—and, second, those who always lived here—the Gujaratis, people from Cambaia, the Bannyan (*Benjanen*), Brahmins, people from the Deccan, and the Rajputs.[11] This list shows that premodern Europeans had not one consistent pattern to differentiate the Indian society, but used different competing categories. Until late eighteenth century most Europeans had problems developing a (to them) comprehensible order for these mixed religious, geographic, and social elements.

The following analysis focuses on ethnic, social, and religious factors, and weighs their relevance against each other. I here employ all three terms in their modern sense, rather than in the forms found in my sources. If we wish to use terms like "social status" and "religion" in a premodern and non-European context, we have to be very careful to avoid anachronism.[12] Regarding the category of ethnicity, the situation is even more complicated. Recent concepts of ethnicity understand it often as a kind of collective identity, based on a shared religion, culture, or origin.[13] Here, however, I use it as a category for an ascription of a group identity by others, most of all the European typology of Indian society. In that context ethnicity is understood as a category besides religion and social status, a category that encompasses most of all outer appearance (for example, skin color) and regional origin.[14]

Many European males, but few females, came to India on the ships of the trading companies. Not surprisingly, therefore, marriage, concubinage, and casual affairs with Indian women were ubiquitous. Equally common was prostitution.[15] Nevertheless, prostitution is curiously missing from the travel accounts analyzed here. Hardly anyone wrote about his own experiences, although there was a tendency to accuse other Europeans, especially those from places competing with the VOC for access to the Asian markets, of frequenting prostitutes. Most travelers, and especially those within the Calvinist-oriented VOC, were apparently reluctant to talk about their own experiences in the sex market for fear of damaging their reputations. Prostitution was sometimes mentioned when describing the Indian dancing girls, whom they often equated with the temple dancers who were part of cultic practice (*devadasis*). Whether prostitution was part of this phenomenon, *devadasis* were distinct from travelling dancing girls.[16] More often the travel accounts mentioned "affairs" with female slaves, but usually as something other Europeans did rather than as a normal practice in their own community. The French traveler and official of the French East India Company, Pierre Poivre, wrote in the eighteenth century that every Dutchman in Batavia had several concubines, all of whom were slaves from Bengal or Malaysia; the ones from Makassar were both the most beautiful and the most expensive.[17] A Dutch report about the Guinea Gold Coast from the early seventeenth century describes a similar Portuguese practice: because the Portuguese could not bring their own women to Africa, they took "reasonable black women" (*verständige Möhrinnen*) as their mates. According to the Dutch report, this practice proved more convenient for the men than a legitimate marriage, because they could simply purchase their "wives." Thus, too, they could easily be rid of them, simply selling them or abandoning them and buying a new one.[18]

We should reject the impression, however, that relationships that lasted only a short time and lacked all sense of commitment where the normal case or even the only kind of unions. The assumption that Europeans mostly used only slaves, concubines, and prostitutes to satisfy their sexual needs and that emotionally profound or legalized interethnic or interracial relations were exceptions that faced enormous legal and social difficulties is based on a nineteenth-century perspective. It was the nineteenth century, strongly affected by a full-blown colonial mentality, that made it difficult for Europeans to conceive the existence of long-term interethnic unions while denying them social acceptance. The idea of marriage in the early modern world did not always bear the same meaning it does today. In premodern Europe, marriage practices were also not identical in all social groups. For instance, European couples without sufficient economic resources often only married semilegally. Church and state often criticized and condemned such clandestine marriages, but the practice did not change even after the introduction the Reformation and Tridentine reform.[19] Thus, European social practice sanctioned different levels of institutionalization for marital unions in the Dutch diaspora in India; each level corresponded to the social status of the parties involved. The VOC employee Christoff Frikens, for example, explained that a European man (*Europäer*) who wanted to marry an Indian woman (*Indianerin*) had to seek official permission.

Frikens described this special procedure: He and his wife-to-be had to make an appointment at the city hall in Batavia. For this appointment they needed "official papers prepared by a solicitor and procurator", and friends to accompany them, probably as witnesses. Frikens further explained that these formalities were only necessary if the couple possessed some property or capital; otherwise, a simple application to the city council or VOC president without special papers sufficed. In both cases, however, the couple had to wait for permission before they could wed; most successful applicants married about two weeks after applying.[20] Frikens's account, it should be noted, described an administrative procedure and its rules; he did not address marriage as a religious act. It is significant, however, that the writers of the travel accounts refer to this relationship as a marriage (*Ehe*) and refer to the man and woman as a married couple. Certainly there were other terms available to describe such a union. It can be concluded that in the authors' conception there were different kind of legitimate marriages possible, amongst others depending on social status, and that the legitimacy of a marriage did not depend on a religious ritual.[21]

Ordinary married Europeans (the many European VOC employees who remained in Asia) and not the European elite (the higher ranks of the VOC administration) are the subject here. For elites, the rules and the opportunities to circumvent this was much greater; indeed the whole situation differed.[22] They, unlike the common employees, often brought their families with them to Asia or they married the few European women there.[23] Common employees had to look for other solutions, such as a mixed marriage, if they did not want to live alone. Christian Burckhardt described how they solved the problem of too few European women: "The common man and the artisans mostly turn to black women that they buy out of slavery and then marry."[24] The Italian traveler Pietro della Valle also depicted comparable practices, explaining how on their way to Batavia, many Dutch stopped in the Indian harbor town Surat, to find a wife "and because they can find no European women, take Indian, or Armenian, or Syrian [women] or those from all other nations if they are Christians or are willing to accept Christian beliefs."[25] While della Valle's words could be understood as polemic and perhaps not true, other travel accounts confirm them.

As mentioned, one thing that astounded German travelers in Asia was the diversity of Asian trading towns' population in general and in particular the large number of mixed marriages they found there. The mixed population of Portuguese towns particularly attracted comment. The German VOC employee Jürgen Andersen, emphasized how ubiquitous Portuguese-Indian offspring were in Goa: "The Portuguese marry not only women from their nation," he noted, "but also [marry] Indians, Moors and others. The children they produce with them are called Mastys."[26] That a unique name existed for the offspring of these unions—Mastys, itself a pidgin version of *mestizo*—suggests strongly that they were many of them as well as that they were perceived as distinct group. It could be argued, of course, that Portuguese-ruled Catholic Goa was often used as a negative foil in the Protestant German or Dutch travelogues.[27] But Catholic travelers, like Francesco Carletti, penned similar descriptions of the Goan population.[28] More important, the German and Dutch travelogues describe similar circumstances in Asian or Indian towns where there was found a German-Dutch majority or where they ruled. When attempts to bring Dutch women to Asia failed, the Dutch authorities adopted the Portuguese policy of allowing interethnic relationships.[29] Still, the situation was less free in the Dutch colonies. For example, VOC employees who were married to Indian women were not allowed to bring them or their children back to Europe.[30] Nevertheless, in some of the trading towns where the Dutch represented the majority of European settlers, such as in Palicat, relationships between Dutch men and native women resembled those described for Goa. Jürgen Andersen, a VOC servant from Schleswig-Holstein, compared Palicat's population with that in Goa. Offspring in Palicat were called *Mestysen*, as in Goa, and the grandchildren were called *Castyse*. In Palicat these two groups constituted the majority of the population.[31] Johann Jacob Merklein, writing in the middle of the seventeenth century, noted that many Dutch people living in Palicat, including merchants, soldiers, and officials, were mostly married to Indian women, or lived with them without marrying them.[32] Similar narratives can also be found concerning Batavia, where many Christians are described as having married Europeans and many others took Indian women as wives.[33] That is, also in Batavia, the capital of the VOC in Asia and therefore with much more European population than towns ruled by Indian governments, mixed marriages were addressed as a common phenomenon. Mixed marriages and mixed populations in Indian towns were, therefore, quite common.

Despite these differences being reducing to a category, which I have labeled "ethnic" in this chapter, this is not the only category that is frequently used. In della Valle's text, ethnicity was subordinated to religion: The Dutch married many kinds of women "as long as they were Christians." Moreover, many of the Indians involved in such relationships did not come from Indian families with some social reputation. As della Valle explained, it was difficult to find Indian women willing to leave their families. Therefore the Europeans had to buy slaves, free them from their bondage, and then marry them.[34] The inequality in mixed marriages thus was not only ethnic, but also social: husbands and wives came from very different social backgrounds. At the beginning of the Dutch diaspora, most women involved in such mixed matches were described as former slaves, but in the course of time this changed: newcomers from Europe may still have bought Indian slaves and married them, but the clearly defined link between ethnic origin and social status changed over time and with it the undisputed social superiority of free European men marrying enslaved Indian women. The offspring of Europeans who stayed in Asia, together with their indigenous wives and children, formed a new society with its own social hierarchy. Daughters of these families generally did not marry newcomers from Europe.[35] Indeed, the opposite was true: marrying into such a family indicated a form of social advancement for a newcomer. In this case, ethnic and social hierarchies had shifted substantially and now individual situations and individual aims became more important. Ethnic boundaries and social hierarchies had become more flexible in this mixed society than they were in Europe.

Christoff Frikens reported an incident that makes this change clear. In his travelogue he reports that an old and rich Indian woman wanted to marry a young German man. He debated in his own mind for a long time about what to do. In the end he decided against the marriage because she was ugly, referring to her sarcastically as a "so beautiful image . . . that resembled a hundred-year-old ape." Moreover, such a marriage would have forced him to stay in Asia.[36] This young man had to weigh many criteria. The proposed marriage would have given him a higher social status in colonial society and quite a lot of money. He finally decided against the connection, supposedly, according to his own account, because the woman was old and unattractive. The ethnic difference seemed only important because it would have forced him to stay in Asia. The relevance of ethnic origin could be negotiated, but was not unimportant. One also must consider why a European would travel to Asia with a company. The sheer love of adventure certainly impelled some to take the leap, but most went because distress of some kind drove them to leave their native land. Certainly, most did not belonged to higher social circles.[37] Just as significant, however, is the fact that issues of ethnic and social differences are described almost exclusively in gendered terms; it was the woman who was native or of mixed origin.

Yet it is even more important to mention that this precolonial diasporic society had no access to Indian families of high social rank. Far from being dominant on the Indian subcontinent in the sixteenth and seventeenth centuries, the Europeans had great difficulty gaining access to Asian trade and to Indian power centers. The lack of interethnic unions with powerful or noble Indian families underscores this point. Family alliances binding together noble or powerful mercantile families of differing ethnic backgrounds existed in the pre-European world of the Indian Ocean and persisted even in the first years after the arrival of the Portuguese. The Portuguese author Tomé Pires described interethnic marriages in South Asia before 1500: Chinese and Islamic merchants, for example, often had married into the local elite. These marriages, and thus the process of ethnic mingling, characterized the precolonial societies of the Indian Ocean and also typified Islamized areas.[38] The Portuguese entered into similar unions at the beginning of their expansion. These unions, however, mostly occurred in Africa or Persia and not in India. Even then, non-Europeans expressed reservations about such unions. The Austrian traveler named Georg Christoph Fernberger reported that the elite of the Persian town Hormuz regarded their ruler with suspicion because he had given his daughter in marriage to a Portuguese noble. There may have been more cases like that, but rejection as an equal marriage partner is not a topic that Europeans liked to write or read about. Thus, Fernberger did not report a story about a mixed marriage, but rather narrated a romantic tale: the daughter of the Persian ruler died because she had so missed her husband while he was away; the husband died of a broken heart when he learned of his spouse's demise.[39] Furthermore, it was certainly easier to marry into an Muslim elite than into the so-called Hinduistic elite.[40] That remained true in eighteenth-century India under English rule.[41] The socially constructed boundaries of what Europeans generally call the caste society were more difficult to transgress than those dividing up the European social order. Moreover, it was perhaps easier for Portuguese or English men with noble backgrounds to be accepted as social equals and thus to be able to gain access to the Indian elites than it was for Dutch merchants or German sailors. Finally, although Indian society comprised many social groups, the Dutch and German VOC officials did not intermarry with any members of the Indian merchant class either or, at least, such marriages were not mentioned in any of the sources analyzed.

Thus, as we have seen, ethnic considerations were not the only major issues concerning interethnic unions in India; the question of social equality was just as important. Moreover, Europeans encountered several social and cultural barriers to mixed marriages. Unions that appeared socially equal from a European perspective, were simply unacceptable from the point of view of Indian families that refused to allow them.

In addition to the inequality deriving from varied ethnic and social backgrounds and status, the relevance of religious affiliation also played a major role. Religion, or confession, formed an important element in the structure of socially acceptable European marriage circles. Mixed marriages, between partners of different confessions, for instance, were not easily accepted, and the conversion of one spouse was usually required.[42] If a European man desired to marry an Indian woman, she had to be Christian. Many travel accounts highlight this requirement. For example, the Italian traveler Pietro della Valle wrote that many VOC officials married Indian women if they were Christians or willing to convert to Christianity.[43] Johann Christian Hoffmann noted that the Dutch authorities forbade some European craftsmen to marry their freed slaves because they were still heathens.[44] This religious barrier pertained not only to formal marriages, but also to more informal unions. Some travel accounts pointed out that this boundary related as well to short-term sexual relations or sex for sale. Both topics generally are not found in most early modern travel accounts, perhaps because they were written to be published for a European, or specifically German, audience. Hence, these texts both describe the traveler's experience in India and project a picture they wanted the audience to see. An anecdote related by Johann Albrecht von Mandelslo demonstrates this well. Mandelslo, a young nobleman from Schleswig-Holstein, traveled to India in the first half of the seventeenth century; he later came to be regarded as an expert on the Indian Mogul Empire. He relates that an Indian innkeeper had offered him female company for the night: "Which courtesy I politely refused ... [so as] not to pollute myself by fleshly conversation with a heathen." The religious barrier was described as crucial for a formal union, but there were also suggestions that different religions, or rather the woman being a heathen, presented a problem even for brief affairs. That is, the religious boundary could not be transgressed; in this case, negotiation was impossible or rather indescribably repellent.

The early modern travelogues here discussed show that there were many interethnic unions in India. Although mixed marriages were common, they still merited mention in the travel accounts. Whether a marriage was considered socially acceptable depended ultimately on a certain equality between the spouses, although inequality within a certain albeit limited range was possible. But equality is a social construct; it changes over time and place, and it even depends on specific situations. Whereas from the colonial perspective of the nineteenth century ethnic or racial boundaries were critical, a different set of boundaries pertained in precolonial India and their relevance and hierarchy were changing in the seventeenth and eighteenth centuries. Many Germans went to India with the VOC, so it can be assumed that many people in the German-speaking territories knew somebody who knew somebody who had been to India. But those who married Indian women mostly remained in India and therefore interethnic unions tended to remain in the realm of the unreal or in the part of the world encountered in literature. German readers did not experience these boundaries immediately or personally. Therefore mixed marriages could serve as a kind of projection screen in fictional texts, as a stage where questions of ethnicity, religion, or social status could be negotiated without actually having much contact with the reality of such unions.

Travelogues, therefore, offer one perspective on mixed matches in the early modern colonial world; belles lettres, in this case, *The Hot Indian Woman*, provide another and a contrasting view. This 1702 novel takes the form of a travelogue in which the narrator, Dacier, recounts his experiences and his adventures while traveling with the VOC. *The Hot Indian Woman* thus represents a fictionalized version of the travelogues analyzed above. In describing his own experiences, Dacier uses another character, Probando, as a foil. Probando had traveled widely, yet his experiences had made him a xenophobe and a misogynist. Probando used women, their role and position in society, and their morals as a way to describe and define alterity. In order to understand the conditions under which interethnic unions could be accepted, we must situate them in several relevant contexts: the construction of alterity, the drawing of boundaries, and the definition of distinctions. In analyzing travelogues, I argue that the most important criteria for determining differences were ethnic, social, and religious, in that order. That is, religion was the most important boundary, and one that could not be transgressed, whereas social difference, and even more ethnic difference, could be negotiated. Although that hierarchy changed at the beginning of the modern era, before then these formed the most important tropes in how these mixed unions were discussed and negotiated.

The Hot Indian Woman outlined the social status and origin of the several protagonists. Most of the women who appeared in the novel were Europeans of extremely modest social origins; they were represented as whores. The well-traveled Probando maintained that most European women who ventured out to India were whores; respectable women rarely travelled so far.[45] Dacier, however, encountered or learned about Indian women with different—that is, higher—social status. The novel includes, for example, anecdotes about the mughal's daughters, who liked having affairs with European men. Such adventures proved dangerous for the men involved; if discovered, they could forfeit their lives.[46] Another important figure, an attendant with the significant name of Sophia (meaning wisdom) was the enslaved daughter of an Indian raja and was one of the few women presented in positive terms in this book.[47] The novel recounted no stories of legitimate relationships between European men and Indian women of higher or equal social rank. The mughal's daughter was looking for pleasure, while Sophia's former social rank as a raja's daughter was eliminated by her enslavement.

Admittedly, the book mostly focused on illicit sexual affairs; it was not interested in legitimate marriages. Thus, social equality played little role in most of the narratives, which on the one hand is not astonishing because the aim of the novel was not a objective description of the European–Indian encounter, but to entertain the—mostly male—audience. On the other hand, religion was far more important than social status. For Probando, interreligious sexual relations or longer-term cohabitation were outrageous and blasphemous. If a Christian man slept with a heathen woman, Probando considered that the Christian thereby had polluted European blood. Only satanic lust could account for such a deviant practice.[48] One must wonder, however, if this passage really concerned religion. In this context, the terms "Christian" and "heathen" were actually code for "black" and "white" and "Indian" and "European." "Nature," Probando opined, "itself finds such [unions] repugnant and keeps them apart by coloring them black and white in order to drive us to our equals in both flesh and culture. One learns in school, that all friendship comes from lust. Tell me, [then], where is in this point [mixed unions] equality to be found." According to Probando, nature had created different skin colors as the natural sign to human beings so they might know whom to join with sexually and whom to avoid; only the mortal sin of lust blinded people to this all-too-obvious fact. Dacier wondered if the color of a person's skin could be a criterion by which to judge a human being, arguing that "color does not make the man."[49] For Probando, however, who represents a mainstream part of the German discourse on mixed unions, no equality can exist between these different phenotypes, although, of course, he would not have used that word.[50]

The transethnic population of Indian port towns formed an important topic in early modern German travel accounts. European travelers to India and armchair novelists perceived these people as ethnically mixed, and created a special terminology to describe their offspring. But which criteria were most important for evaluating transethnic, Indian–German relationships in early modern German discourse? The ethnic difference was not cast in modern racial terms, but rather depended heavily on the notion of skin color. Moreover, the ethnic difference was not the crucial, all-determining difference. Just as important were social differences. Furthermore, any interpretation of difference must include the fact that the Indian elite never formed any part of these mixed connubial circles. Thus the most common case, that of an Indian wife of a social rank considerably below that of her European husband, resulted from the continued working of socially exclusive Indian strategies. The equality of ethnic affiliation and social status were important, but while ethnic identity, skin color, and social status could all be successfully negotiated at least in some cases, religion could not. A difference in religion effectively prevented marriage; only an affair or concubinage was possible. The German readership did not experience transethnic unions themselves but, for the most part, only read about them. The discussion in *The Hot Indian Woman* represents as much a European misogynistic discourse as it does one constructing ethnic alterity. However, this novel also clearly demonstrates that the difference between Europe and India was more important for those who had remained in Europe than it was for those who ventured abroad. Or perhaps, similarity and equality could be experienced in India, but simply could not be believed in Europe.

Notes

1. Johann Christian Hoffmann, *Reise nach dem Kaplande, nach Mauritius und nach Java: 1671—1676* (The Hague, 1931), 48.
2. Sikora, "Ungleiche Verbindlichkeiten"; idem, "'Mausdreck mit Pfeffer': Das Problem der ungleichen Heiraten im deutschen Hochadel der Frühen Neuzeit," Habilitation Thesis, University of Münster, 2004; and Sikora's contribution to this volume. Still useful is Heinz Reif, "Zum Zusammenhang von Sozialstruktur, Familien- und Lebenszyklus im westfälischen Adel in der Mitte des 18. Jahrhunderts," in *Historische Familienforschung*, ed. Michael Mitterauer et. al. (Frankfurt, 1982), 123–55. In early modern Europe concepts, as well as practices, of marriage changed during the course of Reformation, see Harrington, *Reordering Marriage*; Safley, *Let No Man Put Asunder*;

Susanna Burghartz, "Umordnung statt Unordnung? Ehe, Geschlecht und Reformationsgeschichte," in *Zwischen den Disziplinen: Perspektiven der Frühneuzeitforschung,* ed. Helmut Puff (Göttingen, 2003), 165–86; and Antje Flüchter, "Eine katholische Ordnung der Sexualität? Konkurrierende Deutungsmuster um den Priesterzölibat im 17. Jahrhundert," in *Das Geschlecht des Glaubens: Religiöse Kulturen Europas zwischen Mittelalter und Moderne,* ed. Monika Mommertz and Claudia Opitz (Frankfurt, 2008), 201–28.

3. There were many texts and reprints; cf. Roelof van Gelder, *Das ostindische Abenteuer: Deutsche in Diensten der Vereinigten Ostindischen Kompanie der Niederlande (VOC), 1600–1800* (Hamburg, 2004), 13–16.

4. In Germany there was quite a discussion surrounding these so-called ego-documents—that is, autobiographical texts of all sorts, written by people from a rather unlearned background; see Kaspar von Greyerz, "Ego-Documents: The Last Word?," *German History* 28 (2010): 273–82; and Andreas Bähr, Peter Burschel, and Gabriele Jancke, "Räume des Selbst: Eine Einleitung," in *Räume des Selbst: Selbstzeugnisforschung transkulturell,* ed. Andreas Bähr, Peter Burschel, and Gabriele Jancke (Cologne, 2007).

5. See Donald F. Lach and Edwin J. Van Kley, eds., *Asia in the Making of Europe,* vol. 3, *A Century of Advance* (Chicago, 1993), esp. 533–46; Roelof van Gelder, *Het Oost-Indisch avontuur: Duitsers in dienst van de VOC (1600—1800)* (Nijmegen, 1997) ; Antje Flüchter, "'Aus den fürnembsten indianischen Reisebeschreibungen zusammengezogen': Knowledge about India in Early Modern Germany," in *The Dutch Trading Companies as Knowledge Networks,* ed. Siegfried Huigen, Jan L. de Jong, and Elmer Kolfin (Leiden, 2010), 337–60.

6. André Dacier, *Die hitzige Indianerin oder Artige und courieuse Beschreibung derer ostindianischen Frauens-Personen, welche sowohl aus Europa in Ost-Indien ziehen oder darinnen geboren werden, die sein gleich aus vermischten oder reinem heidnischen Geblüte derer India,* ed. Karl K. Walther (Berlin, 1991). First published in 1701, it was reissued in 1704 under the title *Die erlauchte Sklavin* ("The Illustrious Slave"). For more about the author, see Stefan Sienerth, "Andreas Pinxner, ein Zeitgenosse des Gorgias: Ein schlecht behandelter siebenbürgischer Barockautor," *Südostdeutsche Vierteljahresblätter* 38 (1989): 278–84.

7. The changes in these narratives over time and with the transfer of elements from one kind of text to another, forms the substance of my forthcoming book, *Die Vielfalt der Bilder und die eine Wahrheit: Die Staatlichkeit Indiens in der deutschsprachigen Wahrnehmung (1500-1700)* (Affalterbach, 2014).

8. Compare the situation in Africa under German colonial rule: Ulrike Lindner, "Contested Concepts of 'White' and 'Native': Mixed Marriages in German South-West Africa and the Cape Colony," *Basler Afrika Bibliographien Working Papers* 6 (2008): 1–18; Ann L. Stoler, *Carnal Knowledge and Imperial Power: Race and the Intimate in Colonial Rule* (Berkeley, 2002).

9. The terms inter- and transcultural are often used interchangeably or stylized as antithetic concepts; see Wolfgang Welsch, "Transculturality: The Puzzling Form of Cultures Today," in *Spaces of Culture. City, Nation, World,* ed. Mike Featherstone and Scott Lash (London, 1999). In this chapter each term addresses a different perspective: "intercultural" describes the interaction or encounter between two or more as different perceived groups, whereas "transcultural" focuses on practices, institutions, ideas, and so on that evolved as a consequence of an encounter and beyond the participating groups or individuals.

10. This early modern concept of nation has to be distinguished from the modern one. Nonetheless, it is often overlooked that there indeed exists a premodern, humanistic concept of nation. See, for example, Caspar Hirschi, *Wettkampf der Nationen: Konstruktionen einer deutschen Ehrgemeinschaft an der Wende vom Mittelalter zur Neuzeit* (Göttingen, 2005); Herfried Münkler and H. Grünberger, "Nationale Identität im Diskurs der Deutschen Humanisten" in *Nationales Bewußtsein und kollektive Identität*, ed. Helmut Berding (Frankfurt, 1996). However, this concept was not the hegemonic criterion for ethnographic typologies. Rather, it was a learned discourse. The VOC officials used the term "nation" in a less defined and more elusive way; see Antje Flüchter, "'Religions, Sects and Heresy'—Religion on the Indian Subcontinent in Early Modern German Texts," in *Labeling the Religious Self and Others: Reciprocal Perceptions of Christian, Muslims, Hindus, Buddhists, and Confucians in Medieval and Early Modern Times*, ed. Hans Martin Krämer, Jenny Oesterle, and Ulrike Vordermark (Leipzig, 2010), 63.
11. Jürgen Andersen and Volquard Iversen, *Orientalische Reise-Beschreibungen: In der Bearbeitung von Adam Olearius, Schleswig 1669*, ed. Dieter Lohmeier (Tübingen, 1980), 25.
12. On this issue in respect to religion, see Jonathan Z. Smith, "Religion, Religions, Religious," in *Critical Terms for Religious Studies*, ed. Marc C. Taylor (Chicago, 1998): 269–84.
13. See Till van Rahden, "Weder Milieu noch Konfession: Die situative Ethnizität der deutschen Juden im Kaiserreich in vergleichender Perspektive," in *Religion im Kaiserreich: Milieus–Mentalitäten–Krisen*, ed. Olaf Blaschke and Frank-Michael Kuhlemann (Gütersloh, 1996), 413; Steve Fenton, *Ethnicity* (Cambridge, UK, 2003), 12–23; and Marcus Banks, *Ethnicity: Anthropological Constructions* (New York, 1996).
14. In this way, for example, ethnicity is used by Remco Raben in his analysis for Batavia and the Javan population there; see his *Round about Batavia: Ethnicity and Authority in the Ommelanden 1650–1800* (Leiden 2000), esp. 99–100.
15. Pierre Poivre, *Reisen eines Philosophen 1768*, ed. Jürgen Osterhammel (Sigmaringen, 1997), 82. The account appeared in English as *The travels of a philosopher: Being observations on the customs, manners, arts, . . . of several nations in Asia and Africa* (London, 1769). See also Levinus Hulsius, *Siebte Schiffahrt, das ist: In das Goldreiche Königreich Guineam, in Africa gelegen, so sonsten das Goldgestadt von Mina genan[n]t wirdt, welches von den Portugalesern vngefähr vor 200. Jahren erfunden, von den Holländern jnnerhalb 18. Jahren hero bekannt gemacht* (Frankfurt, 1606), 211.
16. About the ritual and social position of the *devadasis* and their Portuguese colonial construction, see Rosa Maria Perez, "The Rhetoric of Empire: Gender Representations in Portuguese India," *Portuguese Studies* 21 (2005): 126–45; for information on the German discourse on dancers, see Antje Flüchter, "Bajadere und Sati—Bilder der Inderin im deutschsprachigen Diskurs der Frühen Neuzeit," in *Gender in Trans-it: Transkulturelle und transnationale Perspektiven*, ed. Martina Ineichen and Anna K. Liesch (Basel, 2009): 159–70. One context in which prostitution was mentioned was the custom of guest prostitution. This ethnographic narrative constructed by Europeans described how the inhabitants of the Malabar coast offered their wives or daughters to their guests as sexual partners; see Folker E. Reichert, "Fremde Frauen. Die Wahrnehmung von Geschlechterrollen in den spätmittelalterlichen Orientreiseberichten," in *Die Begegnung des Westens mit dem Osten*, ed. Odilo Engels and Peter Schreiner (Sigmaringen, 1993), 174–76.
17. Poivre, *Reisen*, 82. Poivre went on to note that these women were not allowed to convert to Christianity.

18. All quotes from Hulsius, *Siebte Schiffahrt*, 211.
19. Jutta Sperling, "Marriage at the Time of the Council of Trent (1560–1570): Clandestine Marriages, Kinship Prohibitions, and Dowry Exchange in European Comparison," *Journal of Early Modern History* 8 (2004): 67–108; Richard Adair, *Courtship, Illegitimacy and Marriage in Early Modern England* (Manchester, 1996), 139–42.
20. Christoff Frikens, *Ost-Indianische Reisen und Krieges-Dienste/Oder eine Ausführliche Beschreibung was sich solcher Zeit–nämlich von Anno 1680 bis Anno 1685, zur See als zu Land in öffentlichen Treffen und Scharmützeln, in Belagerungen, Stürmen und Eroberungen der Heidnischen Plätze und Städte im Marschieren und in Quartieren mit ihm und seinem beigefügten Kameraden hin und wieder begeben, bearbeitet und eingeleitet von Joachim Kirchner* (Berlin, [1692] 1926), 75.
21. Little is known about the manner in which confessionally specific forms of marriage were implemented in non-European context; for some tentative observations concerning the Catholic church, see Tara M. A. Alberts, "Marriage in Southeast Asia: Obstacles to the Tridentine Model and the Development of Local Compromises," conference paper delivered at the Third European Congress on World and Global History, London 14–17 April 2011.
22. For example, those of higher ranks could bring their European families to Asia and it was also easier for them to return home with their Indian families.
23. See Christian Burckhardt, *Ost-Indianische Reise-Beschreibung / Oder Kurtzgefaßter Abriß von Ost-Indien /und dessen angräntzenden Provincien, bevorab wo die Holländer ihren Sitz und Trafiquen manutenieren etc.* (Halle, 1693), 242–43.
24. Burkhardt, *Ost-Indianische Reise-Beschreibung*, 246. Somewhat similarly, Hoffmann observed that there were not enough German women "weßwegen etliche grobe Leute noch Geld /daß man ihnen erlauben möchte mit einigen von den eingekaufften Sclavinnen zu heurathen"; J. C. Hoffmann, *Reise*, 49.
25. Pietro della Valle, *Reiß-Beschreibung in unterschiedliche Theile der Welt / Nemblich in Türckey / Egypten / Palestina / Persien / Ost-Indien / und andere weit entlegene Landschafften / Samt einer außführlichen Erzehlung aller Denck- und Merckwürdigster Sachen* (Geneva, 1674), vol. 4, 9–10.
26. Andersen and Iversen, *Reise-Beschreibung*, 20.
27. That is most significant, if we think about the description here of Goan women as morally degraded and voluptuous. See Andersen and Iversen, *Reise-Beschreibung*, 20–22; Johann Albrecht von Mandelslo, *Des Hoch-Edelgebohrnen Johann Albrechts von Mandelslo Morgenländische Reise-Beschreibung: worinnen zugleich die Gelegenheit und heutiger Zustandt etlicher fürnehmen indianischen Länder, Provintzien, Städte und Insulen . . . beschrieben werden*, ed. Adam Olearius (Hamburg, 1696), 93–95.
28. Carletti visited Goa in the sixteenth century and his description was generally far more positive than later Protestant reports; Francesco Carletti, *Reise um die Welt 1594: Erlebnisse eines Florentiner Kaufmanns*. (Tübingen, 1966), 256–59.
29. Charles R. Boxer, *Mary and Misogyny: Women in Iberian Expansion Overseas, 1415–1815: Some Facts, Fancies and Personalities* (London, 1975), 63–95. Jan P. Coen, the Dutch Governor General in Batavia, was the foremost strategist of the Dutch colonial effort to deport female orphans to Asia. This effort failed, however; see Horst Lademacher, "Batavia," in *Kolonialstädte—Europäische Enklaven oder Schmelztiegel oder Schmelztigel der Kulturen?*, ed. Horst Grüner and Peter Johanek (Münster, 2001), 106–8; Leonard Blussé, "Batavia 1619–1740: The Rise and Fall of a Chinese Colonial Town," *Journal of Southeast Asian Studies* 12 (1982): 166–67; and Jean Gelmann Tay-

lor, *Social World of Batavia: European and Eurasian in Dutch Asia* (Madison, 1983), 12–17.

30. Lademacher, "Batavia," 107. Christoff Frikens related the story of a friend who was considering marrying a Batavian woman. In the end he decided against it, because he would have then been obliged to stay in India forever; Frikens, *Reisen*, 76. See also the report by J. P. Rauschers, quoted in Johann Jacob Merklein, "Reise nach Java, Vorder- und Hinter-Indien, China und Japan, 1644–1653," in *Reisebeschreibungen von Deutschen Beamten und Kriegsleuten im Dienste der Niederländischen West- und Ost-indischen Kompagnien 1602–1797*, 13 vols., ed. Samuel Pierre L'Honoré Naber (The Hague, 1930), vol. 3, 77–78. Rauscher is even more interesting because he offers two reasons for this policy: First, the Netherlands were a small country and, more important, free. Thus, the Netherlanders would not tolerate tyrannical rule. Unfortunately Rauscher did not expand on this argument, that is, he did not explain in detail why Indian women endangered Dutch freedom. His second explanation is a moral judgment: these "Masticen" are said to be very voluptuous.

31. Andersen and Iversen, *Reise-Beschreibung*, 96. One interesting difference exists between Andersen's text and comparable ones. Andersen did not only write about European men marrying Indian women, but also the other way round, discussing Dutch women who married Indian men. In no other travelogue that I have analyzed did this kind of mixed marriage appear as a common case. Several reasons can be adduced to explain that fact. First, there were only very few European women in Asia so there was no need for them to marry Indian men. In fact, they normally wed the most important European men, as Burckhardt pointed out; *Reise-Beschreibung*, 243. Moreover, European social norms concerning spousal equality were much stricter for women than for men. It may be that these formulations in Andersen's text were included by the editor Adam Olearius, who intervened in the texts much more frequently than did other editors. Naber, for example, did not include the reports of Andersen and Iversen in his list of German VOC travelogues; see his introduction to Merklein, *Reise*, viii.

32. Merklein, *Reise*, 53.

33. Ibid., 18. This situation is also thus described in recent research about the Malabar coast, including Anjana Singh, *Fort Cochin in Kerala (1750–1830): The Social Condition of a Dutch Community in an Indian Milieu* (Leiden, 2010), 110, 177.

34. See della Valle, *Reiß-Beschreibung*, part 4, 10, 44.

35. Particularly well-researched is the case of the merchant Pieter Cnoll, whose wife Cornelia von Nijenrode had a Japanese mother. Leonard Blussé, *Bitters bruid: een koloniaal huwelijksdrama in de Gouden Eeuw* (Amsterdam, 1997). A painting of the couple and their daughters hangs in the Rijksmuseum, Amsterdam, and was also printed in an exhibition catalog, *The Dutch Encounter with Asia, 1600* (Zwolle, 2002), 200–201.

36. Frikens, *Reisen*, 76.

37. That may be the reason that some travelogues lament that in diaspora societies only money mattered. Christian Burckardt voiced a similar complaint concerning European women. After they married in India they behaved like noble women, whereas before in the Netherlands they had only sold apples or worse; see Burckhardt, *Reise-Beschreibung* 243. Even more disturbing was the fact that this reversal of the "good old" social order agitated those who stayed in Europe. In the *The Hot Indian Woman*, Dacier explained the situation in Asia as follows: "Who among the free people possesses the most money, he is the mightiest in speech, in appearance, and the most learned and skilled." 78.

38. Pires reported, for example, the history of Malacca that he had heard himself: Islamic traders had married into the royal family and the king had himself become a Muslim. A short time later, seeking to improve his relations with China, he became a vassal of the Chinese emperor and married the daughter of an important Chinese family. He subsequently introduced Chinese customs at his court. Tomé Pires and Francisco Rodrigues, *The Suma Oriental of Tome Pires: An Account of the East, from the Red Sea to Japan, Written in Malacca and India in 1512–1515*, ed. Armando Cortesão (Nendeln, 1967), 242–49. Such relations were also rather common in the South American context. Robinson A. Herrera highlighted the importance of marriage alliances with native noblewomen in Guatemala. In Asia relations with non-noble native women were almost inevitably ones of concubinage. See Herrera, "Concubines and Wives: Reinterpreting Native-Spanish Intimate Unions in Sixteenth-Century Guatemala," in *Indian Conquistadors, Indigenous Allies in the Conquest of Mesoamerica*, ed. Kaura E. Matthew and Michel R. Oudijk (Norman, 2007), 131–33, 137–38.

39. Georg Christoph Fernberger, *Reisetagebuch (1588–1593): Sinai, Babylon, Indien, Heiliges Land, Osteuropa*, ed. Ronald Burger und Robert Wallisch (Frankfurt, 1999), vol. 1, 80.

40. "Hinduism" is much discussed and debated term. It has been argued that it, like the term "caste," was actually an invention of the British in the late eighteenth and nineteenth century. Axel Michaels, *Der Hinduismus: Geschichte und Gegenwart* (Munich, 1998), 27–30; Ines Zupanov and R. Po-Chia Hsia, "Reception of Hinduism and Buddhism," in *The Cambridge History of Christianity*, vol. 6, *Reform and Expansion 1500– 1600*, ed. R. Po-Chia Hsia (Cambridge, UK 2007), 577–97.

41. William Dalrymple's *White Mughals: Love and Betrayal in Eighteenth-Century India* (London, 2002) has provoked much discussion. In a later article, he described the marriage of James Achilles Kirkpatrick with Khair un-Nissa, a daughter of an Islamic high official in Hyderabad, a case of a marriage into Islamic nobility; see his "White Mughals: The Case of James Achilles Kirkpatrick and Khair un-Nissa," in *Unfamiliar Relations: Family and History in South Asia*, ed. Indrani Chatterjee (New Brunswick, NJ, 2004), 122–59.

42. François, *Die unsichtbare Grenze*, discusses the problems of confessional mixed marriages in the Holy Roman Empire, as does Freist, "Crossing Religious Borders." See also Dagmar Freist's contribution to this volume.

43. Valle, *Reiß-Beschreibung*, part 4, 11.

44. J. C. Hoffmann, *Reise*, 49. Pierre Poivre wrote that some Dutch slaves were not allowed to become Christian; Poivre, *Reisen*, 11. That prohibition could indicate that the attitude toward mixed marriages had changed and that the Dutch authorities tried to restrict the practice of marrying non-European, freed slaves.

45. Dacier, *Hitzige Indianerin*, 43.

46. Ibid., 122–24.

47. Ibid., 151–54.

48. Ibid., 221.

49. Ibid., 148–49.

50. Ibid., 221–22.

CHAPTER 10

~: :~

The Meaning of Love
Emotion and Kinship in
Sixteenth-Century Incest Discourses

CLAUDIA JARZEBOWSKI

When Martin Luther married the former nun Katharina von Bora in 1525, contemporaries considered his marriage incestuous.[1] Why? As an Augustinian monk, Luther had vowed to lead a chaste life, a promise regarded as binding, indissoluble, and mandatory. Katharina von Bora had entered the convent of Nimbschen in 1509, at the age of ten. In 1515 she became a regular nun by taking final vows of chastity.[2] Both she and Martin Luther had therefore abjured a worldly life, renounced marriage, and devoted themselves entirely to God. Despite her vows and despite having lived for fourteen years in the cloister, in 1523 Katharina von Bora, along with several of her fellow nuns, fled the Nimbschen cloister. She found safe haven with the Cranach family in Wittenberg, where she lived for two years, weighing various marriage proposals. Her marriage to Luther in 1525—which became possible only after Katharina's plan to marry a Wittenberg student, as well as Luther's designs on a different nun—raised two fundamental problems. From the point of view of the Catholic Church, both had entered into a permanent union with God, which obliged them to renounce sexuality and marriage for the rest of their natural lives.[3] Second, according to contemporary theology, Luther and Bora were already married, not with each other but each with God. This made them spiritual siblings; therefore their marriage not only mocked God, but also violated prohibitions against incestuous unions. In the eyes of the church, all these violations ruptured taboos surrounding marriage, each essential to the defense of godly law.

In so doing, the Luther-Bora marriage also anticipated a series of broader debates over the meaning of kinship and sexuality, marriage law, and—less explicitly—the role of emotions in married life. These concerns transcended the emerging divide between the old and new churches: as Beth Plummer shows in her contribution to this volume, many Protestants also expressed skepticism toward marriages of former monks and priests. The offenders, who included Heinrich Bullinger, Johannes Brenz, and Justus Jonas, argued forcefully against the binding character of celibacy and vows of chastity. The high point in this debate coincided in the 1520s and 1530s with a wave of prominent marriages involving former monks, nuns, and priests.[4] Despite the growing number of such unions, however, no unified line of argument emerged in their defense.[5] Most arguments focused on legal and moral aspects. Some Reformers historicized celibacy, noting that legal restrictions on clerical marriage originated at the Lenten Synod of Rome in 1075 and at the Second Lateran Council in 1139 in Rome.[6] Others objected to the Catholic position that Scripture required clerical celibacy, insisting instead that the Bible endorsed marriage as a way of life pleasing to God. Revoking the sacramental character of marriage, they argued, would allow priests to lead a model life for the people of the community. Advocates of marriage for clergy (including former monks, priests, and nuns) argued that it would do more to advance God's will in the world than demanding a chastity that only a few exceptional individuals were able to achieve.

The marriage of Luther and Bora also challenged the meaning of kinship and raised questions about the significance of spiritual kinship from an evangelical perspective. Spiritual kinship (*cognatio spiritualis*) cannot be consigned to the realm of historical curiosity in considering the question of what constitutes legitimate and illegitimate marriages. In fact, the prohibition against godparents marrying their godchildren or even their godchildren's blood relatives had existed for centuries.[7] During the first half of the sixteenth century, it was widely believed marriages involving spiritual relatives were incestuous because the partners were in fact spiritual siblings—that is, descended from the same spiritual father. As the issue of spiritual relationships suggests, we must inquire into the meaning of love in order to understand how the Reformation understood incestuous marriages.

This chapter analyzes the meanings reformers accorded to emotions, and especially to *love* within kinship, sexuality, and marriage. It ends with a brief consideration of how those changes flowed into the naturalization of love and incestuous desire during the first half of the eighteenth century. Between 1450 and 1550 the essential components of social life were renegotiated.[8] In this revolution of daily life, marriage formed a key issue. The central questions were these: Who was allowed to marry? How was society to ensure its generative continuity and its cherished traditions? How could the worldly order mirror and perform the divine will on earth? Should there be one privileged way of life, and if so, was it to be marriage? What kind of interpersonal relations should be allowed within the set of legitimate relationships? Such questions reveal how deeply disturbed had become the basic beliefs and convictions that held society together. Thus these controversies cannot be understood as simply representing a conflict between the old and the new church: that would vastly oversimplify the situation. Rather, they manifested fissures in the late medieval order of social life throughout Europe. As these changes altered the structures of society, new approaches to the organization of social life appeared as well. One such change was to increase the significance of the emotions in social relationships principally in the direction of taming and softening them. Leadership, for example, was supposed to be gentle and loving (*sanftmüthig* and *lieb*), not wrathful (*zornig*) or terrifying (*furchterregend*). Once godly love (*Gottesliebe*) reentered the world of the emotions, all social relations were open to its influence.[9]

Eros—Amor—Caritas: Love in the Sixteenth Century

Love is crucial to any understanding of late medieval and early modern concepts of power, authority, and relations between rulers and their subjects. The concept of love in question focuses on the love of God as the only means of legitimizing worldly power. Love in the medieval and early modern world did not primarily pertain to intimate or private relations between individuals (as modern historians might presume), but rather reflected God's love in the world. Such love was tangible in social life as an emotion on which the negotiation of social relations hinged.

Charity, or *caritas*, unified this concept of love and enables us to see how love became entwined with the legitimization of interpersonal, marital, and intimate relations during the sixteenth century.[10] This emerges from the rhetoric surrounding of love during the Peasants' War of 1525. In that conflict, love provided basic principles for legitimizing or delegitimizing social action and relations. The rebellious peasants, for example, justified their resistance with the argument that by transgressing the limits of long-established agreements, by increasing taxes too much, by violating common land, and so on, their lords had violated the godly law of love and thus negated their authority.[11] Reestablishing a righteous social order formed the peasants' principal goal: they imagined themselves to be the enforcers of godly love on earth. Luther agreed with their claims at first, but changed his mind once their protest turned bloody and violent.[12] In his tract "Against the Murdering and Thieving Hordes of Peasants," he called for the slaying of the "rebellious peasantry as an act of charitable love, even at the risk of one's own life." To die fighting the rebellious peasants was to perish "obeying the divine Word and commandment . . . and in loving service of your neighbor, whom you are rescuing as from the bonds of hell and the devil."[13] Love had emerged both as a form of social action and, through charity, as an argument to legitimize deadly violence.

In late medieval discourse on power and authority, love was almost always envisioned as male, as a principle that bound powerful men and scholars together.[14] Women figured neither in this construction of love, nor in the networks that produced it.[15] The love among scholars was understood as an erotic, striving love, reminiscent of Plato, and therefore sparked by the wish to reunite spiritually with one's other half.[16] Learned men strove for cognition, completion, and beauty. Friendship accompanied this love and promoted the well-being and self-fulfillment of the other.[17] Semantically, virtually no line separated spiritual love and physical or sexual love. Spiritual love, too, was experienced as a strong bodily sensation.[18] In order to prove the trueness of their love, men had to communicate like lovers and in so doing they actually became "lovers."[19]

This notion points to a major shift in perceptions of spirituality, the body, love, and gender during the Italian and French Renaissances. Dozens of authors, including Marguerite de Navarre, contributed to an outpouring of treatises on the proper relation between love, the body, and desire.[20] These authors treated desire—understood as a bodily experience—as a legitimate human trait within the worldly realm. In his *Gli Asolani* (1505) Pietro Bembo, for example, took the legitimacy of physical desire for granted.[21] Bembo makes it clear that complete fulfillment by spiritual union alone was an experience available to only a few.[22] The price to be paid for such fulfillment was to live a reclusive hermit's life. Bembo did not, however, tell his readers what to do if physical desire interfered with spiritual edification.[23] Rather he advised scholars and theologians to honor the woman for whom they longed as their muse.[24] Noble, learned, and spiritually well-formed women were the proper physical objects for the sexual fantasies of their admirers. Proper love in this sense was love directed toward the correct object and confirmed through reciprocation.

During the Renaissance, in other words, what had been true primarily for relations between men also became a signal feature of male-female relationships. Love became a divinely inspired force referring to class and social descent rather than to gender. It distinguished learned and powerful men and their spouses from those who were supposedly unable to experience it directly, such as artisans and peasants, the common people in general. Love became the exclusive resource of those who were well-educated and noble enough to be able to take on the challenges it presented.[25]

In late medieval times, finally, love was strongly performative. As *caritas*, love shaped the complex relations between rulers and ruled. This model also applied to neighborhood, household, kinship, and parish communities. Mutual love remained the defining principle of relations between rulers and learned men. Here love, above all *eros* in the platonic sense, represented the striving for the achievement of a commonwealth improved by togetherness. In the Renaissance love as physical desire was seen in a new and positive way as a driving force through which one could reach true love. The implications of this obviously elite concept reached far beyond its own social group. The question of legitimate and nonlegitimate desire addressed a general concern.[26] At the core of the matter lay the unsolved problem of reconciling sexual desire and true love. The attempt to answer this question extended the discussion to new topics and explains, as we will see, the salience of Renaissance discourses on love to discussions of incest in sixteenth-century Germany. But the German reformers handled these questions less nimbly than their Italian and French contemporaries, confining their debates on love to the realms of marriage and legitimate sexuality.

Marriage and the Love of God

For a long time historians were convinced that early modern marriages had nothing to do with affection or love, but were concerned solely with material interests.[27] In the 1980s, however, David W. Sabean and Hans Medick suggested that emotional and material interests were two sides of the same coin. On the basis of microhistorical case studies, they showed that matchmaking and marriages did not follow material or emotional interests alone; instead, the partners, parents, and sometimes godparents agreed on a marriage, entwining material interests with bonds of affection.[28] Today no one doubts the key role that affection (*Neigung*) played in matchmaking and in the creation of lasting and happy marriages.[29]

Nonetheless, early modern expectations required a kind of marital love that diverged sharply from modern concepts. Rüdiger Schnell identifies three discourses of love and marriage in the early modern context, each distinguished by its approach to sexuality. Schnell's analysis, however, is flawed because sexuality came to be seen as a separate and distinct facet of human nature only during the nineteenth century. Because commentators did not isolate sexuality as a component of identity separate from other concepts of social interaction, such as love, friendship, kinship, and marriage, it seems that Schnell's attempt to define different discourses on love and marriage based principally on differing ideas of sexuality may not be the best way to approach the problem. This observation applied at the semantic as well as at the practical level. Conceptualizing sexual relations as social relations made them an inherent part of the set of social relations that form a community. Schnell is right, though, in suggesting that the texts and treatises he consulted differed significantly in their normative approach to questions of love and sexual desire.[30]

Undoubtedly the reformers can take considerable credit for reconceptualizing marriage. Almost immediately, the reformers launched into the task of redefining marriage as a legal institution. Bullinger, for instance, argued that despite its effects on the soul, marriage was an "external matter" (*äußeres ding*) and therefore subject to secular authority (*oberkeit*).[31] From here it was a quick step to the conclusion that marriage prohibitions should no longer fall under ecclesiastical jurisdiction. The argument that marriage belonged to a world that God found pleasing paralleled the reformers' repudiation of coerced celibacy and also justified the marriages of evangelical priests. Marriage still appeared to be an obligation, however, rather than a matter of voluntary action or an act that required loving affection as a prerequisite. Especially those who preached "Be fruitful, and multiply" (Gen. 1:28) should lead exemplary lives, which would serve as a guide for parishioners to follow.[32] The reformers in turn never tired of emphasizing the voluntary nature of marriage and underlining the requirement that the partners and their parents should give their agreement. Only such agreement rendered the marriage legally valid.[33] Consequently, the first generation of reformers represented clandestine engagements as the greatest danger to social stability.[34]

Not surprisingly, Luther and his followers wished their own own marriages to be lasting and fruitful. Bullinger explicitly declared the task of raising children as the main purpose of marrying, followed by the necessity of avoiding prostitution and adultery (*hurerey*). He stressed that at "according to the will of God, one should be a companion to the other, a help and a comfort."[35] Bullinger referred to Moses in underlining that "among spouses the greatest attraction and unity should exist and nothing other than death should separate them."[36] Finally, in ranking the different kinds of love he gave priority to marital love as *hertzensliebe*. Love for parents took second place, because spouses were "one flesh and one body."[37] He believed that the solidity of a marriage was determined by the quality of love within it resulting from a closely intertwined bond of *caritas* and *amicitia*.[38]

Still the question remains: Which love did the reformers refer to in their discussions of marriage? Reformation treatises almost always mentioned love as a prerequisite for a successful, lasting marriage with several healthy children. This kind of love was distinct from marital desire (*ehelich begird*), and was linked to the love of God.[39] This position contained a conundrum, however, for only when marriages endured and produced children could the choice of marriage partners be viewed as one approved by God. When a marriage went wrong, the fault must have been with the partners and their parents. Some Reformers suggested that partners in failed marriages had wed without the certainty of true love, which is the love that God plants directly in the heart (*in die hertzen eingepflanzet*) or that they were not capable of accepting the present of love in an appropriate fashion, or that they trusted in a false love.[40] Erasmus Sarcer's question, "Whether it was also a sin, if the bride and groom love one another?" well illustrates the deep conflicts that existed here. In his answer he distinguished two kinds of love:

One transgresses God's law and is unreasonable, that is the love for another [man's] wife. There is however another love that is rooted in the human heart and is neither an affront to God's law or reason; such as the love between a groom and his bride, or between parents and children. Such love is a gift of God and no sin.[41]

The love sparked by God led inevitably to the marriage of righteous partners, who proved their compatibility by regular cohabitation, continuous consolation (*Trost*), and the maintenance of a frugal household.[42]

The love endowed by God could include physical desire (*begird*), provided that it was a desire aimed at producing children and preventing extramarital relations. This latter objective in particular allowed for sexual activities within marriage that were not necessarily procreative: a desire to have no more children, issues of age or ill health, or simply lust. Thus Reformers could differentiate between desirous love (*begird der liebe*), natural affection (*natürlich neigung*), and roguish love (*buebischen liebe*): "Love is the eternal inclination of your heart that you feel for your chosen spouse in marriage. Herein is the difference between the marital inclination and the natural desire."[43] By redefining marriage as worldly, it was necessary to develop reasons for continuing to prohibit certain marriages. In formulating these reasons, concepts of right love and wrong love played key roles.

Kinship and Emotion in Reformation Discourse

When the reformers considered how to justify marriage prohibitions, they had to deal with a background of numerous interdictions, all deriving from the basic taboo of marrying a relative.[44] During the Middle Ages, as kinship structures shifting from a *clan* basis to division of the estate or *primogeniture*, *affinitas* had increased in importance alongside *consanguinitas* as a reason to forbid a marriage. Moreover, *affinitas* became closely attached to the notion of *una-caro*, becoming one flesh through marital coitus.[45] According to this notion, spouses became one flesh and one body and in-laws became blood relatives, thus significantly expanding the prohibitions linked to consanguinity. The notion of *affinitas* also became central to how the reformers thought about marriage prohibitions.[46] Concepts of spiritual kinship (*cognatio spiritualis*) complicated early modern kinship patterns.[47] In 721 Pope Gregory II had declared godparenthood an impediment to marriage. In 743, at the Council of Estinnes, parents were prohibited from stepping in as godparents in cases of emergency baptism.[48] Finally, in 813 the Council of Châlons decided to separate parents who acted as godfathers or godmothers for their own children. Their marriage was no longer considered valid in order to avoid overlapping kinship.[49] The relationship of a Catholic priest to his parishioners also fell within the realm of spiritual kinship. This problem arose in discussions of Luther's marriage to Katharina von Bora. Additionally, *adoptio* functioned as yet another way to create kinship.[50] In his writings Luther would call *adoptio* secular kinship (*weltliche freundschafft*).

Historians have advanced two explanations for why theologians drew these wide definitions of kinship with regard to marriage prohibitions. Social historians focus on the church's financial incentives for increasing the number of impediments, which required prospective husbands to purchase dispensations to protect against the many prohibitions. Scholars informed by cultural studies, such as Joseph Lynch, tend to emphasize the effect of incest taboos, in part because "the rudimentary state of premodern governments" in early medieval Europe could not "create *ex nihilo* a strong sentiment about incest. But if such a sentiment existed already, the law could channel it, reinforce it, diffuse it to new groups or areas, fix its contours, and settle disputes about its limits."[51]

For the reformers, the grounds for the laws regarding incest that they considered excessive were clear: the Catholic Church had pursued illegitimate, intrusive, and extremely exaggerated interventions for material gain. The problem, when Luther addressed it in 1522, was acute.[52] Marriage impediments found in the Bible did not correspond neither to the prevailing logics of kinship nor to Luther's own notion of a marriage as a realm freed from contrived restrictions. Luther pointed out, for example, that Leviticus 18:6–18 strictly distinguished between maternal and paternal kinship. The ban forbidding godparents to wed their "children" had not appeared as prohibitions for stepfathers and stepmothers, nor did it apply to stepsiblings. Luther's suggestion that it should be legal for a person to marry his deceased sister's husband or to wed his brother's wife provoked severe resistance among some of his fellow reformers.[53] The prohibitions as laid out in the Book of Deuteronomy included blood relatives (grandparents to grandchildren), stepmothers, the sisters, half-sisters, and aunts of maternal and paternal descent. They extend as well to paternal uncles, daughters- and sisters-in-law. There existed additional prohibitions against sleeping with a woman and her daughter, or against marrying the sister of one's previous wife if that wife still lived. Luther's plea for limiting these prohibitions according to the principle of *sola scriptura* provoked further discussion. In his compilation of Protestant writings on the matter, Erasmus Sarcer differentiated between divine and human laws. Luther, he wrote, "did not mean thereby that one should throw over the good common law that preserves order and honor, [but only] that not everything is forbidden by God as the greedy papists say there is."[54] Indeed, the Reformers compromised by systematically extending the prohibitions to the third degree by blood and affinity, regardless of maternal and paternal background. They left it to local authorities to determine how to handle marriages in the fourth degree.[55]

Thus the reformers, in accepting the status quo of imperial law while rejecting the extended papal law, allied with a large majority in the German-speaking lands. Yet some theologians continued to regard these prohibitions as more negotiable and less strict. Johannes Brenz, for example, clarified his flexibility. God, he argued, trusted what Brenz calls, "man's natural reason, that is, what the proper authorities, according to customs and civil order ... permit" to specify prohibitions.[56] Luther therefore jettisoned all prohibitions resulting from *adoptio*.[57]

To what extent, then, were emotions bound up with the discussion of incest prohibitions? According to the reformers, marriages should be characterized by the positive emotions men and women felt for each other, such as inclination, attraction, lust, and love (*neigung, anziehung, lust, liebe*), and occasionally desire (*begird*). It was supposed to be that way because God himself "brings people together and awakens the hearts and spirits of persons who should live together in marriage."[58] Yet the Reformers strictly separated this kind of loving from the love they described as animalistic (*viehisch*), childish (*buebisch*), wanton (*hurerisch*), or natural (*natürlich*). Any love not sparked by God's love led humans into temptation by sexual gratification and therefore violated God's will for love in marriage.

By establishing marriage as a model for social life, the Reformation habilitated amorous emotions. No longer was it necessary to restrict marital emotions to the intimate or private sphere. On the contrary, proper emotions justified marriage, intimacy, and lust. This emotional regime applied to relatives, too. In other words: no true or marital love could exist between relatives. God himself guaranteed truthfulness and honesty between future marriage companions, because, as Erasmus Sarcer wrote, he had "poured into human hearts natural laws and feelings, that spouses should love and cherish each other, like they rear and nourish the children of their marriage ... In a wondrous way," he continued, God preserves this affectionate emotion in couples "even though the devil and human evilness try to confuse and tear apart such a feeling."[59] God and his opponent, the devil, competed to win peoples' hearts.

The Reformation treatises on love used striking images to illustrate the destructive capacity of any emotional attachment driven by the devil. In the eyes of the reformers, deviant loving between close blood relatives (*Nechstblutsverwanten*) contradicted God's law of both love and human nature. Brenz observed that imperial law, like Mosaic law, followed the law of Nature in forbidding a marriage between son and mother, son and grandmother, and father and daughter, "all of which natural reason forbids and that is, moreover, abominable" to it.[60] Here Brenz, like most reformers, distinguished between *natural* reason and *natural* law, and between divine love and evil spirits. For him, the limits of forbidden kinship coincide with the third degree of blood kinship. At this juncture *natural* reason and *natural* law should shape social relations. Also, the limits of forbidden blood kinship indicate the space in which "horror and disgust about joining" dominated the emotional régime between relatives.[61]

Reformation marriage prohibitions, however, reached beyond this small group of relatives, narrowly defined. Also forbidden were marriages between step-parents and step-children as well as half-siblings and brothers and sisters-in-law. These relatives were not excluded as marriage partners because they fell within the restrictions of *natural* law. They were, therefore, susceptible to ambiguous emotionality and misleading love. This orientation shifted dramatically over the course of the next two centuries. Already early in the eighteenth century, in-laws were permitted to marry each other without previously seeking formal dispensation. Many made use of that new freedom.[62] Nonetheless, two concepts continued to be important: one defined kinship while the other distinguished legitimate from illegitimate emotion. These two were not identical. The prevalent concept of kinship supported the marriage prohibitions rooted in imperial law. The concept of emotionality set blood kin (grandparents, parents, children, grandchildren, and siblings) aside as a privileged group, different from more distant relatives (in-laws, step-relatives, and so on) This subtle distinction, articulated early in the eighteenth century, eventually developed into the notion of a nuclear family.[63]

Laws that condemned desire between blood relatives were, however, vividly transgressed in literature. As Mary Lindemann's chapter will show, incestuous love became a favored topic for eighteenth-century authors.[64] But they were not the first to do so; rather, they joined an already long tradition.[65] In her *Heptameron*, Marguerite de Navarre (1492–1549) developed her thoughts about incestuous love in ways more reminiscent of Boccaccio's *Decameron* (ca. 1353) and the Renaissance writings discussed above.[66] Several of her stories thematize the topic of forbidden love, and some focus on love between relatives. In particular the thirtieth tale (*nouvelle*) frankly focuses on love between a mother and her son, and between the son and a girl who was at once his sister and his daughter. Through a case of mistaken identity, a young man thought he was seducing his mother's maid, but in fact it was his mother with whom he slept.[67] The mother became pregnant and sent her son away to a foreign country. She herself gave birth abroad and abandoned her daughter there. When her son sought reconciliation, she agreed to meet with him on the condition that he had married before they met. Inevitably, the son meets his sister/daughter; ignorant of their kinship, they fall in love and return to his home as a married couple. When she learned of their union, the devastated mother desperately seeks the pope's advice. He advises her to keep the secret and for reasons that strike us as amazingly modern: they had not sinned, argued the pope, because they did not know their respective identities, let alone their overlapping kinship and blood relationship.[68] No word such as "natural disgust" or "horror" appeared in this *nouvelle*. Indeed, we find exactly the opposite: de Navarre comments on the extreme resemblance of the couple as the compelling reason for their passionate and lasting love. Stories like this tended

to fade over the course of time and resurfaced only in eighteenth-century incest literature.

Conclusions

At the end of this chapter it is useful to survey briefly the further development of attitudes toward incestuous relationships by suggesting the ways these
would differ from the sixteenth century and yet reflect many of the changes
wrought during the Reformation. Although new marriage impediments appeared in both Protestant and Catholic territories during the seventeenth
century, in the eighteenth century virtually all European monarchs and other
authorities purged marriage laws of many restrictive features.[69] In Prussia, for
example, "crime against the blood" (*Blutschande*), a term which previously included all forbidden marriages, now applied only to blood relatives. Prussia's
General Code, ratified in 1794, applied the term *Blutschande* only to relations
among blood kin.[70] Other formerly incestuous relations were grouped under the new heading of seduction (*Verführung*) and included sexual relations
between priests and parishioners or between overseers and their charges (in
schools and in prisons). Dependency and subjection become palpable parts
of a legal judgment on sexual crimes. These laws reveal an awareness of how
similar were sexual offenses among (blood) kin and those in hierarchical relationships.[71] At the same time, they also reduced the scope of incest, allowing,
for example, first cousins and also in-laws in Prussia to marry without a formal
dispensation.[72]

In the eighteenth century, too, incest and love were therefore conceptualized
in new and more intricate ways. Some departed radically from patterns established or reinforced in the sixteenth century and redefined incestuous desire
as the most *natural* longing. In his influential *Mosaic Law* (1774), for example,
the theologian Johann David Michaelis argued that the very "natural horror
[*horror naturalis*] we perceive in such a close union was perhaps not universal."[73]
This approach to the *horror naturalis* turns sixteenth-century discourse on its
head. Thus incestuous desire entered the canon of *natural* sexual appetites and
became subject, at least in theory, to emotional taming and physical discipline.
Sexual drives were thereby transformed into key elements of human nature
and were no longer the subject of divine intervention. Critically, however, the
shift in perceptions of incestuous love indicates a greater transformation: from
a vicious naturalness (*Natürlichkeit*) in sixteenth-century incest discourse, to a
human and therefore acceptable naturalness in eighteenth-century discourse.
The transgression of traditional concepts of marriage and sexuality, of love and
lust, of kinship and spirituality was, on the one hand, a positive contribution

of the early Enlightenment. On the other hand, however, this new contextualization of incest tended also to hinder compliance with useful emotional and sexual norms within families.

Taken together, these transformations of love and incest recommend three conclusions. First, they show that the meaning of incest cannot be understood separately from a broader array of social relationships. Early Reformation thinking took a concept of incest, broadly defined to include all illegitimate connections between the spiritual and the worldly realm, and narrowed it to pertain mostly to incestuous relationships in which marital connections dominated. The once strong implication that incest involved transgressing the limits of spiritual truthfulness faded and was replaced by a rather symbolic understanding of social order. This process was reflected in a dramatically decreased number of incest prohibitions. Reformers recast incest prohibitions as pragmatic and flexible instruments for facilitating rather than hindering marriages.

Essential to the Reformation approach was the differentiation made between relatives who lived together in a social union (such as household, neighborhood, or parish) and those who had lived more distant. Social proximity formed the fundamental basis for calculating prohibitions. The argument of closeness proved to be especially relevant when reformed ideas left the *sola scriptura*–level of Bible reading and adjusted the Levitical rules to the social requirements and cultural sensibilities of the early sixteenth century. The narrow notion of incest promoted by leading reformers such as Luther and the early Bullinger did not appeal to the following generations of scholars, jurists, theologians, and state authorities. It resurfaced, however, in early eighteenth century, when kinship was once again redefined, this time signifying biological blood relations rather than social dynamics. The existence of sexual attraction between members of the nuclear family emerged as a new way of explaining and bolstering warnings against incest. The fear of an irrestible sexual appetite (*Triebhafftigkeit*) drove the prohibitions. The Reformers had devoted considerable thought to the hierarchies of love—the love of God, parents, wife, children, neighbors, enemies, and so on—and therefore can be credited with reendowing the early modern family with binding emotions, as well as with establishing emotional norms. Eighteenth-century scholars and authors who identified with Enlightenment ideas appropriated the incest discourse and simultaneously reframed the larger picture of how emotions, sexual appetite, and family were connected to each other. Emotions became the gateway to sexual transgression within the nuclear family. In their discussions of incest, emotions and sexual appetite were regarded as inescapably natural.

The second major conclusion concerns the role allotted to emotions, as incest was redefined as a social phenomenon with transgressive and sometimes violent potential. Love was not the paramount emotion involved in the rethinking of marriage and sexuality in the seventeenth and eighteenth centuries. Simply put, emotions, and especially love, were conceived as things that needed to be *performed* in order to take effect, as opposed to things that needed to be felt in order be true. This does not mean that material interests and family strategies outweighed emotional attraction. The sources show that what is important here is a modified approach to the *locus* from where love and attraction gained their performative qualities. This locus was not the inner self postulated in modern notions of the individual. Rather, the sources that form the basis of this chapter show that emotions in the specific context of marital, parental, and neighborly relations occupy an intermediary space among men, women, and children, on the one hand, and between human beings and God on the other. This approach offers a new perspective on emotions in the sixteenth century. Early modern discourses on love compellingly highlighted the performative qualities attached to the emotional intermediary. These discourses foregrounded love as a mode of social interaction, rather than as a code, or, alternatively, as modern historians have argued, as an inner feeling.

Third, the rich picture of emotions that early sixteenth-century authors painted demands a contextual approach. If we take seriously the notion that emotions mediate between social, spiritual, and institutional agents, we have to dismiss questions framed as either-or alternatives: cognition versus feeling, rationality versus emotion, inner feeling versus outer appearance and action. Rather than analyzing the history of emotions through a set of predetermined categories, early modern sources recommend an approach in which emotions are understood as a medium that is essentially performative. Approached in this way, it becomes clear that love could not by itself legitimate sexual transgression in sixteenth-century families and households. Incestuous love in the sixteenth century was believed to be sparked by evil spirits and indicated a deeply deceptive relationship. This idea changed dramatically during the second half of the eighteenth century when incestuous love was converted into an undesirable but real form of natural desire. Another reason for adopting a contextual approach is that the meaning assigned to emotions changed dramatically over the course of three centuries. When leading Reformers in early sixteenth century debated whether marital partners should be encouraged to love each other, they worried about the transgressive power often ascribed to love. At the same time, they conceptualized love as a mode of hierarchical interaction. In Renaissance discourses love appears as a fabric woven by spiritual and erotic needs. Any attempt to categorize this ambiguous and conflictual set of emotions among men, women, children, between people and institutions, and between the realms of divine and secular concern can only lead scholars astray. The history of emotions, therefore, contributes to a broader social history interweaving matters of historical anthropology.

Acknowledgments

I wish to express my gratitude to Mary Lindemann and David Luebke for their help in preparing the original essay. Also, my heartfelt thanks goes to Bridget Heal who has invested much time in turning the original essay into a readable chapter.

Notes

1. Thomas A. Fudge, "Incest and Lust in Luther's Marriage: Theology and Morality in Reformation Polemics," *Sixteenth Century Journal* 34 (2003): 319–45.
2. Julius Köstlin, "Bora, Katharina von," in *Allgemeine Deutsche Biographie*, 56 vols. (Berlin, 1876; reprint 1967), vol. 3, 151–52; Oskar Thulin, "Bora, Katharina von," in *Neue Deutsche Biographie*, 24 vols. (Berlin, 1955), vol. 2, 454.
3. Joachim S. Hohmann, *Der Zölibat: Geschichte und Gegenwart eines umstrittenen Gesetzes* (Frankfurt, 1993).
4. Already in November 1520 Philipp Melanchthon had married Katharina Krapp, daughter of a Wittenberg clothier; Ulrich Zwingli had married the widow Anna Reinhart in 1524; and Luther's future opponent, Andreas Bodenstein von Karlstadt, had married Anna von Mochau in 1522.
5. For further reading and additional literature, see Fudge, "Incest and Lust"; and Marjorie Elizabeth Plummer's contribution to this volume.
6. Andreas Karlstadt, *Das die Priester Eeweiber nehmen mügen und sollen. Beschütz red / des würdigen herren Bartholomei Bernhardi / Probsts zu Camberg / so von Bischoff von Meyenburg gefordert / antwurt zu geben / das er in priesterlichem standt / ein junckfraw zu der Ee genommen hat* (Speyer, 1522). For the text of the synod of 1075, see Pope Gregory VII, "Dictatus Papae," in *Das Register Gregors VII*, ed. Erich Casper (Berlin, 1955), 201–8.
7. See also Bernhard Jussen, "Künstliche und natürliche Verwandte? Biologismen in den kulturwissenschaftlichen Konzepten von Verwandtschaft," in *Das Individuum und die Seinen: Individualität in der okzidentalen und der russischen Kultur in Mittelalter und Früher Neuzeit*, ed. Juri L. Besmertny and Otto Gerhard Oexle (Göttingen, 2001), 39–59.
8. Natalie Zemon Davis, *Frauen und Gesellschaft am Beginn der Neuzeit: Studien über Familie, Religion und die Wandlungsfähigkeit des sozialen Körpers* (Berlin, 1986).
9. Claudia Jarzebowski, "Lieben und Herrschen: Fürstenerziehung im späten 15. und 16. Jahrhundert," in *Saeculum* 61 (2011): 39–56.
10. Claudia Jarzebowski, "Liebe," in *Enzyklopädie der Neuzeit*, ed. Friedrich Jaeger (Stuttgart, 2008), 7: 896–905.
11. Susan C. Karant-Nunn, *Reformation of Feeling: Shaping the Religious Emotions in Early Modern Germany* (New York, 2010). See also Peter Blickle, *Die Revolution von 1525*, 4th rev. ed. (Munich, 1993).
12. Martin Luther, "Ermahnung zum Frieden auf die Zwölf Artickel der Bauerschaft in Schwaben (1525)," WA, vol. 18, 291–334, here 295.
13. "Denn du stirbst in Gehorsam göttlichen Wortes und Befehls und im Dienst der Liebe, deinen Nächsten zu retten aus der Hölle und Teufels Banden," in Martin Lu-

ther, "Widder die mörderischen und räuberischen Rotten der Bauern (1525)," WA, vol. 18, 336–61, here 361. English translation by Ernest G. Rupp and Benjamin Drewery, *Martin Luther: Documents of Modern History* (London, 1970), 126.

14. See Andrew Lynch and Philippa Maddern, eds., *Venus & Mars: Engendering Love and War in Medieval and Early Modern* (Nedlands, 1995).

15. Patricia Crawford, "Friendship and Love between Women in Early Modern England," in Lynch and Maddern, eds., *Venus & Mars*, 47–62.

16. Helmut Kuhn and Karl-Heinz Nusser, "Liebe," in *Historisches Wörterbuch der Philosophie*, eds. Joachim Ritter and Karlfried Gründer, 13 vols. (Basel, 1980), vol. 5, 290–310.

17. Gabriele Jancke, "Ritualisierte Verhaltensweisen in der frühneuzeitlichen Gelehrtenkultur—Bettgeschichten," in *Gelehrtenleben: Wissenschaftspraxis in der Neuzeit*, ed. Alf Lüdtke and Reiner Prass (Cologne, 2008), 235–247.

18. See also Mechthild von Magdeburg, *Das fließende Licht der Gottheit* (Frankfurt, 2010).

19. "The dividing line between them [i.e., love and friendship] was not so sharp, so that friendship could be clad in the language of love, and love in the rhetoric of friendship. This remained the case for much of history." Eva Österberg, "Friendship, Love, and Sexuality in Premodern Times," in her *Friendship and Love, Ethics and Politics: Studies in Medieval and Early Modern History* (Budapest, 2010), 32.

20. Marguerite de Navarre, *L'Heptaméron* (Paris, 1960).

21. Pietro Bembo, *Gli Asolani* (Venice, 1505).

22. See Karlstadt, *Das die Priester.*

23. Bembo, *Gli Asolani.*

24. Until the mid-thirteenth century, love formed a subject in medieval school teaching for European nobles; see C. Stephen Jaeger, *Ennobling Love: In Search of a Lost Sensibility* (Philadelphia, 1999), 59–81.

25. See Antonius Beccadelli, *Hermaphroditus*, n.p., 1425; Ioannes Iovanus Pontanus, *De amore coniugali* (Venice, 1518); Michael Tarchaniota Marullus, *Hymni naturales* (n.p., 1515).

26. Österberg, *Friendship, Love, and Sexuality*, 5–23.

27. The historiography on marriage is immense. Essential reading includes several works by Natalie Zemon Davis, among them *Frauen und Gesellschaft;* "Boundaries and the Sense of Self in Early Modern France," in *Reconstructing Individualism*, ed. Ian Watt (Stanford, 1986); "Ghosts, Kin and Progeny: Some Features of Family Life in Early Modern France," in *Daedalus* 106 (1977): 87–114; "The Sacred and the Body Social in Sixteenth-Century Lyon," *Past and Present* 90 (1981): 40–70; and "'Women's History' in Transition: The European Case," *Feminist Studies* 3 (1976): 83–103.

28. Hans Medick and David W. Sabean, eds., *Emotionen und materielle Interessen: Sozialanthropologische und historische Beiträge zur Familienforschung* (Göttingen, 1984). In this sense the bourgeois marriage for love and the premodern marriage of interest are very similar. See three works by Karin Hausen: "Historische Familienforschung," in *Historische Sozialwissenschaft: Beiträge zur Einführung in die Forschungspraxis*, ed. Reinhard Rürup (Göttingen, 1977), 59–95; "Die Polarisierung der 'Geschlechtscharaktere'— Eine Spiegelung der Dissoziation von Erwerbs- und Familienleben," in *Sozialgeschichte der Familie in der Neuzeit Europas*, ed. Werner Conze (Stuttgart, 1976), 363–93; "'. . . Eine Ulme für das schwanke Efeu': Ehepaare im Bildungsbürgertum: Ideal und Wirklichkeiten im späten 18. und 19. Jahrhundert," in *Bürgerinnen und Bürger: Geschlechterverhältnisse im 19. Jahrhundert*, ed. Ute Frevert (Göttingen, 1988), 85–118.

29. Wiesner-Hanks, *Christianity and Sexuality*; Claudia Ulbrich, "Ehe," *Enzyklopädie der Neuzeit*, vol. 3, 38–44; Gadi Algazi, "Scholars in Households: Refiguring the Learned Habitus, 1480–1550," *Science in Context* 16 (2003): 9–42; Safley, *Let No Man Put Asunder*.

30. Rüdiger Schnell, *Sexualität und Emotionalität in der vormodernen Ehe* (Cologne, 2002), esp. 227–65.

31. Heinrich Bullinger, *Der Christlich Eestand: Von der heiligen Ee harkumen / wenn / wo / wie / unnd von waem sy ufgesetzt / und was sye / wie sye recht bezogen were* . . . (Zurich, 1540), esp. chap. 3, "Von rechtmessiger zusammenfuegung Christliche Eelüten." For a discussion of Bullinger's ideas on marriage, see Jutta Eming and Ulrike Gaebel, "'Wie man zwei Rinder in ein Joch spannt': Zu Heinrich Bullinger's "Der Christlich Eestand," in *Eheglück und Liebesjoch: Bilder von Liebe, Ehe und Familie in der Literatur des 15. und 16. Jahrhunderts*, ed. Maria E. Müller (Weinheim, 1988), 125–54.

32. Martin Luther, "Von der Priester Ehe," in WA 50: 249; Martin Luther, "Predigten des Jahres 1545, no. 19 [4. August]," WA 49: 798–99.

33. For example, Johannes Brenz, *Wie in Ehesachen und inn den fellen / so sich derhalben zu tragen/ nach Götlichen billichen rechten / Christenlich zu handeln sey* (Wittenberg, 1531).

34. Hull, *Sexuality, State and Civil Society*, 17–51.

35. Bullinger, *Der Christlich Eestand*, chap. 2, "Was die Ee sy."

36. Ibid., chap. 1, "Von der Ee herkummen."

37. Ibid.

38. See Schnell, *Sexualität und Emotionalität*, 158–99.

39. Brenz, *Wie in Ehesachen* . . . *zu handeln sey*, chap. 1.

40. See Bullinger, *Der Christlich Eestand*, chap. 1, "Von der Ee herkummen."

41. Erasmus Sarcer, *Vom heiligen Ehestande und von Ehesachen mit allen umbstenden / zu diesen dingen gehörig/darinnen zu gleich Natürlich / Göttlich / Keiserlich und / Bepstlich Recht angezogen wird/Zum teil aus vieler Gelerter Theologen Bücher zusammen getragen / Zum teil vom zusammen Zieher selbst geschrieben* (Eisleben, 1556), ciii.

42. Helga Brandes, "Frühneuzeitliche Ökonomieliteratur," in *Die Literatur des 17. Jahrhunderts*, ed. Albert Meier (Munich, 1999), 470–84; Irmintraut Richarz, *Oikos, Haus und Haushalt: Ursprünge und Geschichte der Haushaltsökonomik* (Göttingen, 1991).

43. Bullinger, *Der Christlich Eestand*, chap. 9, "Das die Ee frywillig syn sole."

44. At the same time, the reformers themselves appeared somewhat preoccupied with the issue of incest prohibitions. For example, more than 60 out of 245 pieces of marital legislation provided by Erasmus Sarcer addressed incestuous relations. Almost another fifty cases treated clandestine engagements and marriages.

45. Michael Mitterauer, "Christentum und Endogamie," in *Historisch-anthropologische Familienforschung: Fragestellungen und Zugangsweisen*, ed. Michael Mitterauer (Cologne, 1990), 41–87.

46. Karin Gottschalk, "Niemandes Kind? Illegimität, Blutsverwandtschaft und Zugehörigkeit im vormodernen Recht," *WerkstattGeschichte* 51 (2009): 23–42.

47. For example Hubertus Lutterbach, *Sexualität im Mittelalter: Eine Kulturstudie anhand von Bußbüchern des 6.-12. Jahrhunderts* (Cologne, 1999), 177–90.

48. Lutterbach, *Sexualität im Mittelalter*, 187, 225.

49. David Herlihy, "The Family and Religious Ideologies in Medieval Europe," in *Women, Family and Society in Medieval Europe*, ed. David Herlihy (New York, 1995), 154–73.

50. Bernhard Jussen, *Patenschaft und Adoption im frühen Mittelalter: Künstliche Verwandt-schaft als soziale Praxis* (Göttingen, 1991).

51. Joseph H. Lynch, *Godparents and Kinship in Early Medieval Europe* (Princeton, 1986), esp. 286-88; idem., "Spiritual Kinship and Sexual Prohibition in Early Medieval Europe," in *Proceedings of the 6th International Congress of Medieval Canon Law*, ed. Stephan Kuttner (Vatican City, 1985), 271–88.

52. Martin Luther, "Welche Personen verboten sind zu ehelichen (1522)," WA, vol. 10/II, 263–66.

53. Már Jónsson, "Incest and the Word of God: Early Sixteenth Century Protestant Disputes," *Archiv für Reformationsgeschichte* 85 (1994): 96–119.

54. Sarcer, *Vom heiligen Ehestande*, xlvi.

55. Historically there are two ways of calculating kinship degrees. The counting system of the Roman Law puts the ego at center and determines the degree by the number of steps between the relative and the ego. Siblings were kin in the second degree. Canonical counting focuses on generations and counts step by step in one direction only. Siblings in this system were therefore first degree relatives. See Jack Goody, *The Development of Marriage and the Family in Europe* (Cambridge, UK, 1983), 152–53; Jónsson, "Incest and the Word of God"; and Ulinka Rublack, "'Viehisch, frech vnd onverschämpt': Inzest in Südwestdeutschland, ca. 1530–1700," in *Von Huren und Rabenmüttern: Weibliche Kriminalität in der frühen Neuzeit*, ed. Otto Ulbricht (Cologne, 1995), 171–213.

56. Brenz, *Wie in Ehesachen . . . zu handeln sey.*

57. Luther, "Welche Personen verboten sind zu ehelichen (1522)."

58. Sarcer, *Vom heiligen Ehestande*, vi.

59. Ibid., ii.

60. Brenz, *Wie in Ehesachen . . . zu handeln sey*, cii.

61. Bullinger, *Der Christlich Eestand*, chap. 7, "Von den verbottnen Graden der blut-frynnschaft und magschafft."

62. This statement pertains to Prussia; see Claudia Jarzebowski, *Inzest: Verwandtschaft und Sexualität im 18. Jahrhundert* (Cologne, 2006); see also David W. Sabean, "Inzestdiskurse vom Barock bis zur Romantik," *L'Homme: Zeitschrift für Feministische Geschichtswissenschaft* 13 (2002): 7–28.

63. Otto Brunner, "Das 'ganze Haus' und die alteuropäische 'Ökonomik,'" in his *Neue Wege der Sozialgeschichte. Vorträge und Aufsätze* (Göttingen, 1956), 33–61.

64. Michael Titzmann, "Literarische Strukturen und kulturelles Wissen: Das Beispiel inzestuöser Situationen in der Erzählliteratur der Goethezeit und ihrer Funktionen im Denksystem der Epoche," in *Erzählte Kriminalität: Zur Typologie und Funktion von narrativen Darstellungen in Strafrechtspflege, Publizistik und Literatur zwischen 1770 und 1920*, ed. Jörg Schönert (Tübingen, 1991), 229–81.

65. Jutta Eming, "Inzestneigung und Inzestvorstellung im mittelalterlichen Liebes- und Abenteuerromanen," in *Historische Inzestdiskurse*, 21–45.

66. Elizabeth C. Zegura, "True Stories and Alternative Discourses: The Game of Love in Marguerite de Navarre's Heptameron," in *Discourses on Love, Marriage, and Transgression in Medieval and Early Modern Literature*, ed. Albrecht Classen (Tempe, 2004), 351–68.

67. Navarre, *L'Heptaméron*, 230.

68. Ibid., 233.

69. For example, *Fürstlich-Sächsisch-Altenburgische Landesordnung* (Altenburg, 1705); *Kayserlich Josephinische Peinliche Hals-Gerichtsordnung* (16 July 1707).

70. *Allgemeines Landrecht für die Preußischen Staaten von 1794*, ed. Hans Hattenhauer (Frankfurt, 1970), Part II, Title 20, Section 12, §1039–§1047.
71. One would be mistaken to expect that the legal reformers (*Strafrechtsreformer*) would explain this specific susceptibility with a basic emotional dependancy.
72. "An das Departement der geistlichen Affairen (3. Juni 1740)," in *Acta Borussica: Denkmäler der Preußischen Staatsverwaltung*, ed. Preussische Akademie der Wissenschaften, 42 vols. (Berlin, 1892-1982), vol 6/2, 7, no.6.
73. Johann David Michaelis, *Mosaisches Recht* (Frankfurt, 1774), §104.

CHAPTER 11

~:~

Aufklärung, Literature, and Fatherly Love
An Eighteenth-Century Case of Incest

MARY LINDEMANN

Popular literature in the mid-nineteenth century often took the form of what was, or came to be, known as "mysteries" literature—a genre that took its name from Eugène Sue's famous and extraordinarily popular serialization entitled *The Mysteries of Paris* (Les Mystères de Paris).[1] Sue's *Mysteries* combined melodramatic stories, memorable fictional characters, and social consciousness; other writers, and some significantly greater ones, such as Émile Zola and Charles Dickens, imitated Sue's new form. Not only the *grands écrivains* of the century imitated Sue: a host of epigones and scribblers did so as well.[2] One of these lesser writers was Bernhard Hesslein, doctor of philosophy and erstwhile tutor who, practically simultaneously with Sue, turned his hand—and his pen—to the writing of literary descriptions of cities and historical fiction. From the late 1840s until his death in 1882, Hesslein published over forty volumes of travel literature, city descriptions, historical novels, true-crime stories, and the ever popular moral panoramas (*Sittengemälde*).[3] Among these last was *Hamburg's Famous and Infamous Houses*, in which Hesslein combined fiction, scandal, and topography into captivating vignettes. The raciest of these stories lay concealed under a prosaic title: *The Kaiserhof*.[4] *The Kaiserhof* related the story of the "beautiful Charlotte," a sordid and titillating tale based on a real-life eighteenth-century incident involving father–daughter incest, perjury, and suicide. Hesslein concluded,

> This is a piece of the history of the notorious innkeeper's daughter from the Kaiserhof hotel. Charlotte's father, [Denis] Martin, did not remain untouched by her deceitful nature and her intrigues. But here we will let the curtain fall, and reminisce over a glass of wine in the old Ratskeller under the Kaiserhof the other pleasant and disagreeable histories, which the Kaiserhof witnessed.[5]

It may seem strange to begin an examination of incest and German Enlightenment (the *Aufklärung*) with a discussion of nineteenth-century literature, but such a digression actually carries us right to the heart of the interlocking issues that Charlotte's story raised. One of these, and one that will not be explored in depth here, is how the interplay of true-crime stories, real criminal events, and literature in the eighteenth century continued to shape the historical and literary imaginations well into the nineteenth and even twentieth centuries, as Hesslein's tale suggests. Charlotte's case was by no means the only one that lived on in later literature.[6] More relevant to the concept of transgressive unions in the mid to late eighteenth century are the themes that I propose to treat here and that discuss the ways in which the *Aufklärung* shifted perceptions of incest, affecting how the crime was prosecuted and punished, as well as understood. Cases like that of Charlotte Guyard and her father, Denis Martin, troubled magistrates profoundly and laid bare some paradoxes of the Enlightenment, such as the tension between advocating freedom and condoning license, especially in the world of sexual relations.

First, the crime. The main points of the story can be quickly related. In Hamburg in 1765 a young, recently married woman, Charlotte Guyard, accused her father, an innkeeper and French migrant to Hamburg, Denis Martin, of forcing her to commit incest with him. Alerted by disturbing rumors, the city's magistracy immediately began to investigate the charges. To prevent her subornation, Charlotte was sequestered and interrogated repeatedly. Meanwhile, her husband, the French merchant Jean-François Guyard, demanded that his father-in-law be punished. Charlotte's father denied the crime and blamed his son-in-law for orchestrating the entire affair, compelling his wife, literally at knife point, to conspire in a plot to blackmail her father. For six months Charlotte held steadfastly to her story, embroidering it with further details of where and when the alleged crime took place (in the ice cellar, in the kitchen, in an arbor) and further shocking her audience with lascivious details of greater depravities. Once "debauched," she had wallowed in sin, taking many lovers: eventually she named nine prominent men. Then, suddenly, unexpectedly, she recanted. Flipping her story, Charlotte charged her husband with cooking up the sordid tale to ruin her father. The whole tenor of the case changed; now her spouse came under suspicion. The affair smoldered for more than a year, while Charlotte's father sought restitution of his good name and her husband struggled to regain his lost honor. Three years later, the city silenced her father with a substantial sum; the son-in-law had long since fled.

For her perjury and false witness, the magistracy ordered that Charlotte be confined indefinitely in the city's house of correction (*Zuchthaus*), where she remained for almost fourteen years. But her story does not end with the doors of the prison closing behind her. While in confinement, she began an affair with the young Lutheran pastor assigned to convert her (she, her whole family, and her husband were Catholic; Hamburg was staunchly Lutheran). Within weeks, Charlotte was pregnant. The poor pastor, either seduced or seducer, was fired from his job and soon after committed suicide. Charlotte remained imprisoned for several additional years during which time she had repeated sexual liaisons with other inmates and a guard, resulting in two further pregnancies. She was finally released to her mother's custody in 1778 and spirited away to a convent for her own safety.[7] Here she disappears from the historical record but not, as we have seen, from the literary imagination.

Understanding Incest: Laws and Perceptions

No one has any good idea how common incest was in the eighteenth century. Richard McCabe in writing about early modern England points out that "the statistics for incest in Elizabethan or Jacobean homes are impossible to compile." That holds equally true for eighteenth-century Germany and was not only due to the large dark number of unreported incidents that usually characterizes reporting on the vast majority of sex crimes.[8] As far as I can tell from archival records in Amsterdam, Antwerp, and Hamburg, however, magistrates rarely ignored accusations of child abuse or incest. They investigated them vigorously even, or especially, when victims were quite young.[9]

However, the definition of incest—in German, *Blutschande*—is more complicated than one might expect and had undergone significant changes since medieval times.[10] It was there at the beginning, in the Bible, in Genesis and Exodus, where there can be found "a remarkable number of liaisons between close kin."[11] Most famous perhaps was the story of Lot and his daughters. After the destruction of Sodom and Gomorrah, Lot's daughters got him drunk and then lay with him to preserve their family. But there were many other cases of marriage or sexual relations between near-relatives: Abraham married his half-sister, Nahor married his brother's daughter, and Jacob wed two sisters.[12] The Levitical rules admonished God's people, "None of you shall approach to any that is near of kin to him, to uncover their nakedness: I am Yahweh. The nakedness of thy father, or the nakedness of thy mother, shalt thou not uncover; she is thy mother; thou shalt not uncover her nakedness." Throughout the history of Christianity, theologians glossed and commented on incest; legal authorities defined it; and authorities punished it. Paul, in the New Testament, offered no substantially different view of incest and, when confronted with incest within the new church, quoted the Levitical proscription.[13] Augustine, and Aquinas, too, condemned incest as a worse sin than adultery. In often expanded and more precise forms, these prohibitions formed the basis for black letter law in early modern Europe. Roman law, too, influenced early modern Christian thinking (legal, theological, and moral) on incest. Medieval legend oedipized

Judas, who supposedly—and unwittingly—killed his father and married his mother.

In early modern Europe, incest still figured as an "enormous sin, abominable before God," as the seventeenth-century French theologian Jean Benedicti described it.[14] In Germany the imperial criminal code of 1532, also known as the Carolina, prescribed the death penalty for incest. The Carolina was the basis of legal codes throughout the ancien régime for many (if not all) regions of the Holy Roman Empire, including Hamburg.[15] This does not mean, of course, that every case of incest was punished by death. Despite the threat of capital punishment, far more typical was the penalty meted out to the brother and sister, Jochim Diderich and Johanna Catharina Moll, in 1749 "on the account of incest with one another . . . to which they had [both] confessed." They were whipped and placed on the pillory (*Pranger*). Jochim was sentenced to twelve and Johanna to fifteen years in the city's prison; after their release they were to be banned from the city.[16] Practicing jurists in Hamburg, such as Nicolaus Schuback in the middle of the eighteenth century, noted that "not all [incidents of incest] are equally culpable." Certain cases—such as incest between brothers- and sisters-in-law, for example—Schuback considered merely as "common fornication" and could be dealt with "arbitrarily," that is, summarily. Relations between fathers, daughters, mothers, sons, and siblings "are, however, incestuous." But before initiating a formal investigation he would take the matter directly to the City Council, which is exactly what happened in Charlotte's case.[17]

Thus, even if legal codes set the death penalty for incest, actually imposing it was not usual and, by the eighteenth century, downright *unusual*. Moreover, it does not seem that the authorities, or even neighbors and friends, spent much time worrying about cases of incest, except when they became publicly notorious or when very young women became pregnant. So it was with Charlotte Guyard: only the seriousness and prevalence of rumors about Charlotte and her father, and her own accusation against several respectable men with whom she supposedly had sexual relations, moved the Hamburg authorities to action.

Incest in the European past, of course, was defined and perceived differently from how it is defined and perceived today. Marriage within a prohibited degree of consanguinity, for example, also constituted *Blutschande* and the consent of either party was basically irrelevant. Since the early thirteenth century, canon law had prohibited marriages up to the fourth degree, which included unions between second cousins. The sixteenth-century Reformers tended to restrict these prohibitions to a much tighter circle of kin and in-laws. "Indeed," one scholar has observed, "the modern notion of incest as sexual relations within a small, enclosed family group originates in this period."[18] In normative discourse, and until late in the eighteenth century, incest (or *Blutschande*) meant "sexual relations between relatives, whereby virtually no difference existed between in-laws, step- or blood relatives, or spiritual ones," such as godparents.[19]

Today, certainly, few crimes are more abhorred than incest, which shades over into child abuse. Still, we should be careful not to transport twenty-first century sensibilities into other periods. It is hardly clear that incest in the European past was so defined or that the practice was clearly abhorrent. Even less readily should we assume that incest can inevitably be equated with something we might call domestic violence, although, of course, it may be.[20] Moreover, while all the commonest varieties of incest—sibling, father child, and mother–child—are recognized as transgressive, it is probably the father-daughter version that today evokes the greatest repugnance. Moreover, there seems to be a general agreement that incest is somehow unnatural.

In the age of Enlightenment, however, the prevailing attitudes on both subjects were quite different. During the eighteenth century many prohibitions against marriage between related kin, and especially between brothers- and sisters-in-law, and cousins, began to be repealed or were no longer enforced. At about the same time, new patterns of kinship and marital relations emerged, including more "frequent marriages between increasingly close blood relatives (such as first cousins or uncles and nieces)."[21] The consistory records of the duchy of Braunschweig-Wolfenbüttel are filled with requests for dispensations to allow a widower to marry his deceased wife's sister, for example; increasingly these were granted. And, then, in 1740, Friedrich II ("the Great") of Prussia repealed all existing consanguinity restrictions in his lands.[22]

The treatment of *Blutschande* and *Inzest* in Johann Zedler's *Universal-Lexikon* of the mid-eighteenth century, a bellwether publication of the *Aufklärung*, alerts us to the changes that the perception of incest was undergoing. It documents a significant modification in law and morality (echoed in the literature of the day). Zedler begins with a rather standard definition of *Blutschande* as "the [physical] mixing of persons . . . who share bloodlines . . . [and] generally near in-laws."[23] But Zedler also described a difference of opinion among many commentators on whether natural law (*Naturrecht*), or even divine law, prohibited *Blutschande*. After noting the varied practices in different cultures, he observed that "customs of [many] cultures, however, cannot serve as a rule" and concluded, "incest thus does not contradict nature, as human sex as well as the described customs of peoples demonstrates. Still one cannot only look to nature [for guidance] if society is to be preserved and its good promoted." Thus Zedler's presentation upheld the idea of forbidding incest or *Blutschande* for practical reasons: to prevent marriages of greed, to preserve respect (*Ehrfurcht*) between parents and children, and to avoid "many unchaste deeds." This summary encapsulated the position increasingly common in the eighteenth century that, while incest was not forbidden by nature, its prohibition was nonetheless useful.[24]

The *Aufklärung* redefined the incest taboo (although "taboo" as a word only entered European languages after the voyage of Captain Cook). Enlightened and libertine opinion agreed that the disgust and repulsion incest supposedly evoked was culturally and historically constructed.[25] One culture's crime was another's usual practice. That evil man, Bernhard Mandeville, wrote in the *Fable of the Bees*,

> In the East formerly Sisters married Brothers, and it was meritorious for a Man to marry his Mother. Such Alliances are abominable; but it is certain that, whatever Horror we conceive at the Thoughts of them, there is nothing in Nature repugnant against them, but what is built upon Mode and Custom.

Similarly, Henry St. John, Viscount Bolingbroke, noted that "[the] abhorrence [of incest] is artificial . . . inspired by human laws . . . by prejudice, and by habit." The Marquis de Sade, typically, went much farther, both in elevating incest to the highest planes of love and lust in his *Crimes of Love* (Crimes de l'amour) and *Florville et Courval*, and in calling for a complete abolition of incest penalties and taboos. Incest played a role in numerous writings of the *philosophes*, including contributions, condemnations, analyses, and even apologia from Montesquieu, Lenz, Wieland, Goethe (the famous "Mignon" prologue from *Wilhelm Meister's Apprenticeship* [Wilhelm Meisters Lehrjahre] and his one-act play, *The Siblings* [Die Geschwister]), Prévost, Diderot, Nicolai, Tieck, and Gellert.[26] For the *Aufklärer*, too, incest between siblings or between father and daughter seemed less serious than that between mother and son, and even was "relatively permissible." The eighteenth-century legalist, Johann David Michaelis, expressed the "greatest understanding" for sibling love and offered natural interpretations for incest between father and daughter, although he thoroughly deplored incestuous relations between mothers and sons. For Michaelis, father–daughter incest could be explained, and even partly excused, because a father found it difficult to resist the budding sexuality of his young daughter especially if his marriage was unsatisfactory and his sex life unsatisfying. For the daughter, her natural inclination to obey her father and her tendency to see in him the perfect husband led to her participation in the relationship. Mother–son incest, however, was especially repugnant because it overturned the proper passive and active sexual roles. Most, then, agreed that the taboo against incest should be restricted to members of the nuclear family. But toward the end of the century and early in the next, a re-tabooization occurred within the many dramas set in the bourgeois family, although over the course of the nineteenth century first-cousin marriages became common family strategies.[27]

Although there was considerable variation in how incest was both defined and punished in the eighteenth century, it is also clear that a case like Charlotte Guyard's would provoke a probing investigation. The legal ins and outs of the Guyard incest case, the charges and countercharges that flew in what became a triple set of accusations and, of course, the impossibility of knowing what the actual circumstances of the case were, all complicated the story. Did Denis

Martin force Charlotte into an incestuous relationship with him? Did she lie to her husband about the lack of virginity he discovered on their wedding night and then blame her father? Was it perhaps Guyard himself who concocted the whole story and forced Charlotte to repeat it in order to blackmail her father? Was she a victim—of either father or husband, or both—or was she a willing collaborator, perhaps even the sole source of the charge?

We will never know the answers to these questions. Still, the sheer complexity of the case produced a series of fascinating narratives. There were the legal stories constructed by the magistrates and witnesses as the case was investigated and there were the legal narratives that both Guyard and Martin published to defend themselves and, not incidentally, to accuse each other and Charlotte. Diplomatic narratives crystallized around the case as the French minister-resident intervened on the behalf of his three coreligionists. Martin, who eventually left the city and went to Berlin, gathered the support of the Prussian crown and demanded reparations. Guyard and Martin both appealed to the imperial courts seeking restitution.

The plentitude of these narratives would have been, I think, much less full and the debate less complex if two other factors had not come into play: contradictory, or at least varied, ideas on sexuality, and the limits of moral conduct among the *Aufklärer* and the value of the incest motif for the writing of literature.[28] Sex was then, as it is now, a highly readable topic, and the number of literary works that played, and played on, the incest theme was great. At the same moment when the *Aufklärung* promoted a more expansive education for women, ironically, many also came to view reading, most especially the reading of fiction, as morally corrupting. Moreover, the growing emphasis on the family and on intimacy within the family also contained hidden dangers. These are the themes that Charlotte's case raised and that I will now pursue.

A Dangerous Pastime

In the age of enlightenment, reading was sex and sex was readable. Incest was a very literary event and the stories of Charlotte, her husband, and her father involved reading and writing as well as sordid motives. Yet the sentimental literature of the eighteenth century by no means invented the incest motif. One can trace literary treatments from the Renaissance through today and, of course, back into antiquity. Incest formed the basis of many familiar literary topoi, both in the popular true-crime literature of the day as well as in the novels and romances that an ever-expanding reading public consumed in their thousands. Didactic literature, sentimental novels, erotic prose, legal briefs, true-crime histories, all played with sex and, not least of all, with incest.

In the past several decades historical scholarship has generated a huge body of literature on reading and the enlightenment, on the rise of the public sphere, on education for women, and on the subversive nature of literature that circulated widely—the forbidden bestsellers of the ancien régime. Two particular themes within this broader stream are relevant here: the corrupting influence of reading on women, especially young women like Charlotte, and the storied character of familial love gone wrong.

Over a period of several weeks in 1765 and 1766, as the magistrates in Hamburg attempted to unravel the complicated strands of Charlotte's history, they followed threads they hoped would eventually lead them to the truth of the scandal. As they sought to determine what happened, they also probed the background of the crime and the motives that led to it. Charlotte's own narrative was the starting point. Her account began with a description of her father's "extraordinary regard and exceptional love" for her. Only gradually had she come to perceive that "this reverence and affection on her father's part toward her was not appropriate nor did it remain within the boundaries of propriety, rather it sprang from an unnatural passion and had an [unnatural] goal"—Charlotte herself. She spun out a story of youthful purity intentionally perverted by a treacherous and manipulative parent. Such formed a common theme in eighteenth-century romances. In Charlotte's case, reading had awakened and then further stimulated her latent sexual appetites. Her father had, she told her questioners, given her to read "all sorts of amorous books and novels" that inflamed her "imagination" and "brought her virgin blood to the boil."[29]

The dialogic narrative that emerged from the investigation, therefore, blamed *books:* books had excited Charlotte's passions and implanted carnal thoughts in her brain. What books were these? Charlotte named "erotic stories and novels of all types," specifically *Ninon de l'Enclos, Thérèse philosophe,* the tales of La Fontaine, the tracts of Saint-Évremond, *Les Comtes d'Hoffmann,* and the works of Voltaire, especially his *La Pucelle d'Orléans,* among many others. When asked to describe them, she characterized *Ninon de l'Enclos,* to take one example, as a work "that treated the adventures and love of Ninon, who recounted them herself, and [she revealed] how her own son unwittingly had become enamored of her." *Thérèse philosophe* she represented (accurately!) as "a book with very indecent pictures that narrates amorous adventures . . . and does so vividly." La Fontaine's work was a book "in two volumes of very explicit little stories [illustrated] with lascivious copper-plates." She further mentioned another volume of "novellas with extremely indecent engravings" and, finally, the "religious writings" of Saint-Évremond that, according to her, "contested [religious] belief and at the end make one believe that there is no God." Most scholars would not catalog Saint-Évremond (ca. 1613–1703) as a skeptic, and certainly not as an atheist or libertine, but rather as a moralist who urged a moderate hedonism and pleaded for religious toleration. Nonetheless, Charlotte's perception differed.[30]

Charlotte may have misjudged Saint-Évremond, but not *Thérèse philosophe*—one of the most well-known and widely read pornographic works of the eighteenth century.[31] Charlotte may have been swayed, she suggested, by the episode in which reading "dirty books" so excited Thérèse that she submitted to the count's "dart," which she had previously refused. Here we perceive how Charlotte and her examiners believed her story could be told: giving a young girl dirty books could so arouse her that she would surrender to male lust despite its consequences, in this case, incest. I am not arguing that Charlotte got the idea for her narrative from *Thérèse philosophe* or any other distinctive source, although she may well have taken hints from her interrogators. Rather, the modality by which her sexual excitement was kindled—through reading, specifically the reading of, certain notorious works—formed an accepted part of how Charlotte and her contemporaries perceived and constructed the world about them. Nor am I claiming that Charlotte consciously selected such elements in the hope of having her story believed. She understood her sexuality as easily quickened by reading. Charlotte and her questioners were clearly reading with a range of books available to them.

Just how dangerous knowledge was for the weaker sex, especially the adolescent female, had been long debated. Numerous enlightened publications stressed the necessity of a better education for women. During the eighteenth century discussions on the education of women developed throughout Germany almost simultaneously, and virtually all the enlightened and useful publications of the day took up the topic. The purpose of the program was not to produce "learned ladies" whom, as Gellert observed, "the world . . . hardly needs." Rather, education aimed to produce female companions whose "reason, heart, and taste have been shaped by the reading of good books."[32] This theme—the proper upbringing of women—ranked among the major themes of Germany's most important moral weeklies, *Der Patriot*, published in Hamburg between 1724 and 1726. Laid out in the pages of *Der Patriot* an eighteenth-century bourgeois father might find a veritable catalog of books thought suitable for educating a good and honorable daughter. In the contrast between this *bibliothèque* and the books that Martin prescribed, one immediately recognizes the differences.

Yet the gap may not have been quite so yawning as it first appears. The reading program found in *Der Patriot* was in fact shot through with ambiguities. How, for instance, did one urge women to read and yet control what they read and how? The position of reading in female education, however, and the types of books recommended as well as the *way* in which they were to be read are matters immediately relevant to Charlotte's case. Moral weeklies such as *Der Patriot* regarded the better education of women as an important desideratum, a central part of a much more ambitious program of civic improvement. The

moral weeklies as a whole, and *Der Patriot* in particular, "directed ... pedagogical efforts explicitly and with particular enthusiasm to the female reader."[33] *Der
Patriot* devoted a number of its issues, including several very early ones, to the
subject. The ideal young *Bürgerfrau* portrayed in its pages—chaste, rational,
capable, and modest Araminte (from the Greek term for lofty)—personified
the good results of a well-ordered reading plan for women.[34]

Appropriate literature for women often appeared in the form of publications known collectively as *Frauenzimmer-Bibliotheken*, a term with at least
two meanings. In one sense, the term describes a sort of eighteenth-century
Reader's Digest, a selection intended "to 'spare' women the [necessity] of reading
each original." Two such collections appeared in Hamburg in the second half
of the eighteenth century: a translation of the "Lady's Library," originally published in the English periodical, *The Spectator;* and Karl Friedrich Mückler's
Kleine Frauenzimmerbibliothek (Little Library for Women).[35] The second type
of *Frauenzimmer-Bibliotheken* was a bibliography recommended as the basis of
a woman's library. *Der Patriot* published a catalog of those volumes "that I [the
fictive patriot] found [on the shelves] of the praiseworthy Araminte." Virtually
nothing on this list overlapped with the "reading program" that Denis Martin
had putatively set out for his daughter. The Araminte "library" contained some
eighty-eight titles divided into four categories. Under the rubric "Devotion and
Religious Edification," we find bibles; several works by Luther; the Hamburg
hymnal; and abridged and bowdlerized versions of the Old and New Testaments. Then for "Knowledge and Amusement," there were genealogies, histories (especially religious ones), travel literature, atlases, arithmetic primers,
books on drawing and painting, Fontenelle's *Conversations on the Plurality of
Worlds* (in French); two collections of good literature, one in German and the
other in French; and a *Bibliothèque des Dames* (a French translation of the *Lady's Library*). In order to impart "Practical Wisdom," *Der Patriot* recommended
Montaigne's essays, the works of "Father" Cats (the early seventeenth-century
Dutch moralist), the *Maxims* of La Rochefoucauld, the fables of De La Mothe,
and the *Spectator* in a French translation. Finally, because Araminte was by then
a married woman with a household, she also needed a number of practical
guides on housekeeping, including various *Tisch-Bücher*—household reference
books—on gardening, domestic medicine, and cooking. Last, but not least, *Der
Patriot* recommended both Fenelon and Locke on child-rearing.[36] This compilation dates from the 1720s and, over the course of the century, recommendations shifted to include a series of more modern writers, adding in the 1740s,
for example, Gellert, Hagedorn, and Haller, and some novels, such as Richard-
son's *Clarissa* and *Pamela*, Defoe's best-selling *Robinson Crusoe*, and even Swift,
Fielding, and Sterne.[37]

Of course, historians and literary scholars have often remarked on the vast
increase in the numbers of reading women, the efforts to improve female ed-

ucation and growing concern about reading—and especially the reading of novels—that crested in the late eighteenth century. Many *Aufklärer* considered the reading fever (*Lesewuth* or *Lesesucht*) in women especially perilous not only because of *what* women read, but also because of *how* they read it.[38] Reading alone, and especially reading in bed, they judged to be particularly dangerous. Reading was thought to affect the female organism in two, equally pernicious ways. As a "disease of the soul" (*Seelenepidemie*), it could destroy internal spiritual life. But reading could also disorder the various fluids and tissues that composed the female body. Simply put, "reading accompanies seduction and is directly coupled to the passions and the body." It could, moreover, encourage female masturbation or make a woman "sharp" (*scharf*)—that is, stimulate her lust."[39]

In short, "reading novels, to believe the opinions of certain authors, produces an emotion that is physiological in nature, a sort of over-excitement that is almost pathological."[40] This is clearly the effect that Charlotte described and that her interlocutors accepted as plausible. Thus, Charlotte's discussion of what led her to this incestuous relationship agreed with ideas about reading and its effect on the female body that circulated in enlightened circles. It was an idea equally prevalent in literature. For example, the heroine of La Roche's novel, *Sophie von Sternheim*, burns the "English books"—pornography, one assumes— that had been given to her by her would-be seducer.[41]

The divergences between any of these lists and Charlotte's is marked, to say the least. Despite the ambiguities of *Der Patriot*'s reading agenda, no moral weekly or *Frauenzimmerbibliothek* would have recommended *Thérèse philosophe* as proper reading for any woman, let alone a young girl. This curious convergence expresses well the ambiguities and hidden dangers inherent in the read and reading world of the eighteenth century. Concern about reading and sex, and fears about the damage dirty books could do were, of course, quite old. In 1602, for example, Jean Benedicti condemned all those who "write, compose, or study lascivious and lubricious books for pleasure or with evil intentions."[42] In the early eighteenth century, moralists expressed deep concern about the reading of French novels, *galante* stories, and "wicked books," such as those on fortune-telling, treasure-hunting, "dream-books," and "Doktor Faustus" tales. Especially dangerous counted "all romances" because they endangered "chastity and the purity of heart."[43] Those fears never disappeared, of course, and fulminations against that literature never abated. However, the new worry was a very different one: "Now [1770s] one found himself in a serious predicament regarding literature that should serve to promote virtue, but that at the same time could have deleterious effects" on the mind and conduct. Here one detects the beginnings of a roll-back, perhaps even a reaction against, the program of the early *Aufklärung*, as many began to suggest that reading was a double-edged sword and that less reading (and more contemplation) was a better choice for women.[44] But while it is impossible to ignore the differences between what Charlotte putatively read and what others recommended, it is the *similarities* between her father's reading program and that suggested by the *Aufklärer* that are more intriguing and more insidious. In ways that the next section explores further, Father Martin was actually doing *just* what a father was supposed to do.

A Father's Love

Although incest was by no means solely a product of the new model of close affection between parents and children generally known as the sentimental family, as it developed in the eighteenth century, Charlotte's *story* germinated in just that milieu. The reconciliation scene in Heinrich von Kleist's *Die Marquise von O* pictures tender love between father and daughter but also hints at how such emotions run dangerously close to something more sinister.[45] There exists, of course, a vast amount of work on the development of the affectionate, nuclear family. In the 1970s and 1980s, reigning scholarly orthodoxy accepted the relatively recent emergence of a family that was no longer based mainly on economic considerations or lineage but was far more affective—that is to say, based on deep, binding psychological commitments between wives and husbands, parents and children.[46] Not all scholars accepted this periodization, nor have they seen the emergence of a more affectionate family as an overwhelmingly positive development. Some pointed out its negative implications for the economic and productive life of women; others have noted that the "development, or more particularly the idealizing, of the sentimental domestic family ... provided a new rationale for the subordination of women."[47]

In many ways, Denis Martin fit the contemporary image of a good father, even if we accept that he indeed did all the things that Charlotte first accused him of—sullying her mind with dirty books and forcing her into an incestuous relationship. We have already encountered one way in which Denis Martin and the good father represented in the moral weeklies matched each other. Charlotte's father, like a good parent, had guided her reading. Moral weeklies elsewhere in Germany developed this theme in greater detail. In his dreams for the future, for instance, *The New Upright Observer* (Der neue Rechtschaffene), a moral weekly published in 1767 in Lindau, envisioned the following scene: a fictive observer—the "Upright Observer"—comes upon a girl as she is reading. "Is it possible," he says, "that I am actually meeting a young woman who is also a reader?" In her hands, he discovers to his great satisfaction Gellert's *Lustspiele*.[48] Querying her as to where she got the book and if her mother approved her literary pastime, he learns that "Your mother bought the book for you? And she was actually impelled to so by reading [the advice in] *The New Upright*

Observer!" He went on to praise the "tears of joy" that resulted from Gellert's representation of true sisterly love.[49]

This scene encapsulates the core of the *Aufklärers'* pedagogical project for women; it portrays a program of learning guided by knowledgeable and concerned parents that introduces young female minds to good, that is moral, literature. Yet we should recognize two other important things here. First, it is a parent (here a mother) who chooses the books and, second, that emotions and their physical manifestation, tears, were a perfectly appropriate response to reading. Of course, the author here stresses "good" and "virtuous" books. Nevertheless the means of selection—books chosen by a parent, given to a young woman, and with an expectation of evoking sensations—is exactly the same. One intended "emotion" (*Rührung*) to produce moral improvement. But it was a slippery slope from the evocation of pedagogically useful feelings to the arousal of dangerous passions.[50] While mothers were charged to ensure that their daughters read "good books," the family father bore the chief responsibility for selecting them. Indeed, a father should take as much responsibility for the education of his daughters as for his sons, according to *Der Patriot*. The influential north German pedagogue, Johann Heinrich Campe, writing in the early nineteenth century, summarized decades of expectations for fathers. In his *Paternal Advice for My Daughter* (Väterlicher Rat für meine Tochter), fathers were enjoined to inform their daughters about their proper position in society and also, specifically, to use "carefully selected works [books]" to do so.[51] What Martin was supposed to have done was rather different. The method, however, was identical and was closely allied to what were perceived and preached as the proper duties of a father in the sentimental and affectionate family.

Obviously, it would be insane to suggest that the *Aufklärer* were in any way responsible for fostering incestuous relationships within eighteenth-century families. Nonetheless, the actions prescribed for the good father often looked surprisingly like those the evil father (the incestuous father) took. Charlotte's husband, if in overblown and angry prose, showed that he, too, understood the dilemma and perceived how a father could use pedagogic initiatives to deform or mis-form, rather than properly form, a child. In a short note to Denis Martin, Guyard addressed him as an "unnatural father" (*père denaturé*) who had sacrificed his daughter to his own "monstrous desires." Charlotte, here, was the "unfortunate child" and "the victim of an incestuous and infamous lust."[52] In a long pamphlet published in his defense, one that fiercely attacked Martin, Jean François Guyard characterized Charlotte's father as a corrupter of his daughter's morals. Guyard portrayed his new wife as an inexperienced, naïve, and, at the same time, a frivolous young woman, possessing little or no knowledge of the world. She was, in his words, a tabula rasa, and wax in the hands of a depraved parent. Denis Martin had then deliberately shaped, or twisted, her education to suit his sexual purposes:

This young woman had only recently left the cloister and just entered into that time of life when the passions first bud but when her reason was still imperfectly formed. In this moment, Charlotte discovers the confusions of this world. What does her weak process of reason tell her [to do]? To deceive because she has been deceived.[53]

What, he asked rhetorically, had she learned, what had she been taught as she grew through puberty and into a young woman? Her reading told her that "everything was material" and that religion "was only a restraint for the *canaille*." "It was enough," she learned, "when one knew how to conceal his deeds from other people." She thus had become a hypocrite (*Heuchlerin*)—or, more precisely, that is what her upbringing had made her. Her father, who "possessed the ability to explain to her Évremond and the ways of love" was also capable "of indoctrinating his [young] proselyte with this remarkable system." According to Jean François Guyard, Martin's plan was both diabolical and farsighted. He intended "to make himself in her mind a little deity." Even after Charlotte "entered the Temple of Hymen" and Denis Martin had to share her with another, he would remain Charlotte's "high priest" of love and sex. In the end, however, the student surpassed the teacher and took on other lovers of whom her father knew nothing.[54]

Charlotte, in other words, had been raised by a libertine to become one herself. Her father had deliberately sought out the best books for *his* purposes, handed them over to her, allowed her the leisure and privacy to read them, and then reaped his reward, destroying her innocence in the process—or so Jean François Guyard claimed. As this example demonstrates, libertinism and enlightened thought existed in very close proximity.[55] Many scholars have remarked on the dark side of the enlightenment and, in particular, on a sort of freedom that could, in one direction, degenerate into Sadean license and depravity, or, in another, to incongruities between the ideal of liberty and the practice of slavery. To be sure, libertinism was not new in the eighteenth century. By the seventeenth century, the word libertine applied to those who opposed dogma and received wisdoms and was often used in the sense of free-thinking. Zedler's *Universal-Lexikon* gives the original meaning of libertine as one who "in matters of belief or in other things, did not allow himself to be bound by regular guidelines."[56] By the middle of the eighteenth century, however, the understanding of libertine had come to approximate the way we understand it today—that is, as an expression of slack morals and lack of restraint, particularly in sexual matters. Furthermore, contemporaries tended to equate libertine behavior with courts and especially with the French, personified in the sexual notoriety of the French regent, Philip d'Orléans, himself widely reputed to have had an incestuous relationship with at least one of his daughters.[57]

As there were libertine personalities and libertine locales, there were also libertine books.[58] These were just the books, or some of them at least, that

Charlotte had read and that had, according to her husband, predictably evil effects on her mind, soul, and morals. The story of the Guyard incest case, therefore, illustrates the paradoxes of the reading woman and the affectionate family; both were supported and also constructed by the *Aufklärer*. One path led to the rational, chaste, and competent wife—a good *Bürgerin*—while the other led in an entirely different direction, down the dark paths of moral corruption and even into the darker pit of sexual abuse and criminal relationships. Contemporaries set the life history of Charlotte within the broader literary world of true-crime writing as it developed in the early modern world, using it, like other single incidents, as parables and cautionary tales, but also as entertainment. But the entire story of Charlotte's seduction or her corruption also raised a series of troubling issues for respectable burghers, magistrates, judges, parents, and, not least, the protagonists of enlightenment: What could prevent good intentions from careening wildly off the rails, producing not better educated daughters but monsters of depravity? If fathers should rule and direct, what happened when their guidance proved deeply flawed, as perhaps Denis Guyard's was? Could education produce evil results and criminal deeds as well as nurture the flowering of human potential? The Guyard case made it clear that the pedagogic initiatives of the Enlightenment coexisted with just these ambiguities.

Notes

1. *Les Mystères de Paris* appeared from 19 June 1842 through 15 October 1843 in the popular *Journal des Débats*. The serialization was responsible for a major increase in readership of the journal. It appeared in 1843 as a five-volume novel.

2. Francesco Mastiani, *I misteri di Napoli: Studi storico sociali* (Naples, 1869); George W.M. Reynolds, *The Mysteries of London*, 4 vols. (London, 1850–59); and last but not least, Émile Zola's *Les Mystères de Marseille: Roman historique contemporain* (Marseilles, 1867). Many of Charles Dickens's novels are set in London and have a pronounced "mysteries" character to them, as does, of course, also Victor Hugo's *Les Misérables*.

3. On Hesslein, see Art. "Hesslein, Bernhard," in Hans Schroeder, *Lexicon der hamburgischen Schriftsteller bis zur Gegenwart*, 8 vols. (Hamburg, 1851–83). He wrote, for instance, a three-volume social-political novel based on the life of Jefferson Davis (*Jefferson Davis: Social-politischer Roman aus dem amerikanischen Bürgerkriege*, 3 vols. [Leipzig, 1866–67]) and another on Berlin (*Das schwarze Buch von Berlin oder Geheimnissse der protestantischen Metropole: Social-politischer Roman* [Leipzig1865]); biographies (such as his on *Nikolaus I: 30 Jahre aus der Geschichte Rußlands* [Berlin, 1855]); a series of "young man in the city" novels, including one based on Dickens (*Berliner Pickwickier: Fahrten und Abentheuer Berliner Junggesellen bei ihren Kreuz- und Querzügen durch das moderne Babylon*, 3 vols. [Berlin, 1854]); and true-crime (*Bibliothek moderner Räubergeschichten* [Berlin, 1851]), based on the example of François Gayot de Pitaval, *Causes célèbres et intéressantes avec les jugements qui les ont decidés*, 24 vols. (Paris, 1739–70).

4. On *Der Kaiserhof*, see *Hamburgs berühmte und berüchtigte Häuser in historischer, criminalistischer und socialer Beziehung*, 2 vols. (Hamburg, 1850), vol. 2, 72–87.

5. *Hamburgs berühmte und berüchtigte Häuser,* vol. 2, 86–87.
6. See Mary Lindemann, "Eighteenth-Century True Crime Stories, Legal Histories, and the Literary Imagination," *Daphnis* 37 (2008): 131–52; idem "Narratives of Dismembering Women in Northern Germany, 1600–1800," in *Women & Death: Representations of Female Victims and Perpetrators in German Culture, 1500–2000,* ed. Helen Fronius and Ann Linton (London, 2008), 6–92; Susanne Kord, *Murderesses in German Writing, 1720–1860: Heroines of Horror* (Cambridge, U.K. 2009). In The Dutch Republic the politician and author Onno Zwier van Haren had to retire from politics after rumors (probably true) of his incestuous relationship with one of his daughters came out. See the investigation records in Allgemeine Rijksarchief 5477.1, "Stukken inzake Onno Zwier van Haren, grietman van het Bilt, schuldig aan tentamen criminis incesti, 1762." It received a literary treatment in Edgar du Perron, *Schandaal in Holland* (The Hague, 1939), 88–172. See also Pieter van de Vliet, *Onno Zwier van Haren (1713–1779): Staatsman en dichter* (Hilversum, 1996), 201–78.
7. Details of Charlotte's story are taken primarily from the protocols of the Hamburg Senate (City Council) and of Staatsarchiv Hamburg [hereafter StAHbg], and from a number of contemporary works published by her father and husband: StAHbg, Senat Cl. VIII Lit. Xa, from 1766–70; [Jean François] Guyard, *Sendschreiben des Kaufmanns Guyard in Hamburg an seine Mitbürger: Als eine Einleitung zu seinen herauszugebenden Mémoires* ([Hamburg], 1767); [Denis Martin], *Der vertheidigte Denis Martin, wider seinen Schwiegersohn und seine Tochter François Guyard und Charlotta Martin, verheyratete Guyard* (Hamburg, 1766); *Vollständige Acten in der seltenen und überaus wichtigen Sache, Denis Martin, wider seinen unwürdigen Schwiegersohn und unwürdige Tochter, Jean François Guyard und Charlotta Guyard gebohrne Martin, in Hamburg, Criminell-Verläumder; insonderheit itzo wider die Herren Bürgermeister und Rathmänner der Stadt Hamburg, wegen über verwalteter Justiz, ausgeübten Thätlichkeiten, zugefügten harten Beleidigungen und unersetzlichen Schäden an Ehre, Credit und Gütern, auch veranlaßten schweren Kosten, und daher schuldigst zu gebender Genugthuung, Erstattung aller Schäden, Interesse und Kosten, und in der Folge gegen die Verbrecher und Criminell-Verläumder, Ihren schwerden Eiden, Pflicht und Gewissen gemäß, nach deutlicher Vorschrift der Rechte, besser als bisher geschehen, ernsthaft und ohne Ansehen der Person, EX OFFICIO zu verfahren* ([Hamburg?], 1767). These last two titles may be found in the library of the StAHbg, A427/805 and A427/813, respectively.
8. Richard A. McCabe, *Incest, Drama and Nature's Law* (Cambridge, UK, 1993), 25.
9. See, for example, a case from 1777 in StAHbg, Senat Cl. VIII no. Xa (1777), 9, 113 that involved a father and daughter. A case from the following year involved a stepfather and his step-daughter, whom he impregnated and then tried to marry, passing her off as another woman, in ibid. (1778), 158, 166, 177, 191, 203. Authorities in Antwerp, too, investigated a significant number of cases and punished those who perpetrated sexual assaults on children of both sexes. Records of such cases are in Stadtarchiv Antwerpen [hereafter StA], under Vierschar (hereafter V). When two men raped a *jonge dochter* (she was about twelve), the deed was judged "ten uÿtteristen straffbaer [en] is als vallende in een capitael delict," and they were indeed executed; "Proclamation," from 12 February 1728, in StA, V 91, V 162. The rigor with which such crimes could be pursued is demonstrated by the amount of testimony available on another case of child molestation from 1735, in StA, V91, involving one Jan Bouckhol. The authorities took testimony from several witnesses including the twelve-year-old victim, her parents, and numerous neighbors.

10. See, for instance, Christa von Braun, "Die 'Blutschande': Wandelungen eines Begriffs: Vom Inzesttabu zu den Rassengesetzen," in idem, *Die schamlose Schönheit des Vergangenen: Zum Verhältnis von Geschlecht und Geschichte* (Frankfurt, 1989), 81–111.

11. Calum M. Carmichael, *Law, Legend, and Incest in the Bible: Leviticus 18–20* (Ithaca, 1997), 4.

12. Gen. 19:30–38: "Lot and his two daughters left Zoar and settled in the mountains, for he was afraid to stay in Zoar. He and his two daughters lived in a cave. [31]One day the older daughter said to the younger, "Our father is old, and there is no man around here to lie with us, as is the custom all over the earth. [32]Let's get our father to drink wine and then lie with him and preserve our family line through our father." [33]That night they got their father to drink wine, and the older daughter went in and lay with him. He was not aware of it when she lay down or when she got up. [34]The next day the older daughter said to the younger, "Last night I lay with my father. Let's get him to drink wine again tonight, and you go in and lie with him so we can preserve our family line through our father." [35]So they got their father to drink wine that night also, and the younger daughter went and lay with him. Again he was not aware of it when she lay down or when she got up. [36]So both of Lot's daughters became pregnant by their father. [37]The older daughter had a son, and she named him Moab; he is the father of the Moabites of today. [38]The younger daughter also had a son, and she named him Ben-Ammi; he is the father of the Ammonites of today." Carmichael, *Law,* 2, 5.

13. 1 Cor. 5:1. This is a disputed text that some have interpreted as condoning incest. See also Paul's pronouncement in 1 Cor. 7:36–38.

14. Lev. 18: 6–7. McCabe, *Incest,* 29, 43–44; Karl Elliger, "Das Gesetz Leviticus 18," *Zeitschrift für die alttestamentliche Wissenschaft* 67 (1955): 1–25; Katherine Crawford, *European Sexualities, 1400–1800* (Cambridge, UK, 2007), 35, 70, 85 (Benedicti quote).

15. See §117 of *Die Peinliche Gerichtsordnung Kaiser Karls V. und des Heiligen Römischen Reiches von 1532 (Carolina),* ed. Friedrich-Christian Schroeder (Stuttgart, 2000), 76. Susanne Hehenberger points out that the legal situation was more complex and in the Herrschaft Freistadt (in the late eighteenth century) the Leopoldina and Thersiana codes, as well as other single laws and ordinances need to be considered; see Hehenberger, "'. . . Ich bin mit diesem Knecht geschwistrigt Kinder . . .': Der Prozess gegen Maria Stumvollin und Johann Scherb (Friestadt/Weinberg 1783) als Beispiel der Strafpraxis beim Delikt 'Inzest' im 18. Jahrhundert," *Jahrbuch des Oberösterreichischen Musealvereines* 144 (1999): 199–230, here 201.

16. Decision of 10 October 1749, in Staats- und Universitäts-Bibliothek Hamburg (hereafter SUBHbg), Handschriftensammlung, Cod. Hans., II, 144, 1, 57. On the practice of banishment, see Coy, *Strangers and Misfits.*

17. Nicolaus Schuback, "Versuch Einer systematischen Abhandlung vom Richterlichen Ampte in Hamburg . . . Beÿ Gelelgenheit der von Demselben zu übernehmenden und übernommenen Praetur., circa 1747," in SUBHbg, Handschriftensammlung, Cod. Hans. II, 139, 2, fols. 132–33, "Von den Delicitis Carnis."

18. McCabe, *Incest,* 11. The position of Reformers on incest is actually quite complicated, see Jónsson, "Incest and the Word of God."

19. Claudia Jarzebowski, "Eindeutig uneindeutig: Verhandlungen über Inzest im 18. Jahrhundert," *Historische Inzestdiskurse: Interdisziplinäre Zugänge,* ed. Jutta Emig, Claudia Jarzebowski, and Claudia Ulbrich (Königstein, 2003), 164; idem, *Inzest: Verwandschaft und Sexualität im 18. Jahrhundert* (Cologne, 2006).

20. Ulinka Rublack argues that the cases she examined in the Protestant southwest of Germany were indeed what we would today call "innerfamiliärer sexueller Mißbrauch"; Rublack, "'Viehisch, frech und onverschämpt': Inzest in Südwestdeutschland, ca. 1530–1700," in *Von Huren und Rabenmüttern: Weibliche Kriminalität in der frühen Neuzeit*, ed. Otto Ulbricht (Cologne, 1995), 171–213. Others, such as Susanne Hehenberger, have argued that this is too simple; see her "'. . . Ich bin mit diesem Knecht geschwistrigt Kinder . . .'."

21. "Outline and Summaries," in David Warren Sabean, Simon Teutscher, and Jon Mathieu, eds., *Kinship in Europe: Approaches to Long-term Development (1300–1900)* (New York, 2007), 56.

22. "Dispenserteilung in Ehesachen" from 1730–99 in Niedersächsisches Staatsarchiv Wolfenbüttel, 14 Alt Konsistorialakten, Nrs. 695–702; Jarzebowski, *Inzest*.

23. See Art. "Blutschande" in Johann Zedler, *Grosses vollständiges Universal Lexicon Aller Wissenschaften und Künsten*, 64 vols. (Leipzig, 1731–54), vol. 4, 247–57, here 247.

24. See Art. "Blutschande," in *Zedler's Universal Lexicon*, vol. 4, 250-51.

25. Hartmut Nonnenmacher, *Natur und Fatum: Inzest als Motiv und Thema in der französischen und deutschen Literatur des 18. Jahrhunderts* (Frankfurt, 2002), 73.

26. W. Daniel Wilson, "Science, Natural Law, and Unwitting Sibling Incest in Eighteenth-Century Literature," *Studies in Eighteenth-Century Literature* 13 (1984): 249–70.

27. Nonnenmacher, *Natur und Fatum*, 342; Jarzebowski, "Eindeutig uneindeutig," 168–69. On brother–sister incest, see Andrea Bramberger, *Verboten Lieben: Bruder-Schwester-Inzest* (Pfaffenweiler, 1998); Sabean, "Inzestdiskurse"; and idem, "From Siblingship to Siblinghood: Kinship and the Shaping of European Society (1300–1900)," in *Sibling Relations and the Transformation of European Kinship, 1300–1900*, ed. Christopher H. Johnson and David Warren Sabean (New York, 2011).

28. A large number of works treat incest as a literary theme. It was, of course, not only a topic of eighteenth-century literature. See for example "Inzest," in *Themen und Motive in der Literatur: Ein Handbuch*, ed. Horst S. Daemmrich and Ingrid Daemmrich (Tübingen, 1987); and *Violation of Taboo: Incest in the Great Literatures of the Past and Present*, ed. Donald Webster Cory and Robert E.L. Masters (New York, 1963). See also T.G.A. Nelson, "Incest in the Early Novel and Related Genres," *Eighteenth-Century Life* 16 (1992): 127–62; Titzmann, "Literarische Strukturen," 229–89.

29. "Summarische Vernehmung und Aussage Charlotte Guyard, gebohrne Martin, wegen ihres angeblich mit ihrem eigenen Vater sowohl, als merern andern Mannspersonen gepflogenen verbotenen Umgangs," 10 January 1766, in *Vollständige Acten*, unpag. appendix. For the extensive deliberations of the City Council on the case, see StAHbg, Senat Cl. VIII no. X [Senats-Protokoll], 1766–68. An earlier defense had appeared in pamphlet form in late 1766. This was *Der vertheidigte Denis Martin*. The Senate ordered Martin, under penalty of 500 *Thaler*, to halt the distribution of these pamphlets. Martin, however, insisted, "it was printed without his permission and he had no part in it." StAHbg, Senat Cl. VIII no. X (22 and 29 December 1766), 1300–1301, 1311.

30. "Continuatio examinis," 11 February 1766, in *Vollständige Acten*; Claude Tattinger, *Saint-Évremond: ou le bon usage des plaisirs* (Paris, 1990).

31. Robert Darnton, *The Forbidden Best-Sellers of Pre-Revolutionary France* (New York, 1997), 296–97.

32. Christian Fürchtegott Gellert (1715–69) quoted in Christine Mayer, "Erziehung und Schulbildung für Mädchen," in *Handbuch der Bildungsgeschichte*, vol. 2, *18. Jahrhundert: Vom späten 17. Jahrhundert bis zur Neuordnung Deutschlands um 1800*, ed. Notker

Hammerstein and Ulrich Hermann (Munich, 2005), 192. The literature on female education and the *Aufklärung* is large. See, for example, Elke Kleinau and Claudia Opitz, *Geschichte der Mädchen- und Frauenbildung*, 2 vols. (Frankfurt, 1996); *Tugend, Vernunft und Gefühle: Geschlechterdiskurs der Aufklärung und weibliche Lebenswelten*, ed. Claudia Opitz, Ulrike Weikel, and Elke Kleinau (Münster, 2000); Ulrich Hermann, "Erziehung und Schulunterricht für Mädchen im 18. Jahrhundert," *Wolfenbütteler Studien zur Aufklärung* 3 (1976): 101–27; Johanna Höpfner, *Mädchenerziehung und weibliche Bildung um 1800: Im Spiegel der populär-pädagogischen Schriften der Zeit* (Bad Heilbrunn, 1990); *Geschichte der Mädchenlektüre: Mädchenliteratur und die gesellschaftliche Situation der Frauen vom 18. Jahrhundert bis zum Gegenwart*, ed. Dagmar Grenz and Gisela Wilkending (Weinheim, 1997); and Susanne Barth, *Mädchenlektüren: Lesediskurse im 18. und 19. Jahrhundert* (Frankfurt, 2002).

33. Wolfgang Martens, *Die Botschaft der Tugend: Die Aufklärung im Spiegel der deutschen Moralischen Wochenschriften* (Stuttgart, 1968), 521.

34. *Der Patriot* no. 3 (20 January 1724); no. 5 (3 February 1724); no. 6 (10 February 1724); no. 8 (24 February 1724); no. 28 (13 July 1724); no. 68 (19 April 1725); and no. 132 (11 July 1726).

35. The "Lady's [Ladies'] Library" was advertised as "Written by a Lady," that is, Mary Wray, and published/edited by Richard Steele; it has variously been attributed to Wray, Steele, and George Berkeley. It appeared in two German translations in Hamburg.

36. *Der Patriot* no. 8 (24 February 1724). The second edition of *Der Patriot* that appeared in book form in 1728 modified and expanded the list, increasing the total number of works on the list to ninety-five; Peter Nasse, *Die Frauenzimmer-Bibliothek des Hamburger "Patrioten" von 1724: Zur weiblichen Bildung in der Frühaufklärung* (Stuttgart, 1976), 22, note 17; and Martens, *Der Patriot*, 4 : 49–64. Nasse discusses the books at length in ibid., 626–35. Similar compilations can be found in other spectatorial publications, such as the "Lady's Library," first published in *Spectator* no. 37 (1711) and then in the *Vernünfftler* no. 50 (1713). The *Vernünfftler* was, like *Der Patriot*, published in Hamburg.

37. Martens, *Botschaft*, 448–51; Nasse, *Frauenzimmer-Bibliothek*, 668–82. These lists varied with different authors and different journals, of course.

38. The term "*Lesesucht*" probably first appeared in Rudolf Heinrich Zobel, *Briefe über die Erziehung der Frauenzimmer* (Stralsund, 1773), but the debate really got going with the appearance in 1774 of Goethe's *Die Leiden des jungen Werthers*. The north German pedagogue, Johann Heinrich Campe, writing in 1809, spoke of "Die Lesesucht unserer Weiber," in his *Wörterbuch der deutschen Sprache* (Braunschweig, 1807). Those most susceptible to this fever were women and adolescents, especially adolescent females; see Rudolf Schenda, *Volk ohne Buch: Studien zur Sozialgeschichte der populären Lesestoffe 1770–1910*, 3rd ed. (Frankfurt, 1988), 57–66; Domink von König, "Leseucht und Lesewut," in *Buch und Leser: Vorträge des ersten Jahrestreffens des Wolfenbütteler Arbeitskreis für Geschichte des Buchwesens*, ed. Herbert G. Göpfert (Hamburg, 1977), 89–112.

39. Helga Meise, *Die Unschuld und die Schrift: Deutsche Frauenromane im 18. Jahrhundert* (Berlin, 1983), 71–74. On the fluid humoral economy of female bodies, see Barbara Duden, *The Woman Beneath the Skin: A Doctor's Patients in Eighteenth-Century Germany* (Cambridge, 1991).

40. Jean Marie Goulemot, *Forbidden Texts: Erotic Literature and its Readers in Eighteenth-Century France* (Philadelphia, 1994), 56. Goulemot is referring, in particular, to the

physicians Samuel Tissot and D. T. Bienville, who argued that such reading led to female masturbation. That was not its only effect. Young women who read too much tended to grow up vapourish and prove inadequate mothers, unable, for instance to nurse their infants themselves.

41. Meise, *Unschuld*, 71.

42. Benedicti, *Somme des pechez* (Rouen, 1602) quoted in K. Crawford, *European Sexualities*, 85.

43. From the *Frauen-Zimmer-Bibliotheckgen* (1705) quoted in Nasse, *Frauenzimmer-Bibliothek*, 658.

44. Martens, *Botschaft*, 537.

45. See Art. "Kleist, Heinrich von," in *GLBTQ: An Encyclopedia of Gay, Lesbian, Bisexual, Transgender, and Queer Culture*, online ed. at http://www.glbtq.com/, accessed 3 September, 2010; and Irmela Marei Krüger-Fürhoff, "Epistemological Asymmetries and Erotic Stagings: Father-Daughter Incest in Heinrich von Kleist's *The Marquise von O*," *Women in German Yearbook: Feminist Studies in German Literature & Culture* 12 (1996): 71–86.

46. Classic statements are found in Edward Shorter, *The Making of the Modern Family* (New York, 1975); Lawrence Stone, *The Family, Sex and Marriage in England, 1500–1800* (New York, 1977); and Randolph Trumbach, *The Rise of the Egalitarian Family* (New York, 1978).

47. Susan Miller Okin, "Women and the Making of the Sentimental Family," *Philosophy & Public Affairs* 11 (1981): 65.

48. Christian Fürchtegott Gellert, *Lustspiele* (Leipzig, 1747).

49. Quoted in Jürgen Jacobs, *Prosa der Aufklärung: Moralische Wochenschriften—Autobiographie—Satire—Roman: Kommentar zu einer Epoche* (Munich, 1976), 49.

50. Jacobs, *Prosa der Aufklärung*, 66.

51. Johann Heinrich Campe, *Väterlicher Rat für meine Tochter: Ein Gegenstuck zum Theophron, der erwachsenern weiblichen Jugend gewidmet* (Braunschweig, 1809), 56; Annette Kuhn and Gerda Tornieporth, *Frauenbildung und Geschlechtsrolle: Historische und erziehungswissenschaftliche Studien zum Wandel der Frauenrolle in Familie und Gesellschaft* (Gelnhausen, 1980).

52. "Abermahlige Vernehmung der Charlotte Guyard worinne sie alle ihre vorigen Beschuldigungen wiederrufet, solche für falsch und unwahr, und von ihrem Manne extorquirt erkläret, 31. Mai 1766," in *Vollständige Acten*, unpag. appendix.

53. Guyard, *Sendschreiben*, 37–38.

54. Ibid., 37–39.

55. *Der Patriot's* reading program for women reflected the *Aufklärung's* emphasis on the importance of Christianity and the acquisition of "sincere piety" for the development of the female personality. Nasse, *Frauenzimmer-Bibliothek*, 636–37.

56. Zedler, *Universal Lexicon*, vol. 17: 793.

57. Michael Feher, "Libertinisms," in *The Libertine Reader: Eroticism and Enlightenment in Eighteenth-Century France*, ed. Michael Feher (New York, 1997), 10–15.

58. Goulemot, *Forbidden Texts*; Feher, *Libertine Reader*.

~:~

Shifting Boundaries and Boundary Shifters

Transgressive Unions and the History of Marriage in Early Modern Germany

JOEL F. HARRINGTON

M arriage by its very nature comprises not only the relationship between two individuals, but also the relationship of that union to the larger society. It has always involved, in that sense, some combination of both public recognition and private consent. The legal basis for this public approval is in turn based on collective, communal norms, which obviously vary considerably—not just across historical cultures but also within cultures themselves. Every individual, moreover, is simultaneously a member of multiple communities—based on kinship, habitation, ethnicity, and so on—and while the values of these communities often overlap to significant degrees, they are rarely contiguous. Finally, communal disapproval of any given union does not always entail legal invalidation of the same. The definition of social propriety, in other words, is a perplexing and slippery matter where marriage is concerned, involving multiple boundaries, many of them in flux and otherwise difficult to determine.[1]

The preceding chapters on transgressive unions in early modern Germany confirm the complexity of this subject, but at the same time offer some useful insights to these shifting marital boundaries over the *longue durée* from the high Middle Ages to the modern era. Viewed together, the various boundary-crossers we encounter in this volume reveal much about the relative public–private balance in early modern marriage as well as the relationship of the institution to the most important social transformations of the era. In this final chapter I propose to draw on the findings of this collection to address three interrelated questions about the big picture of German marriage during this period. First, how much in fact did the boundaries of propriety vary between 1400 and 1800, and was the sixteenth century truly a turning point in this respect? Second, did transgression of all or some marriage boundaries become more common over the course of the early modern period (suggesting a declining importance for communal approval) or was the situation more complex? Third, what was the respective influence of major social phenomena during this period, particularly the religious reforms of the sixteenth century, the emergence of the nation-state, and the increase in crosscultural, multiethnic encounters? I have put the early modern period at the center of all three questions in part because of the chronological scope of this volume but also because I believe that these chapters challenge the presumption of a definitive redefinition of the public–private balance in marriage during this period.

Addressing the first question, significant changes in the communal boundaries for acceptable marriages, requires a broad chronological perspective. Before the twelfth century, three communities apparently had the most influence on the propriety of marital unions in German lands: the kin group (led by the appropriate senior male), the geographical community (e.g., the village or the urban neighborhood), and the church (at both the local and regional level). All three overlapped to a considerable degree, with the cultural norms of the locality and familial approval having the greatest weight, even on questions of legal validity. Ecclesiastical proscriptions of polygamy and divorce, as well as broader definitions of incest, clearly shaped common practice and belief, but effective enforcement mostly relied on the same familial and local communities. We know little about the latter for most of the Middle Ages, except for aristocratic and royal marriages, where compliance with clerical guidelines was evidently selective at best.[2] Legal validity of a union was thus virtually identical with familial approval. Whatever the role of individual choice or affection, if a marrying individual's father or other male relative did not approve of the union, it would not be considered valid. Obviously a variety of factors might prompt such a veto, primarily the kin group's own material interests, but also traditional signifiers of inappropriateness: unequal social status, disparate ages, foreign birth, or even physical disability. Judging by secular legislation, the social division between free and unfree individuals was the most commonly transgressed boundary of the era, often accomplished through elopement or kidnapping (*Frauenraub*) to evade legal censure. Unequal unions among artisans or between aristocrats of different rank, by contrast, faced legal consequences only if familial authorities disapproved. Transgressions against marriage itself, especially of a sexual nature, were similarly punished according to local standards and the individual's place within that community.

The codification and application of canon law to marriage from the twelfth century onward dramatically transformed this status quo, at least in theory. Some families and localities might have initially welcomed the introduction of episcopal courts to adjudicate disputed marriage vows, especially when decisions reinforced their own preferences. Even then, however, the significant differences between local Germanic customs and the Roman-based canon law were quickly evident, beginning with the very definition of a valid union. In keeping with its sacramental character, a binding marriage was determined by canonists to be based not on parental or communal approval, but rather on the consent of the groom and the bride. Church officials still sanctioned individuals who defied their families and a host of secular statutes added automatic disinheritance and other disincentives, but the genie was out of the bottle. Clandestine marriage vows between two willing adults (defined as fourteen or older)—however much reviled and punished by all communal authorities, including the church—were nevertheless regularly recognized in episcopal courts throughout Germany and all of Europe as valid and indissoluble. Transgressive unions based solely on individual choice now had an unwitting accomplice in church courts and canon law.[3]

By the beginning of the sixteenth century, the perceived imbalance in the public–private nature of marriage had become a public scandal, considered by many to be symptomatic of a larger social disorder.[4] Secular and religious authorities throughout German lands decried the destructive effects of this alleged perversion and launched a defense of marriage campaign, targeting every kind of marital transgression imaginable, from clandestine marriage and concubinage (both lay and clerical), to adultery and fornication, to unruly wedding feasts. Most fundamentally, Protestant and Catholic legislators alike sought a restoration of traditional values and authority, universally defined in patriarchal terms of the *Gottesvater, Landesvater,* and *Hausvater.* In theory, stricter oversight in each of these three realms—church, state, and family—would prevent marital transgressions of every kind. The religious confessions differed on some important questions of definition—to be discussed shortly—but the universal determination among all reformers to bolster patriarchal authority over unions in itself suggests a watershed moment in the history of German marriage.

Did the sixteenth century truly witness a significant hardening of the boundaries of marital propriety and a subsequent decline in transgressive unions? Let us start with the Protestant attempt to make marriage the new religious ideal for all Christians, presumably the change with the most dramatic impact on marital practice in the short term. As the last two decades of scholarship have demonstrated, cultural transformations of this magnitude typically required several generations of assimilation.[5] The deeply entrenched mental boundary between married laity and unmarried clergy, for instance, could not be erased among Protestants with a single proclamation, no matter how theologically indefensible religious celibacy became in a church founded on justification by faith alone and composed of a priesthood of all believers. The pervasiveness of anticlericalism throughout German society was insufficient to produce the expected tidal wave of marriages among evangelical clerics following their break from Rome. In fact, as Beth Plummer describes, there were fewer than a hundred such transgressive unions in all German lands by 1524, and the practice itself was rarely discussed publicly among evangelical leaders during the first decade of the Reformation. Such ambivalence among Luther and other theologians, she suggests, had less to do with any continuing attachment to the celibate ideal than it did with the other social transgressions that often resulted during the first generation of practice, namely crossing boundaries of social rank and even gender roles (e.g., cross-dressing) in the effort to find spouses for aristocratic nuns. In order to justify their own transgressions of such profound cultural boundaries, as well as the traditional clerical-laity divide, Protestants were forced to emphasize the virtual impossibility of sexual abstinence as well as the subsequent immorality of monastic life and the public scandal of priestly concubinage The liberation of the convents proclaimed by Steven Ozment and other sympathetic modern historians thus appears as more of a post facto self-justification in the polemical war of the 1520s than as a genuine motivation among either marrying clerics or suspicious laypeople.[6] Acculturation to the new marital boundaries required time. Although neither Wolfgang Breul nor Plummer describes here the gradual normalization of clerical marriage over subsequent generations, a return to marriage among social equals obviously played a pivotal role in this genuinely transformative achievement.

Ironically, acknowledging the universal power of the sexual drive led to even more attempts to constrain it, thereby broadening the definition of marital transgressions. Both the abolition of clerical celibacy among Protestants and the stricter punishment of clerical concubinage among post-Tridentine Catholics were in fact part of a larger campaign to minimize all sexual activity outside a valid union. Despite rejecting the biblical justification for marriage's sacramentality, Luther and his coreligionists continued to recognize the sanctity of the estate from the very beginning. By the time of the reformer's own union in 1524, as David Whitford and Wolfgang Breul describe, Luther had dropped all his earlier references to the "stench" of a second class *remedium* and wrote consistently of a godly estate preferable to the "tyrannical joke" of clerical celibacy. For Protestant secular and ecclesiastical authorities, *Unehe*—including not only concubinage, but also the *Unzucht* of bigamy, adultery, fornication, and prostitution—was in that sense as much of a threat to marital order as it was an unobtainable chaste ideal. Together with their Catholic counterparts, they attempted to purge their communities of all forms of illicit sexuality, only to confirm the intractability of original sin in all its manifestations. Marital transgressions of this nature, not addressed in this volume, were perhaps more often punished during the late sixteenth and early seventeenth centuries, but appear to have been otherwise minimally affected by reformers' ambitious aspirations.[7]

What about access to marriage itself? Did Protestant and Catholic attempts to readjust the public–private balance make transgressive unions more or less likely? The reforms themselves are contradictory on this question. On the one hand, Protestants seem to have liberalized access to marriage: eliminating spiritual impediments, modifying the definition of consanguinity, and even making divorce and remarriage possible. As Claudia Jarzebowski writes, the objective was to facilitate rather than hinder appropriate unions. On the other hand, most of the impediments in question had always been subject to dispensation in the Catholic church (albeit for a fee) as well as simple disregard without any repercussions (did anyone really worry about marrying a second cousin?). Divorce with the possibility of remarriage, an admitted novelty, was not widely granted by Protestant courts and thus remained an uncommon response to marital transgressions until the nineteenth century.[8] Overall, the continuity of canonical standards in Protestant and Catholic marital legislation of the sixteenth century far outweighed any modifications, at least as far as judicial authorities were concerned.[9]

At the same time, the sixteenth-century schism of western Christianity created the new—or rather, greatly expanded—impediment of heterodoxy. Protestant and Catholic prohibitions of cross-confessional marriage (*matrimonium mixtum*) were able to drawn on a wide array of precedents in both the Old and New Testaments, including the famous Pauline Privilege of divorce from a nonbeliever (1 Cor. 7:10–15). Clearly, confessional endogamy increased as a result of the new religious divisions and the Pauline Privilege was successfully invoked in both Protestant and Catholic marriage courts. As Dagmar Freist's study of the prince-bishopric of Osnabrück demonstrates, however, the rise of confessional cultures over the course of the sixteenth and seventeenth centuries did not in itself create the new, impenetrable marital boundaries that we often assume. Freist resists characterizing trends in early modern mixed marriages in terms of continuity and change, but her evidence seems to provide a much stronger case for the former than for the latter. Many marriage contracts stipulated freedom of conscience for both spouses as well as the common agreement that girls would assume the religion of the mother, boys that of the father. The Catholic Church also regularly issued dispensations for such unions, if they had familial backing. Consequently, up to 20 percent of all marriages in post-1648 Osnabrück were biconfessional. Transgressions of the religious boundary remained controversial, and Freist also describes many conflicts that resulted in kidnapping of children, coercion, or lawsuits. Overall, though, the new confessional boundaries of the post-Reformation world remained porous enough to allow frequent compromise and unpunished transgression, particularly in biconfessional areas.[10]

Transgressions of this nature were particularly common in the political realm, where dynastic and state interests frequently outweighed theologians' concerns over mixed marriages. Alexander Schunka provides a detailed description of the new confessional pragmatism that held sway during the Hanoverian Succession negotiations of 1714, yet flexibility of this nature was evident within the very first generation of the Reformation. Luther famously had a case-by-case approach to many thorny issues that came before him, acting first as a pastor and second—if at all—as a systematic thinker. His suspicion of jurists in general is also well known, arguing that in pursuing justice one must "tear through the law confidently like a millstone ripping through a spider web, and act as if the law had never been born." David Whitford's lively review of Luther's writings on bigamy demonstrates a pragmatic evolution and thus fundamental inconsistency on the subject. Young Luther condemns what older Luther will endorse, providing Phillip of Hesse with the same approval that he denied to Henry VIII or the heretical Münster Anabaptists. When the reformer's casuistic acquiescence in Phillip's bigamy (on grounds of insatiable sexual appetites) became public, Luther was embarrassed but unrepentant about the political expediency of his decision.

Unequal social rank apparently presented a more difficult obstacle in dynastic marriages than did religious considerations, although here too transgressions could be overseen or at least minimized when necessary. In his study of unequal noble matches, Michael Sikora recounts the aristocratic obsession with all questions of rank and status, sometimes involving seemingly minor degrees of difference. Given the legal consequences for both the spouse and any offspring, however, prenuptial negotiations were tense affairs, sometimes involving commissioned *Ahnenproben* to certify a family's claimed status. Yet with sufficient motivation the boundaries could be shifted or even ignored. A wife's rank might be appropriately readjusted over time; a husband's family might make other compensations—virtually all was negotiable.[11]

One of the best illustrations of the selective definition of transgressive unions is the proposed marriage of Queen Christina of Sweden to Elector Friedrich Wilhelm of Brandenburg, adeptly analyzed by Daniel Riches. During fifteen years of negotiations, four potential obstacles surface: one based on unequal status (Sweden was more powerful than Brandenburg), one based on cultural and legal disparities between the two states, one based on gender inequality (an overly independent, perhaps even lesbian bride), and one based on religion—with their queen's prospective union to a Reformed suitor even more worrisome to some Swedes than if he had been a Catholic. As in most dynastic marriages, no one seemed particularly concerned about the incestuous transgression of first cousins marrying. Each of the four transgressions might have been problematic for a marriage at any social level, even if no larger political ramifications were involved. Just as significantly, the otherness that repulsed opponents of the union was in many cases the very foundation for support among the marriage's backers. Depending on the perceived benefits or costs of the union, in other words, differences were respectively interpreted as assets or liabilities.

Riches ascribes this duality to the liminal nature of dynastic marriage, where marriage outside the community is simultaneously desirable and suspicious. But surely this ambivalence is possible at all levels of society, whenever there is both something to be gained and something to be lost from the family's perspective. Perhaps the most influential factor in defining the relative transgressiveness of early modern unions was the highly volatile (and gender-specific) notion of honor. As Ralf-Peter Fuchs writes, the "attribution of identity based on social norms" informed not just the defamation suits he examines, but also virtually every aspect of human interaction, particularly marriage. Symbolic capital could often outweigh economic capital in communal perception of a proposed union, thus rendering all matchmaking attempts risky and subject to innuendos, insults, or outright rejection. Of course the opposite could also apply where financial considerations trumped all others.

Where did all of these financial and political factors leave individual choice and the idea of companionate marriage? Clearly this suggests strong continuity with medieval practices but it does not address the question of the Reformation's patriarchal reaction. Did the religious and legal changes of the sixteenth century truly represent a return to a time when fathers ruled, with love and personal attraction forever subordinate to material interests? Despite all the innovative means for ensuring public propriety—requiring parental and clerical approval, as well as witnesses to marital vows for validity—neither Protestant nor Catholic legal reforms ever intended to eliminate the individual consensual nature of marriage. In fact, many legal codes worried about parental coercion almost as much as they did about clandestine vows; the codes clearly considered a union to be one properly composed of both private consent and public approval. Since historians are left only with court evidence of contested vows from both sides as well as anecdotal material from ego-documents, it is difficult to generalize on the actual impact of sixteenth-century reforms on transgressions of this nature. Still, it seems likely, as Claudia Jarzebowski writes, that both the performative and transactional aspects of marital unions remained intact throughout the early modern period, with individuals (including parents) who excessively valued either the material or emotional dimensions of a marriage treated as transgressors in the court of public opinion, especially in literature.[12]

However great the general continuity in actual marital practice, ideas about the institution and sexuality exhibited considerable dynamism and flux over the course of the seventeenth and eighteenth centuries. Protestant and Catholic debates over the value, or even possibility, of chastity remained heated, despite their fundamental agreement about the limitation of sexual activity to the sacred institution of marriage. Encounters with the wider world had a gradual but cumulatively more profound effect on popular imaginations during the period. Thanks to the ever-expanding presence of the printing press and the continuing growth of literacy, millions of Europeans from the sixteenth century on indirectly encountered alien societies from all parts of the globe. Many of the printed accounts, such as the 1702 novel *Die Hitzige Indianerin*, were written by Europeans who had themselves lived in Asian or American societies where concubinage, polygamy, and diverse sexual practices were common. Antje Flüchter tells us that more than half a million Germans worked for the Dutch East India Company during its peak period, often adapting their own lives to such foreign mores. Europeans who had never traveled abroad tended to be most scandalized by such transgressive unions, especially when another race was involved.[13]

As Mary Lindemann's chapter on the celebrated incest case of Charlotte Guyard and her father Denys in 1765 demonstrates, the subsequent flurry of both titillating literature and philosophical debates about the natural law of marriage had a marked influence on popular imagination.[14] I am not convinced that a so-called new attitude toward incest was more than a conceit of Enlightenment literature, but early modern globalization clearly shaped both Charlotte's telling of her story and the widespread fascination with the case. Which parts of European definitions of sexual and marital propriety were based in nature and which were cultural inventions? Few writers took the relativity of sexual mores to the extent of the Marquis de Sade, but the notion of uncertain and perhaps shifting boundaries of propriety had at least been successfully hatched during the second half of the early modern era.

In the final assessment, this increasing awareness of cultural diversity is perhaps the most distinctive and defining feature of transgressive unions between 1400 and 1800. Conflicts between individual choices and familial and communal approval had ancient roots and never died out entirely in Europe, certainly not by the beginning of the modern era. New legal and religious mechanisms from the sixteenth century on obviously had real-world implications for this question, but it is difficult to posit a definitive shift of the public–private balance to one side. Families, from peasant to aristocratic, continued to shift the boundaries of propriety as it suited their interests, and individuals continued to struggle with the ramifications of such material interests. The growth of confessionalism, on the other hand, as well as many Europeans' increasing awareness of diverse cultures and customs to a significant degree shifted the emphasis on where "the" boundaries of marital propriety should be to a more relative notion of boundaries in general, depending on the community. This move from ideological absolutism, even though it was still nascent and frequently undermined by more immediate material interests, appears both novel and significant.

Notes

1. Although Katherine Lynch focuses on an urban context, I am particularly influenced by her excellent and nuanced description of shifting communities in her *Individuals,*

Families, and Communities in Europe, 1200–1800: The Urban Foundations of Western Society (Cambridge, UK, 2003), esp. 68–102.

2. Rudolf Weigand, *Liebe und Ehe im Mittelalter* (Goldbach, 1993); and Georges Duby, *Medieval Marriage: Two Models from Twelfth-Century France,* trans. Elborg Forster (Baltimore, 1978).

3. Charles Donahue Jr., *Law, Marriage, and Society in the Later Middle Ages: Arguments about Marriage in Five Courts* (Cambridge, UK, 2008); Harrington, *Reordering Marriage,* 105–34, 172–80; Adhémar Esmein, *Le mariage en droit canonique,* 2 vols. (Paris, 1891).

4. Ozment, *When Fathers Ruled,* esp. 1–49; also Harrington, *Reordering Marriage,* 25–47.

5. See esp. Plummer, *From Priest's Whore to Pastor's Wife;* and the earlier approach of August Franzen, *Zölibat und Priesterehe in der Auseinandersetzung der Reformationszeit und der katholischen Reform des 16. Jahrhunderts* (Münster, 1969).

6. Ozment, *When Fathers Ruled,* 14–25. Ozment later reiterates a more nuanced version of this perspective in *Protestants: The Birth of a Revolution* (New York, 1992), 151–58.

7. Susanna Burghartz, *Zeiten der Reinheit, Orte der Unzucht. Ehe und Sexualität in Basel während der Frühen Neuzeit* (Paderborn, 1999) ; Roper, *The Holy Household;* Harrington, *Reordering Marriage,* 215–71.

8. Roderick Philips, *Putting Asunder: A History of Divorce in Western Society* (Cambridge, UK, 1988; Jeffrey Watt, *The Making of Modern Marriage: Matrimonial Control and the Rise of Sentiment in Neuchâtel* (Ithaca, 1992). Even Thomas Safley, who argues for an important Protestant distinction in this respect, concedes that divorce was not widely practiced during the early modern era: *Let No Man Put Asunder: The Control of Marriage in the German Southwest: A Comparative Study, 1550–1600* (Kirksville, 1984).

9. Dieter Schwab, *Grundlagen und Gestalt der staatlichen Ehegesetzgebung in der Neuzeit bis zum Beginn des 19. Jahrhunderts* (Bielefeld, 1967); Harrington, *Reordering Marriage,* 84–100.

10. See Freist's "Crossing Religious Borders: The Experience of Religious Difference and its Impact on Mixed Marriages in Eighteenth-Century Germany," in Scott Dixon, Dagmar Freist, Mark Greengrass, eds., *Living with Religious Diversity in Early Modern Europe* (Farnham, UK 2009), 203–24; also Lynch, *Individuals, Families, and Communities,* 144–50, 163–70.

11. See also Sikora, *Adel;* Hurwich, *Noble Strategies;* Karl-Heinz Spiess, *Familie und Verwandtschaft im deutschen Hochadels des Spätmittelalters: 13. bis Anfang des 16. Jahrhunderts* (Stuttgart, 1993); Jonathan Dewald, *The European Nobility, 1400–1800* (Cambridge, UK, 1996), esp. 168–71.

12. See also Jarzebowski's coedited collection, with Anne Kwaschik, *Performing Emotions: Zum Verhältnis von Politik und Emotion in der Frühen Neuzeit und in der Moderne* (Göttingen, 2012); as well as the still valuable *Interest and Emotion: Essays on the Study of Family and Kinship,* eds. Hans Medick and David Sabean (Cambridge, UK, 1984); and Harrington, *Reordering Marriage,* 197–214.

13. *Structures on the Move: Technologies of Governance in Transcultural Encounter,* ed. Antje Flüchter and Susan Richter (Heidelberg, 2012).

14. In addition to her article in this volume, see *Liaisons dangereuses: Sex, Law, and Diplomacy in the Age of Frederick the Great* (Baltimore, 2006); also Jarzebowski, *Inzest.*

~: BIBLIOGRAPHY :~

Abbreviations

BL: British Library (London)
ChCh: Christ Church College Library (Oxford)
GStA PK: Geheimes Staatsarchiv, Preußischer Kulturbesitz
HStAD: Hauptstaatsarchiv Dresden
HStAS: Hauptstaatsarchiv Stuttgart
LAV NRW R: Landesarchiv Nordrhein-Westfalen, Abteilung Rheinland
LAV NRW W: Landesarchiv Nordrhein-Westfalen, Abteilung Westfalen
LW: *Luther's Works*
RA: Svenska Riksarkiv
RKG: Reichskammergericht
RTA JR: *Deutsche Reichstagsakten: Jüngere Reihe*
SächsHStADres: Hauptstaatarchiv Dresden
StA: Stadtarchiv Antwerpen
StAA: Staatsarchiv Augsburg
StadtAMm: Stadtarchiv Memmingen
StAHbg: Staatsarchiv Hamburg
StAM: Staatsarchiv Marburg
StAN: Staatsarchiv Nuremberg
StAOS: Staatsarchiv Osnabrück
SUBHbg: Staats- und Universitäts-Bibliothek Hamburg
ThHStAW, EGA: Thüringisches Hauptstaatsarchiv Weimar, Ernestinisches Gesamtarchiv
UA: *Urkunden und Actenstücke zur Geschichte des Kurfürsten Friedrich Wilhelm von Branden-burg*
WA: *D. Martin Luthers Werke: Kritische Gesamtausgabe. Schriften / Werke*
WA BR: *D. Martin Luthers Werke: Kritische Gesamtausgabe. Briefwechsel*

Published Sources

Abgemütigste Vorstellung, welche [Anton Ulrich] An Eine Hochlöbliche und Hoachansehnliche Reichs-Versammlung . . . überreichen lassen. N.p., 1744.
Allgemeine Deutsche Biographie. 56 vols. Berlin, 1876. Reprint, 1967.
Allgemeines Landrecht für die Preußischen Staaten. Berlin, 1794.
Arenkow, Joachim. *Geschichte und Thaten Sr. Hochfürstl. Durchl. Leopoldi, Fürstens von An-halt-Dessau etc., al seines wahrhafften Heldens unserer Zeit*. Dessau, 1742.
Beccadelli, Antonius. *Hermaphroditus*. N.p., 1425.
Beckmann, Johann Christoff. *Histoire des Fürstenthums Anhalt*. 2 vols. Zerbst, 1710. Reprint. Dessau, 1993–1998.

Bembo, Pietro. *Gli Asolani*. Venice, 1505.

Blarer, Ambrosius. *Wahrhafft verantwortnng Ambrosij Blauerer,* . . . . , *warub er auß dem Kloster gewichen, vnd mit was geding er sich widerumb, hyein begeben wöl*. Augsburg, 1523.

Brenz, Johannes. *Wie in Ehesachen und inn den gellen / so sich derhalben zu tragen / nach Götlichen billichen rechten / Christenlich zu handel sey*. Wittenberg, 1531.

Brunel, Antoine de. *Voyage d'Espagne curieux, historique et politique*. Paris, 1655.

Bucer, Martin. *Verantwortung M. Butzers uff das jm seine widerwertigen . . . züm ärgsten zümessen. Mit begebung in alle leibs straff, so er mit seinem leben, oder leer nach Götlichem gesatz straffbar erfunden würt*. Strasbourg, 1523.

Bullinger, Heinrich. *Der Christlich Eestand: Von der heiligen Ee harkumen / wenn/ wo/ wie/ unnd von waem sy ufgesetzt / und was sye / wie sye recht bezogen were* . . . . Zurich, 1540.

Burckhardt, Christian. *Ost-Indianische Reise-Beschreibung / Oder Kurtzgefaßter Abriß von Ost-Indien / und dessen angränzenden Provinvien, bevorab wo die Holländer ihren Sitz und Trafiquen maintenieren etc.* Halle, 1693.

Burckhardt, Johann Gottlieb. *Kirchen-Geschichte der Deutschen Gemeinden in London: Nebst historischen Beylagen und Predigten*. Tübingen, 1798.

Campe, Johann Heinrich. *Väterlicher Rat für meine Tochter: Ein Gegenstuck zum Theophron, der erwachsenern weiblichen Jugend gewidmet*. Braunschweig, 1809.

———. *Wörterbuch der deutschen Sprache*. Braunschweig, 1807.

Campeggio, Lorenzo. *Ordnung und Reformation zu abstellung der Mißbreuch, . . . durch Bäbstlicher hayligkait Legate rc: zu Regenspurg aufgericht*. Augsburg, 1524.

Carletti, Francesco. *Reise um die Welt 1594: Erlebnisse eines Florentiner Kaumanns*. Tübingen, 1966.

Carpzov, Friedrich Benedikt. *Dissertation altera . . . de eo, quod consultum est, in nuptiis personarum diversae religionis*. Wittenberg, 1735.

Codex Constitutionem Osnabrugensem. 2 vols. Osnabrück, 1800.

Dacier, André. *Die hitzige Indianerin oder Artige und couriesuse Beschreibung derer ost-indianischen Frauens-Personen, welche sowohl aus Europa in Ost-Indien ziehen oder darinnen geboren werden, die sein gleich aus vermischten oder reinem heidnischen Geblüte derer India*. Ed. Karl K. Walther. Berlin, 1991.

Dawes, William. *An Exact Account of King George's Religion: With the Manner of his Majesty's Worship in the English and Lutheran Church. And the first Rise of the Lutheran Religion. Shewing also, The Difference between them and the Church of England as by Law establish'd, and the Protestant Dissenters therefrom. With a New Prayer for his Majesty*. London, 1714.

Dedeken, Georg. *Thesauri consiliorum et decisionum*. 3 vols. Jena, 1671.

della Valle, Pietro. *Reiß-Beschreibung in unterschiedliche Theile der Welt: Nemlich Jn Türckey, Egypten, Palestina, Persien, Ostindien, und andere weit entlegene Landschafften*. Vol. 4, *In sich haltend eine Beschreibung der anmercklichsten Städte, und Oerter in Indien, und denen höfen jhrer Fürsten*. Geneva, 1674.

Dietenberger, Johannes. *Antwort das Jungfrawen die klöster vnd klösterliche gelübt nümner götlich verlassen möge*. Strasbourg, 1523.

———. *Doctor Johan Dietenberger. Widerlegung des Lutherischen büchlins, da er schreibt von menschen leren zumeiden rc*. Strasbourg, 1524.

Eberlin, Johann. *Eyn freundliches zuschreyben an alle stendt teutscher nation, daryn sie vermanet warden, nit widerstandt zuthun den geystlichen so auß klostern oder pfaffen standt gehen wöllen*. Erfurt, 1521.

[Ferdinand II]. *Entschliesung der hierin benannten Fürsten, . . . zu Regenspurg versamlet, zu handthabung Christenlichs glaubens, vnd euangelischer leere.* Augsburg, 1524.

Fernberger, Georg Christoph. *Reisetagebuch (1588–1593): Sinai, Babylon, Indien, Heiliges Land, Osteuropea.* Vol. 1, *Lateinisch-Deutsch.* Eds. Ronald Burger and Robert Wallisch. Frankfurt, 1999.

Friedberg, Emil, ed. *Corpus Iuris Canonici.* 2 vols. Graz, 1959.

Frikens, Christoff. *Ost-Indianische Reisen und Krieges-Dienst: Oder eine Ausführliche Beschreibung was sich solcher Zeit—nämlich von Anno 1685, zur See als zu Land in öffentlichen Treffen und Scharmützeln, in Belagerungen, Stürmen und Eroberungen der Heidnischen Plätze und Städte im Marschieren und in Quartieren it ihm und seinem beigfügten Kameraden hin und wieder begeben.* Comp. with an introduction by Joachim Kirchner. Berlin [1692], 1926.

Des Gesamten Fürstlichen Hauses Sachsen gründlicher Bericht . . . . N.p., 1745.

Glagau, Hans, ed. *Hessische Landtagsakten: 1508–1521.* Marburg, 1901.

Guyard, Jean-François [Johann Franz]. *Sendschreiben des Kaufmanns Guyard in Hamburg an seine Mitbürger: Als eine Einleitung zu seinen herauszugebenden Mémoires.* Hamburg, 1767.

Hellfeld, Bernhard von. *Beiträge zum Staats-Recht und der Geschichte von Sachsen.* 3 vols. Eisenach, 1785–90.

Hesslein, Bernhard. *Berliner Pickwickier: Fahrten und Abentheuer Berliner Junggesellen bei ihren Kreuz- und Querzügen durch das moderene Babylon.* 3 vols. Berlin, 1854.

———. *Bibliothek moderner Räubergeschichten.* Berlin, 1851.

———. *Hamburgs berühmte und berüchtigte Häuser.* 2 vols. Hamburg, 1850.

———. *Jefferson Davis: Social-politischer Roman aus dem amerikanischen Bürgerkrieg.* 3 vols. Leipzig, 1866–67.

———. *Nikolaus I: 30 Jahre aus der Geschichte Rußlands.* Berlin, 1855.

———. *Das schwarze Buch von Berlin oder Geheimnisse der protestantischen Metropole: Social-politischer Roman.* Leipzig, 1865.

Hierin findest du Das Kaiserlich Mandat zu Nurenberg außgangen . . . Item Hertzog Georgen tzu Sachsen . . . Mandat und Execution. Dresden, 1524.

Hulsius, Levinus. *Siebte Schiffahrt, das ist: In das Goldreiche Königreich Guineam, in Africa gelegen, so sonsten das Goldgestadt von Mina gena[n]t wirdt, welches von den Portugalesern vngefahr vor 200. Jahren erfunden, von den Holländern jnnerhalb 18. Jahren hero bekannt gemacht.* Frankfurt, 1606.

Karlstadt, Andreas. *Von gelubden vnterrichtung . . . . Das Pfaffen, Monche, vñ Nonnen, mit gutem gewissem, vnd gottlichem willen, sich mogen vnd sollen vermelen, vnd yn eelichen stand begeben . . . vñ ynn ein recht Christlich leben tretten.* Wittenberg, 1521.

———. *Das die Priester Eeweiber nehmen mügen und sollen, Beschütz red / des würdigen herren Barholomei Bernhardi / Probst zu Camberg / so von Bischoff von Meyenburg gefordert / antwort zu geben / das er in priesterlichem standt / ein junckfraw zu der Ee genommen hat.* Speyer, 1522.

Kloentrup, Aegidius. *Alphabetisches Handbuch der besonderen Rechte und Gewohnheiten des Hochstifts Osnabrück mit Rücksicht auf die benachbarten westfälischen Provinzen.* 3 vols. Osnabrück, 1798–1800.

Königliche Akademie der Wissenschaften. *Denkmäler der Preußischen Staatsverwaltung im 18. Jahrhundert.* 38 vols. Berlin, 1892.

Lang, Johannes. *Von gehorsam der Weltlichen oberkait, vnd den außgangen klosterleuten, ain schutzred.* Augsburg, 1523.

Lenz, Samuel. *Becamnus enucleatus, suppletus et continuatus* . . . Köthen, 1757.

Lünig, Johann Christian. *Des Teutschen Reichs-Archiv*. 3 vols. Leipzig, 1710–22.

Luther, Martin. *Luther: Letters of Spiritual Counsel*. Trans. Theodore G. Tappert. Louisville, 1955.

———. *D. Martin Luthers Werke: Kritische Gesamtausgabe*. 120 vols. Weimar, 1883–2007.

———. *Luther's Works*. Ed. Jaroslav Pelikan and Helmut T. Lehmann. 55 vols. St. Louis, 1955–86.

———. *Martin Luthers Sämmtliche Schriften*. Ed. Johann Georg Walch. 23 vols. St. Louis, 1890–1910.

Mandelslo, Albrecht von. *Des Hoch-Edelgebohrnen Johann Albrecht von Mandelslo Morgenländische Reise-Beschreibung: worinnen zugleich die Gelegenheit und heutiger Zustandt etlichr fürnehmen indianischen Länder, Provintzien, Städte und Insulen . . . beschreiben warden*. Ed. Adam Olearius. Hamburg, 1696.

Martin, Denis. *Der vertheidigte Denis Martin, wider seinen Schwiegersohn und seine Tochter François Guyard und Charlotta Martin, verheyratete Guyard*. N.p., 1766.

———. *Vollständige Acten in der seltenen und überaus wichtigen Sache, Denis Martin, wider seinen unwürdigen Schwiegersohn und unwürdigen Tocher, Jean François Guyard und Charlotte Guyard gebohrne Martin, . . .* N.p. [Hamburg?], 1767.

Mastinani, Francesco. *I misteri di Napoli: Studi storico sociali*. Naples, 1869.

Mechler, Aegidius. *Apologia oder schutzrede Egidy Mechlery . . . . Jn welcher wyrt grund vnd vusach ertzelt seynes weyb nemens*. Erfurt, 1523.

Meiern, Johann Gottfried, ed. *Acta Pacis Publicationis Publica: Oder, Westphälische Friedens-Handlungen und Geschichte*. 6 vols. Hanover, 1734–36.

Melanchthon, Philipp. *Etliche Propositiones witer die lehr der widerteuffer*. Wittenberg, 1535.

———. *Philippi Melanchtonis Opera quae supersunt omnia*. Eds. Karl Gottlieb Bretschneider and Heinrich Ernst Binseil. 28 vols. Halle, 1834–60.

Michaelis, Johann David. *Mosaisches Recht*. Frankfurt, 1774.

Mirisch, Melchior, Eberhard Weidensee, and Johannes Frtizhans. *Doctor Melchior Mirisch . . . Erbithen sich diese nach gedruckte Artickell, vor eyner gantzen gemeyn mit gegrunter schrifft tzu erhalten, wider alle Papisten Alhye tzu Maydeburgk*. Magdeburg, 1524.

Moser, Johann Jacob. *Ihro Römisch-Kayserlichen Majestät Carls des Siebenden Wahl-Capitulation . . . Erster Theil*. Frankfurt, 1742.

Müller, Philipp. *Der Fang des edlen Lebens durch frembde Glaubens-Ehe*. N.p., 1689.

Navarre, Marguerite de. *L'Heptaméron*. Paris, 1960 (1558).

Newe Zeitung von den wider Teuffern zu Münster. Nuremberg, 1535.

Ochino, Bernardino. *Dialogi XXX in duos libros diuisi*. Basel, 1563. Translated as *A Dialogue of Polygamy, Written Originally in Italian* (London, 1657).

Oxford Dictonary of National Biography. 60 vols. Oxford, 2004.

Der Patriot. Hamburg, 1724–26.

Pfeiffer, Gerhard, ed. *Quellen zur Nürnberger Reformationsgeschichte: Von der Duldung liturgischer Änderungen bis zur Ausübung ds Kirechenregiments durch den Rat (Juni 1524– Juni 1525)*. Nuremberg, 1968.

Philips, Jenkin Thomas. *The History of the Two Illustrious Brothers, Princes of Saxony . . . Ernestus the Pious, First Duke of Sax-Gotha, and Bernard the Great Duke of Sax-Weimar . . .* London, 1740.

Pires, Tomé, and Francisco Rodrigues. *The Suma Oriental of Tome Pires: An Account of the East from the Red Sea to Japan, Written in Malacca and India in 1512–1515*. Ed. Armando Cortesão. Nedeln, 1967.

Planitz, Hans von der. *Bericht aus dem Reichsregiment in Nürnberg, 1521–1523.* Eds. Ernst Wüulcker and Hans Virck. Leipzig, 1899.

Poivre, Pierre. *Reisen eines Philosophen 1768.* Ed. Jürgen Osterhammel. Sigmaringen, 1997.

———. *The travels of a philosopher: Being observations on the customs, manners, arts, . . . of several nations in Asia and Africa.* London, 1769.

Polybius. *The Histories.* Trans. William Roger Paton. 6 vols. New York, 1922.

Pontanus, Iohannes Jovanus. *De amore coniugali.* Venice, 1518.

Pufendorf, Samuel. *Commentariorum de Rebus Suecicis Libri XXVI. Ab expeditione Gustavi Adolfi Regis in Germaniam ad abdicationem usque Christinüæ.* Utrecht, 1686.

Regau, Eike von. *Sachsenspiegel Landrecht.* 2nd ed. Göttingen, 1955.

———. *Sachsenspiegel, mit vil newen addicion.* Augsburg, 1517.

Regensburg, Andreas von. "Chronica de principibus terrae Bavorum." In *Andreas von Regensburg, Sämtliche Werke.* Ed. Georg Leidinger. Munich, 1903.

Reisebeschreibungen von Deutschen Beamten und Kriegsleuten im Dienste der Niederländische West- und Ost-indischen Kompagnien 1602–1797. Ed. S. P. L. Honoré Naber. The Hague, 1930.

Remy, Nicholas. *Daemonolatriae libri tres.* Frankfurt, 1596.

Reuter, Simon. *Ein Christliche frage Simonis Reuters vonn Schlaytz, an alle Bischoffe . . . Warumb sy doch: an priestern: vnnd andern geistlich geferbten leutte, den eelichen standt nicht mügenn leyden.* Bamberg, 1523.

Reynolds, George W. M. *The Mysteries of London.* 4 vols. London, 1850–59.

Sarcer, Erasmus. *Vom heiligen Ehestande und von Ehesachen mit allen umbstenden / zu diesen dingen gehörig / darinnen zu gleich Natürlich / Göttlich / Keiserlich und / Bepstlich Recht angezogen wird / Zum teil aus vieler Gelehrter Theologen Bücher zusammen getragen / Zum teil von zusammen Zieher selbst geschrieben.* Eisleben, 1556.

Schroeder, Hans. *Lexicon der hamburgischen Schriftsteller bis zur Gegenwart.* 8 vols. Hamburg, 1851–83.

Schwennicke, Detlev. *Europäsiche Stammtafeln.* New ser. 28 vols. Frankfurt, 1997–[2011].

Scott, Samuel P, ed. *The Civil Law.* 17 vols. Cincinnati, 1932.

Sehling, Emil, ed. *Die evangelischen Kirchenordnungen des XVI. Jahrhunderts,* vol. 1/1, *Sachsen und Thüringen nebst angrenzenden Gebieten.* Leipzig, 1902.

Spittler, Ludwig Timotheus. *Geschichte des Fürstenthums Hannover: Seit den Zeiten der Reformation bis zu Ende des siebzehnten Jahrhunderts.* Göttingen, 1786.

Thomasius, Christian. *Rechtmäßige Erörterung der Ehe- und Gewissens Frage Ob zwei fürtliche Personen im Römischen Reich deren eine der Lutherischen die andere der Reformierten Religion zugetan ist einander mit gutem Gewissen heirathen können.* Halle, 1689.

Thou, Jacques-Auguste de. *Iac. Augusti Thuani Historiarum sui tempris libri CXXV.* 11 vols. Paris, 1609.

Urkunden und Actenstücke zur Geschichte des Kurfürsten Friedrich Wilhelm von Brandenburg. 23 vols. Berlin, 1864–1930.

Weidensee, Eberhard, and Johannes Fritzhans. *Ein erklerung der achseen artikel, durch die prediger zu Magdeburg außgangen erkleret.* Eilenburg, 1524.

Wrede, Adolf, ed. *Deutsche Reichstagsakten: Jüngere Reihe, Deutsche Reichstagsakten unter Kaiser Karl V.* 20 vols. Göttingen, 1893–1905.

Zedler, Johann. *Grosses vollständiges Universal Lexicon Aller Wissenschaften und Künsten.* 64 vols. Leipzig, 1731–54.

Zobel, Rudolf Heinrich. *Briefe über die Erziehung der Frauenzimmer.* Stralsund, 1773.

Zoepfl, Heinrich, ed. *Die peinliche Gerichtsordnung Kaiser Karls V: Nebst der Bamberger und der Brandenburger Halsgerichtsordnung*. Leipzig, 1883.

Zola, Émile. *Les Mystères de Marseille: Roman historique contemporain*. Marseilles, 1867.

Zycha, Joseph, ed. *Corpus Scriptorum Ecclesiasticorum Latinorum*. Vienna, 1900.

Bibliography

Ackermann, Jürgen. "Graf Antons zu Ysenburg-Kelsterbach Mißheurath hat seiner Gräflichen Familie vilen Unlust verursachet." *Sammlungen zur Geschichte von Wächtersbach* 41, 265 (January 2003): 1–12.

———. *Verschuldung, Reichsdebitverwaltung, Mediatisierung: Eine Studie zu den Finanzproblemen der mindermächtigen Stände im Alten Reich: Das Beispiel der Grafschaft Usenburg-Büdingen 1687–1806*. Marburg, 2002.

Adair, Richard. *Courtship, Illegitimacy and Marriage in Early Modern England*. Manchester, 1996.

Adams, Simon L. "The Protestant Cause: Religious Alliance with the West: European Calvinist Communities as a Political Issue in England, 1585–1630." PhD Dissertation. Oxford University, 1973.

Ahlund, Nils. *Gustav Adolf the Great*. Trans. Michael Roberts. Princeton, 1940.

Alexander, Bobby C. *Victor Turner Revisited: Ritual as Social Change*. Atlanta, 1991.

Algazi, Gadi. "Scholars in Households: Refiguring the Learned Habitus, 1480–1550." *Science in Context* 16 (2003): 9–42.

Amrhein, August. *Reformationsgeschichtliche Mitteilungen aus dem Bistum Würzburg 1517–1573*. Münster, 1923.

Andersen, Jürgen, and Volquard Iversen. *Orientalische Reise-Beschreibungen In der Bearbeitung von Adam Olearius, Schleswig 1669*. Ed. Dieter Lohmeier. Tübingen, 1980.

Armstedt, Richard. *Der schwedische Heiratsplan des Grossen Kurfürsten*. Königsberg, 1896.

Arndt, Jürgen. "Zur Entwicklung des kaiserlichen Hofpfalzgrafenamtes von 1355–1806." *Hofpfalzgrafen-Register*. Vol. 1. Neustadt an der Aisch 1964. Pp. x–xxiv.

Asch, Ronald G. "'Denn es sind ja die Deutschen . . . ein frey Volk': Die Glaubensfreiheit als Problem der westfälischen Friedensverhandlungen." *Westfälische Zeitung* 148 (1998): 113–37.

———. *Europäischer Adel in der Frühen Neuzeit: Eine Einführung*. Cologne, 2008.

———. "Das monarchische Nobilitierungsrecht und die soziale Identität des Adels im 17. und 18. Jahrhundert." In *Die frühneuzeitliche Monarchie in Europa und ihr Erbe: Festschrift für Heinz Duchhardt zum 60.Geburtstag*. Eds. Ronald G. Asch, Johannes Arndt, and Matthias Schnettger. Münster, 2003. Pp. 91–107.

Bahlcke, Joachim, and Werner Korthaase, eds. *Daniel Ernst Jablonski: Religion, Wissenschaft und Politik um 1700*. Wiesbaden, 2008.

Bähr, Andreas, Peter Burschel, and Gabriele Jancke. "Räume des Selbst: Eine Einleitung." In *Selbstzeugnisse der Neuzeit*. Eds. Andreas Bähr, Peter Burschel, and Gabriele Jancke. Cologne, 2007.

Bainton, Roland H. *The Travail of Religious Liberty: Nine Biographical Studies*. Philadelphia, 1951.

Banks, Marcus. *Ethnicity: Anthropological Constructions*. New York, 1996.

Barge, Hermann. *Jakob Strauss: Ein Kämpfer für das Evangelium in Tirol, Thüringen und Süddeutschland.* Leipzig, 1937.

Barkai, Avraham. "Bevölkerungsrückgang und wirtschaftliche Stagnation." In *Deutsch-Jüdische Geschichte in der Neuzeit*, 4 vols. Ed. Avraham Barkai and Paul Mendes-Flohr. Munich, 1996–2000. Vol. 4, Pp. 37–49.

Barth, Susanne. *Mädchenlektüren: Lesediskurse im 18. und 19. Jahrhundert.* Frankfurt, 2002.

Bastress-Dukehart, Erica. *The Zimmern Chronicle: Nobility, Memory, and Self-Representation in Sixteenth-Century Germany.* Aldershot, 2002.

Bäumer, Remigius, and Erwin Iserloh. *Katholische Theologen der Reformationszeit.* 2nd ed., 6 vols. Münster, 1984–2004.

Beach, Alison I. *Women as Scribes: Book Production and Monastic Reform in Twelfth-Century Bavaria.* Cambridge, UK, 2004.

Beem, Charles. "'I Am Her Majesty's Subject': Prince George of Denmark and the Transformation of the English Male Consort." *Canadian Journal of History* 39 (2004): 457–88.

Benker, Gitta. "'Ehre und Schande'—Voreheliche Sexualität auf dem Lande im ausgehenden 18. Jahrhundert." In *Frauenkörper. Medizin. Sexualität.* Eds. Johanna Geyer-Kordesch and Annette Kuhn. Düsseldorf, 1986. Pp. 10–27.

Blackwell, Jeannine. "Marriage by the Book: Matrimony, Divorce, and Single Life in Therese Huber's Life and Works." In *In the Shadow of Olympus: German Women Writers Around 1800.* Eds. Katherine R. Goodman, Edith Waldstein, Marianne Hirsch, Ruth Perry, and Virginia Swain. Albany, 1992. Pp. 137–56.

Blickle, Peter. *Die Revolution von 1525.* 4th rev. ed. Munich, 1993.

———. *Von der Leibeigenschaft zu den Menschenrechten: Eine Geschichte der Freiheit in Deutschland.* Munich, 2003.

Blussé, Leonard. "Batavia 1619–1740: The Rise and Fall of a Chinese Colonial Town." *Journal of Southeast Asian Studies* 12 (1982): 159–78.

———. *Bitters bruid: een koloniaal huwelijksdrama in de Gouden Eeuw.* Amsterdam, 1997.

Boswell, John. *Same-Sex Unions in Premodern Europe.* New York, 1994.

Botham, Fay. *Almighty God Created the Races: Christianity, Interracial Marriage, and American Law.* Chapel Hill, 2009.

Boenicke, Albert. *Die Ehe zur linken Hand.* Berlin, 1915.

Böttigheimer, Christoph. *Zwischen Polemik und Irenik: Die Theologie der einen Kirche bei Georg Calixt.* Münster, 1996.

Bourdieu, Pierre. *Esquisse d'une Théorie de la Pratique, précédé de trois études d'ethnologie kabyle.* Geneva, 1972.

Boxer, Charles R. *Mary and Misogyny: Women in Iberian Expansion Overseas, 1415–1814: Some Facts, Fancies and Personalities.* London, 1975.

Bramberger, Andrea. *Verboten Lieben: Bruder-Schwester-Inzest.* Pfaffenweiler, 1998.

Brandes, Helga. "Frühneuzeitliche Ökonomieliteratur." In *Die Literatur des 17. Jahrhunderts.* Ed. Albert Meier. Munich, 1999.

Braun, Christa von. "Die 'Blutschande': Wandelungen eines Begriffs: Vom Inzesttabu zu den Rassengesetzen." In *Die schamlose Schönheit des Vergangenen: Zum Verhältnis von Geschlecht und Geschichte.* Ed. Christa von Braun. Frankfurt, 1989. Pp. 81–111.

Braun, Manuel. *Ehe, Liebe, Freundschaft: Semantik der Vergesellschaftung im frühneuhochdeutschen Prosaroman.* Tübingen, 2001.

———. "Tiefe oder Oberfläche? Zur Lektüre der Schriften Christian Thomasius über Polygamie und Konkubinat." *Internationales Archiv für Sozialgeschichte der deutschen Literatur*, 30 (2005): 28–54.

Brauner, Sigrid. "Gender and its Subversion: Reflections on Literary Ideals of Marriage." In *The Graph of Sex and the German Text: Gendered Culture in Early Modern Germany 1500–1700*. Ed. Lynne Tatlock. Amsterdam, 1994. Pp. 179–98.

Brecht, Martin. *Martin Luther*, trans. by James L. Schaaf. 3 vols. Philadelphia, 1985–93.

Breit, Stefan. *"Leichtfertigkeit" und ländliche Gesellschaft: Voreheliche Sexualität in der frühen Neuzeit*. Munich, 1991.

Breul, Wolfgang. "Anfänge moderner Toleranz? Philipp und die religiösen Minderheiten." In *Landgraf Philipp der Grossmütige (1504–1567): Hessen im Zentrum der Reform*. Eds. Ursula Braasch-Schwersmann, Hans Schneider, and Wilhelm Ernst Winterhager. Marburg, 2004. Pp. 105–112.

———. *Herrschaftskrise und Reformation: Die Reichsabteien Fulda und Hersfeld ca. 1500–1525*. Gütersloh, 2000.

———. "Vom Humanismus zum Täufertum: Das Studium des hessischen Täuferführers Melchior Rinck an der Leipziger Artistenfakultät." *Archiv für Reformationsgeschichte* 93 (2002): 26–42.

Brunner, Daniel L. *Halle Pietists in England: Anthony William Boehm and the Society for Promoting Christian Knowledge*. Göttingen, 1993.

Brunner, Otto. "Das 'ganze Haus' und die alteuropäische 'Ökonomik.'" In *Neue Wege der Sozialgeschichte: Vorträge und Aufsätze*. Göttingen, 1956. Pp. 33–61.

Bubenheimer, Ulrich. "Streit um das Bischofsamt in der Wittenberger Reformation 1521/22: Von der Auseinandersetzung mit den Bischöfen um Priesterehen und den Ablaß in Halle zum Modell des evangelischen Gemeindebischofs, Teil I." *Zeitschrift der Savigny-Stiftung für Rechtsgeschichte: Kanonistische Abteilung* 73 [104] (1987): 155–209.

Buchholz, Stephan. "Rechtsgeschichte und Literatur: Die Doppelehe Philipps des Großmütigen." In *Landgraf Philipp der Großmütige von Hessen und seine Residenz Kassel*. Eds. Heide Wunder, Christina Vanja, and Berthold Hinz. Marburg, 2004). Pp. 57–73.

———. *Recht, Religion, und Ehe: Orientierungswandel und gelehrte Kontroversen im Übergang vom 17. zum 18. Jahrhundert*. Frankfurt, 1988.

Buckwalter, Stephen E. *Die Priesterehe in Flugschriften der frühen Reformation*. Gütersloh, 1998.

Burghartz, Susanna. "Jungfräulichkeit oder Reinheit? Zur Änderung von Argumentationsmustern vor dem Basler Ehegericht im 16. und 17. Jahrhundert." In *Dynamik der Tradition: Studien zur historischen Kulturforschung* 4. Ed. Richard van Dülmen. Frankfurt, 1992. Pp. 13–40.

———. *Leib, Ehre und Gut: Delinquenz in Zürich, Ende des 14. Jahrhunderts*. Zurich, 1990.

———. "Umordnung statt Unordnung? Ehe, Geschlecht und Reformationsgeschichte." In *Zwischen den Disziplinen: Perspektiven der Frühneuzeitforschung*. Ed. Helmut Puff. Göttingen, 2003.

———. *Zeiten der Reinheit, Orte der Unzucht: Ehe und Sexualität in Basel während der Frühen Neuzeit*. Paderborn, 1999.

Burmeister, Helmut, ed. *Friedrich, König von Schweden, Landgraf von Hessen-Kassel: Studien zu Leben und Wirken eines umstrittenen Fürsten (1676–1751)*. Hofgeismar, 2003.

Butte, Heinrich. *Stift und Stadt Hersfeld im 14. Jahrhundert mit einem Anhang: Die Stadt Hersfeld bis zum Beginn des 15. Jahrhunderts*. Marburg, 1911.

Carlin, Claire. "Perfect Harmony: Love and Marriage in Early Modern Pedagogy." In *The Art of Instruction: Essays on Pedagogy and Literature in 17th-Century France: Études de*

Langue et Littérature Françaises. Ed. and intro. by Anne Birberick. Amsterdam, 2008. Pp. 201–24.

Carmichael, Calum M. *Law, Legend, and Incest in the Bible: Leviticus 18–20.* Ithaca, N.Y., 1997.

Clark, Christopher. "Religion and Confessional Conflict." In *Imperial Germany, 1871–1918.* Ed. James Retallack. Oxford, 2008. Pp. 83–105.

Classen, Albrecht. *Der Liebes- und Ehediskurs vom hohen Mittelalter bis zum frühen 17. Jahrhundert.* Münster, 2005.

Cory, Donald Webster, and Robert E.L. Masters, eds. *Violations of Taboo: Incest in the Great Literature of the Past and Present.* New York, 1963.

Coy, Jason P. *Strangers and Misfits: Banishment, Social Control, and Authority in Early Modern Germany.* Leiden, 2008.

Crawford, Katherine. *European Sexualities, 1400–1800.* Cambridge, UK, 2007.

Crawford, Patricia. "Friendship and Love between Women in Early Modern England." In *Venus & Mars.* Eds. Andrew Lynch and Philippa Maddern. Pp. 47–61.

Currie, Mark. *Difference.* London, 2004.

Czech, Vinzenz. *Legitimation und Repräsentation: Zum Selbstverständnis thüringisch-sächsischer Reichsgrafen in der frühen Neuzeit.* Berlin, 2003.

Dalrymple, William. "White Mughals: The Case of James Achilles Kirkpatrick and Khair un-Nissa." In *Unfamiliar Relations: Family and History in South Asia.* Ed. Indrani Chatterjee. New Brunswick, 2004. Pp. 122–59.

———. *White Mughals: Love and Betrayal in Eighteenth-Century India.* London, 2002.

Dalton, Hermann. *Daniel Ernst Jablonski: Eine preußische Hofpredigergestalt in Berlin vor 200 Jahren.* Berlin, 1903.

Darnton, Robert. *The Forbidden Best-Sellers of Pre-Revolutionary France.* New York, 1997.

Davis, Natalie Zemon. "Boundaries and the Sense of Self in Early Modern France." In *Reconstructing Individualism.* Ed. Ian Watt. Stanford, 1986. Pp. 53–63.

———. *Frauen und Gesellschaft am Beginn der Neuzeit: Studien über Familie, Religion und die Wandlungsfähigkeit des sozialen Körpers.* Berlin, 1986.

———. "Ghosts, Kin and Progeny: Some Features of Family Life in Early Modern France." *Daedalus* 106 (Spring 1977): 87–114.

———. "The Sacred amd the Body Social in Sixteenth-Century Lyon." *Past & Present* 90 (1981): 40–70.

———. "'Women's History' in Transition: The European Case." *Feminist Studies* 3 (1976): 83–103.

De Jong, Mayke. "To the Limits of Kinship: Anti-Incest Legislation in the Early Medieval West (500–900)." In *From Sappho to de Sade: Moments in the History of Sexuality.* Ed. Jan Bremmer. London, 1989.

Delius, Walter. "Berliner kirchliche Unionsversuche im 17. und 18. Jahrhundert." *Blätter für Berlin-Brandenburgische Kirchengeschichte* 45 (1970): 7–121.

Dewald, Jonathan. *The European Nobility, 1400–1800.* Cambridge, UK, 1996.

Dieterich, Hartwig. *Das protestantische Eherecht in Deutschland bis zur Mitte des 17. Jahrhunderts.* Munich, 1970.

Dinges, Martin. "Die Ehre als Thema der historischen Anthropologie: Bemerkungen zur Wissenschaftsgeschichte und zur Konzeptualisierung." In *Verletzte Ehre: Ehrkonflikte in Gesellschaften des Mittelalters und der Frühen Neuzeit.* Eds. Klaus Schreiner and Gerd Schwerhoff. Cologne, 1995. Pp. 29–62.

———. "Die Ehre als Thema der Stadtgeschichte—Eine Semantik im Übergang vom Ancien Régime zur Moderne." *Zeitschrift für historische Forschung* 16 (1989): 409–440.

———. *Der Mauerermeister und der Finanzrichter: Ehre, Geld und soziale Kontrolle im Paris des 18. Jahrhunderts.* Göttingen, 1994.

———. "'Weiblichkeit' in 'Männlichkeitsritualen'? Zu weiblichen Taktiken im Ehrenhandel in Paris im 18. Jahrhundert." *Francia* 18 (1991): 71–98.

Dixon, C. Scott. *The Reformation and Rural Society: The Parishes of Brandenburg-Ansbach-Kulmbach, 1528–1603.* Cambridge, UK, 1996.

Dolan, Frances E. *Marriage and Violence: The Early Modern Legacy.* Philadelphia, 2008.

Donahue, Charles Jr. *Law, Marriage and Society in the Later Middle Ages: Arguments about Marriage in Five Courts.* Cambridge, UK, 2008.

Douglas, Mary. *Purity and Danger: An Analysis of Concepts of Pollution and Taboo.* London, 1966.

Driver, Tom F. *Liberating Rites: Understanding the Transformative Power of Ritual.* Boulder, 1998.

Duby, Georges. *Medieval Marriage: Two Models from Twelfth-Century France.* Trans. Elborg Forster. Baltimore, 1978.

Duchhardt, Heinz. *Handbuch der Geschichte der internationalen Beziehungen.* Vol. 4, *Balance of Power und Pentarchie: Internationale Beziehungen 1700–1785.* Paderborn, 1997.

Duden, Barbara. *The Woman Beneath the Skin: A Doctor's Patients in Eighteenth-Century Germany.* Cambridge, Mass., 1991.

Dutch Encounter with Asia, 1600. Exhibition catalog. Zwolle, 2002.

Ehrenschwendtner, Marie-Luise. "Virtual Pilgrimages? Enclosure and the Practice of Piety at St. Katherine's Convent." *Journal of Ecclesiastical History* 60 (2009): 45–73.

Elliger, Karl. "Das Gesetz Leviticus 18." *Zeitschrift für die alttestamentliche Wissenschaft* 67 (1955): 1–25.

Emig, Jutta. "Inzestneigung und Inzestvorstellung im mittelalterlichen Liebes- und Abenteuerromanen." In *Historische Inzestdiskurse: Interdisziplinäre Zugänge.* Eds. Jutta Emig, Claudia Jarzebowski, and Claudia Ulbrich. Königstein, 2003. Pp. 21–45.

Emig, Jutta, and Ulrike Gaebel. "'Wie man zwei Rinder in ein Joch spannt': Zu Heinrich Bullinger's *Der Christlich Eestand.*" In *Eheglück und Liebesjoch: Bilder von Liebe, Ehe und Familie in der Literatur des 15. und 16. Jahrhunderts.* Ed. Maria E. Müller. Weinheim, 1988. Pp. 125–54.

Enzyklopädie der Neuzeit. Ed. Friedrich Jaeger. 16 vols. Stuttgart, 2005–2012.

Ésmein, Adhémar. *Le mariage en droit canonique.* 2 vols. Paris, 1891.

Feher, Michael. "Libertinisms." In *The Libertine Reader: Eroticism and Enlightenment in Eighteenth-Century France.* Ed. Michael Feher. New York, 1997.

Feine, Hans Erich. *Kirchliche Rechtsgeschichte: Die katholische Kirche.* Cologne, 1964.

Fenton, Steve. *Ethnicity.* Cambridge, UK, 2003.

Fleck, Michael. "Luther in Hersfeld: Zur Chronologie der letzten Tage von Luthers Rückreise vom Wormser Reichstag." *Zeitschrift des Vereins für Hessische Geschichte und Landeskunde* 102 (1997): 7–14.

Flüchter, Antje. "'Aus dem fürnembsten indianischen Reisebeschreibungen zusammengezogen': Knowledge about India in Early Modern Germany." In *The Dutch Trading Companies as Knowledge Networks.* Ed. Siegfried Huigen, Jan L. de Jong, and Elmer Kolfin. Leiden, 2010. Pp. 337–60.

———. "Bajadere und Sati—Bilder der Inderin im deutschsprächigen Diskurs der Frühen Neuzeit." In *Gender in Trans-it: Transkulturelle und transnationale Perspektiven.* Ed. Martina Ineichen and Anna K. Liesch. Basel, 2009. Pp. 159–70.

———. *From Diversity of Images to a Single Truth: Indian States in German Early Modern Discourse (1500–1750).* Forthcoming.

———. "Eine katholische Ordnung der Sexualität? Konkurrierende Deutungsmuster um den Priesterzölibat im 17. Jahrhundert." In *Das Geschlecht des Glaubens: Religiöse Kulturen Europas zwischen Mittelatler und Moderne.* Eds. Monika Mommertz and Claudia Opitz. Frankfurt, 2008. Pp. 201–28.

———. "'Religions, Sects and Heresy'—Religion on the Indian Subcontinent in Early Modern German Texts." In *Labeling the Religious Self and Others: Reciporcal Perceptions of Christians, Muslims, Hindus, Buddhists, and Confucians in Medieval and Early Modern Times.* Eds. Hans Martin Krämer, Jenny Oesterle, and Ulrike Vordermark. Leipzig, 2010.

François, Étienne. *Die unsichtbare Grenze: Protestanten und Katholiken in Augsburg, 1648–1806.* Sigmaringen, 1991.

Frank, Michael. "Ehre und Gewalt im Dorf der Frühen Neuzeit: Das Beispiel Heiden (Grafschaft Lippe) im 17. und 18. Jahrhundert." In *Verletzte Ehre.* Eds. Klaus Schreiner and Gerd Schwerhoff. Pp. 320–38.

Franke, Myriam. "Die höfische Hochzeit." In *Erden Götter: Fürst und Hofstatt in der Frühen Neuzeit im Spiegel von Marburger Bibliotheks- und Archivbeständen.* Eds. Eva Bender, Petra Niehaus, and Jörg-Jochen Berns. Marburg, 1997.

Franzen, August. *Zölibat und Priestehe in der Auseinandersetzung der Reformationszeit und der katholischen Reformation des 16. Jahrhundert.* Münster, 1971.

Franz, Günter. "Ein Gutachten über Georg Witzel und seine Lehre." In *Festschrift zum 60. Geburtstag von Karl-August Eckhardt.* Ed. Otto Perst. Marburg, 1961.

Freist, Dagmar. "Crossing Religious Borders: The Experience of Religious Difference and its Impact on Mixed Marriages in Eighteenth-Century Germany." In *Living with Religious Diversity in Early Modern Europe.* Eds. Dagmar Freist, C. Scott Dixon, and Mark Greengrass. Aldershot, 2009. Pp. 203–23.

———. "Der Fall von Albini: Rechtsstreitigkeiten um die väterliche Gewalt in konfessionell gemischten Ehen." In *In eigener Sache: Frauen vor den höchsten Gerichten des Alten Reiches.* Ed. Siegrid Westphal. Cologne, 2005. Pp. 245–70.

———. "One Body, Two Confessions: Mixed Marriages in Germany." In *Gender in Early Modern German History.* Ed. Ulinka Rublack. Cambridge, UK, 2002. Pp. 275–304.

Freud, Sigmund. *Gesammelte Werke.* Ed. Anna Freud, Marie Bondaprte, E. Bibering, W. Hoffer, E. Kris, and O. Osakower. 19 vols. London, 1940–52.

———. *Group Psychology and the Analysis of the Ego.* Trans. and ed. James Strachey. New York, 1989.

———. *Das Unbehagen in der Kultur.* Vienna, 1930.

Frey, Linda, and Marsha Frey. *Frederick I: The Man and his Times.* New York, 1984.

Fricke, Waltraut. *Leibniz und die englische Sukzession des Hauses Hannover.* Hildesheim, 1957.

Friedberg, Emil. *Das Recht der Eheschliessung in seiner geschichtlichen Entwicklung.* Leipzig, 1865.

Fuchs, Ralf-Peter. *Hexerei und Zauberei vor dem Reichskammergericht: Nichtigkeiten und Injurien.* Wetzlar, 1994.

———. "Schmähschriften unter Männern: Ein Blick auf den Kampfstil eines frühneuzeitlichen Juristen." In *MannBilder: Ein Lese- und Quellenbuch zur historischen Männerforschung.* Ed. Wolfgang Schmale. Berlin, 1998. Pp. 57–77.

———. *Um die Ehre: Westfälische Beleidigungsprozesse vor dem Reichskammergericht 1525–1805.* Paderborn, 1999.

Fuchs, Thomas. *Traditionsstiftung und Erinnerungspolitik: Geschichtsschreibung in Hessen in der Frühen Neuzeit.* Kassel, 2002.

Fudge, Thomas A. "Incest and Lust in Luther's Marriage: Theology and Morality in Reformation Polemics." *Sixteenth-Century Journal* 34 (2003): 319–45.

Füssel, Marian. "Rang und Raum: Gesellschaftliche Karthographie und die soziale Logik des Raumes an der vormodernen Universität." In *Raum und Konflikt: Zur symbolischen Konstituierung gesellschaftlicher Ordnung in Mittelalter und Früher Neuzeit.* Eds. Christoph Dartmann, Marian Füssel, and Stefanie Rüther. Münster, 2004. Pp. 175–98.

Gädeke, Nora. "Die Rolle des Historikers: Gottfried Wilhelm Leibniz und der Aufstieg des Welfenhauses." In *Hannover und die englische Thronfolge.* Ed. Heide Barmeyer. Bielefeld, 2005.

Gay, Peter. *The Bourgeois Experience, Victoria to Freud.* Vol. 2, *The Tender Passion.* New York, 1986.

Gayot de Pitaval, François. *Causes célèbres et intéressantes avec les jugements qui les ont décidés.* 24 vols. Paris, 1739–70.

Gelder, Roelof van. *Das ostindische Abenteuer: Deutsche in Diensten der Vereinigten Ostindischen Kompanie der Niederland (VOC), 1600–1800.* Hamburg, 2004. Dutch edition. Nijmegen, 1997.

Gellert, Christian Fürchtegott. *Lustspiele.* Leipzig, 1747.

Gess, Felician. *Akten und Briefe zur Kirchenpolitik Herzog Georgs von Sachsen.* Cologne, 1985.

———. *Die Klostervisitationen des Herzog Georg von Sachsen nach ungedruckten Quellen dargestellt.* Leipzig, 1988.

Geyken, Frauke. *Gentlemen auf Reisen: Das britische Deutschlandbild im 18. Jahrhundert.* Frankfurt, 2002.

———. "'Ohne seiner frau todt witwer zu warden, ist doch etwas rares': Folgen des ehelichen Ungehorsams—Sophie Dorotheas Verbannung nach Ahlden." In *Mächtig—verlockend—Frauen der Welfen.* Exhibition catalog. Celle, 2010. Pp. 167–85.

Ginzel, Christof. *Poetry, Politics and Promises of Empire: Prophetic Rhetoric in the England and Neo-Latin Epithalamia on the Occasion of the Palatine Marriage in 1613.* Göttingen, 2009.

GLBTQ: An Encyclopedia of Gay, Lesbian, Bisexual, Transgender, and Queer Culture. Middletown, UK, 2006.

Goldgar, Anne. *Impolite Learning: Conduct and Community in the Republic of Letters, 1680–1750.* New Haven, 1995.

Goody, Jack. *The Development of Marriage and the Family in Europe.* Cambridge, UK, 1983.

Gottschalk, Karin. "Niemandes Kind? Illegitimät, Blutsverwandschaft und Zugehörigkeit im vormodernen Recht." *WerkstattGeschichte* 51 (2009): 23–42.

Goulemot, Jean Marie. *Forbidden Texts: Erotic Literature and Its Readers in Eighteenth-Century France.* Philadelphia, 1994.

Gregg, Edward. *The Protestant Succession in International Politics, 1710–1716.* New York, 1986.

Grenz, Dagmar, and Gisela Wilkending, eds. *Geschichte der Mädchenliteratur und die gesellschaftliche Situation der Frauen vom 18. Jahrhundert bis zum Gegenwart.* Weinheim, 1997.

Greyerz, Kaspar von. "Ego-Documents: The Last Word?" *German History* 28 (2010): 273–82.

Grisar, Hartmann. *Luther.* Trans. M. Lamond. 3 vols. London, 1913.

Groß, Barbara. *Hexerei in Minden: Zur sozialen Logik von Hexereiverdächtigungen und Hexenprozessen (1584–1684)*. Münster, 2009.

Großkinsky, Martin, ed. *Sammlerin und Stifterin—Henriette Amalie von Anhalt-Dessau und ihr Frankfurter Exil*. Frankfurt, 2002.

Häberlein, Mark. "Tod auf der Herrenstube: Ehre und Gewalt in der Augsburger Führungsschicht (1500–1620)." In *Ehrkonzepte in der Frühen Neuzeit: Identitäten und Abgrenzungen*. Eds. Sibylle Backmann, Hans-Jörg Künast, Sabine Ullmann, and B. Ann Tlusty. Berlin, 1998. Pp. 148–69.

Handelman, Dan. *Models and Mirrors: Towards an Anthropology of Public Events*. Cambridge, UK, 1990.

Handwörterbuch zur deutschen Rechtsgeschichte. 5 vols. Berlin, 1964–98.

Harding, Elizabeth. "Warum der Adel seine Ahnen über die Schwelle trägt: Zur Symbolik ritterschaftlicher Aufschwörungen." In *Symbolik in Zeiten von Krise und gesellschaftlichem Umbruch*. Eds. Elizabeth Harding, and Natalie Krentz. Münster, 2011.

Harding, Nicolas. "Hanoverian Rulership and Dynastic Union with Britain, 1700–1760." In *Die Personalunionen von Sachsen-Polen 1697–1763 und Hannover-England 1714–1837: Ein Vergleich*. Ed. Rex Rexheuser. Wiesbaden, 2005.

Harrington, Joel F. *Reordering Marriage and Society in Reformation Germany*. Cambridge, UK, 1995.

Harris, Bob. "Hanover and the Public Sphere." In *The Hannoverian Dimension in British History, 1714–1837*. Eds. Brendan Simms and Torsten Riotte. Cambridge, UK, 2007. Pp. 183–212.

Hatton, Ragnhild. *Georg I: Ein deutscher Kurfürst auf Englands Thron*. Frankfurt, 1982.

Hausen, Karin. "Historische Familienforschung." In *Historische Sozialwissenschaft: Beiträge zur Einführung in die Forschungspraxis*. Ed. Reinhard Rürup. Göttingen, 1977.

———. "Die Polarisierung der 'Geschlechtscharaktere'—Eine Spiegelung der Dissoziation von Erwerbs- und Familienleben." In *Sozialgeschichte der Familie in der Neuzeit Europas*. Ed. Werner Conze. Stuttgart, 1976. Pp. 363–93.

———. "'... Eine Ulme für das schwanke Efeu': Ehepaare im Bildungsbürgertum, Ideale und Wirklichkeiten im späten 18. Und 19. Jahrhundert." In *Bürgerinnen und Bürger: Geschlechterverhältnisse im 19. Jahrhundert*. Ed. Ute Frevert. Göttingen, 1988. Pp. 85–118.

Heck, Kilian. *Genealogie als Monument und Argument*. Munich, 2002.

Hehenberger, Susanne. "'... ich bin mit diesem Knecht geschwistrigt Kinder ...': Der Prozess gegen Maria Stumvollin und Johann Scherb (Freistadt/Weinberg 1783) als Beispiel der Strafpraxis beim Delikt, 'Inzest' im 18. Jahrhundert." *Jahrbuch des Oberösterreichischen Musealvereines* 144 (1999): 199–230.

Heinig, Paul-Joachim. "Fürstenkonkubinat um 1500 zwischen Usus un Devianz." In *"... wir wollen der Liebe Raum geben": Konkubinate geistlicher und weltlicher Fürsten um 1500*. Ed. Andreas Tacke. Göttingen, 2006. Pp. 11–37.

———. "'Omnia vincit amor'—Das fürstliche Konkubinat im 15./16. Jahrhundert." In *Principes: Dynastien und Höfe im späten Mittelalter*. Eds. Cordula Nolte, Karl-Heinz Spiess, and Ralf-Gunnar Werlich. Stuttgart, 2002. Pp. 277–314.

Henze, Barbara. "Kontinuität und Wandel des Eheverständnisses im Gefolge von Reformation und katholischer Reform." In *"In Christo ist weder man noch weyb": Frauen in derZeit der Refomation und der katholischen Reform*. Ed. Anne Conrad. Münster, 1999.

———. *Aus Liebe zur Kirche Reform: Die Bemühungen Georg Witzels um die Kircheneinheit*. Münster, 1995.

Herlihy, David. "The Family and Religious Ideologies in Medieval Europe." In *Women, Family and Society in Medieval Europe*. Ed. David Herlihy. New York, 1995. Pp. 154–73.

Hermann, Ulrich. "Erziehung und Schulunterricht für Mädchen im 18. Jahrhundert." *Wolfenbütteler Studien zur Aufklärung* 3 (1976): 101–27.

Herre, Paul. *Die geheime Ehe des Erbprinzen Wilhlem Gustav von Anhalt-Dessau und die Reichsgrafen von Anhalt*. Zerbst, 1933. Reprint. Dessau, 2006.

Herrera, Robinson A. "Concubines and Wives: Reinterpreting Native-Spanish Intimate Unions in Sixteeenth-Century Guatemala." In *India Conquistadors, Indigenous Allies in the Conquest of Mesoamerica*. Eds. Laura Matthew and Michel R. Oudijk. Norman, 2007. Pp. 127–44.

Hinschius, Paul. *System des katholischen Kirchenrechts mit besonderer Rücksicht auf Deutschland*. 5 vols. Berlin, 1869.

Hippel, Theodor Gottfried von. *Ueber die Ehe*. 5th ed.. Berlin, 1828.

Hirschi, Caspar. *Wettkampf der Nationen: Konstruktionen einer deutschen Ehrgemeinschaft an der Wende vom Mittelalter zur Neuzeit*. Göttingen, 2005.

Historisches Wörterbuch der Philosophie. Eds. Joachim Ritter and Karlfried Gründer. 13 vols. Basel, 1980.

Hoberg, Hermann. *Die Gemeinschaft der Bekenntnisse in kirchlichen Dingen: Rechtszustände im Fürstentum Osnabrück vom Westfälischen Frieden zum Anfang des 19. Jahrhundert*. Osnabrück, 1939.

Hoffmann, Johann Christian. *Reise nach dem Kaplande, nach Mauritius und nach Java: 1671–1676*. The Hague, 1931.

Hoffmann, Julius. *Die "Hausväterliteratur" und die "Predigten über den christlichen Haussstand": Lehre vom Hause und Bildung für das häusliche Leben im 16., 17. und 18. Jahrhundert*. Weinheim, 1959.

Hohmann, Joachim S. *Der Zölibat: Geschichte und Gegenwart eines umstrittenen Gesetzes: Mit einem Anhang wichtiger kirchlicher Quellentexte*. Frankfurt, 1993.

Höjer, Torgny. "Brandenburgs Brytning med Sverige Efter Gustav Adolfs Död." *Historisk Tidskrift* 68 (1948): 197–238.

Holenstein, Pia, and Norbert Schindler. "Geschwätzgeschichte(n): Ein kunsthistorisches Plädoyer für die Rehabitierung der unkontrollierten Rede." In *Dynamik der Tradition*. Ed. Richard van Dülmen. Pp. 41–108.

Homing, Elisabeth. "Konfession und demographisches Verhalten: Oberkassel, 1670–1810." *Historical Social Research / Historische Sozialforschung* 23 (1998): 275–98.

Höpfner, Johanna. *Mädchenerziehung und weibliche Bildung um 1800: Im Spiegel der populär-pädagogischen Schriften der Zeit*. Bad Heilbrunn, 1990.

Hotson, Howard. "Irenicism in the Confessional Age: The Holy Roman Empire, 1563–1648." In *Conciliation and Confession: The Struggle for Unity in the Age of Reform, 1415–1648*. Eds. Howard P. Louthan and Randall C. Zachman. Notre Dame, 2004. Pp. 228–85.

Huber, Alfons. "Ein bislang unbekanntes Meisterlied, die älteste faßbare literarische Bearbeitung des Bernauerstoffes." *Jahresbericht des Historischen Vereins für Straubing und Umgebung* 86 (1984): 453–66.

Hull, Isabel V. *Sexuality, State and Civil Society in Germany, 1700–1815*. Ithaca, N.Y., 1996.

Hurwich, Judith J. "Marriage Strategy among the German Nobility, 1400–1699." *Journal of Interdisciplinary History* 29 (1998): 169–95.

———. *Noble Strategies: Marriage and Sexuality in the Zimmern Chronicle*. Kirskville, 2006.

"Inzest." In *Themen und Motive in der Literatur: Ein Handbuch.* Eds. Horst S. Daemmrich and Ingrid Daemmrich. Tübingen, 1987.

Iwand, Fritz Georg. *Die Wahlkapitalationen des 17. und 18. Jahrhunderts und ihr Einfluß auf die Entwicklung des Ebenbürtigkeits- und Prädikatsrechts des deutschen hohen Adels.* Biberach, 1919.

Jacobs, Jürgen. *Prosa der Aufklärung: Moralische Wochenschriften—Autobiographie—Satire—Romane: Kommentar zu einer Epoche.* Munich, 1976.

Jaeger, C. Stephen. *Ennobling Love: In Search of a Lost Sensibility.* Philadelphia, 1999.

Jancke, Gabriele. "Ritualisierte Verhaltensweisen in der frühneuzeitlichen Gelehrtenkultur—Bettgeschichten." In *Gelehrtenleben: Wissenschaftspraxis in der Neuzeit.* Eds. Alf Lüdtke and Reiner Prass. Cologne, 2008. Pp. 235–47.

Jarzebowski, Claudia. "Eindeutig uneindeutig: Verhandlungen über Inzest im 18. Jahrhundert." In *Historische Inzestdiskurse: Interdisziplinäre Zugänge.* Eds. Jutta Emig, Claudia Jarzebowski, and Claudia Ulbrich. Königstein, 2003.

———. *Inzest: Verwandschaft und Sexualität im 18. Jahrhundert.* Cologne, 2006.

———. "Lieben und Herrschen: Fürstenerziehung im späten 15. und 16. Jahrhunderts." *Saeculum* 61, 1 (2011): 39–56.

Jarzebowski, Claudia, and Anne Kwashik, eds. *Peforming Emotions: Zum Verhältnis von Politik und Emotion in der Frühen Neuzeit und in der Moderne.* Göttingen, 2012.

Jäschke, Kurt-Ulrich. "Ein Hersfelder Stadtbuch aus dem Jahre 1431 als Quelle zur Geschichte von Stift und Stadt Hersfeld im 1. Drittel des 15. Jahrhunderts." *Archiv für Diplomatik* 13 (1967): 313–457.

Jónsson, Már. "Incest and the Word of God: Early Sixteenth Century Protestant Disputes." *Archiv für Reformationsgeschichte* 85 (1994): 96–118.

Jussen, Bernhard. "Künstliche und natürliche Verwandte? Biologismen in den kulturwissenschaftlichen Konzepten von Verwandtschaft." In *Das Individuum und die Seinen: Individualität in der okzidentalen und der russischen Kultur in Mittelalter und Früher Neuzeit.* Eds. Juri L. Nesmertny and Otto Gerhard Oexle. Göttingen, 2001. Pp. 39–59.

———. *Patenschaft und Adoption im frühen Mittelalter: Künstliche Verwandschaft als soziale Praxis.* Göttingen, 1991.

Kantorowicz, Ernst H. *The King's Two Bodies: A Study in Mediaeval Political Theology.* Princeton, 1957.

Kaplan, Benjamin J. *Divided by Faith: Religious Conflict and the Practice of Toleration in Early Modern Europe.* Cambridge, Mass., 2007.

Karant-Nunn, Susan C. *Reformation of Feeling: Shaping the Religious Emotions in Early Modern Germany.* New York, 2010.

Karant-Nunn, Susan C., and Merry E. Wiesner-Hanks, eds. *Luther on Women: A Sourcebook.* Cambridge, UK, 2003.

Karras, Ruth Mazo. *Unmarriages: Women, Men and Sexual Unions in the Middle Ages.* Philadelphia, 2012.

Kathrein, Werner, Karlheinz Diez, Barbara Henze, and Cornelius Roth, eds. *Im Dienst um die Einheit und die Reform der Kirche: Zum Leben und Werk Georg Witzels.* Frankfurt, 2003.

Kawerau, Waldemar. *Die Reformation und die Ehe: Ein Beitrag zur Kulturgeschichte des sechszehnten Jahrhunderts.* Halle, 1892.

Klauber, Martin I. *Between Reformed Scholasticism and Pan-Protestantism: Jean-Alphonse Turretin (1671–1737) and Enlightened Orthodoxy at the Academy of Geneva.* Selinsgrove, 1994.

Klein, Thomas. "Die Erhebungen in den weltlichen Reichsfürstenstand, 1550–1806." *Blätter für deutsche Landesgeschichte* 122 (1986): 137–92.

Kleinau, Elke, and Claudia Opitz, eds. *Geschichte der Mädchen- und Frauenbildung.* 2 vols. Frankfurt, 1996.

Klocke, Friedrich von. *Justus Möser und die deutsche Ahnenprobe des 18. Jahrhunderts.* Leipzig, 1941.

Knöfel, Anne Simone. *Dynastie und Prestige: Die Heiratspolitik der Wettiner.* Cologne, 2009.

Kober, Ulrich. *Eine Karriere im Krieg: Graf Adam von Schwarzenberg und die kurbrandenburgische Politik von 1619 bis 1641.* Berlin, 2004.

Köhler, Hans-Joachim. "Erste Schritt zu einem Meinungsprofil der frühen Reformationszeit." In *Martin Luther: Probleme zeiner Zeit.* Eds. Volker Press and Dieter Stievermann. Stuttgart, 1986.

Kohnen, Joseph. "Ehestreit unter Freunden: Johann Georg Hamann als 'Korrektor'des Buchs *Über die Ehe*." *Recherches germaniques* 18 (1988): 47–65.

Kollmer, Gert. *Die Familie Palm: Soziale Mobilität in ständischer Gesellschaft.* Ostfildern, 1983.

König, Domink von. "Lesesucht und Lesewut." In *Buch und Leser: Vorträge des ersten Jarhes treffens des Wolfenbütteler Arbeitskreis für Geschichte des Buchwesens.* Ed. Herbert F. Göpfert. Hamburg, 1977.

Kord, Susanne. *Murderesses in German Writing, 1720–1860: Heroines of Horror.* Cambridge, UK, 2009.

Koser, Reinhold. *Geschichte der brandenburgischen Politik bis zum Westfälischen Frieden von 1648.* Stuttgart, 1913.

Krais, Beate. "Soziales Feld, Macht und kulturelle Praxis: Die Untersuchungen Bourdieus über die verschiedenen Fraktionen der 'herrschenden Klasse' in Frankreich." In *Klassenlage, Lebensstil und kulturelle Praxis: Theoretische und empirische Beiträge zur Auseinandersetzung mit Pierre Bourdieus Klassentheorie.* Ed. Klaus Eder. Frankfurt, 1989. Pp. 47–70.

Kramer, Karl-Sigismund. *Grundriß einer rechtlichen Volkskunde.* Göttingen, 1974.

———. "Hohnsprake, Wrakworte, Nachschnack und Ungebühr: Ehrenhändel in holsteinischen Quellen." *Kieler Blätter zur Volkskunde* 16 (1984): 49–85.

———. "Würzburger Volk des 16. Jahrhunderts vor Gericht." *Bayerisches Jahrbuch für Volkskunde* 3 (1955): 141–56.

Krauske, Otto. "Die Verlobung Friedrich Wilhelms I." In *Beiträge zur brandenburgischen und preußischen Geschichte: Festschrift zu Gustav Schmollers 70. Geburtstag.* Leipzig, 1908.

Kretzschmar, Johannes. "Die Allianzverhandlungen Gustav Adolfs mit Kurbrandenburg im Mai und Juni 1631." *Forschungen zur Brandenburgischen und Preußischen Geschichte* 17 (1904): 341–82.

Krug-Richter, Barbara. "'Du Bacchant, quid est grammatica?' Konflikte zwischen Studenten und Bürgern im frühneuzeitlichen Freiburg/Br." In *Praktiken des Konfliktaustrags in der Frühen Neuzeit.* Eds. Barbara Krug-Richter and Ruth-E. Mohrmann. Münster, 2004. Pp. 79–104.

Krüger-Fürhoff, Irmela. "Epistemological Asymmetries and Erotic Stagings: Father-Daughter Incest in Heinrich von Kleist's *The Marquise von O.*" *Women in German Yearbook: Feminist Studies in German Literature & Culture* 12 (1996): 71–86.

Kruse, Hans. "Wilhelm von Oranien und Anna von Sachsen: Eine fürstliche Eheträgodie des 16. Jahrhunderts." *Nassauische Annalen* 54 (1934): 1–184.

Kruse, Jens-Martin. *Universitätstheologie und Kirchenreform: Die Anfänge der Reformation in Wittenberg 1516–1522.* Mainz, 2002.

Kuhn, Annette, and Gerda Tornieporth. *Frauenbildung und Geschlechtsrolle: Historische und erziehungswissenschaftliche Studien zum Wandel der Frauenrolle in Familie und Gesellschaft.* Gelnhausen, 1980.

Kunstmann, Friedrich. *Die gemischten Ehen unter den christlichen Konfessionen Teutschlands.* Regensburg, 1839.

Küppers-Braun, Ute. *Frauen des hohen Adels im kaiserlich-freiweltlichen Damenstift Essen (1605–1803).* Münster, 1997.

Kvačala, Johann, ed. *Neue Beiträge zum Briefwechsel von D.E. Jablonsky und G. W. Leibniz.* Jurjew, 1899.

Lach, Donald F., and Edwin J. Van Kley, eds. *Asia in the Making of Europe.* Vol. 3, *Century of Advance.* Chicago, 1993.

Lademacher, Horst. "Batavia." In *Kolonialstädte—Europäische Enklaven oder Schmelztiegel der Kulturen?* Eds. Horst Grüner and Peter Johanek. Münster, 2001.

Late-Medieval German Women's Poetry: Secular and Religious Songs. Trans. Albrecht Classen. Rochester, 2004.

Laurent, Françoise, ed. *Serment, promesse et engagement: Rituels et modalités au Moyen Âge.* Montpellier, 2008.

Leonard, Amy. *Nails in the Wall: Catholic Nuns in Reformation Germany.* Chicago, 2005.

Lévi-Strauss, Claude. *The Elementary Structures of Kinship.* Boston, 1969.

Lindemann, Mary. "Eighteenth-Century True Crime Stories, Legal Histories, and the Literary Imagination." *Daphis* 37 (2008): 131–52.

———. *Liaisons Dangereuses: Sex, Law, and Diplomacy in the Age of Frederick the Great.* Baltimore, 2006.

———. "Narratives of Dismembering Women in Northern Germany, 1600–1800." *Women & Death: Representations of Female Victims and Perpetrators in German Culture, 1500–2000.* Eds. Helen Fronius and Ann Linton. London, 2008. Pp. 76–92.

Lindner, Ulrike. "Contested Concepts of 'White' and 'Native': Mixed Marriages in German South-West Africa and the Cape Colony." *Basler Africa Bibliographien Working Papers* 6 (2008): 1–18.

Lischka, Marion. *Liebe als Ritual: Eheanbahnung und Brautwerbung in der frühneuzeitlichen Grafschaft Lippe.* Paderborn, 2006.

Loewe, Victor. *Ein Diplomat und Gelehrter: Ezechiel Spanheim (1629–1710).* Berlin, 1924.

Logan, F. Donald. *Runaway Religious in Medieval England, C. 1240–1540.* Cambridge, UK, 1996.

Lohse, Bernhard. *Luthers Theologie in ihrer historischen Entwicklung und in ihrem systematischen Zusammenhang.* Göttingen, 1995.

Lowenstein, Steven M. "Jewish Intermarriage and Conversion in Germany and Austria." *Modern Judaism* 25 (2005): 23–61.

Luebke, David M. "Making Marriages Mixed: Religious Pluralization, Ritual, and the Formation of Intra-Christian Marriage Barriers in Germany." In *Gemischte Ehen im Europa: Politik und Praxis der religiösen Pluralität (14.-19. Jh.).* Ed Cecilia Cristellon. Forthcoming.

Luebke, David M., Jared Poley, Daniel C. Ryan, and David W. Sabean, eds. *Conversion and the Politics of Religion in Early Modern Germany.* New York, 2012.

Luhmann, Niklas. *Liebe als Passion: Zur Codierung von Intimität.* Frankfurt, 1982.

Lutterbach, Hubertus. *Sexualität im Mittlalter: Eine Kulturstudie anhand von Bußbüchern des 6.-12. Jahrhunderts.* Cologne, 1999.

Lynch, Andrew, and Philippa Maddern, eds. *Venus & Mars: Engendering Love and War in Medieval and Early Modern Europe.* Nedlands, 1995.

Lynch, Joseph H. *Godparents and Kinship in Early Medieval Europe.* Princeton, 1986.

———. "Spiritual Kinship and Sexual Prohibition in Early Medieval Europe." *Proceedings of the 6th International Congress of Medieval Canon Law.* Ed. Stephen Kuttner. Vatican City, 1985. 271–88.

Lynch, Katherine. *Individuals, Families, and Communities in Europe, 1200–1800: The Urban Foundations of Western Society.* Cambridge, UK, 2003.

MacHardy, Karin J. *War, Religion and Court Patronage in Habsburg Austria: The Social and Cultural Dimensions of Political Integration.* Basingstoke, 2003.

McKay, Derek. *The Great Elector.* Harlow, 2001.

Magdeburg, Mechthild von. *Das fließende Licht der Gottheit.* Frankfurt, 2010.

Malmström, Oscar. *I. Änkedrottning Maria Eleonora och hennes Flykt till Danmark: II. Underhandlingarna om ett Giftermål mellan Kristina af Sverige och Friedrich Wilhelm af Brandenburg.* Helsingborg, 1895.

Marra, Stephanie. *Allianzen des Adels: Dynastisches Handeln im Grafenhaus Bentheim im 16. und 17. Jahrhundert.* Cologne, 2007.

Martens, Wolfgang. *Die Botschaft der Tugend: Aufklärung im Spiegel der deutschen Moralischen Wochenschriften.* Stuttgart, 1968.

Mauss, Marcel. *Die Gabe: Form und Funktion des Austausches in archaischen Gesellschaften.* Frankfurt, 1990.

McCabe, Richard A. *Incest, Drama and Nature's Law.* Cambridge, UK, 1993.

McCutcheon, Allan. "Denominations and Religious Intermarriage: Trends among White Americans in the Twentieth Century." *Review of Religious Research* 29 (1988): 213–227.

Medick, Hans, and David W. Sabean, eds. *Emotionen und materielle Interessen: Sozialanthropoligische und historische Beiträge zur Familienforschung.* Göttingen, 1984.

Meininghaus, August. "Von der morganatischen Ehe des niederen westfälische Adels." *Westfälische Zeitschrift* 95 (1939): 194–212.

Meise, Helga. *Die Unschuld und die Schrift: Deutsche Frauenromane im 18. Jahrhundert.* Berlin, 1983.

Merkel, Kerstin. "Ein Fall von Bigamie: Landgraf Phillip von Hessen, seine beiden Frauen und deren drei Grabdenkmäler." In *Grabmäler: Tendenzen der Forschung an Beispielen aus Mittelalter und früher Neuzeit.* Eds. Wilhelm Maier, Wolfgang Schmid, and Michael Viktor Schwarz. Berlin, 2000. Pp. 103–26.

Meyer, Christine. "Erziehung und Schulbildung für Mädchen." In *Handbuch der Bildungsgeschichte.* Vol. 2, *18. Jahrhundert: Vom späten 17. Jahrhundert bis zur Neuordnung Deutschlands um 1800.* Eds. Notker Hammerstein and Ulrich Hermann. Munich, 2005.

Michaelis, Karl. *Das abendländische Eherecht im Übergang vom späten Mittelalter zur Neuzeit.* Göttingen, 1989.

Michaels, Axel. *Der Hinduismus: Geschichte und Gegenwart.* Munich, 1998.

Mikat, Paul. *Die Polygamiefrage in der frühen Neuzeit.* Opladen, 1988.

Mitterauer, Michael. "Christentum und Endogamie." In *Historisch-anthropologische Familienforschung: Fragestellungen un Zugangsweisen.* Ed. Michael Mitterauer. Cologne, 1990. Pp. 41–87.

Moeller, Bernd. "Die Brautwerbung Martin Bucers für Wolfgang Capito." In *Die Reformation und das Mittelalter: Kirchenhistorische Aufsätze.* Ed. Johannes Schilling. Göttigen, 1991. Pp. 151–60.

———. "Kleriker als Bürger." In *Die Reformation und das Mittelalter.* Ed. Johannes Schilling. Pp. 35–52.

———. "Zwinglis Disputationen." *Zeitschrift der Savigny-Stiftung für Rechtsgeschichte. Kanonistische Abteilung* 86 (1970): 275–324; 91 (1974): 213–364.

Moraw, Peter, and Volker Press. "Fürstentümer, Geistliche." In *Theologische Realenzyklopädie.* Ed. Horst Robert Balz. 36 vols. Berlin, 1876–2007. Vol. 11, Pp. 711–19.

Muir, Edward. *Ritual in Early Modern Europe.* 2nd ed. Cambridge, UK, 2005.

Müller, Jan-Dirk. "Von der Subversion frühneuzeitlicher Ehelehre: Zu Fischarts 'Ehezuchtbüchlein' und 'Geschichtklitterung." In *The Graph of Sex and the German Text:* Ed. Lynne Tatlock. Pp. 121–56.

Müller, Walter. *Entwicklung und Spätformen der Leibeigenschaft am Beispiel der Heiratsbeschränkungen: Die Ehegenoßsame im alemannisch-schweizerischen Raum.* Sigmaringen, 1974.

Münch, Paul. "Grundwerte der frühneuzeitlichen Ständegesellschaft? Aufriß einer vernächlässigten Thematik." In *Ständische Gesellschaft und soziale Mobilität.* Ed. Winfired Schulze. Munich, 1988. Pp. 53–72.

Münkler, Herfried, and H. Grünberger. "Nationale Identität im Diskurs der Deutschen Humanisten." In *Nationales Bewußtsein und kollektive Identität.* Ed. Helmut Berding. Frankfurt, 1996.

Mutschler, Thomas. *Haus, Ordnung, Familie: Wetterauer Hochadel im 17. Jahrhundert am Beispiel des Hauses Ysenburg-Büdingen.* Darmstadt, 2004.

Nasse, Peter. *Die Frauenzimmer-Bibliothek des Hamburger "Patrioten" vom 1724: Zur weiblichen Bildung in der Frühaufklärung.* Stuttgart, 1976.

Nelson, T.G.A., "Incest in the Early Novel and Related Genres." *Eighteenth-Century Life* 16 (1992): 127–62.

Neuhaus, Helmut. *Das Reich in der Frühen Neuzeit.* 2nd ed. Munich, 2003.

Newman, Aubrey. "Two Countries, One Monarch: The Union England/Hanover as the Ruler's Personal Problem." In *Die Personalunionen von Sachsen-Polen 1697–1763 und Hannover-England 1714–1837: Ein Vergleich.* Wiesbaden, 2005.

Nischan, Bodo. *Lutherans and Calvinists in the Age of Confessionalism.* Aldershot, 1999.

Nonnenmacher, Hartmut. *Natur und Factum: Inzest als Motiv und Thema in der französischen und deutschen Literatur des 18. Jahrhunderts.* Frankfurt, 2002.

Oberhammer, Evelin. "Gesegnet sei dies Band: Eheprojekte, Heiratspakten und Hochzeit im fürstlichen Haus." In *Der ganzen Welt ein Lob und Spiegel: Das Fürstenhaus Liechtenstein in der frühen Neuzeit.* Ed. Evelin Oberhammer. Vienna, 1990. Pp. 182–203.

Okin, Susan Miller. "Women and the Making of the Sentimental Family." *Philosophy & Public Affairs* 11 (1982): 65–88.

Opitz, Claudia, Ulrike Weikel, and Elke Kleinau, eds. *Tugend, Vernunft und Gefühle: Geschlechterdiskurs der Aufklärung und weibliche Lebenswelten.* Münster, 2000.

Österberg, Eva. *Friendship and Love, Ethics and Politics: Studies in Medieval and Early Modern History.* Budapest, 2010.

Oßwald-Bargende, Sybille. *Die Mätresse, der Fürst und die Macht: Christina Wilhelmina van Grävenitz und die höfische Gesellschaft.* Frankfurt, 2000.

Owens, Samantha. "'Und mancher grosser Fürst kann ein Apollo seyn': Erbprinz Friedrich Ludwig von Württemberg (1698–1731)." *Musik in Baden-Württemberg* 10 (2003): 177–90.

Ozment, Steven. *When Fathers Ruled: Family Life in Reformation Europe*. Cambridge, UK, 1983.

Pascoe, Peggy. *What Comes Naturally: Miscegenation Law and the Making of Race in America*. Oxford, 2009.

Patterson, William B. *King James VI und I and the Reunion of Christendom*. Cambridge, UK, 1997.

Die Peinliche Gerichtsordnung Kaiser Karls V. und des Heiligen Römischen Reiches von 1532 (Carolina). Ed. Friedrich-Christian Schroeder. Stuttgart, 2000.

Perez, Rosa Maria. "The Rhetoric of Empire: Gender Represtnations in Portuguese India." *Portuguese Studies* 21 (2005): 126–45.

Perron, Edgar du. *Schandaal in Holland*. The Hague, 1939.

Pfanner, Josef, ed. *Die "Denkwürdigkeiten" der Caritas Pirckheimer (aus den Jahren 1524–1528)*. Landshut, 1962.

Plummer, Marjorie Elizabeth. *From Priest's Whore to Pastor's Wife: Clerical Marriage and the Process of Reform in the Early German Reformation*. Farnham, 2012.

Prestwich, Menna. *International Calvinism 1541–1715*. Oxford, 1985.

Prodi, Paolo, and Elisabeth Müller-Luckner, eds. *Glaube und Eid: Treuformeln, Glaubensbekenntnisse, und Sozialdisziplinierung zwischen Mittelalter und Neuzeit*. Munich, 1993.

Rabe, Horst. *Reich und Glaubensspaltung: Deutschland 1500–1600*. Munich, 1989.

Raben, Remco. *Round about Batavia: Ethnicity and Authority in the Ommelanden 1650–1800*. Leiden, 2000.

Rahden, Till van. "Weder Milieu noch Konfession: Die situative Ethnizität der deutschen Juden im Kaiserreich in vergleichender Perspektive." In *Religion im Kaiserreich: Milieus–Mentalitäten–Krisen*. Eds. Olaf Blaschke and Frank-Michael Kuhlemann. Gütersloh, 1996.

Ranieri, Filippo. *Recht und Gesellschaft im Zeitalter der Rezeption: Eine rechts- und sozialgeschichtliche Analyse der Judikatur des Reichskammergerichts im 16. Jahrhundert*. 2 vols. Cologne, 1985.

Reichert, Folker E. "Fremde Frauen: Die Wahrnehmung von Geschlechterrollen in den spätmittelalterlichen Orientreiseberichten." In *Die Begegnung des Westens mit dem Osten*. Eds. Odilo Engels and Peter Schreiner. Sigmaringen, 1993. Pp. 167–84.

Reif, Heinz. "Zum Zusammenhang von Sozialstruktur, Familien- und Lebenszyklus im westfälischen Adel in der Mitte des 18. Jahrhunderts." *Historische Familienforschung*. Eds. Michael Mitterauer and Reinhard Seider. Frankfurt, 1982.

Richarz, Irmintraut. *Oikos, Haus und Haushalt: Ursprunge und Geschichte der Haushaltsökonomik*. Göttingen, 1991.

Richter-Uhlig, Uta. *Hof und Politik unter den Bedingungen der Personalunion zwischen Hannover und England: Die Aufenthalte Georgs II. in Hannover zwischen 1729 und 1741*. Hanover, 1992.

Riedenauer, Erwin. "Zur Entstehung und Ausformung des landesfürstlichen Briefadels in Bayern." *Zeitschrift für Bayerischer Landesgeschichte* 47 (1984): 609–73.

Roberts, Michael. *Gustavus Adolphus: A History of Sweden 1611–1632*. 2 vols. London, 1953–58.

Rockwell, William Walker. *Die Doppelehe des Landgrafen Philipp von Hessen*. Marburg, 1904.

Rogge, Joachim. *Der Beitrag des Predigers Jakob Strauss zur frühen Reformationsgeschichte.* Berlin, 1957.

Rohrschneider, Michael. *Johann Georg II. von Anhalt-Dessau (1627–1693): Eine politische Biographie.* Berlin, 1998.

———. "Leopold I. von Anhalt-Dessau, die orangische Heeresreform und die Reorganisation der preußischen Armee unter Friedrich Wilhelm I." In *Die preussische Armee zwischen Ancient Régime und Reichsgründung.* Eds. Peter Baumgart, Bernhard R. Kroener, and Heinz Stübig. Paderborn, 2008. Pp. 45–71.

Roper, Lyndal. *The Holy Household: Women and Morals in Reformation Augsburg.* Oxford, 1989.

———. "Luther: Sex, Marriage and Motherhood." *History Today* 33, no. 12 (December 1983): 33–38.

———. "'Wille' und 'Ehre': Sexualität, Sprache und Macht in Augsburger Kriminalprozessen." In *Wandel der Geschlechterbeziehungen zu Beginn der Neuzeit.* Eds. Heide Wunder and Christina Vanja. Frankfurt, 1991. Pp. 180–97.

Rose, Anne C. *Beloved Strangers: Interfaith Families in Nineteenth-Century America.* Cambridge, Mass., 2001.

Rösener, Werner, ed. *Adelige und bürgerliche Erinnerungskulturen des Spätmittelalters und der Frühen Neuzeit.* Göttingen, 2000.

Rublack, Hans-Christoph. *Gescheiterte Reformation: Frühreformatorische und protestantische Bewegungen in süd- und westdeutschen geistlichen Residenzen.* Stuttgart, 1978.

Rublack, Ulinka. "'Viehisch, frech und onverschämpt': Inzest in Südwestdeutschland, ca. 1530–1700." In *Von Huren und Rabenmüttern: Weibliche Kriminalität in der frühen Neuzeit.* Ed. Otto Ulbricht. Cologne, 1995. Pp. 171–213.

Russell, James. *Observations on the Testicles.* Edinburgh, 1883.

Sabean, David Warren. "From Clan to Kindred: Kinship and the Circulation of Property in Premodern and Modern Europe." In *Heredity Produced: At the Crossroads of Biology, Politics, and Culture, 1500–1970.* Eds. Staffan Müller-Wille and Hans-Jörg Rheinberger. Cambridge, Mass., 2007. Pp. 37–59.

———. "Inzestdiskurse vom Barock bis zur Romantik." *L'Homme: Zeitschrift für feministische Geschichtswissenschaft* 13 (2002): 7–28.

———. "From Siblingship to Siblinghood: Kinship and the Shaping of European Society (1300–1900)." In *Sibling Relations and the Transformation of European Kinship, 1300–1900.* Eds. Christopher H. Johnson and David Warren Sabean. New York, 2011.

———. *Kinship in Neckarhausen, 1700–1870.* Cambridge, UK, 1998.

Sabean, David Warren, and Simon Teuscher. *Kinship in Europe: Approaches to Long-Term Development (1300–1900).* Ed. by David Warren Sabean, Simon Teuscher, and Jon Mathieu. New York, 2007.

———. "Kinship in Europe: A New Approach to Long Term Development." In *Kinship in Europe: Approaches to Long-Term Development (1300–1900).* Eds. David Warren Sabean, Simon Teuscher, and Jon Mathieu. Pp. 1–32.

Safley, Thomas M. *Let No Man Put Asunder: The Control of Marriage in the German Southwest, A Comparative Study, 1550–1600.* Kirksville, 1984.

Sames, Arno. *Anton Wilhlem Böhme (1673–1722): Studien zur ökonomischen Denken und Handel eines Halleschen Pietisten.* Göttingen, 1990.

Schäufele, Wolf-Friedrich. *Christoph Matthäus Pfaff und die Kirchenunionsbestrebungen des Corpus Evangelicorum 1717–1726.* Mainz, 1998.

Schenda, Rudolf. *Volk ohne Buch: Studien zur Sozialgeschichte der populären Lesestoffe 1770–1910.* 3rd ed. Frankfurt, 1988.

Schevill, Ferdinand. *The Great Elector.* Chicago, 1947.

Schilling, Johannes. *Klöster und Mönche in der hessischen Reformation.* Gütersloh, 1997.

Schindling, Anton. "Reformation, Gegenreformation und Katholische Reform im Osnabrücker Land und im Emsland." *Osnabrücker Mitteilungen* 94 (1989): 35–60.

Schirch, Lisa. *Ritual and Symbol in Peacebuilding.* Boulder, 2005.

Schlip, Harry. "Die neuen Fürsten." In *Liechtenstein: Fürstliches Haus und staatliche Ordnung.* Eds. Volker Press and Dietmar Willoweit. Munich, 1987. Pp. 249–92.

Schlumbohm, Jürgen. *Lebensläufe, Familien, Höfe: Die Bauern und Heuerleute des Osnabrückischen Kirchspiels Belm in protoindustrieller Zeit, 1650–1860.* Göttingen, 1994.

Schmidt, Karl. *Die Confession der Kinder nach dem Landesrechten im deutschen Reiche.* Freiburg, 1890.

Schmidt, Walther. *Prinzessin Henriette Amalie von Anhalt-Dessau, die Begründerin der Fürstlichen Amalienstiftung in Dessau (1720–1793): Ein Lebensbild aus der Zeit des Rokoko.* Dessau, 1937. Reprint. Dessau-Roßlau, 2009.

Schmugge, Ludwig, Patrick Hersperger, and Béatrice Wiggenhauser. *Die Supplikenregister der päpstlichen Pönitentiarie aus der Zeit Pius II. (1458–1464).* Tübingen, 1996.

Schnath, Georg. *Georg Ludwigs Weg auf den englischen Thron: Die Vorgeschichte der Thronfolge 1698–1714.* Hildesheim, 1982.

———. *Sophie Dorothea und Königsmarck: Die Ehetragödie der Kurprinzessin von Hannover.* Hildesheim, 1979.

Schnell, Rüdiger. "Liebesdiskurs und Ehediskurs im 15. und 16. Jahrhundert." In *The Graph of Sex and the German Text.* Ed. Lynne Tatlock. Pp. 77–120.

———. *Sexualität und Emotionalität in der vormodernen Ehe.* Cologne, 2002.

Schreiber, Arndt. "Einleitung." In *Wilhelm von Humboldt: Briefe an Christine Reinhard-Reimarus.* Ed. Arndt Schreiber. Heidelberg, 1956. Pp. 11–78.

Schulte, Regina. "'Bevor das Gerede zum Tratsch wird." *Journal für Geschichte* 2 (1985): 16–21.

Schulze, Richard. *Das Project der Vermählung Friedrich Wilhelms von Brandenburg mit Christina von Schweden.* Halle, 1898.

Schulze, Winfried, ed. *Ständische Gesellschaft und soziale Mobilität.* Munich, 1988.

Schunka, Alexander. "Brüderliche Korrespondenz: Konfession und Politik zwischen Brandenburg-Preußen, Hannover und England im Wendejahr 1706." In *Daniel Ernst Jablonski: Religion, Wissenschaft und Politik um 1700.* Wiesbaden, 2008. Pp. 123–50.

———. "Irenicism and the Challenges of Conversion in the Early Eighteenth Century." *Conversion and the Politics of Religion in Germany.* Eds. David M. Luebke, Jared Poley, Daniel C. Ryan, and David W. Sabean. New York, 2012.

———. "Konfessionelle Liminalität: Kryptokatholiken im lutherischen Kursachsen des 17. Jahrhunderts." In *Migration und kirchliche Praxis: Das religiöse Leben frühneuzeitlicher Glaubensflüchtlinge in alltagsgeschichtlicher Perspektive.* Eds. Joachim Blaschke and Rainer Bendel. Cologne, 2008. Pp. 113–31.

———. "Union, Reunion, or Toleration? Reconciliatory Attempts among Eighteenth-Century Protestants." In *Diversity and Dissent: Negotiating Religious Difference in Central Europe, 1500–1800.* Eds. Howard Louthan, Gary B. Cohen, and Franz A. J. Szabo. New York, 2011. 309–34.

———. "Zwischen Kontingenz und Providenz: Frühe Englandkontakte der halleschen Pietisten und protestantische Irenik um 1700." *Pietismus und Neuzeit* 34 (2008): 82–114.

Schwab, Dieter. *Grundlagen und Gestalt der staatlichen Ehegesetzgebung in der Neuzeit bis zum Beginn des 19. Jahrhunderts.* Bielefeld, 1967.

Schwerhoff, Gerd. *Köln im Kreuzverhör: Kriminalität, Herrschaft und Gesellschaft in einer frühneuzeitlichen Stadt.* Bonn, 1991.

———. "Kriminalitätsgeschichte im deutschen Sprachraum: Zum Profil eines 'verspäteten' Forschungszweiges." In *Kriminalitätsgeschichte: Beiträge zur Sozial- und Kulturgeschichte der Vormoderne.* Eds. Andreas Blauer and Gerd Schwerhoff. Constance, 2000. Pp. 21–68.

Shorter, Edward. *The Making of the Modern Family.* New York, 1975.

Sienerth, Stefan. "Andreas Pinxner, ein Zeitgenosse des Gorgias: Ein schlecht behandelter siebenbürgischer Barockautor." *Südostdeutsche Vierteljahresblätter* 38 (1989): 278–84.

Sikora, Michael. *Der Adel in der Frühen Neuzeit.* Darmstadt, 2009.

———. "Dynastie und Eigensinn: Herzog Georg Wilhelm von Celle, Eleonore d'Olbreuse und die Spielregeln des Fürstenstandes." In *Hof und Medien im Spannungsfeld von dynastischer Tradition und politischer Innovation zwischen 1648 und 1714.* Ed. Heiko Laß. Munich, 2008. Pp. 19–30.

———. "Eleonore d'Olbreuse—die Herzogin auf Raten." In *Mächtig—verlockend—Frauen der Welfen.* Exhibition catalog. Celle, 2010. Pp. 17–43.

———. "Ein kleiner Erbfolgekrieg: Die sachsenmeiningische Sukzessionskrise 1763 und das Problem der Ebenbürtigkeit." In *Menschen und Strukturen in der Geschichte Alteuropas.* Eds. Helmut Neuhaus and Barbara Stollberg-Rilinger. Berlin, 2002. Pp. 319–39.

———. "'Mausdreck mit Pfeffer': Das Problem der ungleichen Heiraten im deutschen Hochadel der Frühen Neuzeit." Habilitation Thesis. Münster, 2004.

———. "Eine Missheirat im Hause Anhalt: Zur sozialen Praxis der ständischen Gesellschaft in der ersten Hälfte des 18. Jahrhundert." In *Die Fürsten von Anhalt.* Eds. Werner Freitag and Michael Hecht. Halle, 2003. Pp. 248–65.

———. "'. . . so muß man doch dem Kindt ainen Nahmen geben': Wahrnehemungsweisen einer unstandesgemäßen Beziehung im 16. Jahrhundert." In *Adel in Hessen: Herrschaft, Selbstverständnis und Lebensführung vom 15. bis ins 20. Jahrhundert.* Eds. Eckart Conze, Alexander Jendorff, and Heide Wunder. Marburg, 2010. Pp. 571–93.

———. "Über den Umgang mit Ungleichheit: Bewältigungsstrategien für Mesalliancen im deutschen Hochadel der Frühen Neuzeit—das Haus Anhalt als Beispiel." *Zwischen Schande und Ehre: Erinnerungsbrüche und die Kontinuität des Hauses: Legitimationsmuster und Traditionsverständnis des frühneuzeitlichen Adels in Umbruch und Krise.* Eds. Martin and Horst Carl. Mainz, 2007. Pp. 97–124.

———. "Ungleiche Verbindlichkeiten: Gestaltungsspielräume standesverschiedener Partnerschaften im deutschen Hochadel der Frühen Neuzeit." *Zeitenblicke* 4, 3 (13 December 2005). http://www.zeitenblicke.de/2005/3/Sikora

Singh, Anjana. *Fort Cochin in Kerala (1750–1830): The Social Condition of a Dutch Community in an Indian Milieu.* Leiden, 2010.

Smith, Hannah. *Georgian Monarchy: Politics and Culture, 1714–1760.* Cambridge, UK, 2006.

Smith, Jonathan Z. "Religion, Religions, Religious." In *Critical Terms for Religious Studies.* Ed. Marc C. Taylor. Chicago, 1998. Pp. 269–84.

Sommer-Mathis, Andrea. *"Tu felix Austria nube": Hochzeitsfeste der Habsburger im 18. Jahrhundert.* Vienna, 1994.

Sperling, Jutta. "Marriage at the Time of the Council of Trent (1560–1570): Clandestine Marriages, Kinship Prohibitions, and Dowry Exchange in European Comparison." *Journal of Early Modern History* 8 (2004): 67–108.

Spieß, Karl-Heinz. *Familie und Verwandschaft im deutschen Hochadel des Spätmittelalters, 13. bis 16. Jahrhundert.* Stuttgart, 1993.

Steinke, Barbara. *Paradiesgarten oder Gefängnis?: Das Nürnberger Katharinenkloster zwischen Klosterreform und Reformation.* Tübingen, 2006.

Steinmetz, Susanne. "The German Churches in London, 1669–1914." In *Germans in Britain since 1500.* Ed. Panikos Panayi. London, 1996. Pp. 49–72.

Steinwascher, Gerd. "Die konfessionellen Folgen des Westfälischen Friedens für das Fürstbistum Osnabrück." *Niedersächsisches Jahrbuch für Landesgeschichte* 71 (1999): 51–80.

Stoler, Ann L. *Carnal Knowledge and Imperial Power: Race and the Intimate in Colonial Rule.* Berkeley, Calif., 2002.

Stollberg-Rilinger, Barbara. "Der Grafenstand in der Reichspublizistik." In *Dynastie und Herrschaftssicherung in der Frühen Neuzeit.* Ed. Heide Wunder. Berlin, 2002.

———. "Rang vor Gericht: Zur Verrechtlichung sozialer Rangunterschiede in der frühen Neuzeit." *Zeitschrift für historische Forschung* 28 (2001): 385–418.

———. "Symbolische Kommunikation in der Vormoderne: Begriffe—Thesen—Forschungsperspektiven." *Zeitschrift für historische Forschung* 31 (2004): 489–527.

Stone, Lawrence. *The Family, Sex and Marriage in England, 1500–1800.* New York, 1977.

Stüve, Carl. *Geschichte des Hochstiftes Osnabrück von 1508–1623.* 3 vols. Osnabrück, 1970.

Sykes, Norman. *William Wake: Archbishop of Canterbury 1657–1737.* 2 vols. Cambridge, UK 1957.

Tacke, Andreas, ed. *". . . wir wollen der Liebe Raum geben": Konkubinate geistlicher und weltlicher Fürsten um 1500.* Göttingen, 2006.

Tanner, Norman P. *Decrees of the Ecumenical Councils.* 2 vols. London, 1990.

Tatlock, Lynne, ed. *The Graph of Sex and the German Text: Gendered Culture in Early Modern Germany 1500–1700.* Amsterdam, 1994.

Taylor, Jean Gelmann. *The Social World of Batavia: European and Eurasian in Dutch Asia.* Madison, 1984.

Testino-Zafiropoulos, Alexandra. "Les alliances royales franco-espagnoles au XVIIe siècle: Propagande et raison d'état." In *Le mariage dans l'Europe des XVIe et XVII siècles: réalités et représentations.* 2 vols. Nancy, 2003. Vol. 1, pp. 175–90.

Thompson, Andrew. *Britain, Hanover and the Protestant Interest: 1688–1756.* Woodbridge, UK, 2006.

Titzmann, Michael. "Literarische Strukturen und kulturelles Wissen: Das Beispiel inzestuöser Situationen in der Erzählliteratur der Goethezeit und ihrer Funktionen im Denksystem der Epoche." In *Erzählte Kriminalität: Zur Typologie und Funktion von narrativen Darstellungen in Strafrechtspflege, Publizistik und Literatur zwischen 1770 und 1920.* Eds. Jörg Schönert and Konstantin Imm. Tübingen, 1991. Pp. 229–81.

Trepp, Anne-Charlott. *Sanfte Männlichkeit und selbständige Weiblichkeit: Frauen und Männer im Hamburger Bürgertum zwischen 1770 und 1840.* Göttingen, 1996.

Trumbach, Randolph. *The Rise of the Egalitarian Family.* New York, 1978.

Tulchin, Allan. "Same-Sex Couples Creating Households in Old Regime France: The Uses of Affrèrement." *Journal of Modern History* 79 (2007): 613–47.

Turner, Victor. *Blazing the Trail: Way Marks in the Exploration of Symbols.* Tucson, 1992.

———. *The Forest of Symbols: Aspects of Ndembu Ritual.* Ithaca, N.Y., 1967.

———. *The Ritual Process: Structure and Anti-Structure.* Chicago, 1969.

Ulbrich, Claudia. "Unartige Weiber: Präsenz und Renitenz von Frauen im frühneuzeitlichen Deutschland." In *Arbeit, Frömmigkeit und Eigensinn: Studien zur historischen Kulturforschung.* Ed. Richard van Dülmen. Frankfurt, 1990. Pp. 13–42.

Unterburger, Klaus. *Das Bayerische Konkordat von 1583.* Stuttgart, 2006.

Vasella, Oskar. "Über das Konkubinat des Klerus im Spätmittelalter." In *Melanges d'histoire et de litterature offerts á Charles Halliard.* Lausanne, 1944. Pp. 269–83.

Van de Vliet, Pieter. *Onno Zwier van Haren (1713–1779): Staatsman en dichter.* Hilversum, 1996.

Vocelka, Karl. *Habsburgische Hochzeiten 1550–1600.* Vienna, 1976.

Vögeli, Alfred, ed. *Jörg Vögeli: Schriften zur Reformation in Konstanz, 1519–1538.* Tübingen, 1972.

Volkmar, Christoph. *Reform statt Reformation: Die Kirchenpolitik Herzog Georgs von Sachsen, 1488–1525.* Tübingen, 2008.

Walther, Stefanie. *Die (Un-)Ordnung der Ehe: Normen und Praxis ernestinischer Fürstenehen in der Frühen Neuzeit.* Munich, 2011.

Walz, Rainer. *Hexenglaube und magische Kommunikation im Dorf der Frühen Neuzeit: Die Verfolgungen in der Grafschaft Lippe.* Paderborn, 1993.

———. "Das Hexengerücht im Dorf und bei den Gebildeten." In *Kloster—Stadt—Region: Festschrift für Heinrich Rüthing.* Ed. Johannes Altenbehrend. Bielefeld, 2002. Pp. 315–33.

———. "Der Hexenwahn im Alltag: Der Umgang mit verdächtigen Frauen." *Geschichte in Wissenschaft und Unterricht* 43 (1992): 157–68.

Ward, Adolphus William. *The Electress Sophia and the Hanoverian Succession.* London, 1909.

Warmbrunn, Paul. *Zwei Konfessionen in einer Stadt: Das Zusammenleben von Katholiken und Protestanten in den paritätischen Reichsstädten Augsburg, Biberach, Ravensburg, und Dinkelsbühl von 1548 bis 1648.* Wiesbaden, 1993.

Weber, Max. *Wirtschaft und Gesellschaft: Grundriß der verstehenden Soziologie.* 5th rev. ed. Tübingen, 1972.

Wehler, Hans-Ulrich, ed. *Europäischer Adel, 1750–1950.* Göttingen, 1990.

Weiß, Ulrike. "'Gefährliche Liebschaften': Die Affäre—Mittel der Karriere oder Katastrophe?" In *Mächtig—verlockend—Frauen der Welfen.* Exhibition catalog. Celle, 2010. Pp. 132–65.

Wallenstein, Peter. "Interracial Marriage on Trial: Loving v. Virginia (1967)." In *Race on Trial: Law and Justice in American History,* ed. Annette Gordon-Reed. Oxford, 2002. Pp. 177–196.

Weller, Thomas. "'Ius sybselliorum templorum': Kirchenstuhlstreitigkeiten in der frühneuzeitlichen Stadt zwischen symbolischer Praxis und Recht." In *Raum und Konflikt:* Eds. Christoph Dartmann, Marian Füssel, and Stefanie Rüther. Münster, 2004. Pp. 199–224.

Wellmann, "Der historische Begriff der 'Ehre'—sprachwissenschaftlich untersucht." In *Ehrkonzepte in der Frühen Neuzeit.* Eds. Sibylle Backmann, Hans-Jörg Künast, Sabine Ullmann, and B. Ann Tlusty. Pp. 27–39.

Welsch, Wolfgang. "Transculturality: The Puzzling Form of Cultures Today." In *Spaces of Culture: City, Nation, World.* Eds. Mike Featherstone and Scott Lash. London, 1999.

Welser, Johann Michael von. *Die Welser.* 2 vols. Nuremberg, 1917.

Wiegand, Paul. *Liebe und Ehe im Mittelalter.* Goldbach, 1993.

Wiesner-Hanks, Merry E. *Christianity and Sexuality in the Early Modern World: Regulating Desire, Reforming Practice.* London, 2000.

Willoweit, Dietmar. *Standesungleiche Ehen des regierenden hohen Adels in der neuzeitlichen deutschen Rechtsgeschichte.* Munich, 2004.

Wilson, W. Daniel. "Science, Natural Law, and Unwitting Sibling Incest in Eighteenth-Century Literature." *Studies in Eighteenth-Century Literature* 13 (1984): 249–70.

Winkelbauer, Thomas. *Fürst und Fürstendiener: Gundaker von Liechtenstein, ein österreichischer Aristokrat des konfessionellen Zeitalters.* Vienna, 1999.

Winston-Allen, Anne. *Women Writing About Women and Reform in the Late Middle Ages.* University Park, 2004.

Witte, John, Jr. *Law and Protestantism: The Legal Teachings of the Lutheran Reformation.* Cambridge, UK, 2002.

Wrede, Martin, and Host Carl. Eds. *Zwischen Schande und Ehre: Erinnerungsbrüche und die Kontinuität des Hauses: Legitimationsmuster und Traditionsverständnis des frühneuzeitlichen Adels in Umbruch und Krise.* Mainz, 2007.

Wunder, Bernd. "Die Sozialstruktur der Geheimratskollegien in den süddeutschen protestantischen Fürstentümern (1660–1720)." *Vierteljahrschrift für Sozial- und Wirtschaftsgeschichte* 58 (1971): 145–220.

Wunder, Heide, ed. *Dynastie und Herrschaftssicherung in der Frühen Neuzeit: Geschlechter und Geschlecht.* Berlin, 2002.

Würgler, Andreas. *Medien in der Frühen Neuzeit.* Munich, 2009.

Zanger, Abby E. *Scenes from the Marriage of Louis XIV: Nuptial Fictions and the Making of Absolutist Power.* Stanford, 1997.

Zegura, Elizabeth C. "True Stories and Alternative Discourses: The Game of Love in Marguerite de Navarre's *Heptameron.*" In *Discourses on Love, Marriage, and Transgression in Medieval and Early Modern Literature.* Ed. Albrecht Classen. Tempe, 2004. Pp. 351–68.

Zschoch, Helmut. *Klosterreform and monastische Spirtualität im 15. Jahrhundert.* Tübingen, 1988.

Zschunke, Peter. *Konfession und Alltag in Oppenheim: Beiträge zur Geschichte von Bevölkerung und Gesellschaft einer gemischtkonfessionellen Kleinstadt in der Frühen Neuzeit.* Wiesbaden, 1984.

Zupanov, Ines, and Ronnie Po-Chia Hsia, "Reception of Hinduism and Buddhism." In *The Cambridge History of Christianity.* Vol. 6, *Reform and Expansion 1500–1600.* Ed. Ronnie Po-Chia Hsia. Cambridge, UK, 2007. Pp. 577–97.

~: CONTRIBUTORS :~

Wolfgang Breul is professor of church history at the Johannes Gutenberg Universität in Mainz, Germany. He has specialized in the social and cultural history of Pietism (17th and 18th Century). His publications include *Herrschaftskrise und Reformation: Die Reichsabteien Fulda und Hersfeld ca. 1500–1525* (Gütersloh, 2000), and *Generalreform: August Hermann Franckes Universalprojekt und die pietistische Neuordnung in der Grafschaft Waldeck* (Göttingen, 2012). He is editor of *Der radikale Pietismus* (Göttingen, 2012), and *'Der Herr wird seine Herrlichkeit an uns offenbahren': Liebe, Ehe und Sexualität im Pietismus* (Halle, 2011). He has also published many articles on Martin Luther, the Protestant Reformation, and marriage and sexuality in Protestantism.

Antje Flüchter is associate professor in the Department of Culture Studies and Oriental Languages at the University of Oslo. She has specialized in the history of the formation of religious denomination in Germany, of gender, state building, religions, and Indian–European relations. She has published *Der Zölibat zwischen Norm und Devianz. Kirchenpolitik und Gemeindealltag in Jülich und Berg im 16. und 17. Jahrhundert* (Cologne, 2006); the edited volume, *Structures on the Move: Technologies of Governance in Transcultural Encounter* (Heidelberg, 2012); and many articles, including "Eine katholische Ordnung der Sexualität? Konkurrierende Deutungsmuster um den Priesterzölibat im 17. Jahrhundert," in *Das Geschlecht des Glaubens: Religiöse Kulturen Europas zwischen Mittelalter und Moderne*, ed. Monika Mommertz and Claudia Opitz (Frankfurt, 2008), 201–28; and "'Aus den fürnembsten indianischen Reisebeschreibungen zusammengezogen': Knowledge about India in Early Modern Germany," in *The Dutch Trading Companies as Knowledge Networks*, ed. Siegried Hulgen, Jan L. de Jong, and Elmer Kolfin (Leiden, 2010).

Dagmar Freist is professor of early modern history at the Carl-von-Ossietzky-Universität in Oldenbourg and has focused her research on the study of absolutism, political culture and the public sphere, religious pluralization, and the experience of diaspora in early modern Europe. In addition to many articles, book chapters, and edited volumes, her publications include *Glaube—Liebe—Zwietracht: Konfessionell gemischete Ehen in Deutschland der Frühen Neuzeit* (Munich, 2014); *Elisabeth I: Eine Biographie* (Stuttgart, 2014); and *Governed* by Opinion: Politics, Religion, and the Dynamics of Communication in Stuart London, 1637–1645 (London, 1997).

Ralf-Peter Fuchs is an associate of the Institute of Modern History at Ludwig-Maximilians-Universität in Munich. He has published on topics as diverse as the histories of witchcraft, honor, the Imperial Chamber Court, and the history of jazz in postwar Germany. His most recent project focuses on the means of peace-making before, during, and after the Thirty-Years-War (*Ein Medium zum Frieden. Die Normaljahrsregel und die Beendigung des Dreißigjährigen Krieges* (Munich, 2010). His other publications include *Hexerei und Zauberei vor dem Reichskammergericht* (Wetzlar 1994), and *Um die Ehre: Westfälische Beleidigungsprozesse vor dem Reichskammergericht (1525–1805)* (Paderborn, 1999). He is also coeditor with Winfried Schulze of *Wahrheit, Wissen, Erinnerung: Zeugenverhörprotokolle als Quellen für soziale Wissensbestände der Frühen Neuzeit* (Münster, 2002) and with Arndt Brendecke and Edith Koller of *Die Autorität der Zeit in der Frühen Neuzeit* (Berlin, 2007).

Joel F. Harrington is professor of history at Vanderbilt University and specializes in the social history of early modern Germany. His publications include *The Faithful Executioner: Life and Death, Honor and Shame in the Turbulent Sixteenth Century* (New York, 2013); *The Unwanted Child: The Fate of Foundlings, Orphans, and Juvenile Criminals in Early Modern Germany* (Chicago, 2009), winner of the 2010 Roland H. Bainton Prize in History; *Reordering Marriage and Society in Reformation Germany* (Cambridge, UK, 1995); and *A Cloud of Witnesses: Readings in the History of Western Christianity* (Boston, 2001).

Claudia Jarzebowski is junior professor of early modern history and the history of emotions at the Freie Universität Berlin. Her publications include *Inzest: Verwandtschaft und Sexualität im 18. Jahrhundert* (Cologne, 2006) and several articles, including "Loss and Emotion in Funeral Works on Children in Seventeenth Century Germany," in Lynne Tatlock, ed., *Loss in Early Modern History* (Leiden 2010). She is currently copublishing a volume of collected essays entitled *Performing Emotions: Zum Verhältnis von Emotionen und Politik in der Frühen Neuzeit und in der Moderne* (forthcoming). Her next book will be on childhood and emotion in early modern Germany.

Mary Lindemann is professor and chair of the department of history at the University of Miami. She is the author of five books: *Patriots and Paupers: Hamburg, 1712–1830* (New York, 1990); *Health and Healing in Early Modern Germany* (Baltimore, 1996); *Medicine and Society in Early Modern Europe* (Cambridge, UK, 1999; 2nd ed. 2010); *Liaisons dangereuses: Sex, Law, and Diplomacy in the Age of Frederick the Great* (Baltimore, 2006); and *The Merchant*

Republics: Amsterdam, Antwerp, and Hamburg, 1648-1790 (forthcoming). She continues to work on a shorter study: *Charlotte's Web: Literature, History, and the Pleasures of the Imagination* and has embarked on another research project: "The Fractured Lands: Northern Germany in An Age of Unending War, 1620-1721."

David M. Luebke is professor of history at the University of Oregon and has specialized in the history of social protest movements in early modern Germany, as well as the formation of religious denominations during and after the Protestant Reformation. His publications include *His Majesty's Rebels: Factions, Communities and Rural Revolt in the Black Forest* (Ithaca, N.Y., 1997) and many articles, most recently "Confessions of the Dead: Interpreting Burial Practice in the Late Reformation," *Archive of Reformation History/Archiv für Reformationsgeschichte* 101 (2010). He is also editor of *The Counter-Reformation: Essential Readings* (London, 1999) and coeditor of *Conversions and the Politics of Religion in Early Modern Germany* (New York, 2012). He is completing a book that bears the provisional title *Hometown Religion: Conflict and Coexistence among the Christian Religions of Germany, 1553-1650*.

Marjorie Elizabeth Plummer is associate professor of history at Western Kentucky University. She specializes in the history of the impact of the early reform movement on family and gender roles and on the changing legal definitions of social norms and religious identity in early modern Germany. Her publications include *From Priest's Whore to Pastor's Wife: Clerical Marriage and the Process of Reform in the Early German Reformation* (Farnham, 2012) and a number of articles, including "'Partner in his Calamities': Pastors' Wives, Married Nuns and the Experience of Clerical Marriage in the Early German Reformation," *Gender & History* 20 (2008): 207–227. She is also coeditor of *Ideas and Cultural Margins in Early Modern Germany: Essays in Honor of H.C. Erik Midelfort* (Farnham, 2009).

Daniel Riches is associate professor of history at the University of Alabama, where he has taught since receiving his PhD from the University of Chicago in 2007. His main research interests center on the impact of intellectual, cultural, and religious forces on early modern European politics and diplomacy, especially in central and northern Europe. He has published work in the journals *Central European History, Scandinavian Studies,* and *German History,* as well as in various volumes of collected essays. He is currently completing a book manuscript entitled *Protestant Cosmopolitanism and Diplomatic Culture: Brandenburg–Swedish Relations in the Seventeenth Century,* while beginning work on a new project that will investigate the continuing role of pan-Protestant sentiment in European diplomacy following the Peace of Westphalia.

Alexander Schunka is professor of European cultures of knowledge at the Forschungszentrum Gotha, which is affiliated to the Universität Erfurt. He earned his doctorate in history at the Ludwig-Maximilians-Universitaet in Munich and has specialized in the history of migration and mobility, cultural transfers, and religious history of early modern Europe. His most recent project focuses on religious contacts between Great Britain and Protestant Germany around 1700. Publications include *Soziales Wissen und dörfliche Welt* (Frankfurt, 2000), *Gäste, die bleiben* (Münster, 2006), and a number of journal articles and book chapters. He is coeditor of *Migrationserfahrungen—Migrationsstrukturen* (Stuttgart, 2010), and of *Orientbegegnungen deutscher Protestanten in der Frühen Neuzeit* (Frankfurt, 2012).

Michael Sikora is adjunct professor of history at the Westfälische Wilhelms-Universität Münster and has written widely on military discipline, nobility, and marriage in early modern Germany. His many publications include *Disziplin und Desertion: Strukturprobleme militärischer Organisation im 18. Jahrhundert* (Berlin, 1996); *Adel in der Frühen Neuzeit* (Darmstadt, 2009); and an edition of the private and official letters of Gerhard von Scharnhorst. He is also preparing for publication a monograph on socially unequal marriages among German aristocracy, entitled *"Mausdreck mit Pfeffer": Das Problem der ungleichen Heiraten im deutschen Hochadel der Frühen Neuzeit.*

David M. Whitford is professor of Reformation history at Baylor University and is interested in the impact of the Reformation on social and political questions. He is an editor of *The Sixteenth Century Journal* and the author of *The Curse of Ham in the Early Modern Era: The Bible and Justifications for Slavery* (Farnham, 2009) and *Luther: A Guide for the Perplexed* (London, 2010). He has edited a number of volumes, including *Early Modern Europe: A Guide to Research* and *T&T Clark Companion to Reformation Theology.* He has published articles in the *Archive for Reformation Research/Archiv für Reformationsgeschichte, Renaissance Quarterly,* and *Milton Quarterly.*

~: INDEX :~

SPEKTRUM: *Publications of the German Studies Association*
Series Editor: David M. Luebke, University of Oregon

www.ingramcontent.com/pod-product-compliance
Lightning Source LLC
Chambersburg PA
CBHW072104040426
42334CB00042B/2309